The ETF Book

Books by Richard A. Ferri

The ETF Book
All About Index Funds
All About Asset Allocation
Protecting Your Wealth in Good Times and Bad
Serious Money: Straight Talk About Investing for Retirement

The ETF Book

ALL YOU NEED TO KNOW ABOUT EXCHANGE-TRADED FUNDS

Richard A. Ferri, CFA

Foreword by Don Phillips

John Wiley & Sons, Inc.

Published by John Wiley & Sons, Inc., Hoboken, New Jersey.
Published simultaneously in Canada.

For general information on our other products and services or for technical
support, please contact our Customer Care Department within the United States at
(800) 762-2974, outside the United States at (317) 572-3993 or fax (317) 572-4002.

Wiley also publishes its books in a variety of electronic formats. Some content that
appears in print may not be available in electronic formats. For more information
about Wiley products, visit our Web site at www.wiley.com.

Library of Congress Cataloging-in-Publication Data:

Ferri, Richard A.
   The ETF book: all you need to know about exchange-traded funds / Richard A.
Ferri.
        p. cm.
   Includes indexes.
   ISBN 978-0-470-13063-6 (cloth)
  1. Exchange traded funds. I. Title.
   HG6043.F47 2008
   332.63′27—dc22

                                                       2007028123

Printed in the United States of America.
10 9 8 7 6 5 4 3 2 1

The ETF Book *is dedicated to all the brave men and women in the armed forces who protect our country, our freedoms, and our way of life. They give everything and ask for nothing except our unwavering support.*

The author's royalties from the sale of this book are donated to a nonprofit organization assisting wounded veterans and their families.

Semper Fi

Contents

Foreword

There's no topic in personal finance today that's hotter than exchange-traded funds (ETFs). Die-hard believers in passive investing love the low costs and broad diversification available through ETFs. Traders and market timers love the ability to buy and sell on an intraday basis, and they cherish the growing number of highly specialized offerings that allow them to execute far more sophisticated strategies than ever before. Even active managers are getting in on the scene, using ETFs to "equitize" their cash positions and imagining a future where actively managed ETFs will be widely available. Never before have so many investors embraced a financial concept so rapidly and for such a wide variety of reasons as they have with exchange-traded funds.

The ETF phenomenon is perhaps most revolutionary from the individual investor's perspective. For years, there was a gulf between what was possible for institutional investors and what the little guy could do. Like many small investors, I recall reading about the global wanderings of legendary investor Jim Rogers, author of *Investment Biker* and other significant investment books. Rogers would observe global events and turn them into investment ideas, often shorting certain currencies, going long various commodities, and making bets on specific subsectors of a market, such as Japanese small companies. I was dazzled by his insight, but was frustrated by my own inability to act upon such insights even if I could be as clever as Rogers in identifying them. Sure, I could buy shares in an international equity fund or a precious metals fund, but I couldn't be sure that the fund's manager was making the bets that I wanted. And even if I did identify a manager who seemed to have his portfolio aligned the way I wanted it to be, there was no guarantee that positioning would stay in place. Simply put, there was no way that I could do what Rogers did, even if I had the right ideas.

Exchange-traded funds have changed all that. Today the toolkit available to individual investors is bigger and better than ever before. Highly specialized precision investment instruments are now part of the small investors' arsenal. If you want to bet on the fortunes of pharmaceutical stocks or regional banks, there's an ETF for you. If you want to play the real estate market, there are multiple ETFs available for that purpose, investing in either domestic or international real estate. If you want to bet on companies that might find a cure for cancer or invest only in companies that don't do business in Somalia, there's an ETF for you. If you want to bet on companies known for innovation, ones that are leaders in their field, or ones that are followed by only a small number of analysts, there's an ETF for you. And all of these bets can go in either direction, as ETFs can be bought long or sold short. There's little to no limit to what an investor may do today; almost any choice is possible.

Of course, more choices don't guarantee better results. Some highly respected investment commentators, most notably Vanguard founder Jack Bogle, have criticized the narrow focus of many ETFs and the overall push toward more frequent trading that some investors adopt when given greater opportunity to adjust their portfolios. Indeed, the basic concept of indexing is to buy and hold the entire market, something that seems at odds with the product proliferation and intraday trading of ETFs. So, while ETFs benefit from the goodwill created by the index movement, they can clearly be used for purposes that range far from the basic premise that underlies indexation. Bogle graphically captures the dual possibilities of ETFs when he likens them a finely honed shotgun that can be used either for survival or for murder.

The reasons that ETFs have become so specialized so quickly are easy to understand. In the actively managed fund world, every shop can have its own broadly diversified large-cap stock fund, as the chance that it may outperform may make it an economically viable offering. In the ETF world, where passive strategies dominate, there's less reason for each shop to have a broad-based equity index fund. Once a handful of these funds exist, there's little reason for more. Accordingly, newer players in the market move quickly to fill more esoteric niches in order to be the first player in a new part of the market. The result has been a rush toward producing more narrowly defined funds that tend to have higher volatility than broadly diversified ones. Indeed, the volatility of the ETF market has moved systematically higher over the past decade, with the most volatile offerings, ones that leverage or short the market, coming in the past 12 months.

Call it the dark side of choice. With greater fragmentation comes greater volatility. Take a look at the quarterly leaders and laggards lists that many personal finance publications run. You'll see that ETFs take up a disproportionate number of slots on lists that combine ETFs with open-end funds. Sadly, these funds that soar way to the top and then crash to the bottom are the very funds that investors are least likely to deploy successfully. We've done a lot of work recently at Morningstar concerning what we call investor returns. Simply put, investor returns take into account investors' purchases and sales to determine collectively how much money funds actually make for their shareholders. What we've found is that highly specialized funds tempt investors to buy high and to sell low, producing bad performances. Investors fare far better with more broadly diversified offerings like the traditional balanced mutual fund or a total stock market index fund. Bogle's warnings about the potential for misuse of ETFs should not be ignored. Power tools can help a skilled carpenter create beautiful furniture. They can also cause an amateur to lose a finger.

So what's the individual investor to do? On the one hand, there's reason to rejoice that many of Wall Street's artificial barriers are coming down. On the other hand, many of those barriers offered valuable protections that may be missed. I think that the only solution is to recognize that ETFs are here to stay and to plot a prudent path. And it always helps to have a reliable guide when exploring new terrain. There are few more able navigators than Richard Ferri. Rick is a fee-only investment advisor who knows the ins and outs of asset allocation, wealth protection, and index funds. He's a great choice to help investors evaluate the growing number of ETF choices. In *The ETF Book*, Rick covers the nuts and bolts of ETFs, the nuances of index creation, and even strategies for putting into place a financial plan based on ETFs. He even goes so far as to suggest an innovative new means of classifying and thinking about these new vehicles. In short, he's done the heavy lifting and the background research that investors need to go forth knowledgably into this exciting new world.

I think investors will benefit from this book. Its portfolio focus is refreshing amid the sea of get-rich-quick hype that too often distracts investors from their mission. Rick is a prudent and thoughtful investor who clearly has his readers' best interests at heart. Whether you're brand-new to ETFs or you're already a seasoned veteran, Rick is exactly the kind of informed guide you want by your side.

Safe travels!

DON PHILLIPS
MANAGING DIRECTOR
MORNINGSTAR, INC.

Acknowledgments

The *ETF Book* could not have been written without the support of a large number of people. I truly appreciate the advice, guidance, and inspiration from those mentioned here and those I may have accidentally left off the list. Several people contributed directly to the success of the book while others contributed indirectly through their published writings and informative personal conversations that I had the pleasure to engage in.

Special thanks goes to Don Phillips of Morningstar who provided the wonderful forward. In alphabetical order, I appreciate the help of Dr. David Blitzer of Standard & Poor's, Robert Brokamp of the Motley Fool, Ron DeLegge of ETFguide.com, Srikrant Dash of Standard & Poor's, Matt Hougan of Indexuniverse.com, Dodd Kittsley of Barclays Global Advisors, Ron Krisko of the Vanguard Group, Tom Lydon of Global Trends Investments, Christian Magoon of Claymore Securities, Brian Megibbon of Citigroup Global Markets, Richard Ranck of PowerShares, Tony Roache of State Street Global Advisors, Scott Salaske of Portfolio Solutions, Robert Tull of MacroMarkets, Jim Wiandt of indexuniverse.com, Brad Zigler, and of course, all the Bogleheads.

Introduction

Look up in the sky!...It's a bird!...It's a plane!...No, it's *Exchange-Traded Funds!*

Exchange-traded funds are flying high. Better known by the acronym ETFs, each week new funds are launched on Wall Street exchanges and land in the portfolios of investors across the nation. While the hype surrounding an ETF launch may not compare to the glitz of an action-packed Superman sequel, some promoters of these investment vehicles make it sound as if their product could leap tall buildings in a single bound. A few ETF companies have even attempted to empower their funds with superpower-sounding names such as *PowerShares, WisdomTree, ProFunds,* and *XShares.*

Are PowerShares powerful? Are WisdomTree funds a wise investment choice? Do ProFunds perform like pros? Well, that remains to be seen. What we do know is that ETFs are an important evolution in the investment industry that may help you achieve financial success, and for that reason astute investors are learning all they can about them. *The ETF Book* gives you a broad and deep understanding of this revolutionary investment structure and provides the tools needed to become a more successful investor.

ETFs have many advantages and a few disadvantages over traditional open-end mutual funds. The advantages range from lower investment costs to increased trading flexibility. The disadvantages include a commission cost on each ETF trade and the arduous task of sorting out all the industry data and jargon (made easier by this book).

ETFs are an important step in an investment revolution that began in 1924 with the first open-end mutual fund offering. Since that time there have been many changes in the mutual fund industry closely watched by a burgeoning regulatory environment.

At their core, ETFs are a simple idea. They represent a basket of securities that you can buy or sell over a stock exchange. However, under the hood, ETFs have a more complex operating structure that require a bit more study to understand, and that makes investment analysis and selection more difficult than traditional open-end mutual funds. Whether ETFs will work for you in a portfolio depends on your dedication to understanding this product and coming to an unbiased assessment of the benefits and drawbacks.

The one criticism that I have about the ETF industry is the unfounded claim of superiority that a few fund companies are promoting. Without mentioning names, some companies are trying to send a message to investors that their custom index ETFs will generate significantly higher returns than traditional index funds that follow common market indexes. In addition, a few newsletter writers are urging their readers to sell all their open-end mutual funds and buy only ETFs because they will offer far better returns.

Claims of higher returns from ETFs are grossly exaggerated. There are some savings in costs over traditional open-end mutual funds, but the savings are not large enough to make a significant difference in returns. Barring any cost differential, there is no reason to expect a basket of stocks to achieve a higher return in an ETF structure than they would return in a traditional open-end mutual fund structure. There are many different ways to design the indexes that ETFs follow, but no clearly superior strategy can guarantee consistently higher returns. Simply put, there is no Lake Wobegon ETF company where "the women are strong, the men are good looking, and all their ETFs are above average."

ETFs are account structures, not investment strategies. Various types of ETF structures have been approved by the Securities and Exchange Commission. Those structures are operational engines to be used by investment companies to create and manage many different types of index funds, using a multitude of investment styles and strategies. It is not the ETF structure that leads to a good or bad return, it is the index strategy that each ETF follows.

The important story behind the ETF structure is their unique operations and how those processes can achieve lower overall investment costs, including taxes and increased trading efficiency. Those factors *could* result in increased returns, but that increase should not be overemphasized, and should not be the sole reason to sell your open-end funds and buy ETFs.

Defining ETFs

Exchange Traded Funds (ETFs) are baskets of securities that are traded, like individual stocks, through a brokerage firm on a stock exchange. Shares of ETFs are traded with other investors who are also going through brokerage firms to facilitate their transactions. All-day trading makes ETFs more flexible than their familiar sister open-end mutual funds, where investors must wait until the end of the day to buy or sell shares directly with a mutual fund company.

ETFs can be bought and sold throughout the trading day whenever the stock exchanges are open. Any way you can trade a stock, you can trade an ETF. Shares can also be sold short or bought on margin. That makes these investment vehicles useful for institutional investors and traders who often need to quickly hedge equity positions.

One difference between ETFs and traditional open-end mutual funds is that ETFs do not necessarily trade at their net asset value (NAV). That is the combined market value of the underlying security and cash holdings. Although the supply and demand for ETF shares is driven by the values of the underlying securities in the index they track, other factors can and do affect ETF market prices. As such, the market price for ETF shares is determined by forces of supply and demand for those ETF shares, and the price occasionally gets off track from the underlying values in the fund. But not by much. ETFs have a mechanism that controls price discrepancy and stops discounts or premiums from becoming large or persistent.

The discrepancy between ETF prices and their underlying values creates a potential profit opportunity for a special set of investors. The market price of an ETF is kept close to its NAV by allowing a few large institutional investors called authorized participants (AP) to buy or redeem ETF shares in-kind (using the underlying securities rather than cash). When a small price discrepancy occurs between an ETF and its underlying securities, APs conduct a risk-free arbitrage trade. The arbitrage trade allows APs to exchange individual securities for large blocks of ETF shares and vice versa. The arbitrage mechanism brings the market price of ETF shares in line with the fund's true value, and brings the AP a small profit. The arbitrage can happen very quickly and is effective in keeping ETF shares in line with the true value.

ETFs are organized as open-end mutual funds. However, the companies that issue ETF shares have agreed with the Securities and Exchange Commission (SEC) that they will not advertise or market their products as open-end mutual funds, or even as mutual funds in general. They are marketed only as exchange-traded funds and exchange-traded securities.

According to the SEC, mutual funds are issued and redeemed by a mutual fund company dealing directly with the public. ETF issuers do not deal directly with the public. They buy and sell only from APs. By regulation, the prospectuses and advertising materials for ETFs must prominently disclose that fact, and state that individual ETF shareholders do not buy or sell shares directly with a fund company. When individual shareholders acquire shares on a stock exchange, they are purchasing part of a creation unit owned by an AP.

Sound complicated? Don't worry. After reading this book you will be well versed in ETF operations. In fact, you will likely know much more about these unique investments than a large number of advisers who are in the financial services business.

Exchange Traded Portfolios

The *Wall Street Journal* lists several types of exchange traded portfolios in their "Money & Investing" section. I prefer the phrase "exchange traded portfolios" because it better describes what is covered in *The ETF Book*. Several investment products discussed in these chapters are not "exchange traded funds" by the strict definition of the word. But those investments do act like ETFs, trade like ETFs, and are often referred to as ETFs in the investment industry.

One example of an investment product that is not a fund by definition is an innovative security from Barclays Bank called iPaths. These unique investments are not ETFs; they are Exchange Traded Notes (ETNs). ETNs are unsecured debt obligations of Barclays Bank that track the performance of certain market indexes.

Debt usually means interest is paid, but that is not the case with ETNs. These unique securities pay no interest, no dividends, and have no performance guarantees. ETNs track the total return of markets, and investors receive whatever the total return of the market is, minus fees. ETNs trade like ETFs on a stock exchange but are not taxed like ETFs. That is an important distinction that we will discuss in detail in Chapter 4.

There are other types of exchange traded portfolios that are not technically ETFs. Those securities are also covered in this book. However, for practical reasons, when there is no reason to distinguish these other exchange traded portfolios from ETFs, they are all referred to as ETFs.

The Growth of the ETF Marketplace

The ETF marketplace is growing at a torrid pace, and that growth will likely continue for a number of years to come. ETF issuance has expanded exponentially every year since 2000. There were over 1,000 ETFs trading on the U.S. markets by 2008, with assets well over $1 trillion in investor dollars. That is 20 percent of the value of traditional open-end mutual funds. By 2010, there could be close to 2,000 available ETFs on U.S. exchanges, with assets nearing $2 trillion. It is feasible that the number and asset level of ETFs could equal that of open-end mutual funds over the next ten years, and that could be a conservative estimate.

ETFs have the potential to become the largest segment of the mutual fund marketplace by 2020. You, as an informed investor, should know what makes ETFs unique, how they work, where to get the information on new funds, and which funds may help you achieve your financial objectives. That is what *The ETF Book* is all about.

Overview of the Contents

The ETF Book is divided into four parts, with each part containing five to seven chapters. Each chapter is fairly concise for easy reading and comprehension. At the end of the book there is an *ETF Resource List* where you can find more information on ETFs, a *Glossary of Terms* to help you with definitions, and an *Index* to quickly find the information you are looking for.

Part I: ETF Basics

The benefit of owning ETFs can be appreciated only after their internal workings are understood. It is the structure that makes them different.

Chapter 1 begins with the evolution of ETFs from their early beginnings to where the market is today. It is said that necessity is the mother of invention, and ETFs are no exception. Understanding how the ETF marketplace evolved and grew over the years is an important step in understanding the benefits they may bring to your portfolio.

Chapter 2 examines the nuts and bolts of managing ETFs, and those mechanics differ significantly from open-end mutual funds. The chapter offers an introduction into the rules-based index strategies that ETFs follow, the calculation of ETF market prices, the calculation of intraday values, the role of authorized participants (AP) in the creation and redemption of ETF shares, individual investor trading in shares, and settlement differences between ETFs and other investment securities.

Chapter 3 examines the fundamental differences between different exchange traded portfolios. While all index-based ETFs follow rules, not all ETFs function in the same way. In fact, some investments that are commonly referred to as exchange traded funds are not funds at all.

Chapter 4 explores the advantages and disadvantages of ETFs over the traditional open-end mutual fund. People commonly refer to open-end mutual funds as traditional because there are nearly 7,000 open-end funds on the market. It is a structure investors are familiar with. Included in the chapter is an overview of ETF tax benefits when shares are placed in a taxable investment account.

Chapter 5 examines the future of actively managed ETFs. An actively managed ETF does not follow a rules-based index. Rather, the securities are chosen by a portfolio manager or committee, using their discretion. The Securities and Exchange Commission now allows a limited form of actively managed ETFs, which will lead to an abundance of new issues.

Part II: ETF Indexes

Most ETFs follow securities indexes. As such, studying the rules and methodology of index construction and maintenance is an important part of ETF analysis. The section differentiates between market indexes and custom indexes. It also introduces a novel method of categorizing ETFs by the type of indexes they follow. *Index Strategy Boxes* are an easy way to understand index construction and how a fund is investing your money.

Chapter 6 divides ETFs into two main types. The first type of index is a market index. That is the classic method of replicating the performance of widely recognized stock and bond indexes. Market indexes use passive security selection weight stocks using market capitalization. The second type is a customized index. A custom index differs from a market index in that the index provider is actively involved in managing the security selection process or modifying the security weighting process, or both.

Chapter 7 introduces the new and simple way to view index strategies using a tic-tac-toe box. *Index Strategy Boxes* have two dimensions. One axis of the box is security selection and the other is security weighting. How securities are selected for an index and how the securities are weighted in an index has a profound effect on the risk and return characteristics of the index.

Chapter 8 further examines the first dimension of *Index Strategy Boxes*, which is security selection. Index security selection is based primarily on one of three strategies: passive, screening, or quantitative. Choosing securities for index is obviously important. What is left out is also important. This chapter gives you in-depth coverage of security selection methods and their impact on performance.

Chapter 9 examines the second dimension of *Index Strategy Boxes*, which is security weighting. Security weighting is based on one of three strategies: capitalization, fundamental, and fixed. How securities are weighted in an index can have a profound effect on the risk and return characteristics of the index. There is a detailed discussion of the various methods and their impacts on returns.

Part III: ETF Selections

The financial markets are divided into many asset classes and many global regions. Part Three divides the world into U.S. stocks, international stocks, bonds, and alternative asset classes. Examples of ETF strategies are provided in each category.

Chapter 10 summarizes the U.S. equity market, the largest component of the ETF marketplace. The chapter covers total market funds, growth and value funds, and those based on the size of companies. Chapter 10 also provides an overview of style and size methodologies used by various index providers.

Chapter 11 goes global by expanding the scope into international equity markets. Global equity ETF issuance is growing as more international indexes are created and U.S. stock exchanges form global alliances. Emerging country ETFs are expanding into parts of the world that were once very difficult to gain access to.

Chapter 12 looks at U.S. and global industry sectors, the fastest-growing part of the ETF equity marketplace. Industry sectors cover broad markets and micro markets, both in the United States and globally. Industry sectors are being sliced thinner and thinner, offering ETF investors access to niche markets that do not exist in the open-end fund universe.

Chapter 13 introduces the interesting field of special equity ETFs. These unique funds include theme investing, sector rotation strategies, leveraged ETFs, and short funds. The theme investment ETFs section covers a variety of areas, including clean energy, infectious disease, social responsibility, and corporate dynamics. Leveraged and short funds are used to market hedge risk and make leveraged market bets in one direction or another. They can be useful when trying to hedge an illiquid stock position.

Chapter 14 covers fixed income ETFs, including government bonds, corporate bonds, and preferred stocks. Fixed income ETF development was slow for several years. Fund providers have recently introduced several fixed income ETFs, ranging from high yield bonds to preferred stocks.

Chapter 15 explores the growing popularity of alternative asset class ETFs, including gold, oil, commodity indexes, and currencies. It is an interesting and often controversial area of investing. Academic research agrees that alternative investments help reduce portfolio risk, but the debate continues over the potential long-term return of these asset classes.

Part IV: Portfolio Management Using ETFs

Part Four offers advice on how you can develop an ETF portfolio and what you can reasonably expect to achieve from it. The section explores many strategies from buy-and-hold to market timing and sector rotation. Regardless of your beliefs, the key ingredients that are critical to the success of any portfolio management strategy is to have a belief, establish a plan based on that belief, implement the plan, and stick to it.

Chapter 16 is a broad overview of the various strategies. The major investment styles are the passive asset allocation strategies of buy-and-hold and life-cycle investing, and the active strategies of market timing and sector rotation. Special strategies include hedging and building around illiquid stock positions.

Chapter 17 introduces a simple and effective portfolio management in strategic asset allocation using a buy-and-hold strategy. This prudent ETF diversification technique is favored by cost-conscious investors who wish to achieve the benefits of market returns without having to predict the markets. The concept of asset class correlation and portfolio rebalancing is introduced.

Chapter 18 provides tools and directions when developing a mix of ETFs based on our journey through life. A person who has just entered the workforce typically invests differently from one who is retiring from the workforce. Life cycle investing directs more weight to aggressive asset classes early in life and more weight to conservative asset classes later in life.

Chapter 19 is an introduction to the world of active portfolio investment strategies. Many different types of portfolio strategies are discussed, including fundamental methods and technical methods. The goal of active investing is to achieve greater returns than the markets outright or on a risk adjusted basis. A successful active strategy does not need to achieve higher returns than the markets if the strategy achieves substantially lower risks than the market.

Chapter 20 focuses special uses for ETFs in portfolio management. Those uses may include hedging a specific risk in a portfolio, such as a concentrated position in one industry. Pairs trading invests long and short in sectors or styles simultaneously in an attempt to capture cycles in the economy. A market neutral strategy invests either a long or short position in an industry, and invests the opposite way with a market index. Tax swapping is a conservative strategy for boosting after-tax returns.

Chapter 21 includes several cost-saving ideas for ETF investors. The chapter includes tips on opening accounts and trading that lower your overall cost. In addition, information is provided on professional portfolio management services available for hire.

Summary

The ETF Book is your guide to creating a winning portfolio strategy. Whether you are just getting started with ETFs or are a seasoned investor, *The ETF Book* will help you get to the next level of understanding. Armed with the knowledge in this book plus other information as outlined in the appendix, you will have the tools necessary to build the right portfolio that fits your needs.

The ETF Book

PART

I

ETF BASICS

1

ETFs from Evolution to Revolution

Exchange-traded funds (ETFs) have emerged from their fledgling beginnings in 1993 to a full-blown revolution in the mutual fund industry. The number of ETF offerings is accelerating each year. Since 2004, the number of ETFs available for investment has doubled in number about every eighteen months. It is not possible to predict when the growth will slow. There are reasons to believe, however, that the total number of ETFs will double or triple again before any slowdown occurs. As more people understand the benefits of ETFs and invest in them, other investors want to know how these unique products might fit into their portfolios.

The best place to begin a study of ETFs is at the beginning. This chapter highlights the events that lead to the creation of ETFs, and how the marketplace has evolved over the decades. The chapter takes us to a point in the evolution where we are today, and looks at where the industry is likely to go in the future.

ETFs Are a Growth Industry

At the end of 1993, there was only one ETF on the market, with assets of $464 million. By the end of 1997, there were still only two ETFs trading on U.S. exchanges, with assets totaling $6.2 billion. Then the idea started to catch on. ETF issuance began to accelerate as more investment companies entered the marketplace. There are more than 25 companies currently issuing ETFs, offering more than 700 choices in the United States, with a total market value exceeding $600 billion. Several hundred more offerings await SEC approval.

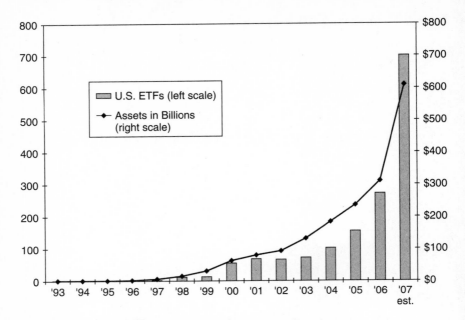

Figure 1.1   Growth of the U.S. ETF Marketplace
Source: Strategic Insight and Investment Company Institute

The acceleration in the growth of the ETF marketplace has been impressive, as is illustrated in Figure 1.1.

ETFs are the big growth story in the mutual fund industry. At the present time, more than 50 percent of all U.S.-traded ETFs have been on the market for less than two years, and the new product pipeline is filled to the brim as hundreds of new funds await SEC approval. New ETF companies are being created by venture capital firms looking to gain a foothold in the industry. A few of those new companies will stay independent, but most will be gobbled up by large mutual fund providers as they scramble to get into the business. Table 1.1 lists the major players in the market and their position in the industry.

Certainly there will be fund failures and fund mergers as the number of ETFs outstrips demand. There is a critical level of assets needed to make a fund profitable. That level of assets, however, tends to be lower than for other types of mutual funds because ETF operational expenses are lower (see Chapter 4). So far, the number of ETFs that have closed is surprisingly low.

Table 1.1   Major U.S. ETF Providers

Manager	Number of ETFs	Assets (Millions U.S. $)	Market Share
BGI & Barclays Capital	137	282,122	59%
SSGA	59	102,093	21%
Vanguard	32	32,257	7%
PowerShares	82	12,276	3%
Bank of NY	6	26,721	6%
ProShares	52	6,490	2%
Rydex	25	4,939	1%
WisdomTree	37	3,996	1%
Claymore	28	926	1%

Source: State Street Global Research, June 2007

A Short History of Mutual Funds

Understanding how ETFs evolved begins with a brief history of the mutual fund industry and the laws that govern it. Mutual funds are not a new investment. In fact, historians believe the idea is as old as the country itself. The first mutual fund originated in the Netherlands at the same time the United States was fighting for its independence from Great Britain.

Where it Began

The introduction of the mutual fund and the American Revolution had nothing to do with each other, except that after the Revolution, some of the money needed for U.S. reconstruction was financed by mutual fund investors from abroad. At that time, the United States was a fledgling emerging market, and foreign investors were speculating that the country would succeed. The idea is no different from U.S. investors today placing money in emerging countries that have just come through a political revolution.

A 2004 paper titled *The Origins of Mutual Funds* by K. Geert Rouwenhorst of the Yale School of Management documents the industry through the early 1900s. Rouwenhorst found that in 1774, a Dutch merchant and broker invited subscriptions from the public to form a pooled investment trust named Eendragt Maakt Magt, "Unity Creates Strength." The creation of the trust followed a financial crisis that occurred in that country during 1772 and 1773. It is common in the financial trade for innovation to follow financial crisis. We will later see how a financial crisis in the twentieth century lead to the innovation of ETFs in the United States.

Eendragt Maakt Magt was created to provide small investors with limited means to invest in profitable ventures and control risk through diversification. The trust was surprisingly transparent and well managed. The fund was composed of securities from Austria, Denmark, Germany, Spain, Sweden, Russia, and a variety of colonial plantations in Central and South America. More than one hundred different securities were regularly traded on the Amsterdam exchange, and at one time or another, most of those investments were part of the trust. Prices of the most liquid securities were made available to the general public in a biweekly publication. The publication also listed local real estate transactions, the announcements of dividends paid by securities traded on the Amsterdam exchange, and any new security offering.

The trust existed for nearly 120 years and still holds the record for the longest investment of its kind to have existed. The fund survived many financial and political crises, including a steep decline in the value of U.S. assets as that emerging market engaged in a costly civil war. The trust also passed through several management changes and a number of name changes. It was officially dissolved in 1893.

Eendragt Maakt Magt was not the only way for foreigners to invest in emerging markets. During the 1780s and 1790s more than thirty investment trusts emerged with a single objective: speculation on the future credit of the United States. Together with France and Spain, the Netherlands was one of the major financiers of the young United States.

Funds Come to the United States

Investment trusts were first introduced to U.S. investors during the 1890s. The Boston Personal Property Trust was formed in 1893 and was the first "closed-end" fund to trade on the U.S. stock market. The fund operated the same way today's closed-end funds work. The new fund offered shares to the public for a limited time, and then the offering was closed. Investors could not withdraw money from the fund, but they could sell shares on the stock exchange and in private transactions. Investors thus had liquidity when they needed it.

Closed-end mutual funds raise cash for investment by selling a fixed number of fund shares. Then a fund manager invests the cash from the sale of shares in accordance with the fund's investment objective and policies. The shares are then listed on a physical stock exchange or trade in the over-the-counter market.

A closed-end fund does not need to liquidate securities to meet investor demands for cash or to purchase securities to invest the proceeds of investor purchases. Because the fund is not subject to the demands of investors for cash, the fund may invest in less liquid portfolio securities. For example, a closed-end fund can invest in securities traded in countries that do not have fully developed securities markets. Many closed-end funds used leverage to potentially boost returns (and always boost management fees). Leverage is still common in closed-end funds that trade on the markets today.

Like other publicly traded securities, the market price of closed-end fund shares fluctuates on the basis of supply and demand for the fund shares. The market price of a closed-end fund may not be the same as its underlying net asset value (NAV) because demand for the fund may be different from the demand for the underlying securities in the fund. By law, the fund company cannot make a market in its own fund, or issue or redeem shares when there is a difference in price between the shares and the underlying NAV. The premiums and discounts in price that occur in closed-end funds is a major disadvantage of that structure and held them back from becoming more popular.

Open-End Funds Introduced

The creation of the Alexander Fund in Philadelphia, Pennsylvania, in 1907, was an important step in the evolution toward an open-end mutual fund and solving the problem of price discrepancy in the closed-end structure. The Alexander Fund featured semiannual issues and allowed investors to make withdrawals directly from the fund at NAV prices. It was the first time a mutual fund had windows where old shares could be redeemed and new shares created at regular intervals.

The Massachusetts Investors Trust (MIT) became the first U.S. mutual fund with a modern open-end structure in 1924. MIT allowed for the continuous issue and redemption of shares by the investment company at a price that is proportional to the NAV. Each day after the markets closed, open-end mutual fund companies computed the NAV of the underlying stocks, bonds, and cash in their fund, and determined a fair price per share. Investors received the NAV when they redeemed mutual fund shares. The NAV price was also quoted in newspapers on a regular basis.

The open-end method allows each fund company to create or redeem shares as needed to satisfy investor demand. Creation and redemption was done only once per day, at the end of the day, based on the fund's ending net asset value. The open-end structure quickly became the standard for mutual fund organization in the United States as State Street was quick to launch its open-end fund in the same year as MIT.

Investors paid a commission to buy shares of an open-end fund. That commission went to the salesperson selling the shares. During the 1920s, banks were the leading issuers of open-end funds and closed-end trusts. Tellers sold shares to depositors, and sometimes the bank would let the depositors borrow up to 100 percent of the money to buy shares. The liberal lending practices of banks ultimately lead to the demise of many small investors, and the introduction of the first Glass-Steagall Act. For nearly 75 years, banks have been precluded from selling stocks and mutual fund investments.

There continued to be innovation in the mutual fund industry during the Roaring Twenties. Scudder, Stevens and Clark launched the first no-load fund in 1928. A no-load fund has no commission. It is purchased and redeemed by the fund company at its NAV. 1928 also saw the launch of the Wellington Fund, which was the first mutual fund to include both stocks and bonds. Only stock funds existed before that time.

By 1929, there were 19 open-end mutual funds competing with nearly 700 closed-end funds in the United States. After the stock market crash, however, from 1929 to 1932, many highly leveraged closed-end fund investors were wiped out. The deep discounts to NAV at which closed-end funds were sold during the early years of the Depression caused dissent among investors, and that allowed open-end funds that redeemed at NAV to take center stage when the stock market recovered in the mid 1930s.

Government regulators also began to take notice of the antics in the mutual fund and trust industry. The creation of the

Securities and Exchange Commission (SEC) lead to the passage of the Securities Act of 1933 and the enactment of the Securities Exchange Act of 1934. These regulations put safeguards in place to protect investors. Companies issuing stocks had to submit regular financial statements. Mutual funds were required to register with the SEC and to provide disclosure in the form of a prospectus. A few years later, the Investment Company Act of 1940 put in place additional regulations that required more disclosures and sought to minimize conflicts of interest between fund issuers and the shareholders.

The Mutual Fund Industry Expands

Over the next few decades, the mutual fund industry continued to expand. During the 1950s, some 50 new funds were introduced. By 1954, the financial markets overcame its 1929 peak, and interest by a new generation of post–World War II investors emerged. The 1960s saw more investors coming into the marketplace as companies like Merrill Lynch, Pierce, Fenner, and Smith opened local offices on every street corner. Hundreds of new funds were established and billions of dollars in new asset inflows.

A bear market in 1969 cooled the public's appetite for stocks, and the reversal of fortune ended the industry's enthusiasm for issuing new funds. Money flowed out of mutual funds as quickly as investors could redeem their shares.

Crisis breeds innovation in the financial markets, and in the early 1970s, wise investors noticed that the performance of most mutual funds were lower than the return of the stock market. Investment costs became an important element of expected return. The concept of cost-cutting had an enormous impact on the direction of the mutual fund industry.

In 1971, Wells Fargo Bank established the first low-cost index fund, a concept that John Bogle would use in 1975 as a foundation on which to build the Vanguard Group. An index fund achieves the return of the stock market, minus a small amount for administrative costs.

The 1970s also saw the rise of the no-load fund. Several fund companies offered only no-load funds, and more traditional fund companies launched no-load alternatives to their existing load funds.

No-load funds and low-cost index funds, coupled with industry deregulation that in 1976 eliminated fixed commission rates at brokerage houses, saved investors billions of dollars annually. Lowering investor cost was a major contribution to the fund industry's turnaround later in the decade.

Boom-Bust

The 1980s and 1990s brought one of the longest bull markets in history. Interest in the stock market and mutual fund investing became a passion for many Americans. Many fund companies became household names, such as Fidelity and American Funds. Some mutual fund managers became public figures and icons in the industry as money poured into their funds.

The Munder Net Net Fund was an example of the boom. The fund was launched in 1995 to track the fledgling Internet industry. The fund manager was not an analyst or a money manager. He was the company's in-house technology installer. The guy was literally setting up workstations one day, and managing a portfolio the next day. There was not a lot of interest in the fund at the time because no one knew what the Internet was. But that did not last. By early 2000, the Munder NetNet Fund had over $12 billion in assets.

Just when it seemed that every barber and shoe store salesperson was a self-proclaimed expert on tech stocks, the bubble broke. Over a period of months, the technology market deflated to a mere fraction of its peak size as many once high-flying technology companies entered bankruptcy. Of course, Munder fired the manager of the NetNet fund, as if the guy had anything to do with the bubble or the collapse.

The burst of the tech bubble in 2000 was followed by a string of mutual fund scandals that took the shine off the mutual fund industry's reputation. Shady trading patterns by fund managers and other behind-the-scenes dealings demonstrated that mutual fund companies were not always acting in their shareholders' best interests. It was clear that the fund companies were not the squeaky clean entities that they promoted themselves to be. What was needed was more transparency, more disclosure, and more accountability, all of which played right into the market for exchange-traded funds.

Back to the Crash of 1987

On Black Monday, October 19, 1987, the Dow Jones Industrial Average (DJIA) fell by more than 20 percent in a single day. It was the second-largest one-day percentage decline in stock market history. The largest one-day decline occurred on December 12, 1914, when the DJIA fell 24 percent. But there is an explanation for the 1914 event. The New York Stock Exchange had been closed for six months since the outbreak of World War I, and many people were waiting to sell on the opening bell.

Unlike the 1914 crash, the 1987 decline seemed to start from nothing of importance. No major news or events occurred before the drop and the political situation in Washington was relatively benign. President Reagan was in his seventh year in office, and aside from the Soviet occupation of Afghanistan, no major conflicts were threatening world peace.

The most popular excuse for the 1987 crash was selling by program traders. Program trading is an automated buy/sell system based on computer tracking of market movements. The strategy involved instantaneous execution of orders in large blocks of stocks and futures. Some economists theorized the collapse was caused by program trading, while others argued that the programs had little to do with it. Either way, the strategy was the scapegoat that ended up taking most of the blame.

In the aftermath of Black Monday, it became clear that large institutional investors did not have the liquidity they needed to quickly hedge positions. Consequently, markets around the world were put on restricted trading. When stock went down, the futures and options markets were closed temporarily, and if stock went down more, the stock exchanges were closed.

The options and futures markets were included because liquidity can dry up quickly in those markets during a crisis, and that can drive equities lower. Closing those markets was the first circuit breaker to stop the cascade of stock selling. If that did not work, the regulators decided that stock exchanges should simply stop trading.

Circuit breakers were a knee-jerk reaction to the problem of limited liquidity in a crisis, but there was no quick or easy way to solve the problem. What was needed was a simple and reliable way to hedge a portfolio of stocks, using an exchange traded vehicle.

Closed-end funds trade on a stock exchange, but there was a problem using them to hedge against rapidly falling stock prices. The market price of a closed-end fund is determined by supply and demand for that fund, not the underlying NAV of the stocks in the fund. Consequently, the market price of a closed-end fund can become severely discounted to its NAV when the markets fall. Depending on the fund and the suddenness of the decline, the discount to NAV could become as high as 30 percent, and it could persist for a long time. Sellers using closed-end funds as a hedge against stock positions could be selling at a built-in loss.

The reason closed-end funds frequently can have a discount or premium is because the fund cannot issue more shares to new investors when the fund is at a premium, or redeem shares from selling investors when the fund is at a discount. Nor can closed-end fund companies self-deal in their own funds. Since the number of shares is basically fixed, there is no ability to arbitrage the difference between the fund price and the NAV. If there were such a mechanism, it would bring the market price of the closed-end fund in line with the underlying NAV, as traders arbitrage fund shares for stock shares and vice versa.

Closed-end fund discounts and premiums would disappear if arbitrage were allowed to occur. For example, if a fund were allowed to redeem closed-end shares when those shares are selling at a discount to NAV, the manager could simultaneously sell the underlying securities that make up the fund at current market prices and make a risk-free profit for remaining shareholders in the fund. Or, if the market price of the fund was selling at a premium to NAV, the manager could sell more closed-end fund shares on the open market while simultaneously buying the underlying securities that make up the fund at a lower market price, resulting in a profit from risk-free arbitrage.

If the SEC allowed arbitrage in closed-end funds, that would be a great vehicle for institutions to hedge their portfolio market risks. They could sell closed-end fund shares in a decline, knowing that the price of those shares would be trading close to their NAV. Closed-end funds were not to receive that exemption, however, from the SEC. Thus, an entirely new vehicle was needed for traders to hedge their positions.

The First Exchange-Traded Funds

In the wake of the market crash of 1987, and by request of the law firm of Leland, O'Brien and Rubinstein (LOR), the U.S. Securities and Exchange Commission started reviewing and rewriting securities regulations to make way for a new type of exchange-traded vehicle. In 1990, the SEC issued the Investment Company Act Release No. 17809, which ultimately paved the way for the formation of mutual funds that allowed for share creation and redemption during the day.

Specifically, the Release No. 17809 granted LOR the right to create and file for a new security called a "SuperTrust." The product was an index fund of sorts designed to give institutional investors the ability to buy or sell an entire basket of S&P 500 stocks in one trade on a stock exchange. The SuperTrust structure had the share creation and redemption characteristics of an open-end fund and the trading flexibility of a closed-end fund.

SuperUnits traded on an exchange just like a closed-end fund. But unlike closed-end funds, if SuperUnits started to sell at a discount to its NAV, institutional investors would arbitrage the situation and profit risk-free. They would purchase the underpriced Super-Units on the open market and simultaneously sell the individual securities in the unit. They would then turn in SuperUnits to the fund manager and receive the underlying stocks. Those stocks would cover the short position in the stocks that were previously sold. This risk-free arbitrage trade locked in a small profit for the institutional investor.

Although arbitrage sounds like a lot of work, it is actually quick, easy, and practically fully automated. The entire transaction can be accomplished in a few moments by running a computer program and making a phone call to a trading desk. A byproduct of the arbitrage was to neatly eliminate any discount and premium between the exchange-traded SuperUnit and its underlying securities.

LOR filed for their SuperTrust securities in 1990, and on November 5, 1992, the SEC completed their regulatory review. Long delays are common at the SEC when filing for any new security product. More on that point later.

The first SuperTrust was launched in December 1992 and had a maturity of three years. At that time, a new SuperTrust was to replace the maturing units. Unfortunately for LOR, there was no second issue. Although the concept was a unique solution for institutional investors, one detriment to success was that SuperUnits had only institutional appeal. A large minimum investment size, the complexity of the product, and adverse tax rulings turned individual investors cold to the idea.

Where there is opportunity, there is innovation, and by the time SuperUnits hit the street, something better was already brewing. The American Stock Exchange took advantage of the Investment Company Act Release No. 17809 and petitioned the SEC to allow the creation of the first Standard & Poor's Depositary Receipts (SPDRs). The official name is SPDR Trust, Series 1, but they are better known as SPDRs S&P 500. State Street Global Advisors (SSGA) manages the fund, which began trading on the American Stock Exchange in January 1993.

The market value of SPDRs S&P 500 is kept very close to the underlying index through an arbitrage mechanism described earlier. Institutional investors have the opportunity to profit from a small mismatch in price between the market value of SPDRs S&P 500 and the stocks in the S&P 500 index. If one value is greater than the other, the expensive one is sold and the cheap one is bought. The arbitrage trade would be repeated over and over until the discrepancy between the ETF and its underlying value was so small that there is no profit left from arbitrage.

SPDRs S&P 500 was an immediate success. The fund brought in about $500 million in assets during the first year. One reason SPDRs succeeded where the SuperUnit failed is because individual investors could afford to buy them. Each unit trades at approximately one tenth the index value of the S&P 500 index. If the S&P 500 was quoted at 1600, the price of one SPDR unit is $160. That is a simple and elegant pricing structure that everyone understands, and at a price per unit that all investors can afford.

SPDRs also filled a big void in the brokerage industry. Stockbrokers needed a way to invest their clients' money in index funds because during the mid and late 1990s, their clients were transferring billions of dollars out of their firms to a low-cost Vanguard 500 Fund. SPDRs S&P 500 gave brokers an alternative to the Vanguard 500, which slowed the outflow of assets.

SPDRs S&P 500 are still the most popular ETF on the market today. Over $60 billion in assets are invested in the product.

Advances in ETF Structure

Morgan Stanley joined forces with Barclays Global Investors in 1996 to launch World Equity Benchmark Shares (WEBS) on the AMEX. The series of thirteen ETFs were benchmarked to different world equity markets ranging from Australia to Belgium.

The significant difference between SPDRs and WEBS is their structures. SPDRs are operated as a unit investment trust (UIT) while WEBS are organized as an investment company under the Investment Company Act of 1940. Under a UIT structure, SPDRs must replicate exactly the index they are designed to track. That means SPDRs S&P 500 must own all 500 of the S&P stocks in the appropriate weights. WEBS were organized as an investment company, and that gave the managers the flexibility to modify their holdings.

The investment company structure of WEBS allows fund managers the discretion to change their fund holdings as needed to work around difficult indexes that the funds were supposed to track. Some indexes are dominated by a few companies and cannot be replicated under UIT rules. In addition, many securities in broad stock and bond indexes are illiquid. Rather than buying all the securities in an index, a manager can sample the index using computer-driven optimization models. The ability to modify fund holdings under the investment company structure was an important innovation for the ETF market.

A second difference between a UIT structure and an investment company structure is the way company dividends paid into the fund are handled. Under the UIT structure, cash dividends paid by the underlying stocks are retained in a non-interest-bearing account until the end of the quarter and then distributed to shareholders as one lump sum. The investment company structure has more flexibility by allowing dividends to be reinvested in more stocks immediately after they are received by the fund. The investment company still pays quarterly dividends to shareholders like the UIT structure, but the reinvestment feature allows for a closer tracking to the indexes.

WEBS are responsible for other important innovations in ETFs. They made a specific advance in a method of arbitrage that acts to reduce the tax liability of individual investors holding WEB shares. SPDRs initially did not petition the SEC to use those tax-reducing strategies, but that has since been changed. The details of those tax benefits are discussed in Chapter 4. In another important market change, WEBS were allowed to use the terms *index fund* and *ETF* together in their sales literature, a combination the SEC had not previously allowed with SPDRs.

The SEC approved the registration of Diamonds (symbol: DIA) in 1997, an SSGA-managed ETF benchmarked to the Dow Jones Industrial Average (DJIA). Diamonds incorporate the tax benefits of WEBS even though it was filed as a unit investment trust. The name recognition of the Dow Jones Industrial Average made DIA attractive to many individual investors. It was easy to invest in and easy to follow. Literally every newspaper, radio station, and television news program reports the performance of the Dow. That has driven DIA to the position of the fifth-largest ETF on the market with nearly $3 billion in assets and two million shares traded daily.

State Street changed ETF structures in 1998 when they filed for industry sector SPDRs. The firm opted to organize Sector SPDRs as an investment company to give the new funds all the tax benefits and dividend reinvestment benefits of an investment company. The nine ETFs are benchmarked to nine S&P 500 sectors, and only stocks included in the S&P 500 are included. The sectors are materials, health care, consumer staples, consumer discretionary, energy, financial, industrial, technology, and utilities (see Chapter 12 for more information).

The most popular ETF among individual investors in the later 1990s was a NASDAQ-100 index-tracking stock with the original symbol of QQQ. The fund was renamed PowerShares QQQ in 2007 and now has the symbol QQQQ. The security has the nickname Cubes. The heavy weighting in technology and communications stocks made the security an ideal speculative investment during the technology and communications boom of the late 1990s. Cubes was an immediate hit with brokers and the public. It was the first ETF that many individual investors bought.

After the tech bust in 2000, Cubes fell out of favor with individual investors and with it ETF investing lapsed into obscurity in the minds of the public. That did not stop the innovation, however. The ETF market was rapidly evolving, and between 2000 and 2003, many new products were introduced and new ETF companies were established.

Vanguard Weighs in with VIPERs.   Vanguard introduced its first ETF in 2001 and called the product Vanguard Index Participation Equity Receipts (VIPERs). Up until this point, all ETFs were stand-alone funds. Vanguard made VIPERs a share class to its existing mutual fund. It was the first time an ETF and an open-end fund were linked.

The difference between Vanguard's open-end Total Stock Market Index Fund and the new VIPERs share class is that the ETF trades during the day when the stock market is open and the open-end fund shares trade after the market is closed. Another difference is the settlement time of the trade. Open-end shares settle the next day whereas VIPER shares settle in three days. That created some accounting challenges for Vanguard that they have managed to work around.

In January 2002, Vanguard launched its second ETF offering, the Vanguard Extend Market VIPERs. This fund tracks the performance of the Wilshire 4500 Index, which includes all stocks except those in the S&P 500.

During 2006, Vanguard dropped the VIPERs name from all their ETFs and now refers to those shares as simple ETFs. At the beginning of 2007, Vanguard launched fixed income ETFs that are share classes of the existing open-end fixed income index funds. When the decision was made to launch fixed income funds, the word VIPERs no longer fit. Recall the E in VIPER stood for "equity."

No other mutual fund has launched an ETF share class in an existing index fund. Perhaps the reason why is that it would have to pay Vanguard a royalty on the product because Vanguard owns a patent on the structure. Perhaps some mutual fund companies will license the structure when actively managed ETFs become commonplace.

Cheaper by the Dozen. Another interesting event took place in May 2000 that was to become a trend in the ETF marketplace. Barclays Global Investors (BGI) launched 50 new iShares ETF products in one day. The funds covered a wide variety of U.S., international, and global stock benchmarks.

BGI's multifund launch was the start of quantity over quality in the ETF industry. Many flood-the-market ETF launches have since occurred from several fund companies. Rydex broke the record in 2006 by filing for nearly 100 new funds on a single day. The flood-the-market model is designed to get as much product on the street as possible as quickly as possible and let the chips fall as they may. Many of us in the industry describe the process as throwing Jell-O against a wall and seeing how much sticks. As of this writing, the quantity-over-quality model is still alive and well as over 300 new funds await SEC approval.

The Quants Have Their Day.   In 2002, PowerShares was founded by former Nuveen Investments sales and marketing executive H. Bruce Bond. His idea was to use quantitative indexes as benchmarks for ETFs.

Quantitative methods are designed to find securities that are believed to have superior performance potential. The strategies use sophisticated *black box* methods to analyze and rank securities from greatest potential to least potential. The highest-ranked securities are optimized to find the best combination that has the highest probability of beating the market.

The engine used in the first PowerShares ETF is called Intellidex methodology. The system uses 25 selection criteria broken into four main groups: risk factors, momentum, fundamental growth, and stock valuations. The methodology was initially developed by Bond and fine-tuned by Robert Tull and others at the American Stock Exchange (AMEX) at the time. The indexes are maintained by the AMEX to satisfy the SEC requirement for separation of index provider and fund manager.

Bond's timing was perfect. The ETF industry was ripe for the next evolution and quantitative offerings were it. PowerShare funds attracted more than $1 billion in assets by 2006, and the company's successes lead to a several-hundred-million dollar buyout by Amvescap, PLC.

What seemed like an incredibly high price paid for PowerShares caused mutual fund providers and asset managers who were not in the ETF industry to step back and rethink their future. Something had changed. The ETF industry was evolving at a faster pace that many realized. In retrospect, Amvescap probably got a very good deal when it bought PowerShares. Traditional mutual fund companies that were not in the ETF market were going to fall behind, and that has created an opportunity for new ETF companies with innovative ideas to grab market share.

Alternative Funds Debut.   Commodities markets have been in existence for centuries. There are price indexes on commodity products going back thousands of years. Occasionally, there is a surge in commodities prices that last a few years. When those spikes occur, it draws a lot of investor attention.

The mid 2000s was a boom time in commodity prices. The price of oil skyrocketed to over $70 per barrel in the summer of 2006, while gold flirted with $700 per ounce. The boom drew instant interest from individual and institutional investors, and that pushed ETF companies into action. New funds were launched that tracked the price of oil, gold, and silver. In addition, a number of ETFs were launched that tracked various commodities indexes such as the S&P GSCI (formally the Goldman Sachs Commodities Index) and the Dow Jones AIG Commodities Index.

Currency funds were introduced with the launch of Rydex CurrencyShares ETFs in 2005. The Euro Currency Trust (symbol: FXE) was designed to rise in value when the Euro strengthens in relation to the U.S. dollar and fall when the Euro weakens. Additional currency market ETFs were added by Rydex in 2006 and 2007. Barclays Bank joined the currency party with the launch of its iPath ETNs, which is an innovative product that converts ordinary income into long-term capital gains.

Figure 1.2 illustrates the number of new ETFs launched each year since SPDRs' inception in 1993. The ETF issuance boom has accelerated every year since 2002, with tremendous growth occurring in 2007. As of mid 2007 there were nearly 400 new funds in SEC registration.

There is no reason to believe the number of ETFs launched will abate for several years, especially with the introduction of actively managed ETFs (see Chapter 5). Morningstar reports that there are over 6,000 distinct open-end mutual fund portfolios on the market and several of those portfolios have multiple share classes. If the open-end marketplace is any indication of where ETFs are heading, there are many years of rapid growth ahead for this industry.

The Future of ETFs

The ETF market is moving at such speeds that today's unique innovations will likely be overshadowed by tomorrow's new and bold idea. The opportunity for new ETFs is limited only by the imagination and ingenuity of the minds of those who create them. Here are some categories for growth:

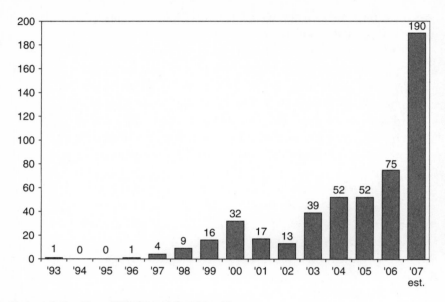

Figure 1.2   New ETFs Launched by Year
Source: Strategic Insight and Investment Company Institute

- Inexpensive hedge fund ETFs could be an era of opportunity for fund providers. Hedge fund investing is a hot topic in the news today, and the opportunities for investment are moving downstream toward individual investors. Academics have already simulated the returns of sophisticated hedge fund strategies, using widely traded derivatives such as futures and options. Those are the tools ETF companies can use to create synthetic hedge fund strategies for the masses.
- Are you buying or selling a home? Home price ETFs that track the housing market may be coming soon. There are already indexes that track housing markets, and derivatives that trade on that data. The indexes are divided into geographical regions and home types, such as condominiums in Miami and single family homes in Phoenix. ETFs benchmarked to these indexes would allow you to hedge against a rise in the price of your future home, or protect home equity from decline in the event of a housing slowdown.
- Worried about your job and making that mortgage payment? Or are you betting against others making their payment?

Perhaps we will see mortgage default ETFs based on increased home mortgage defaults or a decrease in defaults.

• Scared about college tuition increases? Maybe ETFs will be available to hedge tuition increases and allow you to lock in junior's college costs. What about grocery ETFs for those who believe the price of food will increase, or drug ETFs to bet on the price of pills? How about Social Security or Medicare ETFs to hedge a cut in benefits? The sky could be the limit with airfare ETFs to hedge the future price of airline tickets.

Some of these ideas may seem far-fetched, but they are possible. If there is demand, money management fees can be made. The only four factors needed for ETF creation are: a market index to use as a benchmark, liquid and marketable underlying securities that make up the ETF, successful passage of the idea through SEC registration, and market participants.

The biggest delay is SEC approval of new products. Many times existing regulations need to be changed to accommodate the idea, and that can take many months. Table 1.2 lists the time in registration for three different ETF structures. SPDRs took the SEC 28 months to approve. After the regulators studied the concept and approved it, follow-on ETFs using the UIT format were approved much faster. Things get easier once the SEC understands. Details on the three structures are listed in Table 1.2.

Why does it take the government so long to approve a new fund? It is the SEC's responsibility to protect the investing public from unscrupulous investment practices. That is why every new security must operate according to certain standards and meet certain levels of disclosure. It takes regulators time to learn about new products, and they are very thorough. In addition, the SEC asks for input from other governmental departments that might be affected.

The Future for Actively Managed ETFs. As of 2007, only a couple of dozen investment firms have launched products into the ETF marketplace. But I predict many more companies will join the race in the next few years, especially when the SEC allows full-fledged actively managed ETFs.

Actively managed ETFs do not follow an index. Instead, funds are invested in an actively managed portfolio of securities that is subjectively chosen by a fund manager. Active management is

Table 1.2   SEC Review Times for New ETF Structures

Product	Symbols	Structure	Year Filed	Months in Registration Review
SPDRs S&P 500	SPY	UIT	1990	28
Diamonds	DIA	UIT	1997	6
NASDAQ-100 Tracking Stock*	QQQQ	UIT	1998	6
Country Baskets (WEBS)**	Various	1940s Act	1994	19
Barclays iShares	Various	1940s Act	1999	12
Vanguard ETFs	Various	1940s Act	2000	6
streetTRACKS Gold	GLD	1933 Act	2003	18
iShare GSCI Commodities	GSG	1933 Act	2005	13

*Now PowerShares QQQ
**Now iShares
Source: SEC Filings

practiced by a majority of mutual fund companies and accounts for 90 percent of all open-end mutual funds on the market.

Many open-end companies spent many years and many dollars persuading their clients not to use index funds. So it would be close to heresy for many of those active management firms to launch ETF products benchmarked to index funds. But I suspect those active firms are anxiously awaiting an SEC-approved active ETF structure.

While the industry is eager to launch actively managed ETFs, the SEC has been very slow to approve the structure. The regulators expressed doubts about how the products would handle important issues like holdings disclosure and pricing.

Under current law, the index used as a benchmark for ETF management must disclose to the public the securities holdings and their weightings in the index while active open-end mutual fund holdings are only disclosed periodically, usually several weeks or months later. Using an ETF structure for active management means securities would be disclosed daily, and that might be a big disadvantage for actively managed ETFs because the manager's trading strategies would be completely exposed and could be exploited by other market participants.

Nonetheless, some firms have filed for actively managed ETFs that are transparent, in that they showed their holdings in real time. Those firms contend to offer full transparency of the fund's holdings on a daily basis, despite the disadvantage of exposing its strategy. Chapter 5 provides more information on the budding actively managed ETF marketplace.

Summary

Exchange-traded funds (ETFs) are a revolutionary investment product that is taking Wall Street and Main Street by storm. Part stock and part traditional open-end mutual fund, ETF investors buy ETF shares on a stock exchange and receive a proportionate share of a professionally managed portfolio.

Each ETF is managed differently and each in accordance with the benchmark it follows. Like stocks, ETFs offer investors the flexibility to buy and sell shares during the day anytime the exchanges are open. Like open-end mutual funds, ETFs offer broad security diversification in a professionally managed account.

The ETF marketplace is evolving, even though the growth in the number of ETFs has been unprecedented in the last few years. Each year, the structure and depth of the offerings expand. There are now over 500 ETFs traded in the United States with a total value rapidly approaching $1 trillion in assets. It is my belief that there will be more than 1,000 ETFs on the U.S. market by 2010, and perhaps more than half of all mutual funds will be exchange traded by 2020. The ETF marketplace is an exciting industry, and the revolution is just beginning.

CHAPTER 2

The Nuts and Bolts of ETFs

An ETF is bought and sold like a company stock during the day when the stock exchanges are open. Unlike a company stock, the number of shares outstanding of an ETF can change daily because of the continuous creation of new shares and the redemption of existing shares. The ability of ETF companies to issue and redeem shares on an ongoing basis keeps the market price of ETFs in line with their underlying security values. The arbitrage mechanism ensures that the price investors pay for ETF shares is close to the true net asset value (NAV) of the underlying securities that make up the fund.

Chapter 2 covers the operations and management behind ETFs, including important participants that make the ETF market efficient. It also covers the share creation and redemption process, the trading of ETF shares on exchanges, and the symbology used in the ETF industry. There is a lot of useful information packed into these pages.

Acts like a Fund, Trades like a Stock

Assume for a moment that you have decided to buy an S&P 500 index fund. There are many funds available that track the return of the S&P 500, including open-end mutual fund and ETFs. You have narrowed your search down to two candidates: the open-end Vanguard 500 Index—Admiral Shares (VFIAX) or the iShares S&P 500 ETF (IVV). How similar are these funds and what makes them different from one another?

There are more similarities than differences between a traditional open-end fund and an ETF that tracks the same index. They both issue shares that represent ownership interest in the funds. Both funds hold an underlying basket of S&P 500 stocks. The expense ratios charged to shareholders in both VFIAX and IVV is 0.09 percent. Both funds can be bought or sold any day the stock exchange is open. And for all practical purposes, the return expectations of both types of funds are identical. So, what is the difference?

The first and most significant difference is how investors acquire shares of each fund. VFIAX is an open-end fund, and its shares trade directly with Vanguard, the mutual fund company that manages the fund. IVV trades on a stock exchange. Shares are purchased from other investors and sold to other investors. At no time does an individual investor buy ETFs from a fund company or sell back to a fund company.

When buying shares of open-end VFIAX, money is placed directly into the fund by you or your brokerage firm. Vanguard does not charge a commission to invest in their funds, but a commission will be charged by a brokerage when shares of Vanguard funds are purchased through the broker. Either way, the mutual fund company takes in cash and issues new open-end mutual fund shares. That is done at the close of business each day.

If you deal directly with Vanguard to buy VFIAX, the shares you acquire are held at Vanguard in an account in your name. You will receive regular statements from Vanguard as well as tax information. If shares are purchased through a brokerage firm, your shares are still held at Vanguard, but in an omnibus account that holds all shares for that brokerage firm. You will still receive a monthly statement and annual tax information on your prorated shares, but that will come from the brokerage firm, not from Vanguard.

Shares of an ETF are always purchased through a brokerage firm on a stock exchange. The shares you buy already exist in someone else's portfolio. They are not created for you by the mutual fund company. Like buying individual stocks, you are acquiring shares already in the public domain. The only people authorized to trade ETFs directly with the fund company are special institutional investors called authorized participants (APs). We will discuss their important role shortly.

The exchange-traded operations of ETFs have a major impact on the way ETFs are marketed. The exchange-traded fund companies have agreed with the SEC not to advertise or market their products as mutual funds even though many ETFs are legally registered as open-end mutual funds. The SEC has concluded that since investors in ETFs do not deal directly with the mutual fund companies, the ETF shares should not be called mutual funds in any marketing material. Thus, according to the letter of the law, there are mutual funds and there are ETFs, and never shall the two names be used in the same sentence. I am not as strict in this book.

If individuals do not buy from fund companies, where do the shares they buy come from? APs can trade directly with the fund company, and that means ultimately ETF shareholders acquire their shares from a larger block called a creation unit, which is owned by an AP. In essence, individual ETF investors own their shares indirectly as part of a larger block that is owned by a third party. It is a fine distinction, but an important one that aids in operational efficiency and keeps administrative costs down. More details on creation units are provided later in this chapter.

A second important difference between open-end funds and ETFs is the pricing of the shares. Open-end mutual funds are priced once per day at their closing net asset value (NAV) for the day. To the contrary, ETF shares are priced continuously during the day whenever the stock market is open. Rarely is the market price of an ETF the same as the intraday value, which is similar to its NAV.

The main element of a fund's NAV is the current market value of its underlying securities. A fund may also hold cash, other assets, and have liabilities. The fund liabilities are subtracted from its assets to find the total value, and then that number is divided by the total shares outstanding to find the NAV per share. The process for finding a fund's net asset value is the same for an open-end fund as it is for an ETF. The formula is as follows:

$$\frac{\text{Underlying value of a fund}}{\text{Number of shares outstanding}} = \text{Net Asset Value (NAV)}$$

For example:

$$\$100,000,000 \ \text{total fund value} = \$10 \ \text{per share NAV}$$

Each afternoon after the markets close, Vanguard calculates the NAV for each of its open-end mutual funds and then divides that amount by the number of open-end shares outstanding. The firm publishes the NAV about 5:00 PM Eastern Time each day. That is the price all investors would pay per share to purchase the fund on that day, and the price paid for each share redeemed on that day. There is no interday NAV calculation of open-end share prices and no interday trading of those shares.

Continual ETF pricing is very different than open-end fund pricing because shares are constantly trading during the day at different prices. ETFs are bought during the day on a stock exchange from other investors. The price paid for ETF shares is the market price of those shares at the time of sale. The NAV of all ETFs is still calculated only once per day, but an estimate of intraday value is calculated for all ETFs every 15 seconds. The exchange that trades an ETF is responsible for providing the estimate of an intraday value and making those amounts available to the public.

The intraday value estimate is used by investors and APs as a guide to how much an ETF should be trading near. The intraday value is not an absolute number. There could be discrepancies from delayed pricing of securities trades or the ETF may hold securities that have not traded that day. ETFs that invest in foreign securities will often have intraday value estimates that are not a true reflection of NAV because during most trading hours in the United States, the overseas markets are closed.

Since the intraday value is an estimate of NAV, ETFs typically trade at a premium or a discount to their intraday value as illustrated in the table that follows. There are several theories behind ETF premiums and discounts. Perhaps an ETF price is a better estimate of NAV that the intraday value at the time or perhaps an ETF is simply selling at a premium or discount to its NAV because of liquidity issues with the underlying securities. In either case, ETF share pricing is independent of their intraday value, even though most of the time, shares trade close to that value.

The ETF Market Price Discount/Premium formula is:

$$\frac{\text{Market Price} - \text{Intraday Value}}{\text{Intraday Value}} = \frac{\text{Discount or Premium}}{(\text{Discounts} < 0, \text{Premium} > 0)}$$

For example:

$$\frac{\$112.11 - \$111.00}{\$111.00} = 1.0\% \text{ Premium}$$

The third major difference between open-end funds and ETFs is the trade settlement period. Open-end funds have a one-day settlement and ETFs have a three-day settlement.

When you buy or sell open-end shares of VFIAX from Vanguard, the account is settled on the next business day. If you are buying shares, you will need to have your money at Vanguard the next day or you are delinquent. When you sell open-end shares, the money is available to you the next day.

ETF purchases have a three-day settlement. If you buy shares of IVV from your broker on Monday, the money needs to be in your brokerage account by Thursday. You have two extra days to pay for shares. On the other hand, if you sell ETF shares, it takes two extra days to get the money.

I bring up the point about settlement differences because some people find themselves in a pickle when they sell ETF shares and buy open-end shares on the same day. The difference in settlement time can leave an account short of capital for two days. Brokerage firms do not take kindly to investors not paying for their security purchases on time, and most brokers will charge interest for the two-day delay in paying for the open-end fund. If that occurs in your brokerage account, you will likely get a nasty note from the brokerage firm telling you that your account is restricted from trading for a certain period of time. A restricted account must have hard cash on hand or the brokerage firm will not execute your buy orders.

The fourth difference between open-end funds and ETFs is trivial, but might make you sound smart in conversation. It is the difference in the number of symbols used to designate the fund. A security symbol is more than just a market designator. It also identifies the type of fund and where you can find pricing for the fund.

You can tell that from the five letters in the designator, VFIAX, that the Vanguard 500 Index is a traditional open-end mutual fund. Open-end funds always have five letters (no numbers) and the last letter is always an X. Five letters with an X on the end means the price of the fund can be found in the mutual fund section of the newspaper.

You know iShares S&P 500 (IVV) is an exchange traded security because ETFs typically have three letters in their symbol. A one-, two-, or three-letter designator means that a security trades on either the New York Stock Exchange (NYSE) or the American Stock Exchange (AMEX). On rare occasions, you will see an ETF with four letters, such as QQQQ for PowerShares QQQ. Four letters means the security trades over the counter on the NASDAQ. Pricing for ETFs are found either in the stock section of the newspaper, or in a separate section for exchange traded portfolios. You will not find any ETFs that have five letters ending in an X.

Here are four major differences between open-end funds and ETFs that have been covered:

1. The only buyer and seller of open-end shares is the fund company, while individual ETF shares are bought and sold from other investors on an exchange. Those shares are part of a creation unit owned by an authorized participant.
2. Open-end shares are priced once per day at their NAV and all buyers and sellers receive the NAV price while the estimated intraday value of an ETF is calculated every 15 seconds. The intraday value is not the price at which an ETF trades. ETFs trade at a price based on supply and demand for the fund at the time of the trade.
3. The settlement of open-end shares is the next business day, while the settlement of ETF shares is three business days. Be careful when selling ETFs and buying open-end funds because you could find yourself short of capital.
4. The market designator for open-end funds is always five letters, with an X as the last letter, while the market designator for an ETF is typically three letters and occasionally four letters, depending on which exchange it trades on.

Closed-End Fund Issues

Chapter 1 covered a short history of mutual fund investing, including the problem of using closed-end funds (CEF) as a market hedge. Both CEFs and ETFs trade on the stock exchange at prices that are independent of the underlying securities in the funds. Unlike an ETF, a CEF frequently develops large and persistent price differences between the price of a fund and the intraday value of securities and cash that compose the fund.

Wide premiums and discounts to NAV occur in CEFs because the fund company is restricted from changing the number of shares available on the market. The number of shares issued is determined on the first day a CEF is launched. After that, the number of shares in the hands of investors is fixed. The CEF would need SEC and shareholder approval to change the number of shares. That can take a long time and it can be quite costly.

Since the number of CEF shares outstanding does not change, the market price of shares is subject to the supply and demand of those shares. Many times the market of the CEF shares gets far off track from the value of the underlying securities and cash. Odd as it sounds, CEF price premiums and discounts may persist for several years because there is no method to bring the price closer to its NAV.

The gap between CEF prices and the NAVs could easily be closed with a rewrite of securities law. If changes were made to permit fund managers to increase or decrease the number or shares outstanding, the premiums and discounts would immediately disappear. That would allow the fund manager to issue more CEF shares when a premium developed and redeem CEF shares when a discount developed.

For example, when CEF shares are selling at the premium, the fund manager would create more CEF shares and sell them into the market. The proceeds from the sale of new CEF shares would go into the fund and be used to buy the individual stocks that make up the fund. The selling of new CEF shares and the buying of the underlying securities would drive the two prices together. This arbitrage trade would be repeated again and again until the CEF share price and its underlying value were so closely reduced that doing arbitrage would no longer be profitable.

Why doesn't the SEC allow fund managers to do arbitrage trades and eliminate CEF discounts and premiums? Recall from Chapter 1 that the SEC's mission is to protect the investing public. Its concern is that closed-end fund companies will abuse the creation and redemption privilege and attempt to manipulate prices for the benefit of the firm itself. If the fund company can control the market price of CEFs by widening or narrowing discounts and premiums, that could become very lucrative to a fund company.

It is easy to justify the SEC's caution in the wake of many mutual fund scandals that have been uncovered over the past decade. Several once reputable firms and their officers have been implicated on a number of securities violations. Several mutual fund executives have been barred from the business and paid large fines, and even gone to jail.

ETFs to the Rescue

ETFs avoid persistent premiums and discounts inherent in closed-end funds because the pioneers petitioned the SEC to allow ETF managers to create or redeem shares during the day as needed. To avoid self-dealing, however, an independent third party initiates the arbitrage trades and oversees the distribution of newly created ETF shares. The third party also decides when new ETF shares will be created and when existing ETF shares will be redeemed.

The independent third party in the ETF creation and redemption process is called an authorized participant (AP). APs include market makers such as Goldman Sachs, Smith Barney, and Merrill Lynch and market specialist firms that few people outside of Wall Street have heard of. Involving specialists and market makers in the ETF creation and redemption process shifts the arbitrage profit from the fund companies to the APs. Since there are several APs that cover each ETF, the competition between APs for business tends to deter abusive trading practices by ensuring transparency is high and arbitrage profits stay within reason.

Government oversight occurs at every level, including the daily transaction of individual stocks and ETF shares through the Depository Trust Clearing Corporation (DTC). DTC is the U.S. government agency that records securities transactions. They also record ETF transfers just as they do any other exchange traded security.

ETF Share Creation and Redemption

The creation and redemption process that sets ETFs apart from all other mutual funds starts when an investment company sponsors a new fund. First, they record the fund's investment objective and then submit a detailed filing to the SEC for approval. The filing contains legal information about the fund, including fees, objectives, risks, symbols, and how it is responsible. That information is eventually used in the ETF's Prospectus and Statement of Additional Information. Among many other items, it discloses how much shareholders will pay for investment management and administrative costs.

ETFs track securities indexes, the only exception being actively managed ETFs that are forthcoming (see Chapter 5). Most ETF companies license their indexes from an outside vendor such as S&P, Russell, Dow Jones, and MSCI. In addition to those big names, there are dozens of smaller index providers that create and track niche indexes. An index can also be one item, such as the price of one once of gold or a barrel of oil.

A useful index for benchmarking has clear procedures for determining index constituents and the weighting of those constituents. The methodology for managing an index must be consistent, and the pricing of the index must be disseminated in real time. The index provider makes money by charging licensing fees to fund companies that create ETFs. Licensing costs are part of the expense of an ETF, but the actual amount paid to license an index is not disclosed. The fee is typically based on a percentage of assets in an ETF. For example, S&P might charge 0.02 percent for the licensing rights to the S&P 500 while a niche index such as Intellidex may charge 0.08 percent.

One way some ETF companies lower costs is to create their own indexes, thereby keeping the licensing fee that would have to be paid to the third party. The SEC does require, however, that in-house index providers hire an outside management company to manage their ETF, which adds cost back in. WisdomTree Investments, Inc. formed its own dividend and earnings indexes that their ETFs are benchmarked to. The firm hired the Bank of New York to manage the WisdomTree ETFs in order to satisfy SEC requirements.

The lending of securities is one way many large investment firms earn revenue from the ETFs. State Street, the Vanguard Group, and Barclays Global Investors (BGI), for example, hold enormous quantities of stock on behalf of their investors. Those stocks can be loaned to APs during the ETF creation process and that earns the investment firm a small interest fee for the duration of the loan.

A minor but important player in ETF management is the custodial bank. A bank physically holds securities for a fund. It is the actual entity that processes and accounts for each security's coming and going. As exchanges are made in a fund, the custodial bank double-checks the type and quantity of securities to ensure they are correct. The bank typically earns a small fee based on the assets in the fund.

The next group to be involved in ETF share creation and redemption are the most important. They are the authorized participants. APs are often referred to as market makers or specialists. A new fund signs participant agreements with several independent AP firms.

When new ETF shares are created, these middlemen either buy or borrow the appropriate basket of stocks and exchange them with the ETF fund manager for those newly created ETF shares. The individual securities and cash basket turned in by the AP must be equal the NAV published holdings from the previous close. Since the closing NAV is a known quantity, using that list prevents the fund company from indirectly profiting on the share creation process and satisfies the SEC's concern over potential abuse.

APs receive one creation unit issued by the fund through the custodian bank in return for turning in a basket of securities and cash. Creation units are large blocks of ETF shares, usually numbering up to 50,000. The actual number of ETF shares in a creation unit varies according to the ETF. Some are as small as 20,000 shares.

After an ETF creation unit is issued to the AP by the custodial bank, the AP has many options. It can either hold the unit in a company account, trading it to another AP, or break it up into individual ETF shares. Individual ETF shares trade on the public markets and are the shares the general public buys. Figure 2.1 illustrates the creation process as shares move from the fund company, through the AP, to the exchanges, and ultimately to individual investors.

The reverse process occurs when an AP redeems a creation unit. The AP buys ETF shares on the open market to form the correct quantity for a creation unit. It then turns the shares over to the fund company. In return, the AP receives individual securities and a

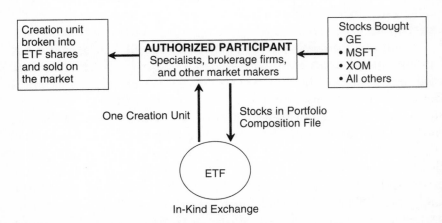

Figure 2.1   The Creation of ETF Shares

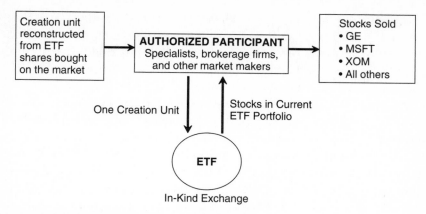

Figure 2.2   The Redemption of ETF Shares

cash portion equal to the exact NAV of the creation unit. Figure 2.2 illustrates the redemption process as shares move from the hands of individual investors, on to the exchanges, through the AP, and finally to the fund company.

There is a small fee charged to the AP by ETF companies every time a creation unit is created or redeemed. That fee is typically about $1,000 per creation unit, depending on the fund. The fee is minuscule compared to the value of the unit, which is typically several million dollars.

Daily Portfolio Composition Files.   How do APs know which securities to include in the basket they turn in for a creation unit? Each evening, after the markets are closed and the NAV of a fund is known, ETF companies publish a portfolio composition file (PCF). The PCF lists the exact names and quantity of the underlying securities and cash that need to be turned in by an AP to receive one creation unit. Cash is part of the list because it often represents the accumulated stock dividends in a portfolio that have yet to be paid or a portion of the fund that is invested in nonliquid securities.

Timely and accurate PCFs are critical to the smooth and orderly flow of the ETF marketplace. ETF managers are responsible for ensuring their PCF files are sent to the National Securities Clearing Corporation (NSCC). The NSCC is then responsible for processing and distributing PCFs to all APs before the opening of the next market day.

As the composition of an underlying index changes, the fund company notifies all APs. The APs are responsible for changing the composition of the creation units they hold. When Standard & Poor's replaces a stock in the S&P 500 index, APs that hold SPDRs S&P 500 creation units are contacted. The APs deliver the newly added security to the fund company through the custodian, and in turn, the custodian sends the AP the security that was deleted from that index. The swap makes all creation units up to date.

The creation, redemption, and management of ETF shares may seem clumsy and complex the first time you study it. The process, however, is actually a very efficient arbitrage mechanism. APs have the ability to create and redeem creation units any time the markets are open by basically hitting a few keystrokes and calling a trading desk. The rest of the transaction is fairly automated. Share creation and redemption has to be efficient and timely because that is the only way APs will make any money on arbitrage. Small profits can add up to big awards for AP firms that use the most sophisticated methods. That helps individual investors, because it keeps ETF prices close to their true NAV price.

Creation and Redemption Arbitrage.   The APs that contract with an ETF are a closed group. They are the only people to have the exclusive right to create and redeem shares with a fund company. There are enough APs assigned to each ETF to ensure a competitive market, as well as the tight spreads between the market price and the NAV. They can make money when ETFs are trading at either a premium or a discount.

If ETF shares are selling at a premium to their intraday value, an AP will buy the securities that make up the fund, add cash according to the PCF, and exchange that basket for a creation unit. The AP will then sell the creation unit for a market price greater than the value of the securities turned in. That generates a risk-free profit. The arbitrage trade is repeated again and again until there is no profit left for the AP. At that point the ETF market price and its NAV are probably in an acceptable range.

If ETF shares are trading at a discount to their intraday value, an AP will sell securities that make up a fund and buy ETF shares on the market. Once the APs buy enough ETF shares to form a creation unit, or trade from their account, they will exchange that unit for its underlying cash and securities. The unit redemption covers the

AP for the stocks they already sold. The price arbitrage generates a small risk-free profit to the AP, and the trades are repeated over and over until the profit incentive is gone.

This provision for arbitrage is what fundamentally differentiates ETFs from closed-end mutual funds. A closed-end mutual fund is much like an ETF—it sells shares representing a basket of securities on a stock exchange, and trades just like a stock, but because it has no legal provision for exchanging the shares of the fund for the securities after the fund is created, the share price of the fund frequently deviates by a large amount from the NAV of the fund.

Getting ETFs into Public Hands. Unlike traditional open-end mutual funds, individual investors have no relationship with the fund itself. Only authorized participants offer ETF shares for sale on the stock exchanges. As such, individual investors own ETF shares that are actually on the books of another investor. There is no risk in this because the AP shares are on the books of the fund company.

As an individual investor, all trades must go through a brokerage firm. When buying ETFs, you need to contact a brokerage firm to purchase shares on a stock exchange. There is a commission to pay as with any brokerage transaction. Most ETF shares trade on the American Stock Exchange (AMEX), with an increasing number trading on the New York Stock Exchange (NYSE) and the NASDAQ exchange. Shares that trade on the AMEX and the NYSE have a three letter symbol and shares that trade on the NASDAQ have a four letter symbol.

Table 2.1 is a summary of the basic differences between ETFs, common stocks, open-end mutual funds, and closed-end mutual funds.

Pricing ETF Shares and Components

The ETF prices printed in the newspaper are the closing price of shares from the previous trading day. They are single price that reflect the last trade of the day. The price does not tell us if that trade was a buy or sell.

Like stocks, ETFs always have two prices: a bid and an ask price. The price you will receive depends on whether you are buying (ask) or selling (bid). The trading spread is the difference between the bid and the ask. A small trading spread of a few pennies means the ETF

Table 2.1   A Comparison of Investment Vehicles

	ETFs	Common Stocks	Open-end Funds	Closed-end Funds
Intraday Liquidity	Yes	Yes	No	Yes
Portfolio Transparency	Yes	Yes	No	No
Tax-efficient	Yes	Yes	Possible	Possible
Diversification	Yes	No	Yes	Yes
Low Expenses	Yes	Possible	Possible	No
Professional Management	Yes	No	Yes	Yes
Fully Invested	Yes	Yes	No	No

is trading close to its intraday value and is typical of the 50 or so most active ETFs. Spreads can become wide when there is uncertainty in the markets, or the underlying securities have less liquidity. When the international markets are closed, trading in ETFs that invest in international stocks will have wider spreads than those that trade in U.S. stocks.

Stock exchanges provide several different ETF component prices and data that you might be interested in. The best way to illustrate information available from an exchange is through an example. Table 2.2 lists all the data and market symbols associated with trading shares of SPDRs S&P 500. Don't be concerned if you do not completely comprehend these indicators because most are relevant to only APs, custodians, fund managers, and other parties involved in ETF operations.

Table 2.2   SPDR S&P 500 Ticker Components

SPDR S&P 500 Components	Frequency	Symbols	Unit Measured
ETF Market Price	Continuous	SPY	Per share
Intraday Indicative Value	Every 15 seconds	SXV	Per share
Net Asset Value	Prior Day	SXV.NV	Per share
Shares Outstanding	Prior Day	SXV.SO	Shares in total
Accumulated Dividend	Prior Day	SXV.DV	Per share
Estimated Cash Component	Prior Day	SXV.EU	Per creation unit
Total Cash Component	Prior Day	SXV.TC	Per creation unit
Index Value	Continuous	SPX	The index

The following list will help sort out all the ETF prices and data that are available from exchanges:

ETF Market Price: The price investors receive when they buy or sell individual ETF shares on an exchange. The market price is a dual quote: the ask price and the bid price. The ask price (or offer price) is the level at which at least 100 shares can be purchased; the bid price is the level at which you would be able to sell at least 100 shares. The difference between the bid and ask is the trading spread.

The spread in some ETFs can be persistently larger than the spread in others. That is due to the securities that make up the underlying ETF. Trading spreads of ETFs reflect a compilation of the trading spreads in the underlying securities of that fund. The trading spread of an S&P 500 ETF will be just a few cents because the stocks that make up the S&P 500 are very liquid and trade constantly. Conversely, the spread in an ETF that invests in emerging market stocks will be wider because some emerging markets are closed when the U.S. stock exchanges are open, and the wider spreads in those underlying stocks reflect extra risk to market makers.

APs are ready to pounce on any opportunity for a risk-free return. Whenever the spread in an ETF becomes inappropriately large, an AP will step in and arbitrage. As a result, the average spread for an ETF tends to reflect very closely the lowest spread that is attainable for that ETF at the time. When markets are volatile, the spread on individual securities can widen, and that causes the spread on ETFs to also widen. Any discrepancy in spreads is an arbitrage opportunity. Stock exchanges track ETF spreads, and that information is available to the public for free on Web sites provided by the exchanges and the fund companies. A list of web sites that track ETF spreads is provided in Appendix B.

Intraday Indicative Value (IIV): Published for every ETF as a reference value to be used in conjunction with other ETF market information. The IIV for an ETF is typically published every 15 seconds and is updated throughout the trading day based on the last sale prices of the securities specified for creation and redemption plus any estimated cash amounts associated with the creation unit, all on a per-ETF share basis. IIV levels are available to the public through any market quote service.

The IIV is designed to give investors a sense of the relationship between a basket of securities that are representative of those owned in the ETF and the share price of the ETF on an intraday basis. Intraday Indicative Value is also referred to as the *intraday value* in this book, and the *Underlying Trading Value* or *Indicative Optimized Portfolio Value* in various places such as the prospectus and ETF marketing materials.

Net Asset Value (NAV): This information is always from the close on the previous trading day. The NAV of an ETF is determined in a manner consistent with other mutual funds. It is calculated by taking the total assets of the ETF minus liabilities, divided by the number of ETF shares outstanding. The official NAV is usually expressed as a value per share and it is calculated officially once a day by most U.S. funds, based on closing prices at 4:00 PM Eastern Time.

Shares Outstanding (in 1,000s): The number of ETF shares issued as of the closing on the previous trading day. It is the number used to calculate the NAV. Since ETFs are constantly being created and redeemed during a trade day, shares outstanding for many ETFs change from day to day.

Accumulated Dividends are per ETF share, net of expenses, through and including the previous day's close. Stocks pay dividends throughout the quarter while ETFs pay dividends only once per quarter. The accumulated dividend is the amount embedded in the share price and IIV waiting to be paid out.

Estimated Cash Amount per current creation unit. The estimated cash amount per creation unit is designed to give APs an idea of approximately how much cash per creation unit will be needed to create or redeem ETF shares on a given day.

Total Cash Required per creation unit for creations and redemptions executed the previous day to ensure that those trades occur at NAV. Cash required ensures that existing ETF shares do not experience any dilution in value as a result of creation and redemption activity.

Index Value: This is the underlying stock, bond, commodity, or other index benchmark that a fund is being managed against. In the case of SPY, it is the S&P 500 Index. It does not include dividend reinvestment.

Although there are a lot of pricing symbols, acronyms, and terminology, the only prices investors should be concerned about are the bid and ask and the Intraday Indicative Value. Based on the type of ETF you are buying or selling, if the spread is within the average spread, and the IIV is close to your trade price, you are probably getting a fair trade.

Individual Investors and ETF Trading

Buy and sell orders for ETF shares can be accomplished with a simple market order, or be conditional using limit orders, stop-loss orders, or many different types of orders that are used for trading common stock. ETFs can also be bought on margin and sold short. The Glossary of Terms explains each of these conditional trades.

ETFs are not subject to the short-sale rules on common stock that require short sales to be executed on an uptick in price. A short sale occurs when an investor borrows stock and sells it on the exchange, hoping to buy it back at a lower price in the future.

The SEC short-sale rule for common stocks was put in place to prevent short sellers from driving the price of a stock down by their trading activity. That does not apply to ETFs because short sellers cannot manipulate the price of an ETF. That is because ETF shares are based on an underlying basket of securities, and when ETF prices get out of line with those underlying securities, APs step in and drive ETF prices higher through arbitrage.

Summary

ETF shares are bought and sold during the day like stocks when the stock exchange is open. The number of ETF shares outstanding can change because of the continuous creation of new shares and redemption of existing shares. Authorized participants closely track ETF prices and underlying securities, looking for a risk-free return. The arbitrage mechanism of ETF shares eliminated the persistent premiums and discounts that are common in the closed-end mutual fund marketplace, and ensures that the price investors pay for ETF shares is close to its Intraday Indicative Value.

The operations behind ETF management involve many participants and can be confusing at times. However, of all the people, processes, terminology, symbols, and prices, the only two things that individual investors should be concerned about are the current ETF bid and ask prices, and the Intraday Indicative Value. Based on the type of ETF you are buying or selling, if the spread between the bid and ask is within a few pennies, then you are probably getting a fair price.

CHAPTER

3

Types of Exchange-Traded Portfolios

Exchange-traded funds trade like stocks on stock exchanges. However, you will not find ETF prices in the stock section of the *Wall Street Journal*. ETF prices are listed in the *Money & Investing* section of the Journal in their own subsection, appropriately titled *Exchange-Traded Portfolios*.

The caption *Exchange-Traded Portfolios* makes a lot of sense because there are different types of exchange traded securities that have the look and feel of an ETF, and are referred to by most people as an ETF, but they are not exchange-traded funds. They are alternatives to ETFs, such as special trusts and notes.

Each exchange-traded portfolio type has similarities and differences with the others. All types trade on a stock exchange. They all attempt to track the performance of an index, a currency, a commodity, or other benchmark. Each one has an arbitrage mechanism of sorts that keeps the market price of the exchange traded share or units in line with its Intraday Indicative Value.

The difference in each type of exchange-traded portfolio is in how they operate and how they are governed. Every new exchange-traded portfolio needs Securities and Exchange Commission (SEC) approval before it is made available to the public. Depending on how a security was filed with the SEC, different government regulations will dictate how that security will operate and report results. There are regulations covering the types of securities that can be held and not held, the way dividends accumulate and are paid to shareholders, and the taxation of those distributions.

It is the mandate of most exchange-traded portfolios to closely track the performance of an index. There are many ways to accomplish that objective. One method is to fully replicate the holdings of an index by matching security for security. A second method is for fund managers to use sophisticated sampling strategies designed to mirror the fundamental characteristics of an index and thus closely track index performance. A third method is to hold derivatives such as futures that closely follow index values in lieu of holding individual securities that make up the index.

This short chapter covers five exchange-traded portfolio structures and their operating differences. By understanding the similarities and differences between structures, you will be better prepared to invest in the security type that makes the most sense for your situation.

The Expanding Exchange-Traded Universe

There are three primary regulatory structures for exchange-traded portfolios discussed in this chapter along with several offshoots of those structures. Some of the differences between structures are slight, while others are large. The difference in structure determines how each exchange-traded portfolio operates, how it is taxed, who regulates it, how it reports financial information and to whom, and how those issues may affect the performance.

There are three primary fund structures commonly referred to as exchange-traded funds; only one structure, however, is organized under laws used for the issuance and governance of mutual funds. The other types of exchange traded structures fall under laws for the issuance and governance of stock and bond offerings.

Investment Company Act of 1940 regulates the operations of investment companies, including open-end mutual funds. ETFs that are organized under the 40s Act are technically created as open-end mutual funds. To avoid confusion, the SEC mandates that ETFs issued as 40s act funds should be called exchange-traded funds rather than open-end mutual funds.

The remaining types of exchange-traded portfolios are not funds. They are registered as trusts or notes under the Securities Act of 1933. That is the same law that stocks and bonds are issued under. Portfolios that are organized under the Securities Act of 1933 may be managed like a fund and trade like an ETF, but they do not report like one, nor are they governed in exactly the same way.

The 1933 Act structure is commonly used when a portfolio is to be concentrated in one single security or just a few securities and does not meet investment company diversification requirements.

Figure 3.1 is a flowchart of the exchange-traded portfolio marketplace. The chart will help you visualize where each structure fits as you read through the next section.

Why are so many different types of exchange-traded portfolios needed? A short history of investment regulations as they relate to pooled investment products will help explain each of the exchange-traded portfolio types in their proper perspective. Each structure had a specific purpose when it was created. Once a security is issued under a new structure, the regulation of the structure persists until there are no longer any securities outstanding.

Government Securities Acts

The first mutual fund was created in 1924 by the Massachusetts Investment Trust Company. Individual investors embraced the new idea of a professionally managed pooled account that was diversified and relatively low cost. By the end of that decade, sixteen more funds were formed. Most of the funds were created by large banks that loaned investors money to buy their funds.

In the 1920s, bank-created funds tended to operate in a rather reckless manner. Banks lent money to fund investors who put little

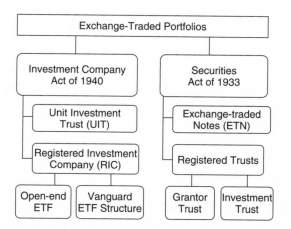

Figure 3.1   Exchange-Traded Portfolio Types
Source: Portfolio Solutions, LLC

down. Leverage of 90 percent was common. The excessive amounts of capital flowing into stock trusts during the Roaring Twenties allowed banks to underwrite stock issues for unproven companies that had no track record of earning and were not entirely creditworthy. The worst of the litter found its way into the bank's mutual funds. On the other hand, when a profitable and creditworthy company issued stocks and bonds, those issues went into the bank's private accounts.

On October 24, 1929, the worst bear market in the history of the U.S. stock market began. Almost immediately, the banks started calling in highly leveraged loans from mutual fund investors. Many did not have the money to pay the bank for their loans. Thus, the bank started dumping stocks on the market while liquidating leveraged mutual fund positions. That led to more declines, more calls to pay off loans, more defaults, and more selling. The downward spiral lasted about three years.

The banking system was in a shambles by 1932. Many large and once reputable banks closed their doors and never reopened. Many individual investors lost everything, especially their faith in banks. People who did not have money in mutual funds also lost when a bank shut its doors. There was no government guarantee of deposits at the time. The financial collapse was followed by a period known as the Great Depression.

The Securities Act of 1933.   Congress went into action and wrote into law, among others, the Securities Act of 1933, the Banking Act of 1933 (the second Glass-Steagall act), and the Securities Exchange Act of 1934. The Securities act regulates initial public offerings that occur when a company issues stock for the first time (also called the primary market). Under this act, every security coming to the primary market had to pass government screening, and had to pledge to keep their investors informed. The Glass-Steagall act separated banks into commercial banks and investment banks. Commercial banks could not be involved in issuing stocks or bonds and investment banks could not make loans for mortgages and other needs. The 1934 Act regulates how securities trade on the stock exchange after they are issued (also called the secondary market). This act also ensures that companies trading on the secondary market publish regular financial statements and other required reports.

The Investment Company Act of 1940. The investing public lost confidence in the financial system after the Crash of 1929. Congress passed the Investment Company Act of 1940 in an effort to restore investors' confidence in the stock market and to protect the public from unscrupulous mutual funds practices of the past. The new law set strict standards by which all registered investment trusts and registered investment companies operated. The 40 Act, as it is often referred to, established regular reporting procedures that each fund had to follow, established minimum diversification requirements, set standards for advertising, and gave regulatory oversight to the Securities and Exchange Commission.

The 40 Act specifically addressed conflicts of interest between investment companies and securities exchanges. It protected the public primarily by legally requiring disclosure of material details and operations about each investment company, and required investment companies to publicly disclose information about their own financial health. However, the act did not go so far as to write strict provisions whereby the SEC could make judgments about how fund managers should or could invest money.

ETFs Organized as 40 Act Funds

ETFs created under the Investment Company Act of 1940 are divided into two types, Unit Investment Trusts (UITs) and Regulated Investment Companies (RIC). Both types of funds are not taxed directly. Rather, they are eligible to pass the taxes on capital gains, dividends, or interest payments on to individual investors. There are differences between the two structures, and of course differences in their offshoot structures.

40 Act Unit Investment Trusts (UITs). ETFs organized as UITs have several telltale characteristics. First, UITs are nonmanaged entities. Nonmanaged means the manager of the fund can have no discretion as to which securities go into a UIT and which do not. The manager must follow the index exactly.

The SPDRS S&P 500 Trust (symbol: SPY) is a UIT structure. Managers of that fund must own all the securities in the underlying index that that fund tracks, which is the S&P 500 Index. The managers of the fund cannot exclude stocks that are in the S&P 500, nor can they add stocks that are not in that index.

UITs are also restricted as to security weightings. Securities that have a weighting of 5 percent or greater cannot compose more than 25 percent of the fund, nor can a UIT hold more than 10 percent of the voting stock of any one company. Funds specializing in industry sectors, or concentrated holdings, cannot compose more than 50 percent of the fund. Weighting restrictions are not a problem for a broadly diversified index such as the S&P 500. Security weight restrictions, however, can be a problem for some industry sectors or country funds where one or two companies dominate that index.

Another restriction in the UIT structure is on the accumulation of dividends paid by stocks in the fund. The UIT manager cannot reinvest cash from dividends paid by the underlying companies in more shares of stock within the security. That cash must go in a non-interest-bearing escrow account where it will sit until paid out to shareholders on a quarterly basis.

Noninvested cash from dividends hurts the total return of a UIT during a bull market in stocks. This phenomenon is known as *cash drag*. The index is assumed to automatically reinvest dividends. Since the UIT does not reinvest, cash becomes a drag on performance during rising prices. Of course, when dividends sit in cash during a bear market it helps the total return. Cash drag is one reason a UIT can never precisely track its index.

The regulations do give some flexibility to managers to make practical portfolio management decisions in a UIT as long as the intent is to best achieve its goal of replicating an index. The flexibility includes the timing of buys and sells, and the distribution of tax lots to authorized participants that are redeeming creation units. A trustee oversees the implementation of the strategy to ensure the fund is in compliance.

Other examples of exchange-traded funds organized as UITs include Diamonds Trust (symbol: DIA), PowerShares QQQ aka Cubes (symbol: QQQQ) and BLDRs. BLDRs are a family of exchange-traded funds based on The Bank of New York ADR Index, a real-time index tracking U.S.-traded international stocks known as depositary receipts.

40 Act Regulated Investment Companies (RIC). A majority of exchange-traded portfolios are organized as regulated investment companies (RIC). This structure is less restrictive than UITs and that provides RICs with several advantages and a few disadvantages.

The most important characteristic of RICs is that the fund manager can modify the holdings of a fund as needed to adhere to the investment objectives. Instead of buying all the stocks in an index, a fund manager can sample an index that is difficult to replicate, and then optimize the portfolio holding so the portfolio tracks close to its index. In addition, the fund manager may use securities in an ETF portfolio that are not included in the corresponding index. Those securities may include other stocks and bonds as well as futures, options, and other derivatives.

The Lehman Brothers Aggregate Bond Market Index holds thousands of bonds. Many of those bonds are illiquid and cannot be included in a fund. Under a RIC structure, a fund manager can selectively choose liquid and tradable bonds from the bond market and create a modified portfolio that has the characteristics of that market. If the bonds are selected carefully, the portfolio will track the LB Aggregate index with minimum error.

The RIC structure also allows the reinvestment of dividends within a fund. Cash is reinvested by the fund manager in more securities after company dividends are paid by underlying stocks. Those dividends are paid to shareholders quarterly. The reinvestment eliminates the cash drag that occurs within a UIT structure.

ETFs registered as investment companies can also participate in securities lending programs. The revenue generated by these activities may help the ETF offset expenses that otherwise could cause the performance of the ETF to lag behind the performance of its index (because an index does not have any expenses). Security lending has become a profitable business for large fund companies such as Vanguard, State Street, and Barclays Global Investors.

ETFs registered as an RIC can also file as a non-diversified fund. That allows the manager to invest up to 50 percent of the fund in single concentrated positions. A fund may hold up to 25 percent in any one security providing it is not more than 10 percent of the voting stock of a company.

There are disadvantages to allowing a RIC manager flexibility and discretion in security selection. It may be the manager's intent to select stocks that track an index, but there is no guarantee that the manager's methods will be successful. You may think you are buying an index tracking fund, but small management decisions in a fund can lead to large tracking errors with the index. In recent years, tracking errors have developed between a number of ETFs structured as RICs and the indexes they are supposed to follow.

Oversight of RIC management is through a Board of Directors. Directors are voted in by the authorized participants that hold shares as part of a creation unit (see Chapter 2). Individual ETF shareholders also vote the shares they own.

Vanguard ETFs are unique RICs. Formerly known as Vanguard Index Participation Receipts (VIPERs), Vanguard ETFs are not stand-alone funds. They are, instead, a separate share class of Vanguard open-end mutual funds.

Vanguard hoped to provide short-term investors and market timers with an attractive means of purchasing shares while helping long-term shareholders in their open-end funds. Unlike Vanguard open-end shares, ETFs can be bought and sold continuously throughout the day at market prices.

Vanguard stated in its application with the SEC that the purchase and redemption requests by short-term investors in its open-end fund classes increased the fund's realization of capital gains, increased fund expenses, and hindered the manager's ability to achieve its investment objective of tracking its index. An ETF class would trade in the secondary market, so the transactions would not involve the open-end fund shareholders. As a result, trading by ETF investors would not disrupt portfolio management or increase the fund's costs.

Vanguard has patented this structure. That means any other open-end mutual fund company can license the concept from Vanguard (as of this writing no other company has). Vanguard ETFs reinvest dividends paid by the underlying securities, which allows the funds to track their indexes more closely.

Some critics have questioned the tax efficiency of Vanguard ETFs. The IRS requires that capital gains generated by other shareholder activities be distributed across all share classes of a mutual fund, even the Vanguard ETF share class. This restriction means that Vanguard ETFs may not be as tax-efficient as stand-alone ETFs such as iShares by BGI. On the other hand, having an ETF share class does help increase the tax efficiency of Vanguard open-end share classes. Chapter 4 covers the tax benefits of ETF structures.

Reports for 40 Act Shareholders. The SEC, under the Investment Company Act of 1940, regulates open-end mutual funds and exchange-traded funds. The SEC requires that investors receive certain information after purchasing shares. A prospectus must be delivered to buyers of open-end mutual fund shares. Since ETFs are listed on a securities exchange, investors are not required to receive a prospectus. Instead, ETF companies have agreed with the SEC that the brokers and dealers selling ETFs will provide investors with a Product Description describing the fund. A Product Description is not intended to be a substitute for a prospectus, although it does contain important information about the fees, objectives, and mechanics of the ETF shares purchased in the secondary market.

The Product Description provides a plain English explanation of the salient features in ETF shares. Part of the language explains that the shares are index-based securities that trade on the secondary market, and that the investor is not buying or selling directly with the fund company. The product description discloses that the ETF shares are not redeemable individually, and that an investor selling the shares in the secondary market may receive less than the NAV of the ETF shares. How creation units are purchased and redeemed is also explained.

The brokers and dealers also provide ETF shareholders with annual and semiannual reports. The reports are made available within sixty days after the end of the fund's fiscal year and within sixty days after the fund's fiscal mid-year. The reports contain updated financial information, a list of securities in the fund, and other information.

Securities Act of 1933 Exchange-Traded Portfolios

Investment firms desiring to launch a highly concentrated nondiversified product are not able to qualify that product as an investment company or unit investment trust under the limitations of the 1940 Act. In those cases, companies file as Registered Trusts under the Securities Act of 1933. Rule 415 of the 1933 act was put in place to allow for the continuous creation and redemption of trust units as needed.

Exchange-traded portfolios issued under the Securities Act of 1933 are also required to follow the Securities Exchange Act of 1934. The 1934 Act regulates how securities trade on a secondary market (stock exchange) after they are issued. The act also ensures investors receive regular financial statements and required reports.

Investment trusts under the Securities Act of 1933 should not be confused with Unit Investment Trusts under the Investment

Company Act of 1940. The two entities are separate and operate under different government regulations.

Investment Trusts.   Investment trusts organized under the Securities Act of 1933 may hold stocks, bonds, or hard assets such as gold or silver, or hold derivatives such as commodity futures. The trust does not provide voting privileges to individual investors or allow redemptions of securities in-kind.

Many investment trusts are commodities linked. The iShares S&P GSCI Commodity-Indexed Trust (symbol: GSG) seeks to track the performance of the S&P GSCIndex (GSCI) Excess Return Index. The index currently tracks 24 different commodities with a heavy weighting in energy. During 2007, over 60 percent of the S&P GSCI was in energy markets. GSG invests in exchange traded futures contracts that track the GSCI index. Those futures contracts are a type of long-term option called a CERF. CERFs are the only investment aside from some cash in the portfolio.

StreetTRACKS Gold Trust (symbol: GLD) is an investment trust with World Gold Trust Services LLC as the sponsor of the trust and the Bank of New York as the trustee. State Street Global Markets is the marketing agent. The investment objective is to reflect the performance of the price of gold bullion, after expenses. The trust holds gold bullion directly (not derivatives). From time to time the trust issues streetTRACKS Gold Shares in baskets in exchange for deposits of gold. The trust distributes gold in connection with redemptions of baskets. A basket equals a block of 100,000 shares of GLD.

Shares of GLD trade on a stock exchange, and baskets of GLD may be created or redeemed by authorized participants (APs). APs follow the procedures for the creation and redemption of baskets and for the delivery of the gold and any cash required for such creations and redemptions. Price arbitrage trading by APs keep the market value of the GLD shares in line with the intraday value of gold.

Exchange-Traded Grantor Trusts.   Exchange traded grantor trusts are registered under the Securities Act of 1933 as nonmanaged investment pools. Grantor trusts are not mutual funds, but they may be broadly diversified in stocks or bonds like a mutual fund.

Grantor trusts trade on a stock exchange like the 1940 Act ETFs. Unlike ETFs, though, grantor trust investors have voting rights in the companies composing the trust. That gives unit holders a say in the management of the fund that individual ETF shareholders do not have. Grantor trust holders can participate in the election of a board of directors, vote on issues the company wants to change, and bring issues to a proxy vote at an annual meeting.

The cash from corporate dividends paid in to a grantor trust are immediately paid out to unit investors. That is different from the 1940 Act securities where dividends are held until the end of each quarter.

Redeeming shares of a grantor trust is also unique. When an individual investor redeems shares of a grantor trust, they can request actual stock certificates for each company in round lots of 100. There may be tax advantages for large individual investors to receive shares in-kind. After the shares are received, the investor can choose which shares to sell and which to keep, based on the cost bases of those shares and the investor's unique tax situation.

Holding Company Depositary Receipts (HOLDRs) are proprietary products of Merrill Lynch. They are a good example of an exchange traded grantor trust. HOLDRs cover a narrow sector of the market, such as the Biotech (symbol: BBH) or Broadband (symbol; BDH). HOLDRs are typically invested in a relatively limited number of stocks and are structured in a manner where investors own the underlying stocks in each unit. Owning the underlying stocks allows investors to vote and receive dividends when they are paid by each company. The disadvantage of direct ownership is that investors are inundated with quarterly and annual reports as well as proxy statements from every company in the HOLDRs.

As stated earlier, HOLDRs investors are permitted to unbundle shares of underlying stocks in a nontaxable exchange, effectively customizing the tax consequences of disposition. Effectively, shareholders can exchange their interest in the units of the trust for an unbundled portfolio of individual stocks, which can then be sold individually to defer or reduce the tax impact.

One disadvantage of the grantor trust structure is that the trusts cannot change securities. New securities cannot be added or old ones deleted. That leads to less diversification over time, as some of the companies grow large and others are bought or head into bankruptcy. Thus, it is inevitable that, over time, these trusts will become less diversified. For example, Internet Holding Co. HOLDRs Trust (HHH) has more than 50 percent of its portfolio invested in just Yahoo and eBay, but not Google because Google didn't have its IPO until after this HOLDR was created.

Exchange-Traded Notes.   When is an exchange traded security not an ETF or a trust? When it is an Exchange-Traded Note (ETN). Unlike other exchange-traded portfolios, ETNs do not represent interest in a pool of securities that is divided among all investors. ETNs are simply direct debt obligations issued by a bank. ETNs pay no interest and offer no principal protection. The bank simply promises to pay holders a certain return based on the return of a securities index or other benchmark, minus annual fees.

Simply put, a bank issues a note and promises to pay the holder of that note whatever the total return of an index is over the maturity of the note, less a fee. The bank may or may not use the cash to invest in the index, and it really does not matter to the investor. All the investor cares about is the return on the note, which will be whatever the index is after fees. As long as the bank is solvent, investors will get the returns they are promised.

ETNs do share several characteristics of other exchange-traded portfolios. They trade on stock exchanges, their returns are linked to the return of a market benchmark, and notes can be shorted like stocks.

Unlike other exchange traded securities, ETN investors will not receive any periodic payments. Nor do investors have voting rights or the right to receive dividends or other distributions from a benchmarked index. When selling notes, an investor will always receive cash. Investors have no right to receive delivery of any index component.

The first iPath ETNs were issued by Barclays Bank PLC in 2006. The purpose of iPaths is to create a type of security that combines both the aspects of bonds and ETFs. Rather than buy a share of a fund's indexed assets, ETNs shift index-tracking risk to Barclays. ETNs are registered under the Securities Act of 1933 because they are a security issued by a bank, not an investment company or UIT.

iPath notes trade close to their intraday value because of their unique structure. A holder of the iPath product has three options for redemption of the notes: first, hold until maturity (30 years); second, trade on the secondary market; third, participate in a unique, weekly redemption feature built into the ETN structure similar to the creation and redemption process of an ETF (just not daily). Every Thursday, holders of the iPath product could conceivably redeem their shares directly with Barclays Bank. The only caveat is that they would have to redeem a minimum of at least 50,000 units of the iPath notes, which would equate to about a $2.5 million redemption, assuming products are trading around $50 per share. This redemption feature enables the notes to more closely track their underlying index. If pricing was out of line, institutional investors would buy iPath shares during the week, hedge their position, and turn them in to Barclays Bank for cash on Thursday. The ability to redeem creates arbitrage opportunities for market makers, and that keeps ETN market prices in line with intraday values.

Observers say ETNs could end up being more tax efficient than other exchange-traded portfolios. That is because the securities pay no interest, no dividends, and no capital gains until each investor recognizes her own capital gain or loss upon the sale or redemption. The United States federal income tax consequences of ETNs are still uncertain. What is we do know is discussed in Chapter 4.

One factor that affects the ETN value is the credit rating of the issuer. The value of an ETN may drop despite no change in the underlying index because of a downgrade in the issuer's credit rating. iPaths are structured products that are issued as senior debt notes by Barclays, a 300-year-old bank with $1.5 trillion in assets and an AA credit rating from Standard & Poor's. This provides iPaths with a fairly dependable backing, but even with this kind of credibility, there is a remote chance that Barclays will have financial problems and potentially default on their obligations.

Outside of the tax treatment and legal registration, the difference between ETNs and ETFs comes down to credit risk versus index tracking error. An ETF investor has virtually no credit risk from a fund collapsing. ETF investors are always entitled to their share of the creation unit assets. On the other hand, an investor in iPaths may not receive the return he was promised. An ETF has a tracking error risk. In other words, there is a possibility that the ETF's returns will differ from its underlying index. ETNs have no tracking error risk. Barring a default, the bank will pay ETN holders exactly the amount the index performed, minus its fees.

Putting It All Together

The difference between exchange-traded portfolio structures can be confusing. Table 3.1 puts the important elements of various exchange-traded portfolio structures side by side in a feature comparison.

Table 3.1   Exchange-Traded Portfolio Reference

Features	Grantor Trusts	Investment Trust	Exchange-Traded Notes (ETN)	Unit Investment Trust (UIT)	RIC Open-End ETF	RIC Vanguard ETF
SEC Registration Act	1933	1933	1933	1940	1940	1940
Company dividend reinvested	No	No	Implied[1]	No	Yes	Yes
Portfolio pays dividends	Yes	Yes	No	Yes	Yes	Yes
Redemption in-kind option	Yes	No	No	No	No	No
Tracking error	NA[3]	Yes	No	Yes	Yes	Yes
Credit risk of issuer	No	No	Yes	No	No	No
Manager discretion	NA[4]	Yes	No	Restricted[2]	Yes	Yes
Allows concentrated positions	Yes	Yes	Yes	No	No	No
Traditional fund share class	No	No	No	No	No	Yes

Notes:
1. ETN investors receive the total return of an index, which implies reinvestment of dividends.
2. UITs must hold all securities in the index they track.
3. Many grantor trusts are not benchmarked to indexes, that is, HOLDRs.
4. Only in the initial selection. After that, grantor trusts are nonmanaged baskets.
Source: Portfolio Solutions, LLC

Summary

Most financial journalists, investment advisers, brokers, and the investing public lump all exchange-traded portfolios together and call them ETFs. That practice is convenient, but it is far from accurate. There are many exchange traded structures approved by the SEC. Each has different operations, regulatory issues, fees, and taxes.

Exchange-traded portfolios cover a wide range of options. The most common is the 1940 Act funds commonly known as ETFs. Non-ETF exchange-traded portfolios include Exchange-Traded Grantor Trusts, Investment Trusts, and Exchange-Traded Notes (ETNs).

The benefits of each exchange-traded portfolio structure depend significantly on each individual investor's circumstance.

No one structure can be labeled as most favorable under all conditions. You must consider your own situation and determine which type of exchange-traded portfolio will afford you the most flexibility and potential return while minimizing risk and cost. Given the pace of innovation in the marketplace, one can only imagine the new and exciting exchange traded structures that investment providers will invent next.

CHAPTER

4

ETF Benefits and Drawbacks

For nearly a century, traditional mutual funds have offered many advantages over building a portfolio one security at a time. Mutual funds provide investors broad diversification, professional management, relative low cost, and daily liquidity.

Exchange-traded portfolios take the benefits of mutual fund investing to the next level. Compared to traditional open-end funds, ETFs offer flexible trading, lower operating costs, greater transparency, and better tax efficiency in taxable accounts. There are drawbacks, however, including trading costs and learning complexities of the product. Informed investors agree that the pluses of ETFs overshadow the minuses by a sizable margin.

In this chapter we will review the benefits and drawbacks of ETFs, including the unique tax advantage inherent in each structure. By the end of this chapter, you should have a clear understanding of the advantages ETFs have over traditional mutual funds and some of the disadvantages. Then you can decide whether they fit with your investment plan.

The Positive Aspects of ETFs

ETFs have several advantages over traditional open-end funds. The four most prominent advantages are trading flexibility, low cost, operational transparency, and tax benefits.

Trading Flexibility

Traditional open-end mutual fund shares are traded only once per day after the markets close. All trading is done with the mutual fund company that issues the shares. Investors must wait until the end of the day when the fund NAV is announced before knowing what price they paid for new shares when buying that day and the price they will receive for existing shares they sold that day. Once per day trading is fine for most long-term investors, but some people require greater flexibility.

ETFs are bought and sold during the day when the markets are open. The pricing of ETF shares is continuous during normal exchange hours. Share prices vary throughout the day, based mainly on the changing intraday value of the underlying assets in the fund. ETF investors know within moments how much they paid to buy shares and how much they received after selling.

The nearly instantaneous trading of ETF shares makes intraday management of a portfolio a snap. It is easy to move money between specific asset classes such as stocks, bonds, or commodities. Investors can efficiently get their allocation into the investments they want in an hour and then change their allocation in the next hour. That is not something I recommend, but it can be done.

Making changes to traditional open-end mutual funds is more challenging and can take several days. First, there is typically a 2:00 PM Eastern Time cutoff for placing open-end share trades. That means you do not know what the NAV price will be at the end of the day. It is impossible to know exactly how much you will receive when selling shares of one open-end fund or know how much you should buy of another open-end fund.

The trade order flexibility of ETFs also gives investors the benefit of making timely investment decisions and placing orders in a variety of ways. Investing in ETF shares has all the trade combinations of investing in common stocks, including limit orders and stop-limit orders. ETFs can also be purchased on margin by borrowing money from a broker. Every brokerage firm has tutorials on trade order types and requirements for borrowing on margin.

Short selling is also available to ETF investors. Shorting entails borrowing securities from your brokerage firm and simultaneously selling those securities on the market. The hope is that the price of the borrowed securities will drop and you can buy them back at a lower price at a later time.

Portfolio Completion and Risk Management

Investors may wish to quickly gain portfolio exposure to specific sectors, styles, industries, or countries, but do not have expertise in those areas. Given the wide variety of sector, style, industry, and country categories available, ETF shares may be able to provide an investor easy exposure to a specific desired market segment.

An example would be the First Trust ISE Water Index Fund (AMEX: FWT). An investor might believe that water-related securities have the potential for profits because of the growing population in arid areas and the global shortage of clean water. FWT tracks the ISE Water Index, a cap-weighted index of currently the 36 largest companies that derive the bulk of their revenue from the potable water and wastewater industries.

Contrary to buying an ETF, an investor may already have significant risk in a particular sector but cannot diversify that risk because of restrictions or taxes. In that case, the person can short an industry sector ETF, or buy an ETF that shorts an industry for him (see Chapter 13).

For example, an investor may have a large number of restricted shares in the semiconductor industry. In that situation, the person may want to short shares of the SPDR S&P Semiconductor (XSD). That would reduce one's overall risk exposure to a downturn in that sector. XSD is an equal-weighted market cap index of semiconductor stocks listed on the NYSE, American Stock Exchange, NASDAQ National Market, and NASDAQ Small Cap exchanges.

Lower Costs

Operating expenses are incurred by all managed funds regardless of the structure. Those costs include, but are not limited to, portfolio management fees, custody costs, administrative expenses, marketing expenses, and distribution. Costs have historically been very important in forecasting returns. In general, the lower the cost of investing in a fund, the higher the expected return for that fund.

ETF operation costs are streamlined compared to open-end mutual funds. Lower costs are a result of client service–related expenses being passed on to the brokerage firms that hold the exchange-traded securities in customer accounts. Fund administrative costs go down for ETFs when a firm does not have to staff a call center to answer questions from thousands of individual investors.

ETFs also have lower expenses in the area of monthly statements, notifications, and transfers. Traditional open-end fund companies are required to send statements and reports to shareholders on a regular basis. Not so with ETFs. Fund sponsors are responsible for providing that information only to authorized participants who are the direct owners of creation units. Individual investors buy and sell individual shares of like stocks through brokerage firms, and the brokerage firm becomes responsible for servicing those investors, not the ETF companies.

Brokerage companies issue monthly statements, annual tax reports, quarterly reports, and 1099s. The reduced administrative burden of service and recordkeeping for thousands of individual clients allows ETF companies a lower overhead, and at least part of that savings is passed on to individual investors in the form of lower fund expenses.

The best example of lower expenses for ETFs is the Vanguard Group. Vanguard ETFs are a unique and proprietary structure in that they are a share class of open-end Vanguard funds. The side-by-side comparison of fees in Table 4.1 highlights the annual cost savings to an individual investor who places $25,000 in each fund.

Another cost savings for ETF shares is the absence of mutual fund redemption fees. Shareholders in ETFs avoid the short-term redemption fees that are charged on some open-end funds. For example, the Vanguard REIT Index Fund Investor Shares (symbol: VGSIX) has a redemption fee of 1 percent, if held for less than one year. The Vanguard REIT ETF (symbol: VNQ) is the exact same portfolio and has no redemption fee.

Table 4.1   Vanguard Investor Class Shares and ETF Comparison

Vanguard Total Stock Market Index Fund	Investor Class Shares (VTSMX)	Exchange Trade Fund Shares (VTI)	Ten Year fee savings on $25,000 in VTI,
Expense Ratio	0.19%	0.07%	0.12%
$25,000 at 8% growth less fund fees over 10 years	$53,031	$53,624	$593

Source: The Vanguard Group

Lower Brokerage Firm Costs

Many people hold their investment assets, including mutual funds, at a brokerage firm. Brokers can be divided into two types: discount brokerage firms such as Charles Schwab, Ameritrade, and Fidelity; and full service brokerage firms such as Merrill Lynch, Smith Barney, and AG Edwards.

Discount brokerages charge clients a low commission to buy mutual funds, or they offer clients funds that pay the brokerage firm a fee each year (called a 12b-1 fee). For example, Charles Schwab charges a flat commission to buy shares of the no-load Vanguard U.S. Total Stock Market Fund (symbol: VTSMX). Now, however, investors can buy ETF shares of the same Vanguard fund (symbol: VTI) and pay Schwab a lower commission. Because of intense price competition among discount brokerage firms, the commission to buy or sell ETF shares can be significantly lower than the commission to buy a comparable amount of a no-load mutual fund.

The big winners are clients of full service brokerage firms. Before ETFs, investors at full service brokerage firms had virtually no access to low-cost mutual funds such as Vanguard funds. The only funds brokers were allowed to talk about or sell were higher-cost mutual funds where the brokerage firms earned more money from commissions and fees. Many full service firms pushed their own funds over those of lower-cost competitors. The SEC has been trying to put a stop to that practice.

The evolution of ETFs has forced full service brokerage firms to rethink their mutual fund strategy. Since ETFs are traded on stock exchanges, individual investors can now buy ETFs in their full service brokerage account and pay the broker a one-time commission. That commission is typically much lower than the 4 percent to 8 percent sales loads charged on many open-end mutual funds.

Lower commissions on trades and lower expenses in ETFs are of great benefit to clients of full service brokers, but bad for the revenue stream of those brokerage firms. Some companies have pushed back by encouraging their clients to buy ETFs through a *wrap-fee* management program that can cost up to 2 percent annually. The wrap-fee programs are generally not worth the fee unless you are doing a lot of trading.

Lower Taxes on ETFs

Holding ETF shares in taxable accounts can lead to a lower annual tax bill than if you owned a similar open-end mutual fund. The tax benefit is a byproduct of the authorized participant (AP) arbitrage mechanism described in Chapter 3. The next few paragraphs explain a specific tax advantage inherent in ETFs and other exchange-traded portfolios.

As outlined in Chapter 2, APs are the only investors that can deal directly with a fund company. An AP turns in a predetermined portfolio of individual securities and is issued one creation unit by the fund company. As the fund manager brings in the new securities from the AP, each issue is assigned a cost basis based on the market price of the security when it came into the fund.

Figure 4.1 illustrates how an ETF manager assigns a cost basis to new shares of stock coming into a fund. The ETF is SPDRs S&P 500 and the stock is Microsoft (symbol: MSFT). After an AP turns in MSFT stock to a fund as part of a basket in exchange for a creation unit, whatever the market price of MSFT was at the time the shares booked into the fund becomes the cost basis to the fund.

In the Figure 4.1 example, MSFT was trading at $30 per share at the time an AP turned in shares. These new MSFT shares are added to the already existing shares of MSFT stock in the fund, but accounted for separately for tax reasons. Those shares are added to the manager's book on MSFT at $30 per share. Every time stock comes into an ETF, those shares are given a separate cost basis and added to the manager's book.

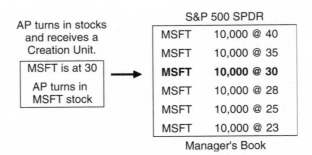

Figure 4.1   Establishing Cost Basis in an ETF
Source: Portfolio Solutions, LLC

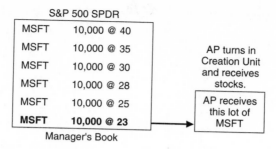

Figure 4.2   Eliminating Low-Cost Basis Stock in an ETF
Source: Portfolio Solutions, LLC

When an authorized participant redeems a creation unit, it receives common stock back based on the NAV of the fund at the time. The shares the AP received, however, are typically not at the same cost basis in the fund manager's book as the shares that were turned in. The ETF manager can issue different shares, which may have a lower cost basis than what the AP originally turned in.

As Figure 4.2 illustrates, there are different tax lots of MSFT stock on the manager's book. The manager chose to distribute the $23 tax lot of MSFT shares to the AP. The manager did not send out the $30 tax lot that was established when the shares came in. If the manager issues low-cost basis stocks back to redeeming authorized participants, the unrealized capital gains in the ETF are practically eliminated.

Table 4.2 illustrates the tax advantage of ETF shares over a traditional open-end mutual fund. In the 1990s, when large cap stock returns were up significantly, S&P 500 SPDRs issued minimal realized capital gains to investors, whereas the Vanguard 500 Index Fund issued capital gains to investors each year.

The redemption of creation units by authorized participants creates an important tax benefit to the holders of ETFs in taxable accounts. It rids a fund of gains that may otherwise eventually have to be distributed to taxable shareholders, and they would have to pay taxes on those gains. The selection of tax lots is perfectly legal and is practiced every day.

To illustrate the power of the ETF tax benefit, we need only to examine 2006. The stock market was up about 15 percent for the year. However, very few U.S. equity ETFs pay any capital gains and those that did were smaller funds, and they paid a minimal amount.

Table 4.2 Capital Gain Distributions as a Percentage of NAV

	S&P 500 SPDRs	Vanguard 500 Index
1994	0.00%	0.47%
1995	0.02%	0.23%
1996	0.16%	0.36%
1997	0.00%	0.66%
1998	0.00%	0.37%
1999	0.00%	0.74%

Source: Bloomberg, Morningstar Principia

The creation and redemption process allowed most of the unrealized capital gains within ETFs to be erased.

The washing of capital gains does not always work perfectly. ETFs may be forced to make an occasional capital gains distribution because they must still sell stocks for cash that are taken private or bought by another company for cash. In addition, the exception to the rule on tax benefits is Vanguard ETFs. Vanguard funds are traditionally tax efficient. However, Vanguard ETFs are a share class of their open-end funds rather than a stand-alone investment vehicle. As such, all share classes of Vanguard funds are treated equally in regard to taxes. Open-end share class investors have the same level of taxable distributions as ETF share investors. Since open-end shares represent over 90 percent of the assets in a fund with an ETF share class, there is a chance that Vanguard ETFs will ultimately not be as tax efficient as they would be if the ETFs were standalones, particularly in the style funds such as the small cap value index.

ETF Dividends

ETFs are still required to distribute all dividends and interest to shareholders. Those distributions are taxed at a rate according to the type of income it is. Most corporate dividends are taxed at a preferred rate, while interest from bonds and money market investments are taxed at an investor's ordinary income tax level.

The federal income tax on qualified stock dividends was lowered to 15 percent in 2003. A dividend qualified for preferred status as long as you held the stock for more than 60 days before the ex-dividend date.

Ironically, unlike stocks, the tax rate you pay on equity ETF dividends is not determined by the length of time you hold the fund. The rate you pay on ETF dividends is determined from when specific tax lots of stock were accepted into the fund, that is, the date the AP turned them in for a creation unit. Once a tax lot of stocks has been held in an ETF for more than 60 days, dividends from that tax lot are taxed at the preferred rate.

The age of an ETF can have a profound effect on the amount of the dividend that is subject to higher ordinary income tax rates. Unlike buying an individual stock, you could buy a seasoned equity ETF in November and all the dividends paid by the fund in December could be at the preferred rate. On the other hand, many ETFs launched near the end of the year hold mostly new securities, and so a higher percentage of paid dividends will not meet the 60-day qualified dividend rule. As such, those dividends are subject to the higher ordinary income tax rates.

Taxable investors in ETFs will eventually pay capital gain taxes, but only after they decide to sell shares that are at a profit. If there are losses on ETF shares, investors are able to write those losses off against other capital gains, and take up to $3,000 in losses against ordinary income (see Chapter 21 for tax harvesting tips). The tax efficiency created by the creation and redemption process, and the ability of each investor to decide when to take gains or losses in ETF shares, gives each person more control over taxes than with traditional open-end mutual funds.

ETN Tax Treatment

If someone wanted to develop a better exchange-traded product, that product would pay the total return of an index, not distribute any taxable capital gains, and not pay taxable income from dividends or interest. It would be a completely tax-free investment until shares are sold by an investor, and then the profits from the sale of shares would be taxed as long-term capital gains.

Barclays Bank appeared to have invented a better exchange-traded product in 2006. Exchange-Traded Notes (ETNs) are a close cousin to ETFs, but they differ in a few key ways: ETNs do not pay any capital gains, dividends, or interest over their lifetime. Instead, Barclays Bank promises investors the return of a benchmark index, minus an annual fee. (See Chapter 3 for complete details.) They can do that because ETNs are a direct obligation of Barclays bank rather than a direct investment in stocks, bonds, or commodities.

Based on Barclays' recommendation, investors should treat ETNs held in an account as prepaid contracts. That means that any difference between the sale and purchase will be classified as a capital gain, and no taxes are due until there is a sale. ETNs are a unique investment that may become very popular in the future because of their superb tax efficiency.

There are two caveats to ETNs: First, as of this writing the IRS had not made a definitive ruling on their tax treatment and a more onerous tax treatment is possible. Second, ETNs are a direct obligation of the issuer. If the issuer files for bankruptcy, ETN holders get in line at bankruptcy court with the rest of the debt holders and there is no guarantee that they will get their money back.

The Negative Aspects of ETFs

The benefits ETFs offered to some investors are often disadvantages to other investors. Trading costs are one example. Depending where you trade, the cost to trade an ETF can be far more than the savings from management fees and tax efficiency. Trading flexibility is a second double-edged sword. The ability to trade anytime and as much as you want are a benefit to busy investors and active traders, but that flexibility can entice some people to trade too much. High turnover of a portfolio increases its cost and reduces returns.

Trading Costs

Trading costs go down for ETF investors who are already using a brokerage firm as the custodian of their assets. On the contrary, trading costs go up for investors who have traditionally invested in no-load funds directly with the fund company and pay no commissions. Investors with a fund company cannot buy ETFs directly. They will have to open a brokerage account and pay a commission to buy shares.

If you plan on making a single, large, lump-sum investment, then paying one commission to buy ETF shares makes sense. Buying small amounts may not make sense. For example, assuming an $8 per trade commission, a single lump-sum investment of $1,000 in the iShares S&P 500 Index would cost 0.8 percent of the investment. A person would be better off investing in the Vanguard 500 Index even though the expense ratio of the Vanguard fund is slightly higher.

The cost of dollar-cost averaging into ETFs may prove to be more expensive than investors hoped for. ETF investors pay a brokerage commission every time they buy or sell ETF shares. Consequently, ETFs tend not to be a good vehicle for investors making frequent, small investments. Staying with a no-load open-end fund is a better option under this scenario.

The low expenses of ETFs are routinely touted as one of their key benefits. But if you are like most people and invest regular sums of money, you may actually spend more on commissions than you would save on ETF management fees and taxes.

Buying High and Selling Low

ETFs have two prices, a bid and an ask. Investors should be aware of the spread between the price they will pay for shares (ask) and the price a share could be sold for (bid). In addition, it helps to know the intraday value of the fund when you are ready to execute a trade.

At any given time, the spread on an ETF may be high, and the market price of shares may not correspond to the intraday value of the underlying securities. Those are not good times to transact business. Make sure you know what an ETF's current intraday value is as well as the market price of the shares before you buy. Chapter 21 has tips to help cut down on ETF trading spreads, fees, and brokerage commissions.

Management Fee Creep

Not all ETFs are low cost. Prospective buyers should look carefully at the expense ratio of the specific ETF they are interested in. They may find the ETF of their choice is quite expensive relative to a traditional market index fund.

Before 2005, the expense ratio of all previously issued ETFs averaged 0.4 percent, according to Morningstar. Since 2005, the average expense of new funds has jumped to over 0.6 percent and some new exchange-traded products are charging over 1.0 percent in fees. That is quite expensive compared to the average traditional market index ETFs that charge about 0.20 percent.

Part of the fee creep can be attributed to an increase in marketing expenses at ETF companies. As the proliferation of ETFs continues, competition for funding is forcing companies to spend more money on marketing, and that cost is passed on to current shareholders in the form of higher fees.

Another cost creep factor is the cost to license indexes. Index licensing is a big business in the investment industry. Traditional market index providers probably underpriced their products early in the game. They are now making up for it by revamping their product lines and pushing fees higher. In addition, new, quantitatively manufactured index providers are pushing the upper bounds of licensing fees, and that drives ETF expense ratios higher still.

Tracking Error

ETF managers are supposed to keep their funds investment performance in line with the indexes they track. That mission is not as easy as it sounds. There are many ways an ETF can stray from its intended index. That tracking error can be a cost to investors.

Indexes do not hold cash but ETFs do, so a certain amount of tracking error in an ETF is expected. Fund managers generally hold some cash in a fund to pay administrative expenses and management fees. In addition, the timing of dividends is difficult because stocks go ex-dividend one day and pay the dividend on some other day while the indexes' providers assume the dividend is reinvested on the same day the company went ex-dividend. This is a special problem for ETFs that are organized as UITs, which, by law, cannot reinvest dividends in more securities and must hold the cash until a dividend is paid to UIT shareholders. Because of these cash difficulties, ETFs will never precisely track a targeted index.

ETFs that are organized as investment companies under the Investment Company Act of 1940 may deviate from the holdings of the index at the discretion of the fund manager. Some indexes hold illiquid securities that the fund manager cannot buy. In that case the fund manager will modify a portfolio by sampling liquid securities from an index that can be purchased. The idea is to create a portfolio that has the look and feel of the index, and hopefully perform like the index. Nonetheless, ETF managers that deviate from the securities in an index often see the performance of the fund deviate as well.

Several indexes hold one or two dominant positions that the ETF manager cannot replicate because of SEC restrictions on nondiversified funds. In an effort to create a more diversified sector ETF and avoid the problem of concentrated securities, some companies have targeted indexes that use an equal weighting methodology (see Chapter 9). Equal weighting solves the problem of concentrated positions, but it creates other problems, including higher portfolio turnover and increased costs.

Complexity and Settlement Dates

One disadvantage of investing in any exchange-traded portfolio is the added layer of complexity that comes with the products. Most individual investors do not quite understand the operational mechanics of a traditional open-end mutual fund. As such, it is a leap of faith to expect individual investors to easily comprehend the differences between exchange-traded funds, exchange-traded notes, unit investment trusts, and grantor trusts. These are not easy products to understand.

Another area of investor confusion is settlement periods. The settlement date is the day you must have the money on hand to pay for your purchase, and the day you get cash for selling a fund. The ETF settlement date is three days after a trade is placed, whereas traditional open-end mutual funds settle the next day.

The difference in settlement periods can create problems and cost you money if you are not familiar with settlement procedures. For example, if you sell ETF shares and try to buy a traditional open-end mutual fund on the same day, you will find that your broker may not allow the trade. That is because there is a two-day difference in settlement between the item sold and the item bought. If you try to do that, your account will be short of money for a couple of days, and at best you will be charged interest. At worst, the buy side of the trade will not occur.

Performance Claims

One area that is neither an advantage nor a disadvantage of ETFs over traditional mutual funds is their expected returns. As competition in the industry heats up, some ETF companies increasingly try to set their products apart from traditional market index funds by inferring the indexes they follow are better and as such their products will have better performance. That is simply marketing hype. Aside from any fee difference, there is no reason to believe that one ETF company's products will outperform any other company's products or open-end mutual funds.

All fund companies choose securities from the same financial markets, whether it be for an open-end fund or an ETF. All funds are subject to traditional market risks and rewards based on the securities that make up their underlying value. As securities in a portfolio that makes up the ETF fluctuate, the value of ETF shares will also rise and fall on the exchange, as will the value of open-end mutual funds that are managed using the same strategy. Assuming the fee and investment objectives of a particular ETF and its competitors are the same, the expected return is also the same.

Guide to ETF Characteristics

The following guide summarizes the advantages and disadvantages of ETFs over traditional open-end mutual funds.

Summary

The advantages of ETFs over traditional open-end mutual funds are summerized in Table 4.3. ETFs offer flexible trading, lower operating costs, greater transparency, and better tax efficiency in taxable accounts. Expense ratios tend to be lower, although higher fees have been the norm in recent years. ETFs must publish their holdings every day, which makes them more transparent than traditional funds that must disclose only twice a year. Transparency reduces the likelihood of fraud or abuse by fund managers and their sponsor companies. Finally, ETFs can be traded throughout the day, which is convenient for active traders.

Taxes are a big consideration for many individual investors. ETFs are by design more tax efficient than traditional open-end mutual funds. The arbitrage mechanism allows the fund manager to rid the portfolio of low-cost stock, which increases a fund's tax efficiency.

ETFs are not suited for every investor despite their benefits. The securities are more complex than traditional mutual funds, and many investors do not really understand what they own. In addition, the ease of trading anytime during the day may cause some investors to trade too much, and that could lead to poor investment results. Trading on exchanges comes with a commission cost. The more an investor trades, the higher the overall cost of the portfolio.

Table 4.3   Major Differences between ETFs and Open-End Funds

ETF	Traditional Open-End Mutual Fund
Priced and traded continuously throughout the day.	Priced and traded at NAV and the end of the trading day.
Investors buy and sell shares on an exchange with other shareholders.	Individual redemptions with the fund company at the end of the trading day.
Purchase and sale of shares has no tax effect for other shareholders.	Large redemptions may result in a capital gains tax distribution for nonredeeming shareholders.
The in-kind redemption process reduces the tax liabilities of shareholders.	Fund managers have limited ability to manage taxes because of cash redemptions.
Like stocks, can be traded with limit orders, stop limits, and can be sold short.	Limit order pricing and short selling not available. Transactions are completed at NAV at the end of the trading day.
Can be bought and sold on margin.	Funds cannot be bought and sold on margin.
Low to moderate expense ratios as most client services are shifted to the brokerage firms.	Low to high expense ratios depending on client service costs' possible sales loads.
Can be bought and sold through any brokerage account.	Availability through brokers depends on negotiated selling agreements. Not all funds are available through brokerage firms and must be purchased from the fund company.
Normal brokerage account commissions apply.	No-load funds bought directly with a fund company have no transaction charges. Load funds and no-load funds bought through a broker usually charge a sales load or a commission charge.

Source: Portfolio Solutions, LLC

Buy ETFs for the right reasons. Do not buy ETFs because you expect a higher return than with traditional open-end mutual funds. While ETFs are somewhat more cost efficient and tax efficient than comparable traditional open-end mutual funds, for all planning purposes, the expected return is the same.

Whether you choose to invest in exchange-traded portfolios including ETFs or not, these securities do put more tools in your toolbox. The more knowledge you have about the various advantages and disadvantages of those tools, the better position you will be in to use them wisely.

CHAPTER 5

Actively Managed ETFs

For years, ETFs have been launched that replicate indexes. The golden cow for ETF providers, however, may well be actively managed ETFs that do not follow indexes. Actively managed ETFs will invest in a portfolio of securities that is subjectively chosen by a fund manager rather than follow a rules-based index. The idea is to perform better than an index through active management. And, for their supposed investment skill, actively managed ETFs will likely charge a higher fee than ETFs that follow indexes.

Actively managed ETFs will be registered with the Securities and Exchange Commission (SEC) as an investment company rather than a Unit Investment Trust (UIT), because a UIT cannot be actively managed (see Chapter 3). The actively managed ETF would list its shares on a national securities exchange, and investors would trade the ETF shares throughout the day at various prices in the secondary market. The problem with active ETFs is in the daily reporting of positions and reporting the intraday price without giving away exactly what the fund manager is doing.

Actively managed ETFs should not be confused with ETFs that follow custom indexes that use active strategies (see Part II). An actively managed ETF involves the direct selection of securities by the company that is managing a fund. There is no index to track.

The First Filings

In February 2007, Bear Stearns was the first company to file a full prospectus for an actively managed ETF. The filing outlined a unique money market–type fund that will hold a variety of short-term fixed income instruments such as Treasuries, municipal obligations, bank obligations, and mortgage-backed securities. The Bear Stearns Current Yield Fund uses active strategies in an attempt to deliver yields above the average money-market account yield. If approved by the SEC, the fund will trade on the AMEX (symbol: YYY). The fee will be 0.28 percent per year.

In early May 2007, the Vanguard Group filed for the second actively managed ETF to be included as a share class in their actively managed Vanguard Inflation-Protected Securities Fund (symbol: VIPSX). The new Vanguard TIPS ETF, if approved, will compete with the iShares Lehman TIPS Bond ETF (symbol: TIP). The two offer substantially similar exposure, in part because they draw from a limited universe of fewer than 25 securities.

The Lehman TIPS index includes all securities and is weighted by market capitalization. The Vanguard fund is actively managed but might make a better index than the Lehman TIPS index because the structure is more evenly spread across maturities. The Treasury did not have ETF investor goals in mind when it issued new TIPS. From an investor's view, there is no rhyme or reason to the structure of the Lehman index.

In June 2007, Vanguard filed for three more actively managed ETFs. They are to be a share class of the existing Vanguard Short-term Treasury, Intermediate-term Treasury, and Long-term Treasury funds. The ETF creation and redemption units will be composed of 40 percent to 50 percent of the Treasury bonds in the open-end fund. Since the Treasury market is large and liquid, Vanguard does not believe the introduction of ETFs will have a material impact on market and that means rogue traders will not gain an unfair advantage.

While the industry is eager to launch actively managed equity ETFs, the SEC has been very slow to approve the structure. The regulators express doubts about how the products would handle important issues such as holdings disclosure and pricing. Under current law, the index used as a benchmark for ETF management must disclose to the public the securities holdings and their weightings in the index, while active open-end mutual fund holdings are only disclosed periodically, usually several weeks or months later.

Using an ETF structure for active management means that a fund's holdings would have to be disclosed daily. That shouldn't create a problem for the Bear Stearns Current Yield Fund, which proposes to use cash creation and redemption instead of in-kind, or the Vanguard TIPS ETF where the number of securities to be purchased is limited and extremely liquid. Security disclosure, however, could create a disadvantage for shareholders in actively managed equity ETFs because the manager's trading strategies would be exposed and thus could be exploited by other market participants.

Before the SEC permits the introduction of actively managed ETFs, particularly in equities, the officials must conclude that the changes and exemptions to the Investment Company Act are in the public interest and consistent with the protection of investors. The SEC had not yet approved any actively managed ETFs as of this writing. But the industry changes fast and it is likely that by the time you read these words that the SEC will have approved actively managed ETFs in some form.

The Advantages of Actively Managed ETFs

A few companies have been lobbying for actively managed ETFs in an attempt to make a name for themselves as product innovators and to ultimately license their methods to fund companies. That helps those companies become profitable, however little has been written about what benefits, if any, actively managed ETFs would have for individual investors. Here are several benefits.

1. The most talked-about benefit of actively managed ETFs is the opportunity to outperform indexes that other ETFs follow. Given the poor track record of most actively managed open-end mutual funds compared to index funds, it is hard to support that contention. Nonetheless, hope over reason is the way active management is marketed to the public, and from that perspective, I am sure actively managed ETF providers will be very successful at gathering assets.

2. The biggest benefit in actively managed ETFs will go to investors who would otherwise invest in a comparable actively managed open-end fund. An actively managed ETF would likely charge less than its open-end counterpart because the structure allows ETF companies to eliminate many client services and to reduce the cost of some administrative services (see Chapter 4).

3. If a fund company introduced an actively managed ETF that closely tracked the performance of actively managed open-end

funds, then investors who frequently trade the open-end fund might choose to use the ETF because there would be no minimum required hold time (currently 30 days on most open-end fund purchases).

4. Like index ETFs, the share creation and redemption process would make the actively managed ETF more tax efficient than a traditional active open-end structure (see Chapter 4). This could be the biggest selling point of the funds.

5. Flexibility is another key benefit. Like index ETFs, actively managed ETFs allow investors to trade throughout the day, including short sales and buying on margin.

Disadvantages of Actively Managed ETFs

Actively managed ETF companies will likely benefit greatly from these products, but will individual investors? Fund managers will have difficulty avoiding the daily pitfalls of full disclosure, and those problems could be magnified during volatile trading days. Here are the issues:

1. Fund companies will be required to disclose at least part of their holdings on a daily basis for actively managed ETFs to function properly. The authorized participants need a fund composition file each day that lists the securities to turn in for a creation unit.

   Disclosure is a problem for full active managers and the SEC. Fund managers go to great lengths to conceal their holdings and camouflage trades so that competitors do not take advantage of their activity. Full disclosure hinders an active manager's ability to implement a fund's strategy since other investors figure out the manager's intent and front-run trades, thus diluting potential profit opportunities for ETF shareholders and escalating losses.

   In addition, investors could free-ride and exploit a skilled manager's research at no cost. The public would have access to daily fund information without purchasing ETF shares. Active manager skill is rare and highly valued in the investment management industry. If an actively managed ETF manager had skill, it would not be long before free-riders would tag along and dilute returns.

Finally, actively managed ETF managers may be reluctant to make adjustments in the portfolio for fear of front-runners and other traders in the marketplace. That reluctance could hurt ETF shareholders. All of these issues would reduce the competitive advantage of actively managed ETFs, and reduce investors' incentive to use actively managed ETFs over less-exposed traditional open-end mutual funds.

2. Actively managed ETFs may develop large premiums or discounts to NAV on volatile trading days. With index ETFs, authorized participants (APs) have been able to minimize the possibility of arbitrage by releasing or redeeming shares as a way of controlling inventory and, therefore, prices. Any time a price disparity becomes apparent in an index ETF, it immediately gets traded away. Actively managed ETFs are a concern because the APs may not be able to maintain the same kind of control. It is difficult to hedge positions without knowing exactly what the underlying securities in an actively managed ETF are during the day, and that may lead to wide price disparities.

Large price disparities are particularly likely to happen if an ETF's last trade occurs well before the market close. At that, the underlying securities in the ETF might have already moved the fund's intraday value away from its last trade price. The media will pick up on the large disparities, and the investing public will become outraged. A similar situation happened with emerging market ETFs during a volatile day in March 2007. That bad press was caused mostly by a lack of understanding by the media.

Summary

The next evolution in exchange-traded securities is actively managed equity ETFs. SEC approval of actively managed equity ETFs will unleash a new wave of products that will penetrate the multitrillion dollar actively managed open-end fund marketplace.

Implementing the new actively managed ETFs will be a sharp learning curve for fund managers. One of the issues they will have to deal with will be the daily disclosure of current ETF positions. It is like playing in a poker game where only your cards are dealt face up. Everyone else in the game will be able to take advantage of you.

Despite the challenges of managing actively managed ETFs, the potential for investment firms to gather assets is enormous. That does not, however, necessarily mean a benefit to ETF investors. It is difficult at best for active managers to beat a market index, let alone when that manager must operate under an ETF system that requires the disclosure of fund holdings.

PART II

THE INDEXES ETFs FOLLOW

CHAPTER 6

Market Indexes and Custom Indexes

Exchange-traded funds attempt to track the performance of indexes. Accordingly, knowing how indexes are constructed and maintained are an important part of ETF analysis. Understanding how index providers select securities and weight those securities in an index gives you deep insight into how an ETF is managed, and puts you in a much better position to make an investment decision.

There are two types of indexes: market indexes and custom indexes. A market index is a measurement tool. The intent is to measure the general price level and value of a financial market. A custom index is an investment strategy. The intent is to develop a portfolio management technique that is used as the basis for investment products, including ETFs. Market index and custom index products compete for space in the ETF marketplace. However, there is room for both. Market index–based ETFs and custom index–based ETFs are two different types of investment products. The first earns the return of the markets less fees and the second earns the return of the portfolio strategy less fees.

Part II of this book is all about index construction methodology. This chapter separates market indexes from customized indexes and explores both types in detail including their advantages and disadvantages. This chapter introduces an innovative index classification method called *Index Strategy Boxes*. Index Strategy Boxes and its accompanying tables are designed to give you a quick and easy method for determining how any securities index is constructed and maintained, whether it is a market index or a customized index. Chapter 7 and Chapter 8 expand on Index Strategy Box methodology.

A Definition of Market Indexes

Market measurement began in the late 1800s when Charles Dow published the first general indicator of 12 stock prices. Dow simply added the prices of the 12 stocks together and that became the indicator. Crude as the method seems today, it is still used to calculate the Dow Jones Averages.

Value-weighted methods for measuring the financial markets were introduced in the middle of the twentieth century as methods improved for gathering data and calculating prices. A value-weighted measure of the stock market takes the price of each security and multiplies them by the shares outstanding. This method provides a general price track as well as a valuation yardstick for the wealth of the stock market. Value-weighted methods are the standard around the world for the measurement of market levels and values.

Market indexes track the performance of financial markets. Their purpose is to reflect the value and price changes of a broad sampling of securities that are targeted for measurement. Market indexes tend to be passive in nature, meaning that security selection and security weighting is based on the natural state of a market. An unbiased sampling of securities that regularly trade on a market is used, and their weight in the index is based on the market value of each security relative to the value of all other securities in the index. In a nutshell, market indexes are passively selected and capitalization weighted.

Market indexes are important financial indicators. They are the standard applied throughout the world as valuation yardsticks. They are the benchmarks applied at the highest levels of economic analysis, including the U.S. Federal Reserve. Market index methodology is the preferred method used in research by all top academic institutions. Virtually all asset allocation decisions made use market index data, whether those decisions are being made by individual investors who use simple models or by large institutional investors that use sophisticated modeling. In addition, market indexes are the standard by which active management strategies are measured. Last, but not least, market indexes over the last 30 years have become the dominant benchmarks used in the management of index funds.

A Definition of Custom Indexes

Although market indexes are the preferred financial indicators used in the global markets, customized indexes have captured a big market share in the ETF industry. Custom indexes are not market indexes. They are not intended to measure the value or performance of financial markets, sectors, or styles. Customized indexes are investment strategies. They are designed for whatever specific purpose their creators intend. That goal is accomplished through engineered security selection methodologies or modified security weighting methods, or both.

The providers of customized indexes are not generally interested in creating data for economic study, academic research, or asset allocation. They are most interested in creating and maintaining indexes that can be commercialized into financial products. Custom index providers receive licensing fees from investment companies that use those indexes. The primary licensees of customized index methods are investment management companies, including ETF firms.

There is no lack of indexes available for licensing by ETF companies. There are currently several hundred thousands securities traded worldwide and an infinite number of ways to work those securities into indexes. A study of each index method would be overwhelming. The next few chapters will give you the basic tools needed to analyze any index so that you have meaningful information upon which to base your ETF selections.

Characteristics of a Good Index

In the early 1990s, the CFA Institute established guidelines for the creation of market benchmarks. Market benchmarks are used as the basis for comparing the performance of investment strategies against. The CFA Institute is an organization of more than 80,000 investment analysts who lead the investment profession globally by setting the highest standards of ethics, education, and professional excellence.

The guidelines were published to ensure relevance, clarity, integrity, and consistency in the creation and maintenance of market benchmarks. According to the CFA Institute, benchmarks should have the following characteristics:

Simple and objective selection criteria: There should be a clear set of rules governing the inclusion of bonds, equities, or markets in an index, and investors should be able to forecast and agree on changes in the composition of the securities in an index.

Comprehensive: The index should include all opportunities that are realistically available to be purchased by all market participants under normal market conditions. Both new and existing securities should have frequent pricing available so the index level can be accurately measured.

Replicable: The total returns reported for an index should be replicable by market participants. Over time, an index must represent a realistic baseline strategy that a passive investor could have followed. Accordingly, information about index composition and historical returns should be readily available. It must also be fair to investment managers who are measured against it, and to sponsors who pay fees or award management assignments based on performance relative to it.

Stability: The index should not change composition frequently, and all changes should be easily understood and highly predictable. The index should not be subject to opinions about which bonds or equities to include on any particular day. Conversely, index composition is expected to change occasionally to ensure that it accurately reflects the structure of the market. A key virtue of an index is to provide a passive benchmark. As such, investors should not be forced to execute a significant number of transactions just to keep pace.

Relevance: The index should be relevant to investors. At a minimum, it should track those markets and market segments of most interest to investors.

Barriers to entry: The markets or market segments included in an index should not contain significant barriers to entry. This guideline is especially applicable to an international index in which an included country may discourage foreign ownership of its bonds or participation in its equity market.

Expenses: In the normal course of investing, expenses related to withholding tax, safekeeping, and transactions are incurred. For a market or market segment to be included, these ancillary expenses should be well understood by market participants and should not be excessive. For example, if expenses are unpredictable or inconsistently applied, an index cannot hope to fairly measure market performance.

The CFA Institute guidelines are important and relevant, but they are not rules. It is clearly evident to the casual observer that many index providers to ETFs have shifted far away from the guidelines to creating customized indexes for the purpose of commercialization.

I am not implying or suggesting that any or all ETFs that follow customized indexes are poor investment choices. Nor am I suggesting the ETFs that follow only market indexes are the best choices. To the contrary, there are some excellent ETFs benchmarked to customized indexes and there are other, less-than-desirable ETFs benchmarked to market indexes.

The purpose of this section is to teach you about different index methodologies and how those differences may affect your portfolio. As an informed ETF investor, it is prudent to dig deep into the indexing methodology so that you can make an informed investment decision about the ETFs you are interested in.

Details of Market Indexes

Market indexes are designed to measure, as closely as possible, the performance of a specific financial market or segment of that market. They are stable baskets of stocks, bonds, commodities, or other assets whose overall price level, risk, and return are used as standard measurements worldwide. Market indexes represent the universe of opportunities that all investors have to choose from. Every index should be readily replicated by an investor using the rules set forth by the index provider.

The securities in a market index are generally passively selected. Typically, index providers include a broad selection of securities, with little turnover of those securities. Some indexes include all securities available on the public markets, while others use a sampling of those securities. Sampling methods are typically optimized in an attempt to track the broad market as closely as possible.

Some popular market indexes do not hold all the securities on the broad market. However, enough securities are sampled from the market to qualify as a market index. The S&P 500 index does not hold all large cap stocks, although it holds enough securities so that the index exhibits close to the risk and return characteristics of a broad basket of large cap stocks.

The selection of securities in a market index cuts across all exchanges. For example, Standard & Poor's, MSCI, Russell, and DJ Wilshire equity indexes exhibit a good cross-section of securities. Those indexes are composed of stocks listed on the New York Stock Exchange (NYSE), the American Stock Exchange (AMEX), and the over-the-counter market (NASDAQ). While each exchange has its own indexes that measure the return of securities on that specific exchange, those custom indexes are not designed or intended to measure the return of the broad markets and thus are not market indexes.

Market indexes are capitalization (cap) weighted. In an equity index, each company is weighted in proportion to its market value relative to all other companies in the index. As such, a large company will have more influence on index performance than a small company.

There are four types of capitalization weighted indexes: full cap, free-float, capped, and liquidity. The difference between full cap and free-float is that the former includes the value of all securities outstanding while the latter only includes that portion of securities that are available to individual investors. They represent the shares held by stockholders who are at liberty to sell. For example, a full cap U.S. large company index includes the market value of all Microsoft shares outstanding while a free-float U.S. large company index does not include the market value of restricted Microsoft stock personally held by company executives. By eliminating shares that are not available to trade, free-float indexes reflect the universe of securities available for purchase by all investors on the open market.

Liquidity indexes are a relatively new idea. Stocks are weighted on the basis of the amount of shares that trade regularly rather than free float. The evolution in liquidity indexes is driven by emerging markets, where the liquidity of some issues is too thin despite a sizable number of outstanding shares.

A capped or restrained index may be used when one or more of the securities in a free-float index dominate the index. In those cases, the dominant securities may be capped at 5 or 10 percent, and the remaining allocation spread across all other securities. Capped indexes ensure that an index is not overly influenced by a single security.

Style and Sector Market Indexes

Broad market indexes include a composite of securities, while style and industry indexes slice those broad market securities into different segments. Broad equity market indexes are generally divisible into styles, industry sectors, and types. Examples of styles include small and large cap stocks, value stocks, and growth stocks. Sectors include technology, energy, real estate, health care, and so on. Bond market indexes can be divided into segments, including corporate bonds, mortgages, Treasury bonds, and a long list of others.

Equity styles, sectors, and bond types are segments of a broad market index. Together, those segments add up to be the broad market. It is a hierarchical structure. The Russell 1000 Growth Index and the Russell 1000 Value Index, for example, combine to make the Russell 1000 Index. Adding the Russell 1000 and Russell 2000 equals the Russell 3000. Bond types also combine to form large bond market indexes. The Lehman Brothers investment grade corporate bond index, mortgage index, Treasury bond index, and other investment grade U.S. fixed income indexes add up to the Lehman Brothers Aggregate Bond Market Index.

A broad market index is a sum of its parts. That is an important distinction that differentiates market indexes from most customized indexes. That distinction becomes clearly evident throughout this book and in the Index Strategy Box methodology.

Uses of Market Indexes

Market indexes are used in a variety of ways. The four most common uses of market indexes are:

1. A basis for economic and academic research
2. A basis for asset allocation decisions
3. A benchmark for measuring active portfolio strategies against
4. A benchmark for index fund management

Economists and academic institutions use market indexes to measure and compare value and performance of publicly traded securities worldwide. For economists, the broad stock, bond, commodities, and derivatives markets act as a barometer of expected future business activity. Sector performance reflects the pulse of investor sentiment and may provide clues to the expected prospect of economic sectors, ranging from housing to retail sales. The Federal Reserve uses broad market index performance in several indicators, including the Composite Index of Leading Economic Indicators, a key forecasting gauge for the U.S. economy.

Reliable data on market indexes goes back several decades. Investors and researchers study that long-term market performance data and the historic correlations between markets to assist in asset allocation decisions. Also, many investors compare the current valuations of market indexes to historic levels in an attempt to correctly adjust their portfolios in an effort to reduce risk and increase their returns.

Market indexes represent the investable universe by which active investment strategies are measured against. A broad market index reflects the number and value of all securities that an investor could buy. It is thus the opportunity set for all investors in the public markets.

Style and industry sector indexes are also used as benchmarks for active funds that invest in those segments of the market. For example, a large cap U.S. value index is an appropriate yardstick by which to measure the performance of an actively managed large cap value mutual fund. It is generally the responsibility of an active manager to disclose in advance the defined universe of securities he selects from, and then be measured against that market index.

Market indexes are the primary benchmarks for index funds based on the value of securities invested in them. More money is benchmarked to market indexes worldwide than any other type of custom index strategy. That includes the ETF marketplace. Ironically, there are far more ETF tracking custom indexes than market indexes. The number of custom index ETFs outstanding in an SEC registration outnumbers market index ETFs by about two to one.

Details of Custom Indexes

Today, a majority of new ETFs track custom indexes. These new indexes cannot realistically be compared to market indexes. Customized indexes are not a measure of the value of markets, nor are they used as the basis for economic analysis or asset allocation studies, nor are they used as benchmarks by which to measure active strategies against. Most customized indexes are designed solely for the purpose of creating and managing investment products.

Little academic research is available about customized indexes because they are so diverse in their methodology. Much of the data that is available is generated by the index providers who have a financial stake in the acceptance of their products. As you read over Parts II and III of this book, some custom indexes will strike you as being well thought out and thought provoking, while others border on financial entertainment.

One custom index methodology that has received far more attention than it should have is called fundamental indexing. The methodology focuses on weighting stocks in an index based on fundamental data rather than the value of a company. From an investment strategy standpoint, the idea has merit because it instills a value stock bias in a portfolio, and over the long term, value stocks have provided a long-term premium over growth stocks (see Chapter 9). A majority of positive research on fundamental indexing has been published by the companies promoting those investment strategies. To the contrary, a majority of the negative or neutral writings has been published by academics who have no financial incentive to promote the methodology.

A largest flaw with calling fundamental weighted portfolios an index is that the index cannot be used for anything except as the basis for investment products. No economist is interested in using a fundamentally weighted index as the benchmark for market performance; the Federal Reserve will not be using the method in their leading economic indicators; investment advisors are not going to use fundamentally weighted indexes as the benchmark for active management strategies, and investors are not using fundamentally weighted indexes in asset allocation models.

As an investment strategy, fundamental indexing is a viable way to create a value stock portfolio. That creates alternatives for ETF investors providing they understand what they are buying.

A Different View on Indexes

The SEC does not regulate the definition of an index or how one should be structured. In this author's opinion, the SEC views an index as a basket of securities that are selected, weighted, and managed using any rules-based methodology. Hence, the traditional view of an index as being a passively selected and capitalization weighted basket of securities that represents a market is no longer valid.

Market index providers view their products as measurement devices. They are the yardsticks by which to compare the performance of markets, the level of country wealth, and the success or failure of investment strategies. Market indexes have a rich history of data for economists, analysts, and students to study and ponder. The indexes are also used by all financial institutions as the basis for asset allocation decisions in managed portfolios.

Custom index providers have a different view of the definition of an index. They define an index as any rules-based investment strategy that can be packaged and licensed into an investment product. This definition muddies the water for investors because it is too broad and it has created much confusion. However, that benefits ETF firms that use custom indexes. Those firms are trying to channel money destined for market index ETFs into their own custom index ETFs by inferring that the old definition of an index is inferior or obsolete.

Some market index providers are also custom index providers and they must keep the two types of indexes separate. To those firms, market indexes are the flagships of their index portfolio and the bedrock of their namesake and practice, while custom indexes are managed primarily for the licensing fees they generate.

The custom index business has become very competitive. The providers range from large research firms that also provide thousands of market indexes, to small research companies that only provide a few custom indexes. One of the largest providers of custom indexes is Standard and Poor's (S&P), which ironically is the provider of the bellwether S&P 500 index. Company analysts work with product providers to create custom indexes that emulate a variety of investment strategies. S&P earns fees for developing and maintaining those indexes.

Summary

Market indexes are designed to capture the price and performance of financial markets and segments of markets. Securities tend to be passively selected and reflect a good cross-section of the market. Each security is weighted in accordance with its market capitalization compared to all other securities in the index. Market indexes are used as the basis for academic research, economic analysis, asset allocation decisions, as a yardstick for comparing active strategies, and as the basis for index funds.

Today, customized indexes have come to dominate new ETF issuance. In a custom index one or more subjective decisions are made by the index provider in the areas of security selection, security weighting, or both. The intent of the customized index provider is to create a strategy that does not track the broad market. As a result, ETFs that track custom indexes offer different risk and return characteristics than ETFs that follow the market.

We live in a changing investment environment where old standards are being challenged by new ideas. The popularity of ETFs is a major factor behind those changes and ETF investors are learning and benefiting from those changes. Investing in ETFs that track market indexes or customized indexes is an investor's choice, and more choices are a good thing, as long as there is a reliable method to evaluate the choices and a competent level of understanding. Market index ETFs are not better or worse than custom index ETFs; they are just different. Whether you choose one, the other, or both depends on your assessment of the methodologies because each one may help you achieve your financial goals.

CHAPTER 7

Index Strategy Boxes

Financial indexes were created in the nineteenth century to reflect the price changes of securities that traded on financial markets. The first indexes were calculated using a simple average of a few stock prices and did not consider the value of companies.

As data gathering methods improved during the twentieth century, indexes advanced to include far more securities. The inclusion of more securities improved the reliability of the index as a market indicator. Also, securities were weighted on the basis of their market capitalization compared to all other constituents in the index. The market capitalization of an index is an important measurement tool that is used by economists, researchers, portfolio managers and investment advisors.

In the twenty-first century, the definition of a financial index has expanded far beyond a market indicator. Today, indexes are virtually any basket of securities that are selected and weighted based on a set of predefined rules. Rules for index construction have stretched from the simple and elegant to the complex and cumbersome. Once simple in form and worthy in intent, indexing has grown into an overcrowded, ambiguous, and confusing marketplace.

The SEC's interpretation a financial index is very loose. The agency seems to define an index as any list of publicly traded securities that are selected, weighted, and maintained using a published rules-based methodology. That definition makes index analysis difficult at best.

Traditional methods for mutual fund categorization analysis are not adequate for the plethora of index fund products that have been launched into the ETF marketplace. What is needed is a simple way to categorize indexes so investors can easily differentiate among strategies.

Indexes Follow Rules

One requirement of all indexes that are used as the basis for ETF management is that they follow published rules for construction and maintenance. Adherence by the index provider to those rules is what makes an index credible. If the index provider does not follow its own rules, or if the rules change frequently, then the provider runs the risk of losing credibility among investors.

Detailed rules for index creation and maintenance should be published in the public domain. The rules should be explained in language simple enough and in enough detail so an unsophisticated investor can gain a working knowledge of how each index functions. The rules should be published on an index provider's web site and in an ETF's initial filing with the SEC. In addition, the rules should be adequately explained on the web sites of ETF companies that are using an index as the basis for investment decisions.

Unfortunately, what should happen and what does happen in the ETF business are two different worlds. Although the ETF companies and index providers should be eager to explain how their products work, many explanations of an index are confusing, inadequate, and in many cases, absent. That makes research difficult at times. Investors must dig very deep to get basic information on how some ETFs are invested and managed.

A few ETF companies provide literally no useful information on how securities are selected or weighted in their ETFs. These companies routinely state that the custom index methodology is proprietary and cannot be disclosed. Yet in their marketing material, the same companies will proudly display hypothetical performance charts that infer outstanding results from the super-secret indexing method.

In this author's opinion, ETFs are a fabulous innovation. The evolution of ETFs has lowered investment costs, added trading flexibility, and created tax efficiency. It is too bad that the disclosure practices and marketing tactics at a few ETF companies have not evolved as well.

Index Strategy Boxes

Index rules tend to be similar enough across index providers so that a broad-based categorizing and organizing system of those rules can be created. The rules for index construction generally fall into two broad categories: security selection and security weighting. How securities are selected is the first step in index construction. How those selected securities are weighted in the index is the second step. The two categories of security selection and security weighting are the two dimensions of Index Strategy Boxes.

Index Strategy Boxes makes index security selection and security weighting methodologies easily identifiable. Knowing how securities are chosen and allocated within an index can explain a lot about how it will move in relation to general market trends. The information provided by the Index Strategy Box categorization and accompanying tables will greatly reduce the time it takes to analyze and select the ETFs for your portfolio.

The topic of Index Strategy Boxes spans this and the next two chapters. This chapter introduces the process by describing the three broad security selection methods and three broad security weighting methods. Chapter 8 provides added detail and examples of the security selection. Chapter 9 provides more information and examples of security weighting methods.

Introducing Index Strategy Boxes

In the 1990s, Morningstar Incorporated popularized their Morningstar Style Boxes™ to help investors identify the style of a mutual fund. Style boxes categorize equity and fixed income funds into nine tic-tac-toe boxes. The two axes of an equity style box divide mutual funds into three size and three style categories. Fixed income style boxes classify funds into the nine tic-tac-toe boxes using the average maturity of a bond fund on one axis and the average credit quality of a bond fund on the other. See Chapter 10 and Chapter 14 for more information on Morningstar Style Boxes.

Index Strategy Boxes use a similar tic-tac-toe diagram. There are nine boxes representing different index strategies. The information provided by these Index Strategy Boxes is quite different from Morningstar Style Boxes. Index Strategy Boxes classify indexes based on how an index is constructed rather than the investment style of that index.

On the vertical axis are three broad security selection methods: passive, screened, and quantitative. The horizontal axis categorizes indexes based on three broad security weighting methods: capitalization, fundamental, and fixed-weight. Figure 7.1 illustrates the tic-tac-toe design of Index Strategy Boxes.

Index Strategy Boxes will help you understand how an index is constructed and managed on the basis of its published rules. Which box an index sits in provides clues as to how an ETF that follows the index is expected to perform over various phases of a market cycle.

When you use Index Strategy Boxes, it is assumed that you have already decided on a particular style of equity ETF. You are now interested in the way the indexes are constructed across that style, and will select an ETF based on the index methodology.

For example, once you have already decided to buy a large cap U.S. value ETF that tracks a large cap U.S. value index, the next step is to screen the ETF database at www.etfguide.com to analyze the various indexes available and select the type of index you are looking for. You may decide to invest in a low-cost market index ETF that passively selects stocks and weights those securities according to their market capitalizations. Or, you may select a custom index ETF

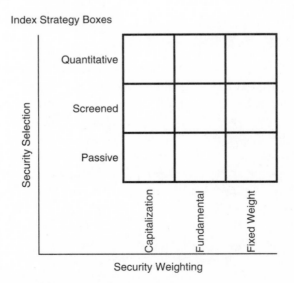

Figure 7.1   Index Strategy Boxes
Source: Portfolio Solutions, LLC

that attempts to enhance returns through a more complex security selection process or a different weighting methodology.

An appealing aspect of Index Strategy Boxes is that they can be used in any asset class. The methodology can be used for equities, fixed income, and commodity indexes.

Also, almost every sector of a broad market index fits cleanly into one of the nine boxes. For example, the Russell 3000 is a market index that passively selects securities and weights those stocks by capitalization. It thus fits into the lower left hand passive selection/capitalization weighted strategy box. The Russell 1000 is a passive cap weighted subset of the Russell 3000. Accordingly, the Russell 1000 also goes into the same strategy box. While there are always exceptions to the methodology, the process is relatively straightforward once you understand the basics.

The Security Selection Axis.   On the vertical axis of Index Strategy Boxes is Security Selection. The category represents the methodology used to select securities from the broad financial markets. The three selection methods are passive, screened, and quantitative. A summary of the three selection levels follows; Chapter 8 explains each level in greater detail.

The first category is passive security selection (see Figure 7.2). Passive selection replicates that broad market or a sector of the market. Most passive indexes do not hold all the securities that trade on a market, although it is the intent of the index provider to

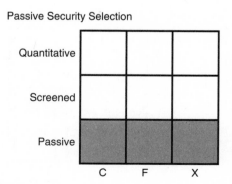

Figure 7.2   Passive Security Selection
Source: Portfolio Solutions, LLC

represent the broad market. Passive indexes typically hold enough securities so that the basket has similar risk and return characteristics in relation to the market as a whole. Also, many ETFs do not hold all the securities that compose the index, although it is the intent of the ETF manager to track the index as closely as feasible.

There are typically few requirements for a security to be a member of a passive index. Those requirements typically include a minimum number of shares outstanding, a certain minimum daily trading volume, and a minimum market capitalization. The constraints placed on some passively selected indexes will not materially affect the performance of the index relative to a complete broad market index.

There are different types of passive selection used by index providers and ETF managers. They include completion methods, sampling and optimization methods, buy-and-hold strategies, and the use of derivatives, such as options, futures, and swaps. The premise behind all security selection is that the composite portfolio replicates the price movement of a broad market of securities, regardless of the underlying method used to replicate those returns.

The second type of security selection is screening (see Figure 7.3). Screening securities eliminates unwanted issues from an index. It starts with a broad market universe of securities and then filters out those that do not meet certain criteria. Screening goes far beyond the requirements for a passively selected index by isolating securities according to fundamental factors, social issues, exchange

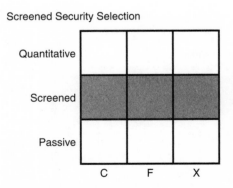

Figure 7.3   Screened Security Selection
Source: Portfolio Solutions, LLC

preferences, or a variety of other items. The idea of screening is to eliminate undesirable securities, thus leaving in the index only those securities that have desirable characteristics.

Dividend screens are a popular fundamental filter. Typically, companies that do not pay a regular quarterly dividend are filtered out of dividend indexes. A second filter could be added to ensure a company has paid dividends for at least three years. A third screen could be put in place that ensures a company has not cut its dividend in the past five years. The remaining securities represent a basket of stocks that meet the index provider's specifications.

Screens can be applied for social reasons. In a socially responsible stock index, companies that are believed to be in a socially harmful business or follow socially unacceptable business practices are eliminated. Undesirable companies that are often screened out are in the tobacco, alcohol, and gaming industries. After screening for social issues, the result is a basket of supposedly responsible companies.

The third type of security selection is quantitative (see Figure 7.4). Securities in a quantitative (or quant) index are selected on the basis of advanced computer models that follow complex mathematical formulas. These models are often referred to as *black boxes* because those on the outside are not supposed to know how the models work.

Quant index providers program their software to isolate what they believe is predictive information in securities data and prices.

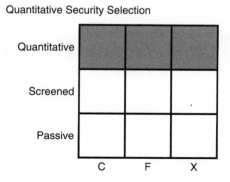

Figure 7.4   Quantitative Security Selection
Source: Portfolio Solutions, LLC

The idea is to separate potentially market-beating securities from potentially market-losing securities. Stocks are ranked into quintiles according to their quantitative scores. The top quintile securities are optimized with one another in an attempt to find an ideal mix of securities to put into a market-beating index. Detailed selection rules of most quantitative models are not made available to the public except on a very limited basis. The fear from index providers and ETF companies is that if people knew the methodology, it would be compromised. The competition would steal their ideas and traders would trade ahead of their index changes. Some seepage of information is inevitable if the system works. So quant index providers may reevaluate their methods occasionally and tweak the models in an attempt to stay ahead of the competition.

The Security Weighting Axis.   Once securities are selected for an index, they need to be given a weight in the index. The horizontal axes of Index Strategy Boxes classify weighting methodologies using three basic methods, which are capitalization weight, fundamental weight, and fixed weight. Weighting methods are important because the fundamental characteristics of a given basket of securities change when using each of the three different methods. A summary of the three weighting methods follows, and Chapter 9 provides more details.

Capitalization weighting is the traditional method for constructing market indexes (see Figure 7.5). Securities in a market index are allocated on the basis of the market value of each security in relation to all of the other securities in the index.

There are four basic methods of capitalization weighting used by index providers. They are full cap, free float, constrained, and liquidity. The difference between full cap and free float is that the former includes the entire value of securities in the index while the latter includes only the value of shares that are available in the public markets.

Unlike full or free-float indexes, liquidity weighting is based on the actual value of securities that trade on a market. Although there may be a large number of shares that could trade based on a securities float, it is the market value of the trades that is the most important component for ETF companies and authorized participants. Liquidity weighting is a particularly useful method of managing index ETFs in hard-to-trade foreign markets.

Capitalization Weighted Index

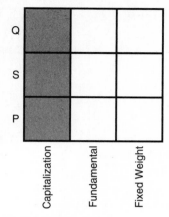

Figure 7.5 Capitalization Weighting Index
Source: Portfolio Solutions, LLC

A constrained (or capped) index simply means that no security is allowed to go above a certain percentage in the index, that is, a maximum of 5 percent or 10 percent per security. Constrained indexes are designed to keep ETFs within strict SEC mutual fund diversification requirements.

The second type of weighting methodology uses fundamental factors (see Figure 7.6). A fundamental weighted index relies on a factor or set of factors other than market capitalization to weight stocks in an index. Information that may be used includes financial factors such as dividend yield or earnings yield, earnings predictions, or other factors such as security price, price momentum, and rankings of social responsibility. An example of a weighting factor can be stock dividend yield, where the greater the dividend yield of an index constituent, the greater that stock's weighting in the index. Another example is a multifactor formula where securities are weighted on the basis of a combination of many fundamental variables. Since fundamentals change over time, fundamental weighted indexes are rebalanced periodically to realign the index with current conditions.

The third weighting category represents fixed weight strategies (see Figure 7.7). There are five basic types: equal, modified equal, leveraged, inverse, and long-short.

Fundamental Weighted Index

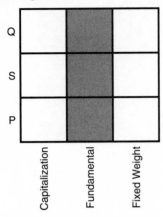

Figure 7.6   Fundamental Weighting Index
Source: Portfolio Solutions, LLC

An equal weight allocation assigns the same percentage to every security. For example, in a 100 bond index, each bond is weighted to 1 percent of the index. Modified equal weights are used to allocate securities among two or more fixed percentages based on some method of priority. Larger stocks might be weighted 2 percent,

Fixed Weighted Index

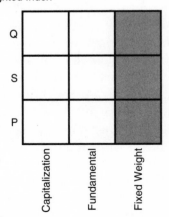

Figure 7.7   Fixed Weighted Index
Source: Portfolio Solutions, LLC

whereas small stocks might get only 1 percent. Securities can also receive a fixed weight based on a ranking system using quantitative methods. For example, securities in the top quintile group might be allocated 2 percent each and securities in the second quintile group might be 1 percent. The weightings in fixed weight indexes are generally realigned every quarter.

The last types of fixed weight indexes are leveraged, inverse (short), and long-short strategies. Leveraged indexes double or triple the daily gains and losses of a broad market index, while inverse indexes go the opposite direction of the broad market. A long-short weighting methodology overweights securities that are believed to provide market-beating returns and shorts securities thought to be underperformers.

Market Indexes and Custom Indexes

Table 7.1 summarizes Index Strategy Boxes and their components. You will see small Index Strategy Boxes next to all ETF symbols throughout this book.

Chapter 6 explained the differences between market indexes and custom indexes. Those differences can be broadly illustrated using Index Strategy Boxes. Figure 7.8 illustrates the boxes where market index, and Figure 7.9 where custom index, strategies fall.

Market indexes are designed to capture the performance of a financial market. Market index ETFs are categorized by passive

Table 7.1   Summary of Index Types and Index Strategy Boxes

Strategy Box	Index Type	Security Selection	Security Weighting
	Market	Passive	Capitalization
	Custom	Passive	Fundamental
	Custom	Passive	Fixed Weight
	Custom	Screened	Capitalization
	Custom	Screened	Fundamental
	Custom	Screened	Fixed Weight
	Custom	Quantitative	Capitalization
	Custom	Quantitative	Fundamental
	Custom	Quantitative	Fixed Weight

Source: Portfolio Solutions, LLC

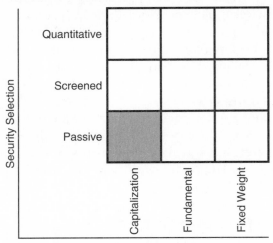

Figure 7.8 Market Index Strategy Box
Source: Portfolio Solutions, LLC

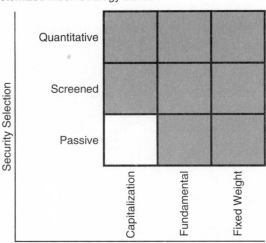

Figure 7.9 Custom Index Strategy Boxes
Source: Portfolio Solutions, LLC

security selection and capitalization weighting. A representation of a market index using Index Strategy Boxes is seen in Figure 7.8.

Customized indexes are set apart from market indexes by their security selection and security weighting methods. Customized index security selection includes screens to filter out undesirable securities, or through complex quantitative methods thought to separate superior securities from inferior ones. Customized security weighting can be in the form of fundamental weighting and various fixed weight methods.

With few exceptions, it is the intent of the customized index provider to deviate from the characteristics of a market index. The providers intentionally seek a different risk and return path than that provided by the market. To accomplish that goal, custom indexes are based on the subjective decisions of the provider, which can be argued is a form of active management.

Summary

Indexes are used as benchmarks for ETFs. Index Strategy Boxes represent a simple way to categorize the security selection and weighting strategies used in the management of those indexes. Index Strategy Boxes can be applied to all asset classes, including stocks, bonds, and commodities.

Indexes are rules-based. Those rules can be categorized into two types: security selection and security weighting. The different methodologies used to select securities and weight those securities in a portfolio can have a profound impact on the risk and return characteristics of an ETF that follows that index.

Index Strategy Boxes are a major step forward in ETF analysis. Knowing how an index is constructed and managed goes a long way toward understanding why an ETF is expected to exhibit certain risk and return characteristics. Incorporating Index Strategy Box analysis into ETF research will greatly reduce the time it takes to analyze ETFs and enhance your search for the right investment vehicles.

8

Index Security Selection

Index Strategy Boxes categorize indexes based on their construction and maintenance rules. The rows represent security selection methodologies and the columns represent security weighting methods. Knowledge of an index's security selection and security weighting mythology are major steps toward understanding the performance of ETFs that track the index.

ETF managers follow indexes in a number of ways. They can use a complete replication of the securities in an index, sample the securities in an index, or use derivatives that trade based on the level of an index. Regardless of the replication method used by a fund manager to replicate the index, the important matter for ETF investors is how the index is managed and the characteristics of the index.

The first part of index analysis is security selection, and the second half is security weighting. This chapter examines security selection methodology in detail, and Chapter 9 will complete the discussion with an examination of security weighting methodologies.

Security Selection Categorization

Each index has published rules for security selection so that an investor can gain a working knowledge of how each index is maintained. Some index providers detail information on how their indexes are constructed. Other providers release woefully inadequate information about their methodology, so be prepared to dig deep for data.

In general, the more complex the selection methodology, the less disclosure is provided about the selection rules. Index providers that use a passive security selection tend to be far more transparent than providers favoring security screens and quantitative security selection strategies.

The three rows in Index Strategy Boxes represent these three weighting methods. Table 8.1 lists the three broad security selection categories and examples of security selection methods used by index providers. See Appendix A for a larger list of selection methods under each category. Appendix A is an abbreviation guide for Index Strategy Boxes. The abbreviations next to the categories and methods are used in the tables in Part III.

Securities are selected for indexes based on rules that are specified in advance and rigorously applied. Index rules state that the securities selected for that index must have certain characteristics. Those characteristics must be maintained for continued inclusion in the index. Some selection rules are incorporated in all indexes, while most are specific to a particular index.

One criterion for security selection that is used for nearly all indexes is adequate liquidity. An active market in index constituents ensures the index maintains a relevant and accurate market value. Adequate liquidity is also important for ETF managers who are attempting to replicate or sample the index. Securities listed on the daily portfolio composition file (PCF) must meet or exceed certain minimum capitalization and trading volume requirements so they can be purchased by the authorized participants (APs). If the securities in the PCF cannot be bought and sold efficiently, then

Table 8.1 Examples of Security Selection Categories and Methods

Passive (P)	Screened (S)	Quantitative (Q)
Full Replication (A)	Exchange (E)	Economic Cycle (E)
Sampling (S)	Fundamentals (F)	Multi-factor (M)
Buy and Hold (B)	Price Trend (P)	Momentum (X)
Single Issue (I)	Thematic (T)	Proprietary* (P)

*Proprietary means not enough public information is available to determine.
Source: Portfolio Solutions, LLC

the APs would not be able to form the basket of securities needed to create ETF shares.

The rules for index security selection can be categorized into three broad classifications: passive, screened, and quantitative. Passive rules are very basic and they tend to eliminate illiquid securities and only a few other types that would have only a minor effect on the performance if included. Screened indexes eliminate broad swaths of the market that the index provider does not want in his custom index. Quantitative analysis is used at the highest level of security selection in that the provider applies deep mathematical analysis to isolate securities he believes will outperform the broad market average.

Passive Security Selection

"I can't decide which securities to buy. Can't I just buy them all?" Sure you can, or at least come close. Simply purchase an ETF that follows an index that uses passive security selection techniques.

Passive security selection is a simple methodology that is the most common in global index construction. Passive is also the traditional form of security selection for indexes, and for several years, was the only type of selection used in ETF management (see Figure 8.1).

Passive selection has been broadly applied to market indexes, including stocks, bonds, commodities, currencies, and real estate. The strategy focuses on representing a market. As such, a passive index holds as many positions as necessary to reflect the general price movement of all stocks that trade on a market or a segment of a market.

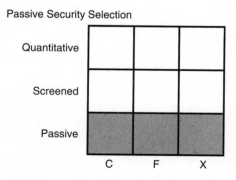

Figure 8.1 Passive Security Selection

There are no biases in a passive selection process that screens out large segments of the market, and there is no forecasting of security performance in an attempt to create a basket that outperforms the market. A passive index does not need to own all of the stocks in a market. There only needs to be enough securities in an index so that the basket reflects the natural price movement of a securities market.

Most rules in passive selection eliminate low volume securities that have infrequent pricing. Additional rules eliminate redundant securities and odd securities that clearly do not belong in the index being created. For example, closed-end mutual funds typically hold securities whose shares are already accounted for in the index. Closed-end funds are consequently excluded because of redundancy. Obvious stocks that do not fit an index are also excluded. For example, a passive U.S. stock index would exclude foreign stocks that trade on U.S. exchanges.

Large index providers typically have a family of passive indexes. At the top of the hierarchy are broad market indexes. They include the securities of all other indexes in the family. Under the broad market indexes are categories including size indexes (large-small), style indexes (value-growth), and industry sector indexes (technology, for example). Below these categories are subsectors (software, hardware, networking, and so on). Some subsectors can be sliced so thin that their components seem almost too narrow to be called an index (nanotechnology, for example).

Indexes using passive security selection have several characteristics. First, they tend be part of an index family hierarchy. Second, they have low turnover in relation to other selection methods. Third, they are not biased to one securities exchange or another.

A family hierarchy of passive indexes has a unique characteristic. All the categories and subcategories can be reformed to equal the broad basket. The providers of passively selected index families give us the opportunity to invest in either the broad market or any piece of that market. The index provider is not biased to one style or another or one industry group or another. All the categories are available to investors as one index or in its pieces. It is up to each one of us to decide which indexes to use in our ETF portfolio.

Passive security selection indexes tend to have the lowest turnover of the three selection methods. New securities invariably go in and out of passive indexes because of general maintenance. However, the number is low in relation to the screened and quantitative security selection methods.

Passive security selection indexes are not exchange specific. Securities are selected across all major exchanges. For example, a passive U.S. equities index includes stocks from the New York Stock Exchange, the American Stock Exchange, and the NASDAQ.

Examples of Passive Security Selection

The major providers of passively selected indexes used in ETF management are Frank Russell & Company (Russell), Morgan Stanley Capital International (MSCI), Morningstar, Standard and Poor's (S&P) including S&P/Citigroup, and Dow Jones & Company, including Dow Jones Wilshire.

Astute readers may question why S&P indexes are placed under the passive selection category given that the S&P selection committee has historically not used a purely passive methodology. Recall that a passive selection strategy attempts to replicate the price movement of securities on an entire market. It is not necessary to include all stocks in a market to achieve that objective. Just include enough to track the market closely. S&P selects hundreds of stocks for each index. The sheer number represents a large cross-section of the markets, and negates practically all of the potential tracking error from subjective decision-making that the S&P committee may impart in security selection.

An Example of a Passive Selection Family

Frank Russell & Company of Tacoma, Washington, created the Russell family of passively selected stock indexes in 1984. Russell calculates the value of 21 indexes daily. Almost all Russell indexes are subsets of the Russell 3000 Index, which represents approximately 98 percent of the investable free-float U.S. equity market. The one exception is the Russell Micro Cap index, which stretches below the Russell 3000.

The rules for Russell index methodology are listed in the text that follows. Reconstitutions of the indexes are done once a year on June 30, based on market data from May 31. A more in-depth description of their index methodology is available at the Frank Russell & Company web site, which lists the rules for deciding how an index should be categorized using Index Strategy Boxes.

Russell eliminates the following securities in their U.S. equity indexes:

- Stocks that do not trade on a major stock exchange
- Stocks that trade below $1
- Closed-end mutual funds, limited partnerships, royalty trusts
- Berkshire Hathaway, Inc. (considered an investment company)
- Non-U.S. domiciled stocks, foreign stocks, ADRs

The securities left are ranked and separated by size:

- Common stocks are listed from the largest to smallest by market capitalization.
- The top 3,000 stocks are included in the Russell 3000 Index.
- The largest 1,000 stocks are included in the Russell 1000 Index.
- The next 2,000 stocks are included in the Russell 2000 Index.
- The smallest 1,000 stocks in the Russell 2000 plus the next 1,000 smallest stocks below the Russell 2000 become the Russell Micro Cap index.

Each Russell index is then divided into style indexes:

- Each stock in the Russell indexes is ranked by price-to-book ratio and its forecasted long-term earnings growth averages.
- Variables are combined to create a composite value score for each stock.
- Stocks are ranked by their score and applied to a mathematical formula to the distribution to determine style membership weights.
- Of the stocks, 70 percent are classified as all value or all growth, and 30 percent are weighted proportionately to both value and growth and are listed in both indexes.

The Russell passive family of indexes is a hierarchy. It is divided into parts and the parts add back up to the whole. The broad market index becomes value and growth indexes, and small stock and large stock indexes. Building back up, those indexes reconnect to form the Russell 3000. Figure 8.2 illustrates the family.

It may not be necessary or feasible for an ETF manager to include all the securities in an index. An ETF manager works around the

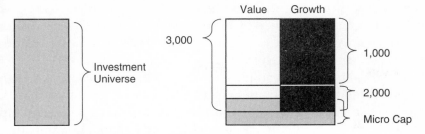

Figure 8.2   Russell Index Security Selection

problem by sampling stocks in the index. By sampling an index, an ETF manager selects liquid securities representing various industries in an attempt to replicate the movement of an index without owning all stocks in that index. Managers who use a sampling technique also tend to employ a sophisticated portfolio optimization process that helps reduce the funds' tracking error with an index. An ETF that uses sampling is still considered to have passive security selection. The intent is to replicate that index as closely as possible.

The iShares Russell Micro Cap ETF (symbol: IWC) is benchmarked to the passively selected Russell Micro Cap index. It cannot be fully replicated in an actual portfolio because many of the smallest 1,000 stocks in the index do not have enough liquidity. Although the Russell Micro Cap index has 2,000 stocks, IWC is composed of only about 1,200 liquid stocks sampled from the index.

Some ETFs follow baskets of securities that are selected once and never changed. An example of ETFs using a buy-and-hold strategy is Holding Company Depositary Receipts (HOLDRs). Stocks in HOLDRs are selected once on the basis of a passive method. Then the basket becomes an unmanaged trust (see Chapter 3 for details). The advantage of this method is its extremely low cost (there is no management fee). The disadvantage is that no new securities can go into a fund. Once the stocks are selected at inception, they become a fixed buy-and-hold basket. Stock can be taken out of the basket because of mergers and acquisitions, but no new companies can replace them.

Screened Security Selection

Security screening is a second type of index security selection methodology. Index providers filter passive baskets of securities to eliminate those that have undesirable characteristics. Screening methodology is only limited by the imagination of the index provider and the information they can gather about the factor they wish to screen for (see Figure 8.3).

An example of screening can be to eliminate securities with certain fundamental qualities or a lack of those qualities, that is, eliminate stocks that have a debt-to-equity ratio over 50 percent and no earnings. Screens can also be designed to eliminate companies that sell unacceptable products based on certain social beliefs, for example, tobacco and alcohol. Screening can limit an index to only those securities that trade on a certain stock exchange, for example, the NASDAQ.

The process can involve the application of many layers of screens. For example, screen for stocks that trade only on the NASDAQ, pay a regular dividend, and provide health care benefits for employees.

Screens are designed specifically by the index provider to eliminate certain securities and to retain others. Screening is thus an active investment management decision. The ETF companies that follow these custom indexes are following an active investment strategy.

Index providers start the screening process with a large universe of securities. To create a U.S. equity index, the starting universe typically holds all the stocks that trade on the NYSE, AMEX, and NASDAQ. Computers filter those securities in a particular order to ensure the results are in accordance with what the provider is seeking. After all the screens are complete and the index provider has the desired list, that list either becomes the index or securities are sampled from the list to form the index.

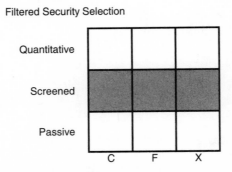

Figure 8.3   Filtered Security Selection

Screened indexes differ from passive indexes in that there is a limited hierarchy, if there is any at all. The various indexes never add up to the starting universe because the undesirable securities are permanently eliminated. Those securities do not go into an index of undesirables. For example, a provider of socially responsible indexes does not maintain socially *irresponsible* indexes. There may be socially irresponsible indexes and ETFs in the future, but they will not be licensed by the companies that sell socially responsible ones. Figure 8.4 illustrates how an index provider permanently eliminates securities through screening.

Custom indexes based on screens are not market indexes and products that follow them should not be bought under the assumption that they will outperform a market index. ETFs that follow filtered indexes are investment products designed for distribution to a specific audience and typically for a specific purpose. That being said, many ETF companies that use these custom indexes attempted to sell their products as a better way to index. That is marketing hype, not investment reality. There is no academic evidence to indicate that screening securities will improve market performance in the long-term after adjusting for portfolio risk.

Examples of Screened Indexes

There are thousands of screens that can be applied to create custom indexes. The list that follows highlights only a few of the more popular ones. By and large, the purpose of these custom indexes is to create and license investment products. Few custom indexes have any relevance in economic analysis, academic research, or asset allocation.

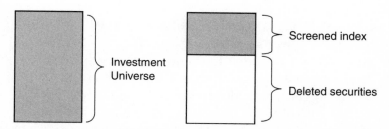

Figure 8.4   Screened Index Security Selection

Dividend Indexes.   Stocks that pay regular dividends became quite popular after the tax law changes of 2003. The top tax rate on stock dividends was lowered to 15 percent if the shares were held more than 60 days. In addition, value stock investing became very popular in the first half of the decade after the growth stock bubble collapse from March 2000 to March 2003. Those two events lead to the creation of many dividend screened indexes followed by the launch of several ETFs that follow those custom indexes.

Dividend indexes have filters designed to sift through a basket of stocks looking for companies that pay regular cash dividends. An index provider typically starts with a universe of stocks composed of all exchanges. For example, the WisdomTree Dividend Index holds cash dividend-paying companies listed on the NYSE, AMEX, and NASDAQ. According to WisdomTree, in 2007, there were approximately 1,500 dividend-paying stocks culled from a 3,500-stock universe that met minimum capitalization and liquidity requirements.

Dividend indexes have strong value stock bias. Compared to non-dividend-paying stocks, companies that pay dividends are typically in mature industries, have lower price-to-earnings ratios (P/E), low price-to-book ratios (P/B), and low price-to-sales ratios (P/S). Dividend indexes also have a higher correlation with a passive value index than with a passive growth index. That means when the passive value index goes higher and the passive growth indexes go lower, custom dividend indexes follow the value index.

See Chapter 9 and Chapter 10 for more information on value investing.

Second and third dividend screens are typically applied to dividend indexes. Those screens may be designed to eliminate companies that have not increased their dividends in recent years, or pay out too much of the earnings as dividends, or have reduced their dividend. Index providers use as many screens as needed to tweak their custom indexes to just the right list of securities that they or their ETF firm client is actively seeking.

WisdomTree Investments, Inc., introduced the first family of domestic and global dividend weighted indexes and ETFs in May 2006. The WisdomTree dividend indexes are composed of companies that pay regular cash dividends and meet other liquidity and capitalization requirements. Stocks are fundamentally weighted (see Chapter 9) in the indexes to reflect the proportionate share of cash dividends projected to be paid by each company in the coming year.

In 2007, WisdomTree introduced the first family of domestic and global earnings weighted indexes and ETFs. The WisdomTree Earnings Indexes are selected companies that have generated positive cumulative earnings over their four most recent fiscal quarters. The indexes are fundamentally weighted to reflect the proportionate share of the aggregate earnings each company contributed.

Exchange Indexes. There are three primary stock exchanges in the United States: the New York Stock Exchange (NYSE), the American Stock Exchange (AMEX), and the National Association of Securities Dealers Automated Quotations system (NASDAQ). Of the three exchanges, the NASDAQ is not a physical exchange. It is a computer network established by the National Association of Securities Dealers (NASD) to facilitate the trading of securities between licensed brokers and dealers. The system provides member firms with current price quotes of over-the-counter securities stocks and some securities listed on the NYSE and AMEX.

Each of the three exchanges has its own set of indexes based exclusively on the stocks that trade on those exchanges. For example, the NASDAQ Composite Index includes stocks that trade only on the NASDAQ, while the NYSE Composite Index includes stocks that trade only on the NYSE. Filters screen out all cross-listed securities that trade primarily on a competing exchange.

Each exchange has several subindexes that may impose special filters to achieve a desired index. The NASDAQ-100 Index includes 100 of the largest domestic and international securities based on the market capitalization of the stocks that trade primarily on the NASDAQ. The custom index includes computer hardware and software, telecommunications, retail and wholesale trade, and biotechnology, but intentionally screens out financial companies and investment companies. The purpose for the industry screen is to give the index a growth stock bias. PowerShares QQQ tracks NASDAQ-100 Index and the trades on NASDAQ (symbol: QQQQ).

Socially Responsible Indexes. Socially responsible indexes are thematic based designs created to reflect the way certain socially conscious investors select companies. As such, the indexes filter out companies involved in alcohol, tobacco, and gambling, as well as controversial industries such as nuclear power, firearms, and weapons-related defense contracting. Some socially responsible indexes also filter for subjective areas such as community relations, diversity, employee relations, environmental stewardship, human rights, product safety and quality, and corporate governance.

The KLD Select Social Index is a service mark of KLD Research & Analytics, Inc. The index has been licensed for use by Barclays Global Investors and is the benchmark for the iShares KLD Select Social Index ETF (symbol: KLD) The fund uses a representative sampling strategy in tracking the KLD Select Social Index.

The KLD Select Social Index consists of approximately 200 to 300 securities drawn from the universe of companies held in the Russell 1000 and the S&P 500 Indexes. Companies that do not meet KLD's financial screens of minimum market capitalization, earnings, liquidity, and stock price are also ineligible for inclusion.

In addition to screening out companies that make products that are offensive to some people, KLD screens for social and environmental performance on the basis of seven qualitative areas. Those areas include environment, community, corporate governance, diversity, employee relations, human rights, and product quality and safety.

Corporate Action Filters.   Initial public offerings (IPOs) are companies that raise capital by selling common shares to investors for the first time. Once issued, those shares trade on a public stock exchange. Index providers can screen the markets to find IPO data and create custom indexes based on IPO information.

The U.S. IPOX Composite Index is managed by the Chicago index firm IPOX Schuster. The IPOX 100 Index measures the performance of the largest 100 companies in the U.S. IPOX Composite as ranked quarterly by market capitalization. The companies included in the index have had their IPO within 1,000 trading days (almost three years). Since one or two large companies such as Google (symbol: GOOG) can dominate the index, individual securities are capped at 10 percent of the fund's holdings. The First Trust IPOX-100 Index Fund (Symbol: FPX) follows the IPOX-100 index.

Commodity Filters.   There are many commodities indexes. Most are only a few years old. Almost all indexes benchmarked by ETF companies are formed using commodity futures contracts (see Chapter 15). Unlike most passive stock market indexes, the dispersion in return between commodities indexes is very large. One index could be reporting a year-to-date return of plus 5 percent while another is reporting a year-to-date return of minus 5 percent. Your performance will depend greatly on which index you chose.

While many indexes track the same commodity futures contracts, there are significant differences in the number of commodity futures contracts tracked by the index providers, and the weight of those contracts, and that is what makes a large difference in index performance.

At one extreme, the Rogers International Commodity Index (RICI) tracks 35 commodities, and at the other extreme, the Deutsche Bank Liquid Commodity Index (DBLCI) tracks just six. In the middle, Goldman Sachs Commodity Index (CSCI), Dow Jones AIG Commodity Index (DJAIG) and the Commodity Research Bureau (CRB) Index track from 17 to 24 commodities.

The index providers that use fewer contracts believe diversification can be achieved with a small number of commodities in each of the major sectors. For that reason, those providers use filters to screen for contracts with the most trading liquidity. They also test to ensure those contracts track the broader sectors closely. DBLCI has screened out all but six highly liquid contracts, each in a different industry sector.

Quantitative Security Selection

Quantitative security selection strategies are designed to find securities that are believed to have superior performance potential (see Figure 8.5). The strategies use sophisticated *black box* methods to analyze and rank securities. Those methods model the markets and predict which securities have the highest probability of beating the market.

Before we move on, it is important to note that quantitative index providers say their returns may not beat the market nominally, but by applying a quantitative risk model to security selection, they hope to achieve better risk-adjusted returns. Adjusting the returns of an index for risk can be done in many different ways. One of the most popular methods, the Sharpe Ratio, is discussed in Chapter 19. ETFs that follow quantitative security selection have definite telltale characteristics. I list here five of the most common ones.

First, a quantitative index holds a relatively small number of stocks, typically between 40 and 100 securities. That is in contrast to

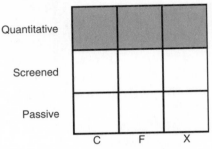

Quantitative Security Selection

Figure 8.5   **Quantitative Security Selection**

hundreds of securities in filtered indexes and sometimes thousands of securities in passively selected indexes. Figure 8.6 illustrates the narrow range of securities that are included in quantitative indexes.

Higher turnover is a second characteristic of quantitative selection. The amount of buying and selling in an ETF depends highly on the frequency at which the index provider recreates the index. An index that is recreated quarterly might turn over securities 100 percent per year. An index that is recreated monthly might turn over three times as much.

The third characteristic of quantitative security selection is that the selection rules provided to the public are vague, at best. Most quantitative index providers intentionally limit the available information on their security selection methodology. According to the CFA Institute, index rules should be transparent enough so that any trained analyst can reconstruct an index and achieve the same investment results using historical data. However, the quantitative indexers say they do not want competitors reconstructing their portfolios and

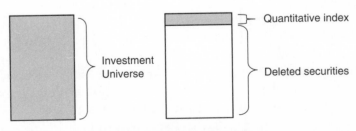

Figure 8.6   **Quantitative Index Security Selection**

stealing their secrets. A fourth characteristic of nearly all quantitative ETF providers is that they advertise comparison of, charts in marketing material that imply that their indexes have achieved superior performance over some benchmark. Realize that these charts do not show the return of the ETF, because most ETFs using quantitative strategies have not been around long enough. They show instead the hypothetical returns of the index, which in several cases do not actually exist either. Does that hypothetical performance have any relevance? Not to a knowledgeable investor, but perhaps the ETF companies are hoping naive investors would not know the difference.

The fifth characteristic of quantitative ETF providers is very important to investors because it is about costs. Universally, ETFs that employ quantitative methods charge the highest fees of any type. Those fees are about three times higher than ETFs that select stocks passively and twice as high as ETFs that follow filtered indexes. Costs matter. All things being equal, higher cost funds are expected to have lower returns because the fee is higher.

When you are investing in quantitative ETFs, you are investing mainly on faith. You hope the strategy works well enough to make up the higher fees and then some. A sense of adventure definitely helps when you put your money down on ETFs that follow complex indexes with very short track records. Prudence is important in the amount you allocate to quantitative strategies.

Examples of Quantitative Security Selection

The following are several examples of quantitative selection. The methods range from complex to eccentric. PowerShares introduced quantitative ETFs in 2002. The idea was quite innovative. The first-to-the-market effort has placed PowerShares as the clear leader in the number of funds and assets benchmarked to quantitative ETFs. Only one company is challenging PowerShares head to head, while several others have introduced ETFs that track niche indexes. Some ideas are unique.

Intellidex Indexes.   In 2002, PowerShares was founded by former Nuveen Investments sales and marketing executive H. Bruce Bond. His idea was to use quantitative indexes as benchmarks for ETFs. The methodology was first developed by Bond and then tweaked by analysts at the AMEX. The indexes are maintained by the AMEX to satisfy the SEC requirement for the separation of index provider and fund manager.

PowerShares' first two funds, Dynamic Market (symbol: PWC) and Dynamic OTC (symbol: PWO) track AMEX Intellidex indexes. The secret recipe of Intellidex indexes is not known. What is known about the formation of the Dynamic Market Intellidex index is that it begins with an initial universe of the 2,000 largest U.S.-domiciled stocks by market and only 100 stocks end up in the index after quantitative methods are applied. The Dynamic OTC Intellidex index (DYO) is similarly constructed and also has 100 stocks, although the initial universe of stocks is the 1,000 largest U.S.-headquartered companies quoted on the NASDAQ.

The Intellidex methodology seeks to select stocks that meet certain quantitative criteria that are indicative of a potential stock growth. The system uses 25 selection criteria broken into four main groups: risk factors, momentum, fundamental growth, and stock valuations. Factors in the model include cash flow, historical trading range, analysts' consensus estimates, earnings growth, fundamental ratios, a consistent record of profitability, and market liquidity. The exact sequence of the process and how much weight is given to each factor is not available to the public.

The component companies of Intellidex indexes change quarterly. As such, PowerShares ETFs that are benchmarked to those indexes can have high turnover ranging from 50 percent to 150 percent annually. That's quite a bit higher than the 2 percent to 4 percent turnover of a comparable passive index. It is a good thing that ETFs are structured to keep capital gains taxes to a minimum, or avoid them altogether.

AlphaDEXes. First Trust's AlphaDEX ETFs were introduced in May 2007 to compete with PowerShares Intellidex ETFs. The 16 new funds are one of the newest entrants in the ever-expanding line of quantitative, beat-the-market ETFs. The AlphaDEX takes existing indexes and tweaks the methodology to try to create a better performing product. The style funds are based on S&P indexes (the S&P 500 for large stocks, S&P Mid Cap 400 for mid cap stocks, and so on), while the sector funds are based on the Russell 1000 Index.

One difference between AlphaDEX and Intellidex is that the former tends to be more transparent in its methodology. Stocks in the earlier-mentioned indexes are divided into growth, core, and value. The growth stocks are evaluated using five metrics and given a score. The value stocks are evaluated by three metrics and also given a score. First Trust then looks at all the scores and assigns the highest weight in each AlphaDEX to the highest scoring stocks. The goal is to create an index that emphasizes the growth and value stocks that have the highest potential for beating the rival market index from which they came.

AlphaDEX ETFs charge 0.70 percent in expenses, placing them among the highest fee for any equity ETF. As expected, First Trust claims that the extra performance will more than compensate for the higher fees. We shall see!

Niche Quantitative Indexes.   There are many niche ETFs that follow an odd assortment of quantitative indexes. Those indexes run the gauntlet from price momentum methodologies to intellectual property rights. As mentioned earlier, many quantitative ETFs are unique and innovative, but there are also concerns. There is little information available about the rules for selecting securities in the index except that the provider uses a proprietary selection methodology, the ETFs benchmarked to those indexes have a higher cost relative to passive market ETFs, and the ETF firms have pushed the limit on marketing by implying that these strategies are superior because they test well in a theory.

Security Selection by Price Momentum.   The PowerShares DWA Technical Leaders Portfolio (symbol: DWA) is based on the Dorsey Wright Technical Leaders Index. That index includes approximately 100 U.S.-listed companies that are believed to demonstrate powerful relative price strength characteristics.

The Index is constructed pursuant to Dorsey Wright proprietary methodology, which means there is not a lot of information available. The prospectus states that the index takes into account, among other factors, the price momentum and performance of each of the 3,000 largest U.S.-listed companies compared to a composite benchmark, and the relative performance of industry sectors and subsectors. The methodology evaluates companies quarterly and ranks them according to a proprietary formula. Stocks that are selected receive a modified equal weighting.

Securities Selected Using Timeliness.   The PowerShares Value Line Timeliness Select Portfolio (symbol: PIV) is based on the Value Line Timeliness Select Index. The index seeks to identify a group of 50 companies that have the potential to outperform the U.S. equity market. The index uses the popular Value Line Ranking System, which is composed of three categories: timeliness, safety, and technical. The equally weighted portfolio is rebalanced and reconstituted quarterly.

The marketing material on the PowerShares web site displays the hypothetical performance of the Value Line Timeliness Select Index versus the S&P 500. As one would expect, the index significantly outperformed the S&P, using hypothetical investment returns.

How reliable is the back-tested comparison of the Value Line Timeliness Select Index? It is interesting to note that over the same period of time the open-end Value Line Fund (symbol: VLIFX) was actually in existence. According to Morningstar data and the fund's prospectus, VLIFX was managed using close to the same methodology as PIV is being managed. The major difference that I can tell between VLIFX and PIV is that the VLIFX holds 100 stocks and the new ETF holds 50.

Unlike the hypothetical superior performance shown in the marketing material for PIV, the actual performance of VLIFX was dismal. Over a same ten-year period that PowerShares shows in their marketing literature that the Value Line Timeliness Select Index beat the S&P 500 by approximately 7 percent, VLIFX underperformed the S&P 500 by more than 4 percent.

What is the explanation for this 11 percent discrepancy between hypothetical performance of the index and VLIFX real performance? It is widely known that the manager of VLIFX did not follow an index closely, although that was the stated investment objective of the fund. An argument can thus be made that PIV will not repeat those mistakes because it will follow the index.

An 11 percent difference seems quite large to ignore. Nonetheless, as I mentioned earlier, investing in quantitative funds is a leap of faith. Proceed with your eyes open.

Security Selection from Spin-Offs.   The Claymore/Clear Spin-Off ETF (symbol: CD) seeks investment results that correspond generally to the performance, before fees and expenses, of an equity index called the Clear Spin-off Index. A spin-off occurs when a public company is separated from its parent firm and subsequently trades on a stock exchange separate from its former parent. The Clear Spin-Off Index tracks those companies, although it is not simply a filtered index of spin-offs. Once the universe of spin-offs is established, each company goes through a rigorous quantitative analysis and only 40 stocks are selected for the Clear Spin-Off Index.

The Clear Spin-off Index selection methodology is designed to identify companies that are believed to provide potentially superior return profiles. The selection model evaluates and selects stocks using a multifactor proprietary selection method that includes composite scoring of several growth-oriented, multifactor filters, and is sorted from highest to lowest. The 40 highest-ranking stocks are chosen and given a modified market cap weighting with a maximum weight of 5 percent. The index is adjusted semiannually.

Security Selection Using Patent Rights. The Claymore/Ocean Tomo Patent ETF (symbol: OTP) seeks investment results that correspond generally to the performance, before fees and expenses, of an equity index called the Ocean Tomo 300 Patent Index. The index is an intellectual property index. It is a quantitatively selected index of 300 companies that own valuable patents.

The evaluation of each company's patent portfolio is done by Ocean Tomo's, which calculates the relative attractiveness of the more than 4 million patents that have been issued by the U.S. Patent and Trademark Office since 1983. If you believe that invention is the mother of future profits, this could be your fund.

When One Selection Method Does Not Fit

There are three broad selection methods: passive, filtered, and quantitative. Each index falls into one of the three categories. However, there are cases when an index could fit into two security selection categories, or even all three. It depends how a person interprets the selection process.

The idea of Index Strategy Boxes is to select one method of security selection and the one method of security weighting that best represents the strategy. For that, we need a holistic approach to security selection. All the factors need to be considered, including the main parts of the selection technique and how that technique forms a basket of stocks that is expected to track a market. There will be borderline cases, and there will be disagreement. But in the end, the objective is to select the one security selection strategy that best represents how securities are chosen, and label that index as such.

Summary

The first part of Index Strategy Box categorization is an analysis in security selection. There are three basic methods used: passive, screened, and quantitative.

Passive security selection is the traditional and dominant method used in indexing. When passive selection is combined with capitalization weighting, the resulting market index is used for many things, including economic analysis, asset allocation decisions, and as a benchmark to measure the performance of other investment strategies against. ETFs that use passive indexes have the broadest security selection, the lowest operating costs, and the lowest turnover of securities in the index.

Screened security selection is the first step toward active indexing. The provider filters a large universe of securities to eliminate the ones that have undesirable characteristics. That phrase can mean different things to different index providers. It could mean no cash dividends for the dividend index manager or a socially unacceptable product according to a provider of socially responsible indexes. ETFs based on filtered indexes tend to have higher turnover and higher expenses than ETFs based on passive selection.

Quantitative security selection follows black-box methods of indexing in an attempt to find securities that will outperform the market. The selection process is in-depth and typically involves many layers of analysis. The rules used by quantitative index providers tend to be scarcely explained by index providers to prevent intellectual property theft. ETFs that follow quant indexes generally have the highest turnover and the highest operating expenses.

9

Index Security Weighting

Security selection is the first half of index construction; security weighting is the second half. The weight allocated to each security in an index is an important characteristic because different weighting schemes applied to the same basket of securities can make a profound impact on performance characteristics of the index.

Index providers allocate securities in their indexes using three basic methods: capitalization weight, fundamental weight, and fixed weight. A capitalization weighted index bases the allocation on the relative market value of each security in that index. Fundamental weighted indexes use financial ratios or qualitative factors to allocate among index constituencies. Fixed weighting assigns a set weight to each security in an index. Leverage, short (inverse), and long-short ETFs are also considered fixed weighted indexes because the weighting of the entire index is changed by a fixed amount.

The three columns in Index Strategy Boxes represent these three weighting methods. Most indexes fit easily into one of the three categories. Table 9.1 provides the three broad security weighting categories and examples of security weighting methods under each category. See Appendix A for a larger list of weighting methods under each category. Appendix A is an abbreviation guide for Index Strategy Boxes. The abbreviations next to the categories and methods are used in the tables in Part III.

There are a few indexes that could fit into two security weighting categories, depending on how a person interprets the process. In those cases, the weighting methodology assigned is the one that best fits the index based on how it compares with the weighting

Table 9.1   Security Weighting Categories and Methods

Capitalization (C)	Fundamental (F)	Fixed Weight (X)
Full Cap (A)	Dividends (D)	Equal (E)
Free Float (F)	Financial (F)	Modified Equal (M)
Constrained (C)	Price (P)	Leveraged (L)
Liquidity (L)	Momentum (M)	Short (S)
Production (P)	Qualitative (Q)	Long/Short (N)

methods used by other indexes. For example, leveraged, inverse, and long-short indexes may seem to be a good fit for the capitalization weighted category. However, it goes in fixed weight because the entire index is either 100 percent short (-1 times the index), 200 percent long ($+2$ times the index), or a fixed percent long and short ($+1.3$ times long securities and -0.3 times short securities.)

Capitalization Weighting

Capitalization weighting is a natural method for security allocation in an index because it reflects the total dollar value of the securities in an index. The basic premise of a capitalization weighting is to let the markets decide what importance each security should have based on how much investors value each company.

The market capitalization of a company is calculated by multiplying the number of common shares outstanding by the current market price for those shares. For example, if a company has 200 million shares of common stock outstanding, and the current market price of that stock is $50 per share, the market capitalization of the company would be $10 billion.

When an equity index is capitalization weighted, a large company has greater influence on the index performance than a small company. A capitalization weighting naturally places a proportionally greater amount of capital in larger companies than in smaller companies. The Russell 3000 has 3,000 stocks, but it is the largest 100 stocks that have the greatest influence on the index return.

Willing buyers and willing sellers enter the securities markets each day to trade securities based upon an agreed fair price. Since the markets are an auction, the value of a company on any given day can be thought of as the consensus price of all global investors. Many theorists will argue that markets do not do a good job of deciding the fair market value of companies. However, with millions of people looking at the same data and coming to an agreement about the price, the market price cannot be far off.

In very broad market indexes, such as the Russell 3000, a single company such as Exxon-Mobil can account for 5 percent of the index value. If Exxon-Mobil went up by 10 percent, the value of the index would increase by 0.5 percent. On the other hand, if the smallest company in the Russell index went up by 100 percent, the gain would hardly register because the index is only published to two decimal places.

Types of Passive Security Weighting

There are four basic types of capitalization weighted indexes: full cap, free float, constrained (capped), and liquidity. The difference between full cap and free float is that the former includes the total value of all securities outstanding while the latter includes only the value of shares that are available in the public markets. Capped indexes preclude a few securities from dominating a narrowly defined index. Liquidity indexes are useful in thinly traded markets to ensure there is enough trading volume of securities to physically create investment products such as ETFs.

Through most of the twentieth century, capitalization weighted indexes were full cap. Every share of company stock outstanding was counted regardless of who owned it. A full cap index counted shares that were restricted from sale, part of a private placement of stock, held by the government, and cross-held by other publicly traded corporations. Full cap weighted indexes have the advantage of reflecting the full market value of a company, which is good for economic study, but have a disadvantage because of shares that are not available in the public market, thus providing an inaccurate yardstick for creating index funds and as measuring the performance of active investment managers.

By the millennium, the trend was to construct free-float indexes. A free-float index includes only those securities that are available for sale in the public markets. Float adjusted indexes more accurately measure investable market capitalization by reflecting only the shares available for purchase by the public. They make easier benchmarks for index fund managers to track, and do a better job of representing the universe of investment opportunities that all investors can choose from. Thus, free-float indexes also represent a better benchmark against which to judge the performance of active management.

Most of the original full cap indexes have switched over to free float. MSCI indexes completed the switch from full cap to free float in 2002 and indexing giant S&P completed its switch in 2005.

Free-float indexes are better benchmarks for index investors, but they are not an ideal solution because the indexes do not measure the liquidity of securities that are needed for maintaining an index product. Some companies that have an adequate amount of free-float shares outstanding do not have adequate liquidity in those shares because they are not actively traded. As such, the next generation of capitalization weighted indexes will likely be liquidity adjusted. A liquidity adjusted index makes good sense in ETF investing, particularly in hard-to-trade emerging markets.

Some niche market indexes are dominated by a few large companies. That creates a problem for some ETF structures, which have to abide by the SEC's requirements for diversification (see Chapter 3). The concentrated security problem can be solved by benchmarking an ETF to a constrained or capped index. Those indexes place maximum percentage caps on large positions in a capitalization weighted index to ensure that index products do not become overweighted in those securities. The cap is typically between 5 and 10 percent on any single security. The amount over the cap is spread across all other securities in the index.

In the United States alone, there are hundreds of capitalization weighted stock indexes covering all corners of the market. Broad capitalization weighted index providers include Dow Jones Wilshire, Russell, MSCI, Morningstar, Citigroup, and Standard & Poor's, to name just a few. Each provider has a slightly different twist from the others, and some of those differences are discussed in Chapter 10.

The largest market in the world is the fixed income market. Most bond index providers use a full capitalization weighting of sorts, although a more appropriate description would be value weighted. The driving factor for weighting bonds in an index is the market value of the bonds rather than the market value of the entity that issued them.

Assume a bond index holds the following bonds: a $200 billion equity market cap value pharmaceutical company that has $100 million in bonds outstanding, and a $40 billion dollar equity market cap automobile company that has $10 billion in bonds outstanding. The equity market value of the pharmaceutical company is 20 times more than the equity market value of the auto company, yet the value of the auto company bonds outstanding is 100 times more than the value of the pharmaceutical company bonds outstanding. Consequently, in a full cap weighted fixed income index, the auto company bonds will have a much greater impact on performance than the pharmaceutical company.

Capitalization weighted bond indexes include U.S. Treasury bonds, corporate bonds, high yield bonds, convertible bonds, mortgages, tax-exempt bonds, and foreign bonds. Some leading providers of bond indexes are Lehman Brothers, JPMorgan, Dow Jones, Salomon Smith Barney, and Merrill Lynch. Since many fixed income indexes are dominated by one or two issues, several fixed income index providers offer both unrestrained and constrained (capped) indexes.

There are no direct market capitalization weighted indexes in the commodities markets, but there are attempts at economic weighting. Commodities are held in a variety of ways: long futures positions, over-the-counter investments, long-term fixed-price purchasing contracts, physical inventory at the producer, and so on. That makes a complete accounting of the stock of commodities outstanding very difficult.

An easier way to achieve a market capitalization like weighting in commodities is to count the amount of the commodity produced. The quantity of each commodity in the index is determined by the average quantity of production in the last five years of available data. The impact that doubling the price of oil has on inflation and on economic growth, for instance, depends directly on how much oil was produced. The appropriate weight assigned to each commodity is in proportion to the amount of that commodity flowing through the economy.

The only problem is that oil and energy-related commodities dominate the markets, and overwhelm any production weighting methodology. Thus, many commodities indexes use restrictive caps on energy levels, or resort to modified equal weighting methodology.

The S&P GSCI^{TM} is a world-production weighted index. It holds as many commodities as possible, with the rules excluding commodities only to retain liquidity in the futures markets. Currently, the GSCI contains 24 commodities from all sectors: six energy products, five industrial metals, eight agricultural products, three livestock products, and two precious metals.

Fundamental Weighting

A fundamental weighted index uses a factor other than market cap to determine the weight of securities in an index. Most fundamental weighted index derived factors are from the corporate financial statements. A weighting factor can be a single variable such as each company's dividend yield, or a complex multifactor model that brings several items of data into the equation. Fundamental weighting can also be qualitative, such as a record of environmental stewardship, workplace issues, and community involvement.

Most fundamentally weighted indexes must be rebalanced periodically to realign the index with changing fundamental conditions. A large number of trades can take place in an ETF during those rebalancing periods. Theoretically, more trading means higher trading costs and less tax efficiency in a portfolio, although ETF managers have other methods to offset those taxable events.

The first U.S. market indicators to use fundamental weighting are also the oldest market indicators known to U.S. investors. Charles Dow began in 1884 with 11 stocks, most of them railroads. Railroads were among the biggest and sturdiest companies in America at that time, which is why they dominated Dow's first average. Few stocks of industrial companies were publicly traded, and those were considered highly speculative. In 1896, Charles Dow renames the first indicator as the transportation average and started The Dow Jones Industrial Average (DJIA) covering 12 large industrial stocks.

At the end of each trading day, Charles Dow simply added up the prices of the stocks in the averages and the sum total became the market average. Realize that stock price has nothing to do with a company's market capitalization. A very large company can have a low stock price while a small company can have a high stock price. However, the computation of the averages were quite simple because the methodology was established during a time when stock price data was all recorded by hand.

Continuous adjustments have been made to the DJIA over the years, in both the number of stocks and the divisor used to best account for stock splits and buyouts. The DJIA gradually increased to 20 in 1916, and again to 30 in 1928, where it remains today. Nonetheless, the way the indicator was computed in the 1800s is the same way it is computed today. The only difference is today the averages are computed nearly instantaneously.

Although the number of stocks in the DJIA has increased, it still cannot be called a practical market index. Thirty stocks are simply not a robust enough number to say that the DJIA tracks the stock market closely. The indicator is not used in academic studies or in economic analysis. Nor is it used in asset allocation decisions. Basically, it is an outdated and antiquated indicator.

The fact is, today the "Dow" as it is nicknamed is used for only two things. First, as a reference point for the media and stock market chatter, "How's the market?" "The Dow's up 30 today!" Second, Dow DIAMONDS (symbol: DIA) are a popular ETF for individual investors because it tracks the familiar Dow Jones Industrial Average. Should you choose DIA as an investment with so many fine alternatives available? You decide.

Table 9.2 looks as the many different ways indexes can be fundamentally weighted, and new products created. Here is a very short list of factors that can be used to weight stocks or bonds in an index.

Dividend weighted indexes have become very popular recently. In the past few years, dozens of ETFs and open-end mutual funds have been launched that focus on some aspect of dividend payout. A few indexes screened companies for cash dividend payments and then weighted those companies based on the dividend yield relative to all other dividend payers. Dividend-paying companies tend to have value characteristics over non-dividend-paying stocks. That has strong implications for dividend index risk and return characteristics (see the analysis that follows).

Weighting securities based on one factor is easy to comprehend. The only problem with this approach is that the value of each security's weighting factor changes from quarter to quarter. For

Table 9.2   Examples of Fundamental Weight Factors

Dividend yield	Price-to-book ratio
Dividend growth rate	Price-to-earnings ratio
Stock price	Price-to-sales ratio
Earnings yield	Price-to-cash flow ratio
Return on equity	Number of employees
Earnings growth rate	Price momentum
Employees to sales	Estimate change momentum
Employees to earnings	Social responsibility ratings

example, quarterly dividend payouts change as companies increase, maintain, or cut dividends. Consequently, fundamental weighted indexes need to be rebalanced frequently to ensure their integrity. Rebalancing is a cost to the portfolio because securities must be traded by the fund manager. Higher maintenance costs may be the reason why ETFs that use fundamental weighting charge more money than an ETF that uses passive security selection and capitalization weighted market indexes.

Fundamental weighting strategies can be done using a simple single factor model or a complex multifactor weighting methodology. The FTSE RAFI US 1000 is a large cap index that employs a sophisticated multifactor fundamental method for weighting stocks. The summary that follows provides an overview of the FTSE RAFI Index Series methodology. It incorporates a selection strategy into the weighting strategy by assigning rankings to each security in a potential universe of stocks, and then uses the ranking for index selection and weighting. A more detailed explanation can be viewed at www.ftse.com.

FTSE RAFI US 1000 Index Security Selection and Weighting

Security Selection:

1. The process starts with the selection of the company universes. The constituents of the FTSE US All Cap Index are used. That index includes large, medium, and small cap stocks that trade on the NYSE, AMEX, and NASDAQ.
2. The universe companies are each ranked by four fundamental measures: company size, book value, cash flow, sales, and dividends. The percentage weight that each company represents of the total value of each fundamental measure is calculated. Trailing five-year averaged data is used to reduce turnover and to minimize the substantial volatility in the index factors that would result from using year-to-year data.
3. A composite fundamental value is given to each company by taking the average weighting of each fundamental measure. If a company has a zero dividend percentage, the average of the other three metrics are taken.

4. The companies are then ranked in descending order of their RAFI fundamental values. The top 1,000 companies derived from the FTSE US All Cap Index then form the constituents of the FTSE RAFI US 1000 Index.

Security Weighting:

5. The weights in the indexes are then set in proportion to their fundamental values. The weighting factor used in the index calculation is derived by dividing the RAFI fundamental value of each company by its free-float adjusted market capitalization. If there are fewer than five years of data available, the average of the years of data that are available are taken. It can be shown that although the results are not materially different from those of their trailing five-year counterparts, portfolio turnover is higher.

6. When converting from company level to stock level factors, the fundamental value is calculated at a company rather than a stock level. If a company has two or more lines of stocks in the relevant index, the company's fundamental value is allocated between these lines of stock in proportion to the free-float adjusted market capitalizations at the date of the rebalancing.

Fundamental weighting strategies can stretch beyond balance sheets and income statements into more esoteric factors. The next few paragraphs describe a couple of indexes that give us an idea of the direction indexing is moving.

The Claymore/Zacks Sector Rotation ETF (symbol: XRO) follows the Zacks Sector Rotation Index. The index is to overweight those sectors that are believed to outperform the S&P 500 on a risk-adjusted basis. The sector allocation methodology strives to overweight cyclical sectors before periods of economic expansion and overweight noncyclical sectors before periods of economic contraction. See Chapter 19 for more information on economic cycles.

The Zacks Sector Rotation Index is composed of 100 stocks selected from a universe of the 1,000 largest U.S.-listed stocks and ADRs based on market capitalization. The index provider selects stocks using quantitative methods. Each quarter, the multifactor proprietary selection rules identify stocks that are believed to offer the greatest potential.

The industry sector allocation methodology weights each sector based on relative value, insider trading, price momentum, earnings growth, earnings estimate revision, and earnings surprise, as well as quantitative macroeconomic factors focusing on the business cycle. Exposure for any one sector may range from 0 percent to a maximum of 45 percent of the index. Individual stock exposure within each sector is determined by relative market capitalization within that sector. Individual issuers are capped at 5 percent of the total index.

Fundamental weighting strategies can become gaseous with the JPMorgan Environmental Index–Carbon Beta bond index (JENI-Carbon Beta). That index covers securities in the JP Morgan U.S. Liquid Index (JULI), a benchmark for the U.S. investment grade corporate bond market. JPMorgan uses a relative carbon beta score to reflect each bond issuer's benefit from or cost of climate change. The JULI constituents are weighted according to the carbon beta scores of issuers to create the JENI-Carbon Beta. For example, the JENI-Carbon Beta would underweight an issuer whose cost of reducing carbon emissions will be especially high and overweighting an issuer that appears to have unusual revenue potential in a carbon-constrained environment.

There are no ETFs benchmarked to the JENI-Carbon Beta bond index, at least not this week. But it is an interesting example of how index providers can weight securities using fundamental methods that are not derived from financial factors.

Limitations of Fundamental Weighting

Fundamental weighted indexes are interesting and at first thought seem intuitive, but they have a very narrow use. Fundamental weighted indexes are not used for economic study or as the basis for asset allocation, and with the exception of the DJIA, fundamental weighted indexes are not used as a measure of market returns or as a benchmark for the performance of active strategies. They are basically only good for one thing—to be applied to baskets of securities for the purpose of creating investment products that are marketed to the public.

There is also an inherent flaw in calculating fundamental weighted indexes that capitalization weighted indexes do not have to deal with. Different companies report fundamental data at different times throughout the quarter. Therefore, the weighting of each stock in a fundamental index should change almost daily as new information flows in. But that is not feasible from an investment point of view. ETFs would generate too much trading activity from daily rebalancing, and the ensuing paperwork would take too much time if the managers had to realign the portfolio every day.

The frequency of realigning an ETF portfolio with a daily calculated fundamental index would be a tradeoff between trading costs and tracking error. Since it is not practical for ETFs to track a daily changing index, the manager would delay rebalancing. However, the longer the time between reallocation, the greater the tracking error versus an index that was compiled daily. On the other hand, greater adherence to the index would cause many more transactions and that would be a cost to investors. What should an ETF provider choose—more trading cost or more tracking error?

Before I answer that question, let's take a critical look at the index providers. The providers of fundamental weighted indexes are in the business of licensing their products. As such, they try to create indexes that are easy for ETF providers and other investment companies to replicate and manage in a portfolio. This makes good business sense.

One advantage that ETF managers have is that fundamental weight index providers understand and accommodate the daily rebalancing dilemma. So, instead of using an accurate daily weighting methodology based on new information from the marketplace, the index providers reallocate security weights in fundamental indexes only once per quarter, or less. In other words, it is not the accuracy of the index that matters; it is the licensing of the index. The providers let their quarterly rebalanced indexes float away from the hypothetically accurate daily rebalanced indexes because it accommodates their clients, that is, ETF companies and other investment firms that are licensing the indexes.

Is this decision by index providers wrong? No. They are in business and they have a right to create and manage indexes any way it makes them a profit. However, as an informed investor, you just need to be aware of how the methodology works, and whether these issues will affect your portfolio.

Fixed Weighting

The third category of security weighting is fixed weight. The category covers a broad spectrum of weighting schemes, including equal, modified equal, leveraged, inverse, and long and short methods.

Equal weighting is the simplest form of weighting. All securities in an index are allocated the same percentage. If there are 100 securities, each gets a 1 percent weighting. If there are 50 securities in the index, they each get a 2 percent weighting.

The Rydex S&P Equal Weight (symbol: RSP) is an excellent example of an ETF that tracks a straight equal weighted index. The fund tracks the S&P Equal Weight Index (EWI), a product of Standard and Poor's. The fund will typically invest at least 90 percent of its assets in the securities of the S&P Equal Weight index. It may also invest in options, futures contracts, options on futures contracts, and swaps related to its underlying index, as well as cash and cash equivalents.

The S&P Equal Weight Index is the equal-weighted version of the widely regarded S&P 500. The index has the same constituents as the capitalization weighted S&P 500, but each company in the S&P EWI is allocated a fixed weight of 0.20 percent, rebalanced quarterly.

When a company is added to the index in the middle of the quarter, it takes the weight of the company that it replaced.

In recent years there have been many ETFs launched that track equal weighted indexes. Many of those funds are thinly sliced sector funds that need to be equal weight or else one or two stocks would dominate. HealthShare ETFs are quantitatively selected health care indexes that track narrow sectors of the health care market. The ETFs track indexes covering autoimmune-inflammation, cancer, cardio devices, cardiology, diagnostics, emerging cancer, enabling technologies, neuroscience, ophthalmology, and several other sectors. Since the indexes are so narrow, the logical weighting method is equal weighting. That ensures that no single issuer dominates a sector index.

Modified equal weight is another method in the fixed weight category. The term may sound like an oxymoron, but it does describe the multilevel fixed weighting methodology. Instead of using one equal weight, there are two or three levels of equal weights. Stocks are assigned to one of the levels based on a rank or size or some other factor. The difference between modified equal weighting and fundamental weighting is that the allocation of stocks using a modified equal weight method is reset to a fixed percentage at rebalancing rather than to an arbitrary number based on the actual value of factors.

For example, an index might use an earnings rank score to assign weights. Stocks that have the highest rank in an index are given a fixed 3 percent weighting each, stocks in the second tier are allocated a fixed 2 percent, and stocks in the third and final tier are allocated a fixed 1 percent. Since turnover is high in a modified equal weight index, those fixed allocations are typically adjusted quarterly or less frequently.

The PowerShares Dynamic Market Portfolio (symbol: PWC) is a good example of modified equal weighting. The ETF follows the Dynamic Market Intellidex Index. The index is a quantitatively engineered basket of 100 stocks thought to have superior investment characteristics. The largest 30 stocks by market capitalization receive 70 percent of the index weighting (2.33 percent each) and the other 70 stocks receive 30 percent of the index weighting (0.43 percent each). The index is reconstructed each quarter. Stock weights are allowed to float between reconstruction periods.

A few ETF providers have ventured into leveraged ETFs and inverse ETFs. These funds follow market indexes that are designed to generate two to three times the return of a market benchmark, or in the case of an inverse index, return the opposite return of a market index. When an ETF attempts to return twice the performance of a market index, it is leveraged two times, or 2X. An ETF that shorts the return of a market receives the inverse return, or −1X. Rydex and ProShares are innovators in these types of funds and have competing leveraged and inverse ETF products. Chapter 13 covers these and other Special Equity ETFs in more detail.

Limitations of Fixed Weighting

Like fundamentally weighted indexes, there is an inherent problem with several fixed weight schemes. Since the value of each stock changes every day, the allocation of an equal weighted portfolio (and other methods) is not equal after the first day of trading. Hence, index providers and portfolio managers should rebalance securities weights daily to regularly realign the portfolio with the index. But that is not feasible.

One advantage ETF managers have is that the index providers accommodate the fund manager's trading dilemma. Instead of using daily reweighting methods, the providers reallocate most fixed weighted indexes once per quarter, or less. Consequently, most fixed weight indexes do not represent a true fixed weight strategy.

The decision by the equal weight index providers to not rebalance daily helps cut down on transaction costs and the ETF manager's time, and that helps make the practice acceptable. However, investors in equal weighted index ETFs need to know that they are not getting true equal weighted results because between quarters (or longer) the indexes can pick up substantial tracking errors.

Modified Security Weighting Schemes and Style Biases

Modified security weighting schemes can have a profound impact on equity index style and size characteristics. The performance of an equity index takes on certain size and style biases as the percent allocated to each security is spread more equally across all securities.

Fundamental weighted indexes result in an equity portfolio with strong value stock characteristics. Those characteristics include lower price-to-earning (P/E) and price-to-book (P/B) ratios and higher dividend yields than weighting the same basket of stocks using marketing capitalization methods. Figure 9.1 illustrates how the style characteristics of an index change as securities weightings move from capitalization to fundamental weighting.

Evidence of the value characteristics in a fundamental weighted index can be seen in a comparison between an ETF that tracks the Russell 1000 Index and a second ETF that tracks the RAFI 1000 Index. Both underlying indexes start with approximately the same largest 1,000 stocks that trade on the NYSE, AMEX, and NASDAQ. The Russell 1000 is a free-float capitalization weighted index. The RAFI 1000 uses a multifactor fundamental weighting method described earlier in this chapter. How do the characteristics of the two indexes differ?

Figure 9.1   Modified Security Weighting and Style Biases

Table 9.3 Fundamental Weight Style Characteristics

ETF Name	Symbol	Exp Ratio	P/E	P/B
iShares Russell 1000	IWB	0.15	17.0	2.9
PowerShares FTSE RAFI 1000	PRF	0.76	15.5	2.4
iShares R1000 Value	IWD	0.20	14.3	2.2

Source: Morningstar, May 2007

Table 9.3 shows the value characteristics that surface as the fundamental weighted PowerShares RAFI 1000 ETF compared to the capitalization weighted iShares Russell 1000. The PowerShares RAFI 1000 ETF has a lower portfolio P/E and P/B ratios, which is a strong characteristic of a value stock heavy portfolio. For more evidence, the characteristics of the iShare Russell 1000 Value ETF are also included. Notice how the PowerShares RAFI 1000 ETF has characteristics that are closer to the iShare Russell 1000 Value ETF than to the style-neutral iShares Russell 1000 ETF.

Equal weighting and modified equal weighting causes a size shift in a diversified index. Applying equal weighting to a broad basket of passively selected stocks creates a portfolio with mid cap stock average capitalization. Figure 9.2 illustrates how the size characteristic of a broad basket of stocks shifts from primarily large cap under capitalization weighted to an average mid cap under an equal weighted methodology.

Table 9.4 offers a good example of the downward shift in the weighted average stock size that occurs when equal weighting is compared to capitalization weighted. The table compares the weighted average size of stocks in a capitalization weighted S&P 500 ETF to an equal weighted S&P 500 ETF called the Rydex S&P Equal Weight.

At the end of 2006, the iShares S&P 500 ETF had a share-weighted market capitalization of $53 billion while the Rydex S&P Equal

Figure 9.2 Size Changes with Equal Weighting

Table 9.4   Equal Weight Style Characteristics

Name	Symbol	Exp Ratio	Geo. Mkt Cap
iShares S&P 500	IVV	0.10	53,062
Rydex S&P Equal Weight	RSP	0.40	14,153

Source: Morningstar, May 2007

Weight ETF has a share-weighted market capitalization of only $14 billion. That put share-weighted equal weighted ETFs at less than one-third the average market capitalization of the S&P 500 index ETF. A share-weighted market cap of $14 billion was just a sliver away from being in the mid cap fund category according to Morningstar's size rating system.

Style Performance Characteristics

Value and mid cap indexes exhibit different risk and return profiles than broad market indexes. To that extent, the way an index is weighted can have a profound impact on its performance. Investors that select modified weight ETFs should be aware that those ETFs will not track the performance of a capitalization weighted ETF most of the time. There will be periods of underperformance and periods of outperformance. That is simply the cycle of size and value factors.

Figure 9.3 illustrates the 2000–2006 annualized return of the Russell 3000 Index, the Russell 3000 Value Index, and the Russell Mid Cap Value Index. Its chart shows that during the six-year period, an investment in mid cap stocks or value stocks would have achieved higher returns than a capitalization weighted broad market fund.

It is little wonder why several index providers created fundamental and fixed weighted indexes during the 2000–2006 period given the rosy scenario for value stocks and smaller stocks. And it is little wonder why ETF companies licensed those indexes soon thereafter. The mutual fund industry is widely known for chasing investment performance, and ETF companies are no exception.

A few ETF companies are marketing the excess returns gained from the value and small stock biases of modified weighted indexes to promote their funds as following superior strategies. But those claims are not supported by unbiased academic research. Several recent independent reports show that the out-performance of modified

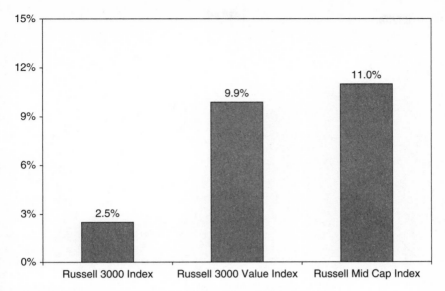

Figure 9.3   Index Return Comparison 2000-2006

weighted custom indexes is entirely a result of company size and value characteristics, not superior indexing strategies.

One only needs to look back to the 1990s to find a period when the returns of smaller stocks and value stocks were not as rosy. Figure 9.4 illustrates the annualized return of the Russell 3000 Index, the Russell 3000 Value Index, and the Russell Mid Cap Value Index from 1993 to 1999.

Based on the data from Figure 9.4, you will understand why there were no ETFs launched in the 1990s that followed modified weighted custom indexes. If one were launched in the mid 1990s, it would have performed poorly in relation to a capitalization weighted index. That means the ETF probably would not have attracted enough assets to survive the decade.

When value stocks slump again as part of a natural economic cycle (see Chapter 19), growth stocks will likely become popular again. Like the open-end mutual fund business, ETF issuance will migrate to the style that performed best recently because that is what the public wants.

As an informed investor, you now understand that investing in an ETF that tracks a style bias custom index is quite different from

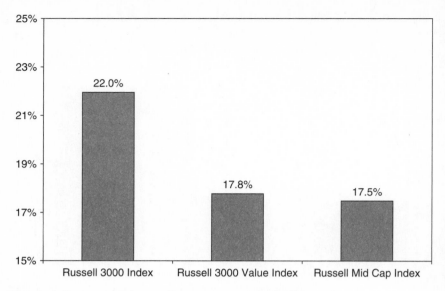

Figure 9.4   Index Return Comparison 1994–1999

investing in an ETF that follows a broad market index. Knowing that index style biases affect performance puts you in a better position to manage your ETF portfolio for the long term.

Summary

Security selection is the first half of index construction and security weighing is the second half. The methodology used in weighting securities can have a profound impact on the style characteristics of an index, which in turn affects the performance of an ETF that tracks the index.

There are three basic categories of security weighting. Capital-ization weighting uses the relative market value of each security in the index. Fundamental weighting uses basic financial data or other factors to allocate securities across an index. Fixed weight methods assign a fixed percentage allocation to each security, or to the entire market using leveraged or inverse strategies.

Fundamental weighting tends to produce value characteristics in a custom index while equal or modified equal weighting increases the exposure to small and mid cap stocks. Value stocks and small-to-mid cap stocks have different risk and return characteristics than large cap stocks, which are prominent in capitalization weighting. Investors in

ETFs that track modified security weighting schemes should keep in mind that the style biases inherent in those underlying investments will often cause large positive and negative tracking errors against a broad market benchmark.

Index Strategy Boxes are an easy method of analysis that categorizes indexing selection and weighting rules. Think in terms of index strategy and you will make more informed decisions about your ETF selections.

PART III

ETF STYLES AND CHOICES

CHAPTER 10

Broad U.S. Equity and Style ETFs

The ETF evolution has its roots in the broad U.S. equity market, and S&P indexes were the earliest benchmarks to be licensed. In December 1992, SuperTrust units were introduced. The exchange-traded units were benchmarked to the S&P 500 Index. One month later, the AMEX launched SPDR Trust (symbol: SPY) and that ETF also tracked the S&P 500 Index. A couple of years later, the AMEX launched the Mid Cap SPDR Trust (symbol: MDY) benchmarked to the S&P 400 Mid Cap index. Industry SPDRs made their debut in 1998 (see Chapter 12) followed by broad market style and size ETFs in 2000. All U.S. equity ETFs were benchmarked to S&P indexes.

In 2000, competing index providers negotiated ETF licensing deals that brought other broad market products to the market. The first competitor to S&P dominance was Frank Russell & Company. Other issues followed that tracked Dow Jones Wilshire indexes, Morgan Stanley Capital International (MSCI) indexes, and Morningstar indexes.

The first ETF benchmarked to a custom index was introduced in 1999. The NASDAQ-100 Trust, now PowerShares QQQ (symbol: QQQQ) is benchmarked to the NASDAQ-100 index. It is a single-exchange index that lists only stocks that trade on the NASDAQ, less financial stocks. In 1999, QQQQ helped promote the NASDAQ as the new market for the millennium.

A series of ETFs based on custom index strategies was launched by newcomer PowerShares in 2003. The PowerShares Dynamic Market Portfolio (symbol: PWC) seeks to replicate, before fees and expenses, the AMEX Dynamic Market Intellidex index. The index uses advanced quantitative methods to create a portfolio of selected U.S. equities. The securities are allocated in the index using a modified equal weighted methodology. PowerShares believes the actively managed Intellidex indexes will generate greater capital appreciation than a comparable broad U.S. market index.

After the successful launch of PowerShares ETFs, custom indexing became a new avenue for index providers and ETF companies to tap into the individual investor market. Individual investors are those who invest their own money as opposed to institutional investors who are paid to manage other peoples' money. The marketplace offers a much larger universe of potential buyers. Custom index ETFs also have higher management fees that generated greater revenue streams to ETF companies.

The economic opportunity in customized indexing has attracted a number of new entrants. Those new index providers include WisdomTree Indexes, Research Affiliates Fundamental Indexes (RAFI) and a variety of other firms. There is now a continuous flow of start-up companies introducing retail ETFs based on custom index strategies.

Broad Market Indexes and Style Components

The amount of information available on broad U.S. equity indexes and ETFs is so large that it could fill an entire book. Because of limited space, only a sampling of market index ETFs and custom index ETFs are discussed in this chapter. For a complete list of all U.S. ETFs, visit www.theetfbook.com for a link to the www.etfguide.com database. Index Strategy Box information is included in the ETF database.

Broad market indexes measure the pulse of the securities market they follow (see Figure 10.1). They are also referred to as all cap or total market indexes. Broad markets are a compilation of passively selected securities that are weighted on the basis of capitalization. Most market indexes and their subsectors include hundreds, if not thousands, of securities. The Dow Jones Wilshire indexes include over 5,000 U.S. stocks. Russell indexes include 4,000 stocks, the MSCI represents 3,500 stocks, and the S&P 1500 represents 1,500 stocks.

Figure 10.2 illustrates several broad market indexes and the number of stocks in the investment universe of each index provider. At least one ETF exists that tracks each of the indexes in Figure 10.2.

Market Index Strategy Box

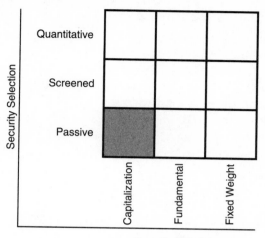

Figure 10.1   Broad U.S. Market Index Strategy Box

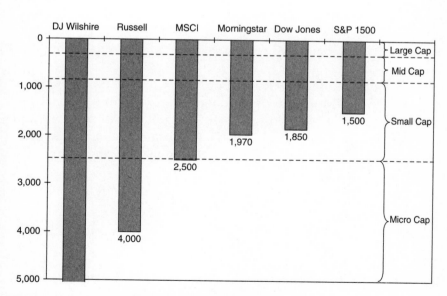

Figure 10.2   Major Market Index Penetration

Source: Dow Jones, Morningstar, MSCI, S&P, Russell, and Wilshire

Broad market indexes are divided into size components based on the average size of the companies they hold. The index providers tend to use roughly the same company size criteria as break points. Indexes that represent predominantly large company stocks are classified as large cap, those that represent smaller companies are labeled mid cap and small cap, and those that invest in the smallest companies are micro cap indexes. If you put all size indexes together in one, you end up with the broad market.

Size reallocation is done periodically to maintain index integrity. Depending on the provider, that period may be annually, quarterly, monthly, or as needed. Fewer reallocations means less turnover of stocks in each size index. Long periods between reallocation, however, also result in portfolio turnover when they do occur. The rules for movement between sizes can also vary significantly from provider to provider. Some index providers move an entire company at once while other providers will adjust in steps.

Style indexes divide broad indexes and size sectors into growth and value components. Each index provider has its own distinct mythology for style divisions. Some index providers have only growth and value sectors, while others have a third, middle style called blended, neutral, or core. The middle style is for stocks that have characteristics of both growth and value or neither growth nor value. Figure 10.3 illustrates one type of style strategy using Morningstar Style Boxes.

Style methodology varies among index providers and is more complex than dividing by size. Russell uses two fundamental factors to separate growth from value; Dow Jones uses six; S&P and S&P/Citigroup uses seven; MSCI incorporates eight; and Morningstar uses ten factors. Index providers generally reconstruct for

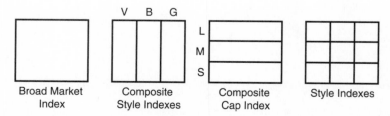

Figure 10.3   Morningstar Size and Style Indexes

Source: Morningstar, Inc.

style when they rebalance for size, which is at different periods. Consequently, the composition and performance of one growth index can vary considerably compared to another, and what may be a value stock in one index could be a growth stock in another.

Market Index ETFs

Recall from previous chapters that traditional market indexes have a broader purpose than just being used as a basis for commercial investment products such as ETFs. Market indexes are used in economic analysis, in asset allocation studies, and as a yardstick to measure the performance of active managers against.

The following information offers brief descriptions of some market index providers. To gain a better understanding of those indexes and the ETFs benchmarked to them, visit each provider's web site and read the prospectus of an ETF that follows the index. Provider web sites can be found in Appendix B.

S&P U.S. Equity Indexes

ETFs benchmarked to the S&P 500 index are the most popular of all U.S. equity funds. More than $1 trillion is invested in S&P 500 products, including the assets in ETFs. There is more money invested in State Street's SPDR S&P 500 than most ETF companies have under management in aggregate.

All index providers have strengths and weaknesses, and the S&P is no exception. While there are strict rules for inclusion and deletion from S&P indexes, at the core of the process is a team of analysts that make the final decision as to which stocks go into the indexes, which come out, and when.

Although the S&P 500 is considered the most important benchmark for large companies, it is not the most complete. A popular misconception about the S&P 500 is that it contains only large companies. First, not all large cap stocks are in the S&P 500, and second, not all stocks in the index are large cap. About 10 percent are in mid cap companies. Actually, there is not a market capitalization limit for inclusion in the index. The guiding principle is that the company must be a leader in an important industry, regardless of its size.

It would seem as though the S&P 500 selection process is highly customized. However, under Index Strategy Box methodology, the S&P 500 is categorized as using passive security selection for three reasons; first, the large number of stocks sampled for in the index; second, the low turnover of stocks in the index; and third, the very high correlation of returns with competing large cap indexes.

The S&P 100 is a subset of the S&P 500 and is an important index followed by institutional investors. The S&P 100 is composed of large U.S. stocks that have exchange-listed options. Although there are only 100 securities, the index represents about 57 percent of the market capitalization of the S&P 500 and almost 45 percent of the entire market capitalization of the U.S. equity markets.

The S&P 400 Mid Cap Index and S&P 600 Small Cap Index are also managed using the same fundamental selection criteria and their big brother S&P 500. Both of those indexes are also categorized as passive selection under Index Strategy Box methodology for the same reason as the S&P 500 is.

Combining the S&P 500, the Mid Cap 400, and the Small Cap 600 indexes makes up the S&P SuperComposite 1500. The combined index represents about 85 percent of the total U.S. equity market capitalization.

To fill in the remaining 15 percent gap in the S&P index series, the S&P Total Market Index (TMI) was created. It includes all common equities listed on the NYSE, the AMEX, the NASDAQ, and the NASDAQ Small Cap exchanges. When the S&P 500 stocks are excluded from the TMI, the result is the S&P Completion Index. That index holds about 4,500 stocks.

S&P divides its 500, 400, and 600 indexes into two groups to create the S&P/Citigroup growth and value style indexes. The methodology employs a multifactor approach to decide value and growth. Three factors measure growth variables and four factors measure value components. Each stock is assigned a style score, and that score is used to assign a company to the value or growth index. The style series is divided by market capitalization so that each side has approximately the same value while limiting the number of stocks that overlap between them. The style series is exhaustive (that is, covering all stocks in the parent index universe) and uses a conventional free-float market capitalization weighting scheme.

Dow Jones and DJ Wilshire U.S. Equity Indexes

The Dow Jones Company has created more than 3,000 proprietary U.S. and international market indexes, including style and industry components. That may seem like a lot, but it is actually fewer than what many other providers have. Dow Jones is trying to catch up by becoming very active in index creation and licensing, especially after teaming with Wilshire Associates.

In 2000, Dow Jones launched the U.S. Total Market Index. The U.S. Total Market Index represents the top 95 percent of the free-float value of the U.S. stock market. The Dow Jones U.S. Total Market Index spans only 1,850 stocks, making it the smallest range of stocks for any index provider using the title of *total market*.

Wilshire Associates is a privately owned investment firm head-quartered in Santa Monica, California. An index powerhouse in its own right, Wilshire began co-branding its index data with Dow Jones and Company in 2004. That gave Dow Jones more depth in the market. The DJ Wilshire 5000 was the first U.S. equity index to capture the return of the entire U.S. stock market. The name does confuse many people who think DJ Wilshire has a goal to maintain the index at 5,000 stocks. The actual number of stocks in the index varies from week to week, depending on the number of new issues, mergers, buyouts, bankruptcies, and trading volume of issues.

When the index was created in 1974, the DJ Wilshire 5000 Total Market Index became the broadest index for the U.S. equity market by measuring the performance of all U.S.-headquartered equity securities with readily available price data. Investors who want the broadest possible breadth of stocks in the U.S. market will find that an ETF benchmarked to the DJ Wilshire 5000 provides it. You will not be able to invest, however, in an ETF that holds all the stocks in the index because some of the smallest stocks in the index do not have enough liquidity for authorized participants to purchase. Thus, ETF managers sample the smallest portion of the stock universe.

The Wilshire 4500 was created in December 1983 to measure the performance of small and mid cap stocks within the Wilshire 5000. Essentially, it is the Wilshire 5000 Index without the companies in the S&P 500. The approximately 4,500 stocks left over provide an excellent benchmark for extended market performance in relation to the S&P 500. ETF managers sample most DJ Wilshire indexes because of the limited liquidity of several small stocks.

DJ Wilshire Style Indexes separate the DJ Wilshire 5000 into four capitalization groups (large, small, mid, and micro), and then divide the large, small, and mid cap issues by float-adjusted capitalization equally into growth and value indexes. Growth and value is defined by analyzing six factors: projected price-to-earnings ratio, projected earnings growth, price-to-book ratio, dividend yield, trailing revenue growth, and trailing earnings growth.

Russell U.S. Equity Indexes

In 1984, Frank Russell & Company created the Russell family of stock indexes to measure the performance of active managers. Today several hundred billion dollars are benchmarked to Russell's stock indexes, and some of that money is invested in ETFs. The most popular ETF is the iShare Russell 2000, which follows an index of small cap stocks.

Russell reconstructs its indexes annually, using market values on May 31. The largest 3,000 stocks are selected and ranked strictly by size. The Russell U.S. indexes are market cap weighted and include only common stocks domiciled in the United States and its territories. The indexes represent the free-float value of U.S. stocks rather than all shares outstanding.

The Russell 3000 Index measures the performance of the 3,000 largest U.S. companies based on total market capitalization, which represents approximately 98 percent of the investable U.S. equity market. There are several tiers of Russell indexes, and all are subsets of the Russell 3000 Index with the exception of the Russell Micro Cap index, which extends from stock number 2,001 down to stock number 4,000. See Chapter 8 for a detailed explanation and illustration of the Russell U.S. equity index family hierarchy.

Russell style indexes are divided into growth value categories by ranking stocks according to their price-to-book ratio and forecast earnings growth rate. Each stock is given a score and allocated to the growth or value index accordingly. Russell splits the market capitalization of many stocks that have both growth and value characteristics. Each index represents 50 percent of the total market value of its respective Russell size index. Of the stocks in a Russell index, about 30 percent have a percentage weighting allocated to both the value index and the growth index depending on the style score. These allocations do not overlap and there is no double counting.

Morgan Stanley Capital International Indexes (MSCI)

Morgan Stanley Capital International (MSCI) U.S. equity indexes are relatively new, but very important. They were created in 2003 with the help of index fund giant Vanguard. At the time, Vanguard was seeking an alternative to S&P indexes, and they ultimately chose MSCI.

MSCI's investable market is composed of three market capitalization segments: large cap, mid cap, and small cap. The company defines Large Cap Index as the 300 largest companies by full market capitalization in the investable market segment. The Mid Cap Index comprises the next 450 companies and the Small Cap Index consists of the remaining 1,750 companies. The large cap and the mid cap indexes are also combined to create a separate index of the 750 largest companies in the investable market segment, as ranked by full market capitalization.

MSCI uses buffer zones to manage the migration of companies from one market capitalization index to another. The purpose is to strike a balance between ensuring that the various indexes continue to accurately reflect the different investment styles and at the same time minimize stock turnover. The process also helps eliminate losses due to front runners. Those are rogue traders that try to anticipate changes in an index and jump in front of large trades before the price of the stock moves. Front running can cost index investors several million per year in lost profits.

The style characteristics for MSCI index construction are defined by using the three value variables and five growth variables. The objective of the value and growth indexes is to divide constituents of an underlying market capitalization index into a value index and a growth index, each targeting 50 percent of the free-float adjusted market capitalization of the underlying market capitalization index. Securities may be partially allocated to both value and growth indexes, depending on their score. The market capitalization of each size index will be fully represented in the combination of the value index and the growth index and will not be double counted.

Morningstar Indexes

Morningstar has a comprehensive family of 16 size and style indexes based on the same methodology used in their popular Morningstar Style Boxes. The indexes target 97 percent coverage of the free-float U.S. equity market. The style methodology incorporates ten factors to identify distinct growth and value attributes. For a complete description of Morningstar's index eligibility requirements, please refer to the Morningstar Rulebook at indexes.morningstar.com.

Morningstar divides its U.S. Market Index into three cap indexes by defining each as a percentage of the market cap of the investable universe. Large Cap equals the largest 70 percent of investable market cap, Mid Cap equals the next 20 percent and Small Cap is the next 7 percent of investable market cap. The final 3 percent are micro cap stocks, which are not represented in style boxes.

Within each capitalization class, index constituents are assigned to one of three style orientations: value, growth, or core, based on the stock's overall style score. A stock's value orientation and growth orientation are measured separately, using five different variables for each. The value score and the growth score determine each stock's composite style score. Stocks are reclassified as style or capitalization only if they move sufficiently beyond the break point between styles. Buffer zones allow stocks to migrate between size categories and style categories over time without affecting the classification.

Customized U.S. Equity Index ETFs

Customized indexes are not market indexes by design. They are investment strategies. Custom indexes are designed and maintained for the purpose of creating investment products rather than for use as economic indicators, research tools, or any other noninvesting purpose. In many cases, a customized index does not exist until a fund company contracts with an index provider to create and maintain the investment strategy (see Figure 10.4).

Custom indexes differ in structure from market indexes. They either have a security selection methodology that eliminates many securities from a market index, or they use a security weighting scheme that differs from a capitalization weight, or both.

The difference in custom index methodology generates risk and return characteristics that also differ from market indexes. All customized indexes fit into one of the eight Index Strategy Boxes that represent some method of construction other than passive selection and capitalization weights.

This second portion of the chapter examines several customized U.S stock indexes including size and style strategies. A sampling of ETFs that follow customized U.S. indexes is provided at the end of the chapter. For a complete list of all U.S. ETFs, visit www.theetfbook.com for a link to the www.etfguide.com ETF database. Index Strategy Box data can be screened and viewed in the ETF database.

Custom Index Strategy Boxes

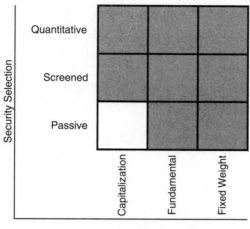

Figure 10.4   Customized U.S. Index Strategy Boxes

Exchange Specific Indexes

Exchange specific indexes are custom indexes. They include only stocks that trade primarily on one particular stock exchange. For example, the NASDAQ Composite index tracks only those U.S. common stocks that trade primarily on the NASDAQ. All other securities are filtered out regardless of their investment quality or standing in the overall U.S. equity market. The Fidelity NASDAQ Composite ETF (symbol: ONEQ) tracks the NASDAQ Composite index.

The NASDAQ-100 Index is a popular exchange specific stock indicator. It has two prominent filters. First, it includes only stocks that trade primarily on the NASDAQ, and second, the index excludes financial companies. PowerShares QQQ (symbol: QQQQ) is a unit investment trust that issues securities that track the NASDAQ-100 Index. Although the NASDAQ-100 Index is limited in its exchange selection and industry coverage, the index is popular with institutions and individual traders because the index tends to be technology stock dominant. There is close to $20 billion invested in QQQQs.

First Trust has two unique ETFs that follow customized NASDAQ indexes. One is an equal weighted NASDAQ-100 (symbol: QQEW) and the other is the NASDAQ-100 that excludes technology stocks (symbol: QQXT). QQXT is an interesting fund because it excludes the stocks that make NASDAQ-100 popular. However, some investors make good uses of industry-excluding ETFs. See Chapter 20 for more details on special ETF uses.

NYSE indexes track only the performance of stocks that trade on the New York Stock Exchange. There are two ETFs benchmarked to the NYSE indexes: the NYSE Composite index and the NYSE 100 index. The iShares NYSE Composite Index (symbol: NYC) tracks all the stocks that trade on the NYSE while the iShares NYSE 100 Index (symbol: NY) tracks the 100 largest companies.

Standard and Poor's is also heavily into the customized indexing business. One popular custom index managed by S&P is the equal weighted S&P 500. The index holds all stocks in the S&P 500 in an equal amount rather than capitalization weights. Rebalancing is done each quarter to maintain the equal weighting. The equal weighted S&P 500 index has a significantly lower-weighted average market capitalization than the capitalization weighted index (see Chapter 9). The Rydex S&P Equal Weight ETF (symbol: RSP) tracks the index. Rydex was the first to introduce an equal weighted ETF and has been rewarded with over $2 billion in assets for their first-to-market effort.

The S&P Pure Style Index Series offers intensified styles exposure. S&P identifies approximately one third of the market capitalization of corresponding S&P/Citigroup indexes as pure growth and another third as pure value. The securities in the middle ground between pure growth and pure value are excluded. Securities in the pure styles indexes are weighted on the basis of a multifactor fundamental methodology. The system ranks the fundamentals attractiveness of each company and assigns weights accordingly.

Fundamental Selection and Weighting Indexes

Selecting and weighting stocks based on fundamental factors became popular after large gains from value stocks that occurred between 2000 and 2006. Fundamental selection and fundamental weighting methods create a strong value stock bias in an index. As such, back-testing of any fundamental selection or weighting method would show outperformance against a broad U.S. market index anytime value stocks achieve higher returns then growth stocks. See Chapter 9 for information on the value style bias created when an index provider uses fundamental selection and weighting.

A complex multifactor security weighting scheme is used by Research Affiliated Fundamental Indexes (RAFI). Each stock in a passively selected basket is given a ranking based on the combined strength of several fundamental factors. Those rankings are then used to assign a percentage to each security in the index. The result is a custom index that is weighted more heavily in value stocks than the broad stock market. Detailed information on RAFI methodology is covered in Chapter 9.

WisdomTree Dividend Indexes use fundamental filters to eliminate stocks that do not pay a regular cash dividend and then weight remaining stocks using dividend data. During 2007, approximately 1,500 dividend-paying stocks meet the screens from a universe of approximately 3,500 companies. WisdomTree slices the 1,500 stocks into various size indexes to create the benchmarks for WisdomTree ETFs. The indexes also use fundamental weighting. Companies that pay higher dividends by cash value have a higher percentage weight.

There are several dividend index providers, including Standard and Poor's and Merchants. All selection and weighting strategies are similar in that they are based on dividend payments. The precise methodologies used by various dividend index providers differ in subtle ways, such as length of time a company has paid dividends, the level of dividends payment in relation to earnings, and so on. All dividend indexes have a value stock bias regardless of the methodology.

Earnings indexes are an offshoot of dividend indexes. WisdomTree Earnings ETFs are benchmarked to WisdomTree Earnings indexes that screen companies for positive cumulative earnings over their four most recent fiscal quarters. Since most U.S. companies have earnings, those screens allow more companies to pass through than dividend screens, thus giving investors a broader slice of the U.S. market.

Quantitative Indexes

There have been several entrants in the quantitative index marketplace since 2003. First on the scene was Intellidex indexes. The Intellidex methodology was originally inspired by Bruce Bond, the founder of PowerShares as a benchmark for a new lineup of ETFs. Since there is an SEC conflict when an ETF company also manages the indexes, Bonds turned to the AMEX. The AMEX is now responsible for Intellidex index upkeep while PowerShares manages the ETFs (see Chapter 1 for a brief history of PowerShares).

Stocks are selected and reallocated quarterly in Intellidex indexes. The AMEX uses 25 different factors in security selection. The system evaluates stocks in four areas: risk factors, momentum, fundamental growth, and stock valuation. After individual securities are ranked, a fixed number at the top of the rankings go into an index. The weighting of stocks in Intellidex indexes is based on a two-tier modified equal weighted method. The largest stocks in the indexes receive a higher fixed weighting and the remaining stocks receive smaller allocations.

An outsider cannot emulate the Intellidex quantitative process because only a summary description of the proprietary black box model is available to investors. Even the authorized participants do not have access to details.

A growing number of index providers are using quantitative methods to choose securities for ETFs. The First Trust AlphaDEX ETFs are one of the more recent entrants into the quantitative, beat-the-market space. The ETFs track an equity index family of custom indexes created and administered by Standard & Poor's. The methodology for creating those indexes is more transparent than Intellidex indexes, but just as complicated.

The S&P Defined Index series takes existing market indexes and tweaks the methodology to try to create a better-performing product. The stocks in existing S&P indexes are divided into growth, core, and value buckets. The growth stocks are evaluated by five metrics and given a score, and the value stocks are evaluated by three metrics and given a score. Core stocks are evaluated on both metrics and the higher of the two scores is taken.

The selected stocks are then split into quintiles based on their score. Stocks are equal weighted within each quintile. First Trust assigns the more weight in AlphaDEX ETFs to the highest quintiles. The top ranked quintile receives five fifteenths (33.3 percent) of the portfolio weight with successive quintiles receiving four fifteenths (26.7 percent), three fifteenths (20.0 percent), two fifteenths (13.3 percent) and one fifteenth (6.7 percent), respectively. The indexes are rebalanced quarterly.

The Customized Dow?

The Dow Jones Industrial Average (DJIA) was introduced in 1896. It was a price weighted index, thus making it, by accident, the second customized index (the first was the Dow Jones Transportation Average started in 1884). Better known as the Dow, the DJIA is still one of the world's most widely followed stock market indicators. The DJIA is currently composed of 30 large U.S. companies.

The security selection of the DJIA is subjective. A committee decides what companies go in and which come out. However, like the S&P 500, subjective security selection does not preclude the DJIA from being categorized as passive as long as those sampled stocks adequately represent the large cap U.S. market.

It is not the security selection of the DJIA methodology that makes the indicator customized; it is, rather, the weighting of the stocks. The securities are fundamentally weighted on the basis of the market price of each stock (as opposed to the market capitalization of each company). A small company with a stock price of $100 per share has 10 times the weight in the index as a gigantic company with a stock price of $10 per share. The price weighting methodology gives the Dow a value bias.

There are several billion dollars benchmarked in the DJIA through Diamonds Trust (symbol: DIA). Most of the money belongs to individual investors.

From Huge Dow to Micro Dow

Everyone recognizes the Dow Jones Industrial Average, but few people have heard of the Dow Jones Select Micro Cap Index. It measures the performance of very small stocks trading on major U.S. exchanges. Dow Jones represents the index as the investable portion of U.S. micro cap companies because there is believed to be liquidity in those stocks.

The DJ Select Micro Cap Index is a custom benchmark. Issues with the smallest market capitalizations and lowest trading volumes are excluded, although the customization categorization is due to fundamental screening. Companies with poor fundamentals are filtered out. The screens exclude stocks with poor operating profit margins, inadequate price-to-earnings ratios, price-to-sales ratios, earnings momentum, and relative performance versus other micro caps.

Sample List of Broad U.S. Equity and Style ETFs

The following table is a sampling of ETFs that track broad U.S. equity indexes and style indexes. It is not a complete list because

Table 10.1 Broad U.S. Equity ETFs, Including Size and Styles

Market Index ETFs—Broad U.S. Equity and Style

Category	Market ETF Name	Ticker	Expense Ratio	Index	Strategy Box	Sec. Select	Sec. Weight
Large Blend	SPDRs (S&P 500)	SPY	0.10	S&P 500		P S	C F
Large Blend	iShares S&P 500	IVV	0.10	S&P 500		P S	C F
Large Blend	iShares S&P 100	OEF	0.20	S&P 100		P S	C F
Large Blend	iShares S&P 1500 Index	ISI	0.20	S&P 1500		P S	C F
Large Blend	Rydex Russell Top 50	XLG	0.20	Russell Top 50		P A	C F
Large Blend	iShares Russell 1000	IWB	0.15	Russell 1000		P A	C F
Large Blend	Vanguard Large Cap	VV	0.07	MSCI U.S. Large Cap		P A	C F
Large Blend	iShares Morningstar Large Core	JKD	0.20	Morningstar Large Core		P A	C F
Large Growth	iShares R1000 Growth	IWF	0.20	Russell 1000 Growth		P A	C F
Large Growth	iShares S&P 500 Growth	IVW	0.18	S&P 500 Growth		P S	C F
Large Growth	Vanguard Growth	VUG	0.11	MSCI U.S. Growth		P A	C F
Large Growth	iShares Russell 3000 Growth	IWZ	0.25	Russell 1000 Growth		P A	C F
Large Growth	iShares Morningstar Large Growth	JKE	0.25	Morningstar Large Growth		P A	C F
Large Growth	SPDR DJ Lrg Growth	ELG	0.21	DJ Lrg Growth		P A	C F
Large Value	iShares R1000 Value	IWD	0.20	Russell 1000 Value		P A	C F
Large Value	iShares S&P 500 Value	IVE	0.18	Russell 1000 Value		P A	C F
Large Value	Vanguard Value	VTV	0.11	MSCI U.S. Value		P A	C F
Large Value	iShares Russell 3000 Value	IWW	0.25	Russell 1000 Value		P A	C F
Large Value	iShares Morningstar Large Value	JKF	0.25	Morningstar Large Value		P A	C F

Table 10.1 *(continued)*

Category	Market ETF Name	Ticker	Expense Ratio	Index	Strategy Box	Sec. Select	Sec. Weight
Large Value	SPDR DJ Wilshire Large Value	ELV	0.21	DJ Wilshire Large Value		P A	C F
Multi Cap Blend	Vanguard Total Stock Market	VTI	0.07	MSCI U.S. Total Stock Market		P A	C F
Multi Cap Blend	iShares DJ Total Market	IYY	0.20	DJ Total Market		P A	C F
Multi Cap Blend	iShares Russell 3000	IWV	0.20	Russell 3000		P A	C F
Multi Cap Blend	SPDRs Total Market (DJW 5000)	TMW	0.21	DJ Wilshire 5000		P A	C F
Mid Cap Blend	Mid Cap SPDR (S&P 400)	MDY	0.25	S&P Mid Cap 400		P S	C F
Mid Cap Blend	iShares S&P 400 Mid Cap	IJH	0.20	S&P Mid Cap 400		P S	C F
Mid Cap Blend	iShares Russell Mid Cap	IWR	0.20	Russell Mid Cap		P A	C F
Mid Cap Blend	Vanguard Mid Cap	VO	0.13	MSCI U.S. Mid Cap		P A	C F
Mid Cap Blend	Vanguard Extended Market	VXF	0.08	DJ Wilshire 4500		P A	C F
Mid Cap Blend	iShares Morningstar Mid Core	JKG	0.25	Morningstar Mid Core		P A	C F
Mid Cap Growth	iShares S&P 400 Mid Growth	IJK	0.25	S&P Mid Cap 400		P S	C F
Mid Cap Growth	iShares Russell Mid Growth	IWP	0.25	Russell Mid Cap Growth		P A	C F
Mid Cap Growth	iShares Morningstar Mid Growth	JKH	0.30	Morningstar Mid Growth		P A	C F
Mid Cap Value	iShares Rusell Mid Value	IWS	0.25	Russell Mid Cap Value		P A	C F
Mid Cap Value	iShares S&P 400 Mid Value	IJJ	0.25	S&P Mid Cap 400		P S	C F
Mid Cap Value	iShares Morningstar Mid Value	JKI	0.30	Morningstar Mid Value		P A	C F
Small Blend	iShares Russell 2000	IWM	0.20	Russell 2000		P A	C F

(continued)

Table 10.1   *(continued)*

Category	Market ETF Name	Ticker	Expense Ratio	Index	Strategy Box	Sec. Select	Sec. Weight
Small Blend	iShares S&P 600 Small	IJR	0.20	S&P 600 Small		P S	C F
Small Blend	iShares Morningstar Small Core	JKJ	0.25	Morningstar Small Core		P A	C F
Small Blend	Vanguard Small Cap	VB	0.10	MSCI U.S. Small Cap		P A	C F
Small Growth	iShares R2000 Growth	IWO	0.25	Russell 2000 Growth		P A	C F
Small Growth	iShares S&P 600 Growth	IJT	0.25	S&P 600 Growth		P S	C F
Small Growth	Vanguard Small Cap Growth	VBK	0.12	MSCI U.S. Small Cap Growth		P A	C F
Small Value	iShares R2000 Value	IWN	0.25	Russell 2000 Value		P A	C F
Small Value	iShares S&P 600 Value	IJS	0.25	S&P 600 Value		P S	C F
Small Value	Vanguard Small Cap Value	VBR	0.12	MSCI U.S. Small Cap Value		P A	C F
Small Value	iShares Morningstar Small Value	JKL	0.30	Morningstar Small Value		P A	C F
Small Value	SPDR DJ Small Value	DSV	0.26	DJ Small Value		P A	C F
Micro Cap	iShares Russell Micro Cap	IWC	0.60	Russell Micro Cap		P A	C F
Average Fee—Market Index ETFs			**0.21**				

Cusom Index ETFs—Broad U.S. Equity and Style

Category	Active Index ETF Name	Ticker	Expense Ratio	Index	Strategy Box	Sec. Select	Sec. Weight
Large Blend	iShares NYSE Composite	NYC	0.25	NYSE Composite		S E	C F
Large Blend	Rydex S&P Equal Weight	RSP	0.40	S&P Equal Weight		P S	X E

Table 10.1 *(continued)*

Category	Active Index ETF Name	Ticker	Expense Ratio	Index	Strategy Box	Sec. Select	Sec. Weight
Large Blend	PowerShares FTSE RAFI 1000	PRF	0.76	RAFI 1000	▦	P A	F F
Large Blend	iShares NYSE 100	NY	0.20	NYSE 100	▦	S E	C F
Large Blend	First Trust Large Cap Core AlphaDEX	FEX	0.70	S&P Defined Large Cap Core	▦	Q M	X M
Large Growth	Powershares QQQ	QQQQ	0.20	Nasdaq-100 Trust	▦	S E	C F
Large Growth	Rydex S&P 500 Pure Growth	RPG	0.35	S&P 500 Pure Growth	▦	S F	F F
Large Growth	PowerShares Dynamic Large Growth	PWB	0.64	Intellidex Dynamic Large Growth	▦	Q M	X M
Large Value	DIAMONDS Trust	DIA	0.18	Dow Jones Industrial Avg	▦	P S	F P
Large Value	WisdomTree Large Cap Div	DLN	0.28	WisdomTree Large Cap Div	▦	S F	F D
Large Value	Rydex S&P 500 Pure Value	RPV	0.35	S&P 500 Pure Value	▦	S F	F F
Large Value	PowerShares Dynamic Large Value	PWV	0.65	Intellidex Dynamic Large Value	▦	Q M	X M
Multi Cap Blend	PowerShares Dynamic Mkt	PWC	0.60	Intellidex Dynamic Mkt	▦	Q M	X M
Multi Cap Value	WisdomTree Total Dividend	DTD	0.28	WisdomTree Total Dividend	▦	S F	F D
Multi Cap Value	First Trust Multi Cap Value AlphaDEX	FAB	0.70	S&P Defined Multi Cap Value	▦	Q F	X M
Multi Cap Growth	First Trust Multi Cap Growth AlphaDEX	FAD	0.70	S&P Defined Multi Cap Growth	▦	Q F	X M
Mid Cap Blend	WisdomTree Mid Cap Div	DON	0.38	WisdomTree Mid Cap Div	▦	S F	F D
Mid Cap Blend	First Trust Mid Cap Core AlphaDEX	FNX	0.70	S&P Defined Mid Cap Core	▦	Q F	X M
Mid Cap Growth	Rydex S&P 400 Pure Growth	RFG	0.35	S&P 400 Pure Growth	▦	S F	F F

(continued)

Table 10.1   *(continued)*

Category	Active Index ETF Name	Ticker	Expense Ratio	Index	Strategy Box	Sec. Select	Sec. Weight
Mid Cap Growth	PowerShares Dynamic Mid Growth	PWJ	0.65	Intellidex Dynamic Mid Growth		Q M	X M
Mid Cap Growth	First Trust IPOX-100 Index	FPX	0.66	IPOX-100 Index		S T	C C
Mid Cap Value	Rydex S&P 400 Pure Value	RFV	0.35	S&P 400 Pure Value		S F	F F
Mid Cap Value	PowerShares Dynamic Deep Value	PVM	0.60	Intellidex Dynamic Deep Value		Q M	X M
Mid Cap Value	PowerShares Dynamic Mid Value	PWP	0.67	Intellidex Dynamic Mid Value		Q M	X M
Small Blend	WisdomTree Small Cap Div	DES	0.38	WisdomTree Small Cap Div		S F	F D
Small Blend	PowerShares Zacks Small Cap	PZJ	0.75	Zacks Small Cap		Q P	X M
Small Blend	First Trust Small Cap Core AlphaDEX	FYX	0.70	S&P Defined Small Cap Core		Q F	X M
Small Growth	Rydex S&P 600 Pure Growth	RZG	0.35	S&P 600 Pure Growth		S F	F F
Small Growth	PowerShares Dynamic Small Growth	PWT	0.65	Intellidex Dynamic Small Growth		Q M	X M
Small Value	Rydex S&P 600 Pure Value	RZV	0.35	S&P 600 Pure Value		S F	F F
Small Value	PowerShares Dynamic Small Value	PWY	0.66	Intellidex Dynamic Small Value		Q M	X M
Micro Cap	First Trust DJ Sel Micro Cap	FDM	0.60	DJ Select Micro Cap		S F	C F
Micro Cap	PowerShares Zacks Micro Cap	PZI	0.72	Zacks Micro Cap		Q P	X M
	Average Fee—Custom Index ETFs		**0.51**				

Source: theetfbook.com

of the large numbers of funds that track U.S. equity markets. For a complete list of current ETFs, including the Index Strategy Box data, visit www.theetfbook.com and www.etfguide.com.

Table 10.1 is divided into two sections. The first section includes a sampling of ETFs that track market indexes, which are categorized as passive security selection and capitalization weighted. The second section includes a sampling of ETFs that track customized U.S. indexes.

The average expense ratio of market index ETFs in the first section is only 0.21 percent. That is the lowest cost group among all remaining Index Strategy Box groups. The average expense ratio of the customized index ETFs in the second section is 0.51 percent. There is no operational reason why custom index ETFs should cost 150 percent more than market index ETFs. In this author's opinion, the fund companies charge more because the buyers of those ETFs tend to be individual investors as opposed to fee-savvy institutional investors.

Appendix A is an abbreviation guide for security selection and weighting methodologies used in each index in Table 10.1. Selection and weighting methodologies are the best fit given information available to the public through the ETF companies by way of each fund's Prospectus.

Summary

This chapter gave you flavor of broad U.S. equity and style ETFs. The important points to remember about this chapter are that there are a variety of ETF strategies to choose from that have a range of costs. The lowest-cost funds tend to follow market indexes where securities are passively selected and capitalization weighted. As the complexity of security selection and weighting increases, so do the expenses of the ETFs that follow those indexes.

The ETF list in this chapter included many examples of broad U.S. market indexes and customized U.S indexes. These samples do not represent a complete list of the ETFs available to the public. For a complete list of broad U.S. equity ETFs, including the Index Strategy Box database, visit www.theetfbook.com and www.etfguide.com.

CHAPTER 11

Global Equity ETFs

International investing adds a new dimension to an otherwise domestic portfolio. International stocks and bonds can expand the frontier in two ways: it increases the number of securities in a portfolio, which reduces portfolio risk, and it diversifies the currencies, which also reduces portfolio risk.

Advantages of Investing Internationally

Markets and currencies around the globe often move in different directions at different times. When that occurs, a globally diversified portfolio naturally hedges one market against another. The occasional rebalancing of international investments and domestic investments puts the portfolio back to its original global target allocation.

The process of regular rebalancing between U.S. and international securities has historically lowered overall portfolio risk and actually inched up portfolio returns. It was the nirvana of modern portfolio theory. There is no guarantee the phenomenon will happen again in the future. Having global diversification, however, shouldn't hurt your portfolio in the long term.

One reason the returns of foreign securities diverge with U.S. securities is due to the underlying native currency movements. International equity ETFs are quoted in U.S. dollars on U.S. exchanges even though the underlying investment in those funds may have a native currency of something else. For example, Japanese equities are valued in yen and converted to U.S. dollars before being quoted on U.S. exchanges on the stock pages of your local newspaper.

The price of Japanese stocks may not change in its native currency, but they could change in U.S. dollars if the value of the dollar changes against the yen. The Japanese stock market could even be closed and ETFs that track the Nikkei and other Japanese market indexes experience sizable price movements on U.S. exchanges because of currency fluctuations. When the U.S. dollar falls in value against the yen, U.S. investors holding Japanese stocks are hedged against the decline. When the dollar rises against the yen, those same investors will experience a loss due to currency differences.

There is a certain nomenclature that goes with investing in foreign securities. Those terms can be redundant or confusing. For example, international securities are also called foreign, overseas, or ex-U.S. securities. Global mutual funds are also called world mutual funds and they hold both international and U.S. securities.

A developed market is an economically and socially advanced country. Emerging markets are countries that may not have a mature economy, an advanced banking structure, or a stable securities market. There tends to be a national output issue that separates developed markets from emerging markets. Generally, about $20,000 per capital in Gross Domestic Product (GDP) is considered the minimum for developed markets.

Disadvantages of Investing Internationally

One disadvantage of investing in overseas stocks is the tax treatment of dividends. When a foreign company pays a cash dividend, the company's home country often taxes that dividend before the cash is sent overseas. You never get that tax withholding back directly. However, according to the U.S. tax code, investors are entitled to a tax credit for the amount of foreign tax withheld but *only* if the security was held in a taxable account. If dividends were withheld in a nontaxable account, such as an Individual Retirement Account (IRA), you are not allowed to claim a foreign tax credit on your U.S. tax return.

Another disadvantage of investing internationally is in understanding the concept of price discovery. The rest of the world's markets are typically closed when international ETFs are trading on U.S. exchanges. That can pose special challenges for U.S. investors and market makers who are trying to establish fair trading prices for international ETFs. The NAV of international securities becomes old or stale as soon as overseas markets close, which means the ETFs trading in the United States are doing so without a concrete number.

International ETF prices and the stale NAV price can separate widely when the global markets are volatile. At that juncture, many investors think the U.S. markets are incorrectly pricing the ETF. But the opposite is true. The U.S. market price probably reflects the best price for the underlying securities overseas at the moment. It represents what would likely be happening to the NAV of the securities that make up the ETF if those overseas markets were open. In that sense, ETFs become an important price discovery vehicle for the global market participants.

Broad International and Global Market Indexes

Broad international and global market ETFs are the topic of discussion in the first part of this chapter. These ETFs follow indexes that cover the entire globe as well as the international component, regional components, and individual country components.

Broad markets also include slicing the international market horizontally into developed market and emerging market indexes. Horizontal slicing also includes global industry indexes that form the basis for global industry ETFs to be discussed in this chapter.

There are many index providers that track the global and international markets. Each provider has its own methodology. The common thread among index providers is that each one builds its broad indexes from the country level up. That means countries are lumped together into regions, regions are lumped together to form international indexes, and international indexes are combined with U.S. indexes to form global indexes. A second methodology lumps developed markets with emerging markets to form international and global indexes.

Style and size indexes are carved from each level of a global index hierarchy to form style indexes. Figure 11.1 is a simplified illustration of the process, whereby countries form regions, regions form developed and emerging markets, and so on.

The providers of global market indexes have created an extensive series of benchmarks, and no two index providers carve up the global markets in the exact same fashion. Tens of thousands of market indicators represent the returns of more than 150 countries,

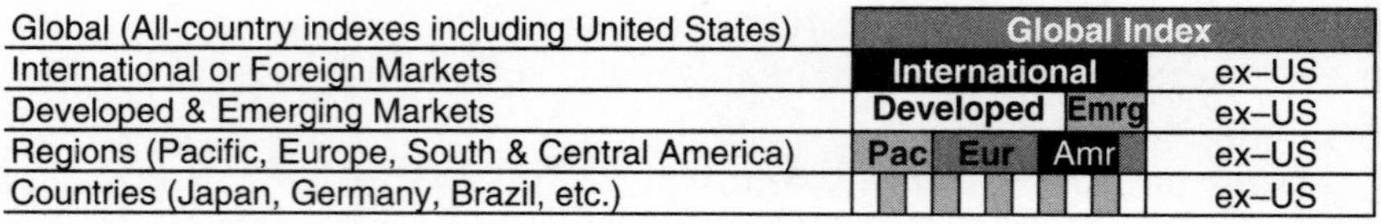

Global (All-country indexes including United States)	Global Index		
International or Foreign Markets	International		ex–US
Developed & Emerging Markets	Developed	Emrg	ex–US
Regions (Pacific, Europe, South & Central America)	Pac	Eur Amr	ex–US
Countries (Japan, Germany, Brazil, etc.)			ex–US

Figure 11.1   Basic Global Index Structure

multiple regions, and various slices of the developed and emerging markets. Those indexes also cover multiple securities types from stocks to bonds to commodities.

It is not possible to completely examine the global marketplace in just one chapter. My intent is to provide a brief overview. The best place to learn the extensive details of global index construction is to visit the web site of each index provider. The main providers of global market indexes include Morgan Stanley Capital Investments (MSCI), Standard & Poor's (S&P), Dow Jones (DJ), and FTSE. Their web sites are in the *ETF Resource List* in Appendix B. Reading a prospectus provided by an ETF that is a benchmark to an index that interests you also provides more detailed information.

MSCI Standard indexes target 85 percent of the free-float adjusted market cap segment of the global equity markets. The size cutoff varies somewhat across countries and regions depending on the extent of the market. To cover most of the other 15 percent, MSCI Small Cap indexes are promoted by the firm as "exhaustively covering" the investable small cap market worldwide. The data include both developed and emerging markets. In total, MSCI has created more than 20,000 style, sector, and regional indexes worldwide. That leaves no shortage of indexes to use as future benchmarks for ETFs.

The S&P Global 1200 Index combines the features of a broad global portfolio with a liquidity screen to make their indexes ideally suited for ETFs benchmarked to larger companies. The S&P Global 1200 is a free-float weighted index covering approximately 70 percent of the global market capitalization. It comprises the S&P 500 for the United States, and five non-U.S. indexes: S&P Europe 350, S&P/TOPIX 150 (Japan), S&P/TSX 60 (Canada), S&P Asia Pacific 100, and S&P Latin America 40.

The S&P Global 100 Index consists of 100 leading companies listed in the S&P Global 1200 whose businesses are global in nature and that derive a substantial portion of their operating income from multiple countries. S&P selects individual companies for the index based on strong fundamentals, industry leadership, market liquidity, and size. The Global 100 does not represent the largest 100 companies globally, although it is close.

The FTSE All-World Index Series was launched in 1987. It provides a single set of ground rules that are applied to FTSE Global Equity Index Series (Large, Mid, and Small Cap), the FTSE All-World Index Series (Large and Mid Cap), and the FTSE Global Small Cap Indexes.

Dow Jones Indexes and Wilshire Associates Incorporated have developed the DJ Wilshire Global Index family. They provide benchmarks that map a broad global market universe covering 59 countries and 98 percent of global market capitalization.

Developed Market Indexes

From a U.S. investor's standpoint, developed markets are large and established countries with large economies, stable governments, a reliable banking system, a functioning legal system for disputing claims fairly, and well-managed financial markets that can be easily accessed. In addition, the GDP per capita is over $20,000 U.S. dollars per year.

The most widely quoted developed market index is the Morgan Stanley Capital International Europe, Australasia, and the Far East Index, better known as the EAFE. The MSCI EAFE index comprises approximately 1,000 large company stocks from 21 developed markets located in Europe and the Pacific Rim. It is a float-adjusted index that includes at least 85 percent of the free-float market value of each industry group within each country.

MSCI slices the EAFE Index into two large geographic regions, forming the MSCI Europe Index and the MSCI Pacific Index. The division of the international indexes into regions allows the formation of index funds benchmarked to those regions. The MSCI Europe Index is made up of approximately 600 common stocks of companies located in 16 European countries. The MSCI Pacific Index consists of approximately 550 common stocks of companies located in Japan, Australia, Hong Kong, Singapore, and New Zealand.

MSCI does not control regional weights in the EAFE index. As a result, the value of the index can swing around from one region to

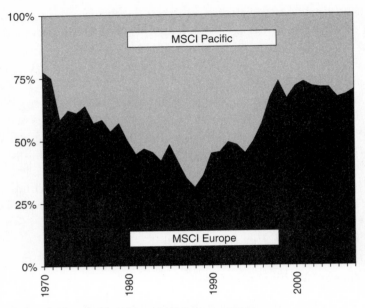

Figure 11.2   MSCI EAFE Market Weight by Region

Source: MSCI

another over time. In 1990, Japan dominated the EAFE with a weight of 70 percent. By 2000, Japan was only about 25 percent of the index. See Figure 11.2 for an illustration of the regional swings that can occur in the EAFE Index between the Pacific Rim and Europe.

There are other broad market benchmarks such as the FTSE All-World ex-U.S. index. It seeks to track the performance of companies located in developed and emerging markets around the world, not including the U.S. markets. The Citigroup Primary Market Index in another developed market benchmark that captures the top 80 percent of the Citigroup Broad Market Index. The deeper Citigroup Broad Market Index captures 95 percent of the market cap in each country.

Emerging Markets

Broadly defined, an emerging market is a less economically advanced country that is making some effort to become developed. The effort might entail attracting global capital, building infrastructure, free trade, job creation, fair labor laws, private ownership of real estate, transparency to business transactions, increased standards of living, advanced educational opportunities for all, and a host of other factors too numerous to mention.

There are more than 150 economies in the world that fit some classification of emerging market status, and over 100 of those have a stock exchange. About 25 percent of those exchanges have opened since 1990.

The S&P Emerging Market Indexes and its underlying database, which Standard & Poor's acquired from International Finance Corporation (IFC) in 2000, has been maintained since 1975. Since their inception, the indexes have grown to cover more than 2,000 companies in 54 established markets.

The MSCI Emerging Markets Index is a free-float-adjusted market capitalization index that is designed to measure equity market performance in the global emerging markets. Designation as an emerging market is determined by a number of factors. MSCI evaluates gross domestic product per capita, local government regulations, perceived investment risk, foreign ownership limits, and capital controls.

ADRs, GDRs, and Emerging Market ETFs

Several international companies trade on U.S. exchanges in the form of an American Depositary Receipt (ADR). Each ADR is issued by a U.S. depositary bank and represents one or more shares of foreign company stock that are held in trust at the bank. The shares are traded in U.S. dollars. A global form of the ADRs is called a global depositary receipt (GDR).

The system of trading international equities on U.S. exchanges allows the opportunity for ADR indexes. Enough ADR and GDRs have been issued so that they can be used to create emerging market indexes. Some of those indexes have been licensed and formed into emerging market ADR ETFs.

BLDRS Emerging Markets 50 ADR (symbol: ADRE) follows the Bank of New York Emerging Market 50 ADR index. The BNY EM 50 ADR index is a free-float composite of the largest and most liquid ADRs and GDRs that trade on U.S. exchanges.

The Claymore/BNY BRIC ETF (symbol: EEB) invests in so-called BRIC countries. The fund follows the Bank of New York BRIC Index. That index is composed of ADRs and GDRs from Brazil,

Russia, India, and China (B-R-I-C). The weights of stocks in the index are based on security capitalization of the ADRs, which means there is a heavy Brazil weighting and a light China and Russia weighting.

Regional Indexes

There are several regional indexes that offer ETF investors broad regional exposure. The MSCI Europe and MSCI Pacific indexes segregate the EAFE market into two indexes that are specific to those regions.

The introduction of the Euro as a common currency through much of Europe created an opportunity for index providers to create more indexes. The iShares MSCI EMU Index seeks to provide investment results that correspond generally to the price and yield performance of the aggregate publicly traded securities in the Eurozone markets, as measured by the MSCI EMU Index.

The Dow Jones STOXX 50 is a subgroup of 50 companies of the Dow Jones European broad index with the aim to mirror the sector leaders. Dow Jones Euro STOXX 50 is a subgroup of the Dow Jones European broad index that excludes those countries not in the EMU.

The MSCI United Kingdom index seeks to provide a benchmark of publicly traded securities in the aggregate in the British markets. The United Kingdom, Sweden, and Denmark are the only developed markets in Europe that are not currently in the Eurozone.

At the core of all global indexes are individual country markets. Many country ETFs are benchmarked to MSCI country indexes. MSCI constructs an index for each country by listing every security on the market based on free float and trading volume. The stocks are also categorized according to industry group. Individual companies are selected from each industry. Industry replication, more than any other single factor, is a key characteristic of a single country market index. MSCI methodology requires at least 85 percent representation of each industry group. As a result, a country index captures at least 85 percent of the market capitalization of that country.

The S&P/TOPIX 150 index includes 150 highly liquid securities selected from each major sector of the Tokyo market. The S&P/TOPIX 150 is designed specifically to give portfolio managers and derivative traders an index that is broad enough to provide representation of the market, but narrow enough to ensure liquidity.

The Russell/Nomura Prime Japan and Small Cap Japan also track the Tokyo markets.

S&P has recently teamed with Citigroup to become more active in regional emerging market indexing. A series of SPDRs was launched in 2007 that tracks several different S&P/Citigroup emerging market regional indexes, including the Middle East and Africa, Latin America, Asia Pacific, and Latin America. Be careful with these ETFs, because there can be a heavy concentration on one company and one country. There is, for example, an SPDR that tracks the entire S&P/Citigroup BMI Emerging Markets Index, and an SPDR that tracks the S&P Emerging Markets ETF (symbol: GMM).

There are a growing number of niche indexes created to follow countries in rapidly growing areas. The FTSE/Xinhua China A50 Index is free-float adjusted and consists of the top 50 Chinese companies by total market capitalization.

Country Indexes

There are several companies that collect price data and develop country indexes. It is an expanding area of ETF issuance, and will likely continue.

MSCI constructs a country index by listing every security on the market, and collects price data, outstanding shares, significant ownership, free float, and monthly trading volume. The stocks are categorized according to industry group, and individual companies are selected from each industry. MSCI methodology requires at least 85% representation of each industry group. Therefore, a country index captures at least 85% of the market capitalization of that country. Industry replication, more than any other single factor, is a key characteristic of a single country market index.

Currently, there are 21 separate iShares country funds, most of which are based on MSCI indexes (two are based on S&P Global Indexes). Some of the funds were originally issued as WEBS shares in 1996.

Other ETF providers are edging into the country fund marketplace. Most have a single country fund targeted to a specific audience. For example, Japan, China, and Russia funds have become popular.

State Street has had success in the global small cap market with its SPDR Russell/Nomura Small Cap Japan ETF (symbol: JSC). It was launched in November 2006 and has assets approaching $200 million. There were only a few small cap international ETFs at the time JSC was launched, and first-to-market ETFs always reap a good harvest if the product is decent.

The SPDR S&P China ETF (Symbol: GXC) is benchmarked to the S&P/Citigroup BMI China Index and is a good example of a niche emerging market offering. The China Index is float adjusted so that only those shares publicly available to investors are included in the index calculation. As of mid 2007, the GXC held approximately 125 securities. The largest position was China Mobile Ltd., with close to 12 percent of the NAV.

The Market Vectors Russia ETF (symbol: RSX) seeks to replicate as closely as possible, before fees and expenses, the performance of the DAXglobal Russia + Index. The index is a modified market capitalization weighted index comprising 30 publicly traded companies domiciled in Russia. Part of the fund holdings include common stocks and depositary receipts of selected companies in Russia that are listed for trading on global exchanges. Oil companies dominate the index.

Customized International Indexes

Customized international indexes do not track international markets. The index provider seeks, instead, to create a basket that offers different risks and returns than broad international securities markets. The providers may modify existing market data in some way to exclude securities, or to weight securities using a different methodology from market capitalization, or a combination of both. There are a growing number of customized international indexes that are being created for the ETF marketplace, and I expect many more in the future.

WisdomTree has taken the lead in customized international index investing. The WisdomTree Dividend Index of Europe, Far East Asia, and Australasia (WisdomTree DIEFA) measures the performance of dividend-paying companies in the industrialized world, excluding Canada and the United States. Foreign companies in the index pay regular cash dividends and meet other liquidity and capitalization requirements. Companies in the DIEFA index are weighted on the basis of annual cash dividends paid. WisdomTree has launched a series of regional and country ETFs that use data derived from the WisdomTree DIEFA.

WisdomTree was first to the market with a small cap international ETF. Its WisdomTree International Small Cap Dividend Fund (symbol: DLS) was launched in June 2006. First to the market funds gather assets quickly. The portfolio had $500 million in assets one year later.

ETF provider PowerShares is also in the international marketplace with customized international ETFs. The PowerShares International Dividend Achievers ETF (symbol: PID) tracks the International Dividend Achievers index. The index is designed to track the performance of dividend-paying ADRs that have increased their annual dividend for five or more consecutive fiscal years. The Golden Dragon Halter USX China index (symbol: PGJ) comprises U.S.-listed securities that derive a majority of their revenue from the People's Republic of China. The index has a modified equal weight structure.

A lineup of PowerShares Dynamic QSG international funds and ETFs that track FTSE RAFI international indexes launched in 2007 greatly expanded that company's presence in the marketplace. The Dynamic QSG portfolios use quantitative methods of stock selection and weighting while the FTSE RAFI funds use a multifactor fundamental approach to weighting stocks in FTSE indexes.

Perhaps the most ambitious ETF benchmarked to a custom international index is the Claymore/Zacks Country Rotation ETF (symbol: CRO). Drawing from the countries included in the MSCI EAFE index plus Canada, the underlying Zacks Country Rotation index selects stocks in countries that it believes have a high potential to outperform the global market, and weights the countries accordingly. Any of the 22 countries can have a weighting ranging from 0 percent to 45 percent of the index, and the index includes just 12 countries at a time. CRO has an expense ratio of 0.65 percent.

Global and International ETFs List

Global and international ETF investing is a rapidly expanding market. Table 11.1 is a partial list of ETFs that cover the international spectrum. The list includes ETFs that are benchmarked to markets as well as custom-made indexes. The list is a good starting point to finding an ETF that suits your needs. For a complete list of global, international, regional, and country ETFs, including the Index Strategy Box database, visit www.theetfbook.com and www.etfguide.com.

Table 11.1 is divided into three sections. The first section includes global, international, and regional ETFs that are benchmarked to market indexes. The second list includes single-country market index ETFs. The third is a list of global, international, regional, and country ETFs that track custom indexes.

Appendix A is an abbreviation guide for security selection and weighting methodologies used in each index in Table 11.1. Selection and weighting methodologies are the best fit given information available to the public through the ETF companies by way of each fund's Prospectus.

Table 11.1   Global, International, and Country ETFs

Market Index ETFs—Global, International, and Regional

Category	Market ETF Name	Ticker	Expense Ratio	Index	Strategy Box	Sec. Select	Sec. Weight
Global—Dev. Large	iShares S&P Global 100	IOO	0.40%	S&P Global 100 Index		P S	C F
Global—Dev. Large	SPDR DJ Global Titans	DGT	0.50%	Dow Jones Global Titans		P S	C F
Int'l—Broad Mkt	SPDR MSCI ACWI ex-U.S.	CWI	0.35%	MSCI ACWI ex U.S.		P S	C F
Int'l—Broad Mkt	SPDR S&P World ex-U.S. ETF	GWL	0.60%	S&P/Citigroup BMI World ex-U.S.		P S	C F
Int'l—Broad Mkt	Vanguard FTSE All World ex-U.S.	VEU	0.25%	FTSE All World ex-U.S.		P S	C F
Int'l— Developed	iShares MSCI EAFE	EFA	0.35%	MSCI EAFE		P S	C F
Int'l—Dev. Grwth	iShares MSCI EAFE Growth	EFG	0.40%	MSCI EAFE Growth		P S	C F
Int'l—Dev. Value	iShares MSCI EAFE Value	EFV	0.40%	MSCI EAFE Value		P S	C F
Int'l—Dev. Large	BLDRs Developed Markets 100 ADR	ADRD	0.30%	BNY Developed Markets 100 ADR		P A	C F
Int'l—Small Cap	SDPR S&P International Small Cap	GWX	0.60%	S&P/Citigroup World Ex U.S. Small		P S	C F
Regional Mkt	BLDRs Asia 50 ADR	ADRA	0.30%	BNY Asia 50 ADR		P A	C F
Regional Mkt	BLDRs Europe 100 ADR	ADRU	0.30%	BNY Europe 100 ADR		P A	C F
Regional Mkt	iShares MSCI EMU	EZU	0.54%	MSCI EMU		P S	C F
Regional Mkt	iShares MSCI Pacific ex-Japan	EPP	0.50%	MSCI Pacific Free ex-Japan		P S	C F
Regional Mkt	iShares MSCI United Kingdom	EWU	0.54%	MSCI United Kingdom		P S	C F
Regional Mkt	iShares S&P Europe 350	IEV	0.60%	S&P Europe 350		P S	C F

Table 11.1 *(continued)*

Category	Market ETF Name	Ticker	Expense Ratio	Index	Strategy Box	Sec. Select	Sec. Weight
Regional Mkt	iShares S&P Latin America 40	ILF	0.50%	S&P Latin America 40		P S	C F
Regional Mkt	DJ EURO STOXX 50 ETF	FEZ	0.33%	Dow Jones EURO STOXX 50		P A	C F
Regional Mkt	Vanguard MSCI European	VGK	0.18%	MSCI European		P A	C F
Regional Mkt	Vanguard MSCI Pacific	VPL	0.18%	MSCI Pacific		P A	C F
Emerging Mkt	BLDRS Emerging Markets 50 ADR	ADRE	0.30%	BNY Emerging Markets 50 ADR		P A	C F
Emerging Mkt	Claymore BNY BRIC ETF	EEB	0.60%	BNY BRIC Select ADR		P A	C F
Emerging Mkt	iShares MSCI Emerging Markets	EEM	0.75%	MSCI Emerging Markets		P S	C F
Emerging Mkt	SPDR S&P Emerging Markets	GMM	0.60%	S&P/Citi BMI Emerging Markets		P S	C F
Emerging Mkt	Vanguard Emerging Markets	VWO	0.30%	MSCI Emerging Markets		P S	C F
Emerging— Regional	SPDR S&P Emerging Latin America	GML	0.60%	S&P/Citi BMI Latin America		P S	C F
Emerging— Regional	SPDR S&P Emerging Middle East & Africa	GAF	0.60%	S&P/Citi BMI Middle East & Africa		P S	C F
Emerging— Regional	SPDR S&P Emerging Europe	GUR	0.60%	S&P/Citigroup BMI Europe		P S	C F
Emerging— Regional	SPDR S&P Emerging Asia Pacific	GMF	0.60%	S&P/Citigroup BMI Asia Pacific		P S	C F
	Median Fee—Market Index ETFs		**0.50%**				

Market Index ETFs—Country Funds

Category	Country ETF Name	Ticker	Expense Ratio	Index	Strategy Box	Sec. Select	Sec. Weight
Developed— Market	iShares MSCI Australia	EWA	0.59%	MSCI Australia		P S	C F
Developed— Market	iShares MSCI Austria	EWO	0.54%	MSCI Austria		P S	C F

(continued)

Table 11.1   *(continued)*

Category	Country ETF Name	Ticker	Expense Ratio	Index	Strategy Box	Sec. Select	Sec. Weight
Developed— Market	iShares MSCI Belgium	EWK	0.54%	MSCI Belgium		P S	C F
Developed— Market	iShares MSCI Canada	EWC	0.59%	MSCI Canada		P S	C F
Developed— Market	iShares MSCI France	EWQ	0.54%	MSCI France		P S	C F
Developed— Market	iShares MSCI Germany	EWG	0.54%	MSCI Germany		P S	C F
Developed— Market	iShares MSCI Hong Kong	EWH	0.59%	MSCI Hong Kong		P S	C F
Developed— Market	iShares MSCI Italy	EWI	0.54%	MSCI Italy		P S	C F
Developed— Market	iShares MSCI Japan	EWJ	0.59%	MSCI Japan		P S	C F
Developed— Market	iShares MSCI Netherlands	EWN	0.54%	MSCI Netherlands		P S	C F
Developed— Market	iShares MSCI Singapore	EWS	0.59%	MSCI Singapore		P S	C F
Developed— Market	iShares MSCI Spain	EWP	0.54%	MSCI Spain		P S	C F
Developed— Market	iShares MSCI Sweden	EWD	0.54%	MSCI Sweden		P S	C F
Developed— Market	iShares MSCI Switzerland	EWL	0.54%	MSCI Switzerland		P S	C F
Developed— Market	iShares S&P TOPIX 150	ITF	0.50%	S&P/Tokyo Stock Price Index 150		P S	C F
Developed— Market	DJ STOXX 50	FEU	0.33%	Dow Jones STOXX 50		P A	C F
Developed— Market	SPDR Russell/Nomura Prime Japan	JPP	0.50%	Russell/Nomura PRIME		P S	C F
Developed— Small	SPDR Russell/Nomura Small Cap Japan	JSC	0.55%	Russell/Nomura Japan Small Cap		P S	C F
Emerging— Market	PowerShares Golden Dragon Halter USX China	PGJ	0.60%	Halter USX China		P S	C F
Emerging— Market	SPDR S&P China	GXC	0.60%	S&P/Citigroup BMI China		P S	C F
Emerging— Market	iShares FTSE/Xinhua China 25 Index	FXI	0.74%	FTSE/Xinhua China 25		P S	C F
Emerging— Market	iShares MSCI Brazil	EWZ	0.74%	MSCI Brazil		P S	C F

Table 11.1 *(continued)*

Category	Active Index ETF Name	Ticker	Expense Ratio	Index	Strategy Box	Sec. Select	Sec. Weight
Emerging—Market	iShares MSCI Malaysia	EWM	0.59%	MSCI Malaysia		P S	C F
Emerging—Market	iShares MSCI Mexico	EWW	0.59%	MSCI Mexico		P S	C F
Emerging—Market	iShares MSCI South Africa	EZA	0.74%	MSCI South Africa		P S	C F
Emerging—Market	iShares MSCI South Korea	EWY	0.74%	MSCI South Korea		P S	C F
Emerging—Market	iShares MSCI Taiwan	EWT	0.74%	MSCI Taiwan		P S	C F
Emerging—Market	Market Vectors—Russia ETF	RSX	0.69%	DAXglobal Russia + Index		P A	C F
	Median Fee—Country ETFs		**0.59%**				

Custom Index ETFs—Global, International, Regional and Country

Category	Active Index ETF Name	Ticker	Expense Ratio	Index	Strategy Box	Sec. Select	Sec. Weight
Int'l—Broad Mkt	Claymore/ Robeco Developed Int'l Equity	EEN	0.65%	Robeco Dev. International Equity		Q M	C F
Int'l Dev.—Value	WisdomTree DEFA Fund	DWM	0.48%	WisdomTree DEFA		S F	F D
Int'l Dev.—Value	WisdomTree DEFA High Yield Equity Fund	DTH	0.58%	WisdomTree DEFA High Yield Equity		S F	F D
Int'l Dev.—Value	WisdomTree International Dividend Top 100	DOO	0.58%	WisdomTree Int'l Dividend Top 100		S F	F D
Int'l Dev.—Value	PowerShares International Dividend Achievers	PID	0.50%	International Dividend Achievers		S F	F D
Int'l Dev.—Large Val	WisdomTree International Large Cap Dividend	DOL	0.48%	WisdomTree Int'l Large Cap Dvd		S F	F D
Int'l Dev.—Mid Value	WisdomTree International Mid Cap Dividend	DIM	0.58%	WisdomTree Int'l Mid Cap Dividend		S F	F D

(continued)

Table 11.1 *(continued)*

Category	Active Index ETF Name	Ticker	Expense Ratio	Index	Strategy Box	Sec. Select	Sec. Weight
Int'l Dev.— Small Val	WisdomTree International Small Cap Dividend	DLS	0.58%	WisdomTree Int'l Small Cap Dividend	▦	S F	F D
Regional— Value	WisdomTree Pacific ex-Japan High Yield Equity Fund	DNH	0.58%	WisdomTree Pacific ex-Japan High Yield Equity	▦	S F	F D
Regional— Value	WisdomTree Pacific ex-Japan Total Dividend	DND	0.48%	WisdomTree Pacific ex-Japan Total Dividend	▦	S F	F D
Regional— Value	WisdomTree Europe High Yield Equity Fund	DEW	0.58%	WisdomTree Europe High Yield Equity	▦	S F	F D
Regional— Small Value	WisdomTree Europe Small Cap Dividend	DFE	0.58%	WisdomTree Europe Small Cap Dvd	▦	S F	F D
Regional— Value Value	WisdomTree Europe Total Dividend	DEB	0.48%	WisdomTree Europe Total Dividend	▦	S F	F D
Country— Value	WisdomTree Japan High Yield Equity Fund	DNL	0.58%	WisdomTree Japan High Yield Equity	▦	S F	F D
Country— Small Value	WisdomTree Japan Small Cap Dividend	DFJ	0.58%	WisdomTree Japan Small Cap Dvd	▦	S F	F D
Country— Value	WisdomTree Japan Total Dividend	DXJ	0.48%	WisdomTree Japan Total Dividend	▦	S F	F D
Country— Rotation	Claymore/Zacks Country Rotation	CRO	0.65%	Zacks Country Rotation	▦	S F	F F
	Median Fee—Custom Index ETFs		**0.55%**				

Summary

The global stock market is a dynamic area of investment. Gaining international stock exposure through ETFs makes sense for today's investors. Going global not only provides more security diversification, it provides currency diversification as well.

More research into international investing is mandatory for astute investors. Check the *ETF Resource List* in Appendix B for starters. Ensure that you know which index each ETF follows so that you will not have redundant country exposure in your portfolio. ETFs that follow customized indexes are also available in an assortment of regions and countries. Look for many more global and international ETFs to be launched in the future.

12

Industry Sector ETFs

Industry sector ETFs are a dynamic and growing market. The number of ETFs that track industries and the depth of the offerings continue to increase. More global industry ETFs are also making their way into investors' portfolios as the world becomes flatter.

There are many uses for industry ETFs. One basic use is to fill an industry gap in a portfolio that is not covered by other investments. Another use is to gain greater exposure to an industry sector that you expect to outperform the broad market. A third use is to use the funds as a hedge against a concentrated stock position. That is accomplished by shorting an industry ETF short and thereby reducing industry exposure in a portfolio.

Whatever the use an investor has for industry sector ETFs, there are plenty of funds to choose from. More than one quarter of all equity ETFs are industry sector funds, and the assets in those funds total about 10 percent of the total assets in all ETFs.

One of the most popular industries for ETF investing is real estate. Nearly $10 billion is invested in a handful of U.S. real estate investment trust (REIT) ETFs. SSGA launched the first international real estate fund in 2006. The SPDR DJ Wilshire International Real Estate ETF (symbol: RWX) attracted more than $1 billion in assets during its first 12 months. A special section on real estate ETFs is provided at the end of this chapter.

The Evolution of Industry ETFs

The first and still leading industry sector ETFs were launched in 1998. Select Sector SPDRs divide the S&P 500 into nine sectors.

Each Select Sector SPDR is designed to track, before expenses, the price performance of a particular Select Sector Index. State Street Bank and Trust Company serves as administrator and custodian of the Trust and SSGA Funds Management serves as the Trust's adviser. The values of Select Sector Indexes are calculated daily by the American Stock Exchange.

Many firms have followed State Street's success in the industry sector arena, and several have introduced global industry ETFs that track industry sectors around the world. Some ETF firms have launched products based on customized indexing strategies. The goal of those indexes is to outperform market industry indexes. PowerShares is the leader in the number of customized industry sector ETF products, including a series that follows quantitative methods and another that follows a fundamental weighting scheme. Other companies are not far behind, however. WisdomTree has dividend weighted industry indexes, Rydex and State Street now have equal weighted industry ETFs, and First Trust has launched the quantitative AlphaDEX series to compete head to head with PowerShares.

Industry Sector Categorization

The stock market is made up of thousands of individual companies. Without an orderly way to classify those stocks, the market would be a quagmire of names and symbols. Classifying companies by what business they are in is a logical method. That allows investors to study the market economy and make industry bets as they anticipate the movement of capital from one industry sector to another.

Competing index providers slice industries in different ways in an attempt to differentiate their products. The dissimilarities in the classification methods, however, are not materially different. All the index providers offer 10 or so industry groups and the holdings in those groups tend to be fairly consistent.

New technology creates new businesses, which are financed in part by an issuance of common stock. The listing of new businesses on stock exchanges leads to new industry sectors and subsectors. At the same time, established industries fade away. Thus, the industry classification system is constantly evolving.

Global Industry Classification Standard (GICS)

MSCI, in collaboration with Standard & Poor's, introduced the Global Industry Classification Standard (GICS) in 2000. Over 34,000 active, publicly traded companies globally are currently classified and maintained using GICS methodology. The system categorizes stocks in each of its indexes according to 10 sectors, 24 industry groups, 67 industries, and 147 subindustries. MSCI has created literally thousands of global industry indexes covering categories at each level and using various global, regional, and country indexes. As a result, there is no shortage of indexes to be created into market index ETFs.

The 10 GICS sectors and examples of industries and subsectors are as follows:

1. Basic Materials—metals, mining, forest and paper products, chemicals
2. Consumer Discretionary—auto, appliances, retail, leisure, home building, media
3. Consumer Staples—food and drug retailing, tobacco, household products
4. Energy—energy equipment, oil and gas exploration, refining, storage
5. Financials—banks, financial services, real estate investment trusts, insurance
6. Health Care—managed care, medical products, drugs, biotech
7. Industrials—capital goods, building, defense, aerospace, all transportation
8. Information Technology—hardware, software, telecom equipment, consulting
9. Telecommunication Services—fixed line, mobile, integrated services
10. Utilities—electric, gas, water, multi-utilities

Select Sector SPDR ETFs unbundle the S&P 500 according to GICS. There are nine SPDRs representing the 10 GICS sectors. The Information Technology and Telecommunication Services sectors are lumped together under the Technology SPDR.

Vanguard industry sector ETFs also use GICS. The MSCI U.S. Investable Market 2500 Index is divided into different sectors according to the standards. Having 2,000 more stocks than the S&P 500 adds mid cap and small cap depth to the Vanguard Sector Index ETFs.

Another difference between Vanguard U.S. Sector ETFs and SPDRs is that Vanguard ETFs are formed under the Investment Company Act of 1940. That allows the management to sample their target indexes rather than fully replicate them as with SPDRs. However, that also leads to greater tracking errors with the index.

iShare Global Sector Industry ETFs are benchmarked to GICS industry subsets of the S&P Global 1200, which covers 70 percent of the global market cap. The index is a free-float weighted index constructed in a joint effort with Morgan Stanley. The S&P Global 1200 Index covers approximately 70 percent of the global market capitalization and comprises the S&P 500 for the United States, and five non-U.S. indexes: S&P Europe 350, S&P/TOPIX 150 (Japan), S&P/TSX 60 (Canada), S&P Asia Pacific 100, and S&P Latin America 40.

Industry Classification Benchmark (ICB)

Dow Jones Indexes and FTSE have a competing industry classification system to GICS called the Industry Classification Benchmark (ICB). The system is supported by the ICB Universe Database, which contains over 40,000 companies and 45,000 securities worldwide from the FTSE and Dow Jones universes. ICB offers broad, global coverage of companies and securities and classifies them based on revenue, not earnings.

The structure of ICB is based on 10 industries, 18 supersectors, 39 sectors, and 104 subsectors. Although many names in ICB are the same as GICS, they are not in the same order. What ICB calls an industry, GICS calls a sector, and what ICB calls a supersector, GICS calls an industry group. Another difference is in the subsectors. For example, airline transportation is classified as Consumer Services under ICB and Industrials under GICS.

Barclays Global Investors (BGI) lists a series of 22 sector iShares based on ICB. Ten funds are benchmarked to the 10 primary ICB industries and the rest are benchmarked to supersectors, sectors, and subsectors.

Morningstar Sector Methodology

A third industry sector methodology is Morningstar, Inc. Morningstar classifies companies into the industry that best reflects each company's underlying business activities based on the largest source of revenue. Each company is assigned to one of 129 Morningstar industries based on the firm's primary source of revenue. The industries are classified into one of 12 sectors. Those 12 sectors are then organized under one of three supersectors: information economy, service economy, and manufacturing economy.

This organization of sectors is designed to mimic the way economies evolve from dependence on the production of physical products to the delivery of services, which culminates in the exchange of information. Index constituents are weighted according to their free float of shares outstanding. The free float is defined as a firm's outstanding shares adjusted for block ownership to reflect only shares available for investment.

Claymore Advisors, LLC, has filed with the SEC to launch ETFs based on the Morningstar Information Economy, Service Economy, and Manufacturing Economy indexes. As of this writing, the funds were still in registration and no ticker symbol or fee information was public. Check the databases listed at the end of this chapter and in Appendix B for updates.

Merrill Lynch HOLDRS

In early 2000, Merrill Lynch introduced a series of unit investment trusts called HOLDRS. These securities are initially in 20 large stocks using an MSCI industry index based on GICS, but are then fixed for the life of the trust. The securities are not updated as the index updates. The securities are equal weighted in the trust at first, then allowed to float thereafter. There is no rebalancing. In addition, there are other unique features of HOLDRS that investors should be aware of:

- Individual investors can turn in round lots of 100 units and receive the underlying stock in return. This allows an investor to sell specific stocks in a fund instead of the entire fund.
- The owners of HOLDRS retain voting rights on the stocks in a fund. That means an investor in one unit will get 20 annual reports and voting proxies stuffed into her mailbox each year.

- There are no management costs, but there is an annual $2 per 100-unit trustee and custody fee that is paid to the Bank of New York from stock dividends.

Customized Industry Indexes

Customized industry ETFs vary considerably from the equal weighting of stocks in a traditional market capitalization index to advanced quantitative methods. There are also HOLDRs, which select stocks one time based on capitalization and equal weight them in a trust, and then just sit there.

Rydex created a series of ETFs benchmarked to Standard & Poor's Equal Weight Industry indexes, which cover S&P 500 stocks. Those indexes comprise the same securities as Select Sector SPDR ETFs. Where each stock's weight in the index is proportionate to its market value in SPDRs, however, each stock included in the Rydex S&P Equal Weight Sector ETF has the same target weighting as every other stock included in that index. Capitalization weighted Select Sector SPDRs cost investors 0.24 percent per year in fees, whereas the equal weighted Rydex ETFs cost investors more than twice that amount at 0.50 percent per year.

S&P has also licensed a different series of equal weighted indexes to State Street for use in niche industries that S&P Select Sector industry groups do not adequately capture. Those narrow markets include biotech, home builders, and semiconductors, to name a few. The fees for these narrowly focused S&P industry SPDR ETFs are 0.35 percent per year.

WisdomTree put an international spin on customized industry indexes with the introduction of a series of international industry ETFs during 2007. WisdomTree screens for dividend-paying stocks and weights those stocks based on the level of dividends paid. The strategy gives WisdomTree international industry ETFs a strong value bias.

PowerShares has almost 40 industry ETFs on the market. One series is based on quantitative analysis and the other series uses a multifactor fundamental weighting method.

The PowerShares Dynamic Industry Sector Portfolio series is based on the AMEX Dynamic Intellidex index series. The AMEX evaluates companies based on a variety of investment merit criteria, including fundamental growth, stock valuation, investments, and risk factors. Securities chosen are believed to possess the greatest capital appreciation potential. Securities are allocated in the index according to a modified equal weighting method. Larger stocks tend to get a greater fixed weight than smaller stocks.

First Trust AlphaDEX ETFs are one of the latest entrants in the ever-expanding line of beat-the-market quantitatively run industry ETFs. The AMEX's StrataQuant model starts with the Russell 1000 indexes and analyzes those securities using several growth factors and value factors. The stocks are then ranked. The bottom 25 percent is eliminated and the top 75 percent is selected for the StrataQuant industry indexes. Stocks are equal weighted within each quartile, however, using a modified equal weight method. The top-ranked quartile receives a higher allocation than the second quartile, and the second receives a higher allocation than the third. There are currently nine First Trust AlphaDEX industry ETFs on the market.

Some narrowly focused industry ETFs are so restrictive that there are a limited number of securities that fit the criteria. In those circumstances, a fund company may put a limit on the amount any company can be represented in a portfolio. The caps ensure that one company does not become overweighted in that product. The cap is typically between 5 percent and 10 percent of the index value.

REIT ETFs

Twenty-five years ago, the only way you could invest in commercial real estate was through direct ownership or a limited partnership. Today, you can buy a large portfolio of commercial real estate with the purchase of one ETF that tracks real estate investment trusts (REITs) index. REITs represent indirect ownership in a group of real properties. You actually own a small part of a publicly traded management company whose purpose is to acquire and manage commercial real estate. That company selects or builds properties, finds tenants, collects rents, and distributes profits to shareholders.

REITs have a unique tax benefit. Management companies do not pay corporate income tax on dividend distributions to shareholders as long as 90 percent of the profits is passed on to shareholders, and at least 75 percent of the income is from rents, mortgages, and the sale of properties. There is one caveat. Since income is not taxed at the company level, most of the dividends paid to you from REIT ETFs are treated as ordinary income, for tax purposes. That means the income is taxed at a higher rate than the dividends paid by ETFs owning only common stocks.

REITs provide diversification benefits in a portfolio. Adding a REIT's ETF tends to reduce portfolio risk and increase portfolio returns over the long term. That is because of the low correlation of returns between REITs, stocks, and bonds. For detailed information on portfolio management, including the data on the benefits of REITs, read *All About Asset Allocation* by Richard Ferri [McGraw-Hill, 2005].

The Vanguard REIT ETF (symbol: VNQ) is benchmarked to the Morgan Stanley U.S. REIT Index. The Morgan Stanley U.S. REIT Index was designed as a broad representation of REITs. The index represents approximately 85 percent of the U.S. REIT universe. It consists of REITs included in the MSCI U.S. Investable Market 2500 Index, excluding specialty equity REITs that do not generate a majority of their revenue and income from real estate rental and leasing operations. The MSCI U.S. REIT index holds approximately 100 companies. It excludes mortgage and hybrid REITs that hold both properties and mortgages.

iShares Dow Jones U.S. Real Estate is benchmarked to the Dow Jones U.S. Real Estate Index. The index seeks to provide a broad measure of the U.S. real estate securities market. It currently holds approximately 93 companies, which make up the real estate portion of the Dow Jones U.S. Total Market Index. Although the U.S. Real Estate Index consists predominantly of REITs, and can hold real-estate operating companies (REOCs), REOCs are subject corporate income taxes. As such, they do not have to distribute 90 percent of their earnings as REITs do and can reinvest those earnings in more projects. DJ Wilshire REIT ETF (symbol: RWR) is benchmarked to the Dow Jones Wilshire REIT Index. Its objective is to provide a broad measure of publicly traded REITs. The index has 85 components. The DJ Wilshire REIT Index does not hold health care REITs or REOCs.

SPDR Dow Jones Wilshire International Real Estate (symbol: RWX) is not exclusively an international REIT fund. Rather, the index is a measure of all types of real estate securities that represent the ownership and operation of commercial or residential real estate, including REOCs. The index is a float-adjusted market capitalization index designed to measure the performance of publicly traded real estate securities in countries excluding the United States. RWX has been a popular attraction for investors, gathering $1 billion in assets during the first six months on the market.

Specialized REIT Indexes

BGI launched three iShares REIT ETFs in 2006 that offer U.S. investors the ability to slice and dice the U.S. equity REIT marketplace into different sectors. Investors can now allocate among different segments of the equity REIT market in an attempt to capture better returns or to reduce risk. The indexes are drawn from the broader cap weighted FTSE NAREIT Composite Index. The submarkets are residential (apartments), industrial/office, and retail (including malls).

The first customized index tracked by an ETF is the Cohen & Steers Realty Majors index. The fund is the iShares Cohen & Steers Realty Majors (symbol: ICF). Securities are selected by a Cohen & Steers investment committee, based on each security's management, portfolio quality, real estate sector, and geographic diversification. There are 30 REITs in the index. Weighting is by restrained free-float market capitalization. No security can be more than 8 percent of the index.

The WisdomTree International Real Estate Sector Fund (symbol: DRW) selects and weights real estate stocks based on cash value of dividends paid. The weighting is primarily in the countries Australia, Hong Kong, and Japan. A third of the ETF is allocated to European countries.

A Partial List of Industry ETFs

Table 12.1 is a partial list of market and custom index industry ETFs, which will give you a sampling of the funds available. It is not a complete list because of space constraints, and several new industry ETFs are launched each year. For a complete list of industry ETFs, including Index Strategy Box data, visit www.theetfbook.com and www.etfguide.com. Additional information on industry ETFs can also be found at www.indexuniverse.com, www.morningstar.com, and from a variety of sources in the ETF Resource List found in Appendix B.

Table 12.1 is divided into three sections. The first section includes ETFs that follow market indexes, the second list includes ETFs that follow custom indexes, and the third list includes REIT ETFs.

Table 12.1 A Sampling of Industry ETFs

Market Index ETFs—Industry Sectors

Industry Category	Market ETF Name	Ticker	Expense Ratio	Index (or Parent Index)	Strategy Box	Sec. Select	Sec. Weight
Consumer Discretionary	Consumer Discretionary Select Sector SPDR	XLY	0.24%	S&P 500 Industry Sector		P A	C F
Consumer Staples	Consumer Staples Select Sector SPDR	XLP	0.24%	S&P 500 Industry Sector		P A	C F
Energy	Energy Select Sector SPDR	XLE	0.24%	S&P 500 Industry Sector		P A	C F
Financial	Financial Select Sector SPDR	XLF	0.24%	S&P 500 Industry Sector		P A	C F
Health Care	Health Care Select Sector SPDR	XLV	0.24%	S&P 500 Industry Sector		P A	C F
Industrial	Industrial Select Sector SPDR	XLI	0.24%	S&P 500 Industry Sector		P A	C F
Materials	Materials Select Sector SPDR	XLB	0.24%	S&P 500 Industry Sector		P A	C F
Technology	Technology Select Sector SPDR	XLK	0.24%	S&P 500 Industry Sector		P A	C F
Utilities	Utilities Select Sector SPDR	XLU	0.24%	S&P 500 Industry Sector		P A	C F
Consumer Discretionary	Vanguard Consumer Discretionary ETF	VCR	0.25%	MSCI U.S. Investable Market		P A	C F
Consumer Staples	Vanguard Consumer Staples ETF	VDC	0.25%	MSCI U.S. Investable Market		P A	C F
Energy	Vanguard Energy ETF	VDE	0.25%	MSCI U.S. Investable Market		P A	C F
Financial	Vanguard Financials ETF	VFH	0.25%	MSCI U.S. Investable Market		P A	C F
HealthCare	Vanguard Health Care ETF	VHT	0.25%	MSCI U.S. Investable Market		P A	C F
Industrial	Vanguard Industrials ETF	VIS	0.25%	MSCI U.S. Investable Market		P A	C F
Info. Tech.	Vanguard Information Technology ETF	VGT	0.25%	MSCI U.S. Investable Market		P A	C F

Table 12.1 *(continued)*

Industry Category	Market ETF Name	Ticker	Expense Ratio	Index (or Parent Index)	Strategy Box	Sec. Select	Sec. Weight
Materials	Vanguard Materials ETF	VAW	0.25%	MSCI U.S. Investable Market	▦	P A	C F
Telecom	Vanguard Telecommunications ETF	VOX	0.25%	MSCI U.S. Investable Market	▦	P A	C F
Utilities	Vanguard Utilities ETF	VPU	0.25%	MSCI U.S. Investable Market	▦	P A	C F
Aero/Defense	iShares Dow Jones U.S. Aerospace & Defense	ITA	0.48%	Dow Jones U.S. Select	▦	P S	C F
Basic Materials	iShares Dow Jones U.S. Basic Materials	IYM	0.48%	Dow Jones U.S. Select	▦	P S	C F
Consumer Goods	iShares Dow Jones U.S. Consumer Goods	IYK	0.48%	Dow Jones U.S. Select	▦	P S	C F
Consumer Services	iShares Dow Jones U.S. Consumer Services	IYC	0.48%	Dow Jones U.S. Select	▦	P S	C F
Energy	iShares Dow Jones U.S. Energy	IYE	0.48%	Dow Jones U.S. Select	▦	P S	C F
Financial	iShares Dow Jones U.S. Financial	IYF	0.48%	Dow Jones U.S. Select	▦	P S	C F
Health Care	iShares Dow Jones U.S. Health Care	IYH	0.48%	Dow Jones U.S. Select	▦	P S	C F
Industrials	iShares Dow Jones U.S. Industrial	IYJ	0.48%	Dow Jones U.S. Select	▦	P S	C F
Technology	iShares Dow Jones U.S. Technology	IYW	0.48%	Dow Jones U.S. Select	▦	P S	C F
Telecom	iShares Dow Jones U.S. Telecommunications	IYZ	0.48%	Dow Jones U.S. Select	▦	P S	C F
Transportation	iShares Dow Jones U.S. Transportation	IYT	0.48%	Dow Jones U.S. Select	▦	P S	C F
Utilities	iShares Dow Jones U.S. Utilities	IDU	0.48%	Dow Jones U.S. Select	▦	P S	C F
Global Consumer Discretionary	iShares S&P Global Consumer Discretionary	RXI	0.48%	S&P Global Industry Sector	▦	P S	C F

(continued)

Table 12.1   *(continued)*

Industry Category	Market ETF Name	Ticker	Expense Ratio	Index (or Parent Index)	Strategy Box	Sec. Select	Sec. Weight
Global Consumer Services	iShares S&P Global Consumer Staples	KXI	0.48%	S&P Global Industry Sector		P S	C F
Global Energy	iShares S&P Global Energy	IXC	0.48%	S&P Global Industry Sector		P S	C F
Global Financial	iShares S&P Global Financials	IXG	0.48%	S&P Global Industry Sector		P S	C F
Global Health Care	iShares S&P Global Health Care	IXJ	0.48%	S&P Global Industry Sector		P S	C F
Global Industrials	iShares S&P Global Industrials	EXI	0.48%	S&P Global Industry Sector		P S	C F
Global Materials	iShares S&P Global Materials	MXI	0.48%	S&P Global Industry Sector		P S	C F
Global Tech	iShares S&P Global Technology	IXN	0.48%	S&P Global Industry Sector		P S	C F
Global Telecom	iShares S&P Global Telecommunications	IXP	0.48%	S&P Global Industry Sector		P S	C F
Global Utilities	iShares S&P Global Utilities	JXI	0.48%	S&P Global Industry Sector		P S	C F
Business to Business	B2B HOLDRS	BHH	0.00%	None – Large Stocks in 2000		P B	C A
Internet	Internet HOLDRS	HHH	0.00%	None – Large Stocks in 2000		P B	C A
Pharmaceutical	Pharmaceutical HOLDRS	PPH	0.00%	None – Large Stocks in 2000		P B	C A
Regional Bank	Regional Bank HOLDRS	RKH	0.00%	None – Large Stocks in 2000		P B	C A
Retail	Retail HOLDRS	RTH	0.00%	None – Large Stocks in 2000		P B	C A
Semiconductor	Semiconductor HOLDRS	SMH	0.00%	None – Large Stocks in 2000		P B	C A
Telecom	Telecom HOLDRS	TTH	0.00%	None – Large Stocks in 2000		P B	C A
Utilities	Utilities HOLDRS	UTH	0.00%	None – Large Stocks in 2000		P B	C A
Wireless	Wireless HOLDRS	WMH	0.00%	None – Large Stocks in 2000		P B	C A
	Average Fee—Market Index ETFs (x-HOLDRS)		**0.37%**				

Table 12.1 *(continued)*

Custom Index ETFs—Industry Sectors

Category	Active Index ETF Name	Ticker	Expense Ratio	Index (or Parent Index)	Strategy Box	Sec. Select	Sec. Weight
Consumer Discretionary	Rydex S&P Equal Weight Consumer Discretionary	RCD	0.50%	Equal Weight S&P 500		P A	X E
Consumer Staples	Rydex S&P Equal Weight Consumer Staples	RHS	0.50%	Equal Weight S&P 500		P A	X E
Energy	Rydex S&P Equal Weight Energy	RYE	0.50%	Equal Weight S&P 500		P A	X E
Financial	Rydex S&P Equal Weight Financial Services	RYF	0.50%	Equal Weight S&P 500		P A	X E
Health Care	Rydex S&P Equal Weight Health Care	RYH	0.50%	Equal Weight S&P 500		P A	X E
Industrial	Rydex S&P Equal Weight Industrial	RGI	0.50%	Equal Weight S&P 500		P A	X E
Materials	Rydex S&P Equal Weight Materials	RTM	0.50%	Equal Weight S&P 500		P A	X E
Technology	Rydex S&P Equal Weight Technology	RYT	0.50%	Equal Weight S&P 500		P A	X E
Utilities	Rydex S&P Equal Weight Utilities	RYU	0.50%	Equal Weight S&P 500		P A	X E
Home builders	SPDR S&P Home builders	XHB	0.35%	Equal Weight S&P Total Mkt		P A	X E
Oil & Gas Ex/Pr	SPDR S&P Oil & Gas Exploration & Production	XOP	0.35%	Equal Weight S&P Total Mkt		P A	X E
Biotech	SPDR S&P Biotech	XBI	0.35%	Equal Weight S&P Total Mkt		P A	X E
Pharmaceuticals	SPDR S&P Pharmaceuticals	XPH	0.35%	Equal Weight S&P Total Mkt		P A	X E
Metals & Mining	SPDR S&P Metals & Mining	XME	0.35%	Equal Weight S&P Total Mkt		P A	X E
Semiconductor	SPDR S&P Semiconductor	XSD	0.35%	Equal Weight S&P Total Mkt		P A	X E
Basic Materials	PowerShares FTSE RAFI Basic Materials	PRFM	0.60%	FTSE RAFI Industry Sector		P A	F F
Consumer Goods	PowerShares FTSE RAFI Consumer Goods	PRFG	0.60%	FTSE RAFI Industry Sector		P A	F F

(continued)

Table 12.1 *(continued)*

Category	Active Index ETF Name	Ticker	Expense Ratio	Index (or Parent Index)	Strategy Box	Sec. Select	Sec. Weight
Consumer Service	PowerShares FTSE RAFI Consumer Services	PRFS	0.60%	FTSE RAFI Industry Sector	⊞	P A	F F
Energy	PowerShares FTSE RAFI Energy	PRFE	0.60%	FTSE RAFI Industry Sector	⊞	P A	F F
Financials	PowerShares FTSE RAFI Financials	PRFF	0.60%	FTSE RAFI Industry Sector	⊞	P A	F F
Health Care	PowerShares FTSE RAFI Health Care	PRFH	0.60%	FTSE RAFI Industry Sector	⊞	P A	F F
Industrials	PowerShares FTSE RAFI Industrials	PRFN	0.60%	FTSE RAFI Industry Sector	⊞	P A	F F
Telecom & Tech	PowerShares FTSE RAFI Telecom & Tech	PRFQ	0.60%	FTSE RAFI Industry Sector	⊞	P A	F F
Utilities	PowerShares FTSE RAFI Utilities	PRFU	0.60%	FTSE RAFI Industry Sector	⊞	P A	F F
Basic Materials	PowerShares Dynamic Basic Materials	PYZ	0.60%	AMEX Intellidex Index	⊞	Q M	X M
Consumer Goods	PowerShares Dynamic Consumer Discretionary	PEZ	0.60%	AMEX Intellidex Index	⊞	Q M	X M
Consumer Services	PowerShares Dynamic Consumer Staples	PSL	0.60%	AMEX Intellidex Index	⊞	Q M	X M
Energy	PowerShares Dynamic Energy	PXI	0.60%	AMEX Intellidex Index	⊞	Q M	X M
Financial	PowerShares Dynamic Financial	PFI	0.60%	AMEX Intellidex Index	⊞	Q M	X M
Health Care	PowerShares Dynamic Health Care	PTH	0.60%	AMEX Intellidex Index	⊞	Q M	X M
Industrial	PowerShares Dynamic Industrials	PRN	0.60%	AMEX Intellidex Index	⊞	Q M	X M
Technology	PowerShares Dynamic Technology	PTF	0.60%	AMEX Intellidex Index	⊞	Q M	X M
Telecom	PowerShares Dynamic Telecom & Wireless	PTE	0.60%	AMEX Intellidex Index	⊞	Q M	X M

Table 12.1 *(continued)*

Category	Active Index ETF Name	Ticker	Expense Ratio	Index (or Parent Index)	Strategy Box	Sec. Select	Sec. Weight
Utilities	PowerShares Dynamic Utilities	PUI	0.60%	AMEX Intellidex Index		Q M	X M
Basic Materials	WisdomTree International Basic Materials	DBN	0.58%	WisdomTree DEFA Index		S F	F D
Communications	WisdomTree International Communications	DGG	0.58%	WisdomTree DEFA Index		S F	F D
Consumer Cyclical	WisdomTree International Consumer Cyclical	DPC	0.58%	WisdomTree DEFA Index		S F	F D
Consumer Noncyclical	WisdomTree International Consumer Noncyclical	DPN	0.58%	WisdomTree DEFA Index		S F	F D
Energy	WisdomTree International Energy	DKA	0.58%	WisdomTree DEFA Index		S F	F D
Financial	WisdomTree International Financial	DRF	0.58%	WisdomTree DEFA Index		S F	F D
Health Care	WisdomTree International Health Care	DBR	0.58%	WisdomTree DEFA Index		S F	F D
Industrial	WisdomTree International Industrial	DDI	0.58%	WisdomTree DEFA Index		S F	F D
Technology	WisdomTree International Technology	DBT	0.58%	WisdomTree DEFA Index		S F	F D
Utilities	WisdomTree International Utilities	DBU	0.58%	WisdomTree DEFA Index		S F	F D
Consumer Staples	First Trust Consumer Staples AlphaDEX	FXG	0.70%	AMEX StrataQuant		Q M	X M
Technology	First Trust Technology AlphaDEX	FXL	0.70%	AMEX StrataQuant		Q M	X M
Financials	First Trust Financials AlphaDEX	FXO	0.70%	AMEX StrataQuant		Q M	X M
Utilities	First Trust Utilities AlphaDEX	FXU	0.70%	AMEX StrataQuant		Q M	X M

(continued)

Table 12.1 *(continued)*

Category	Active Index ETF Name	Ticker	Expense Ratio	Index (or Parent Index)	Strategy Box	Sec. Select	Sec. Weight
Materials	First Trust Materials AlphaDEX	FXZ	0.70%	AMEX StrataQuant	⊞	Q M	X M
Energy	First Trust Energy AlphaDEX	FXN	0.70%	AMEX StrataQuant	⊞	Q M	X M
Health Care	First Trust Health Care AlphaDEX	FXH	0.70%	AMEX StrataQuant	⊞	Q M	X M
	Average Fee—Custom Index ETFs		**0.56%**				

REIT ETFs

Category	REIT ETF Name	Ticker	Fee	Index	Strategy Box	Sec. Select	Sec. Weight
U.S. REITS	Vanguard REIT ETF	VNQ	0.12%	MSCI U.S. REIT	⊞	P A	C F
U.S. REITS	Dow Jones Wilshire REIT ETF	RWR	0.25%	Dow Jones Wilshire REIT	⊞	P A	C F
U.S. REITS	iShares Dow Jones U.S. Real Estate	IYR	0.48%	Dow Jones U.S. Real Estate	⊞	P S	C F
U.S. REITS	First Trust S&P REIT	FRI	0.50%	S&P REIT Composite Index	⊞	P A	C F
Int'l REITS	SPDR DJ Wilshire International Real Estate	RWX	0.59%	DJ Wilshire Ex-U.S. Real Estate Sector	⊞	P S	C F
Sector U.S. REITs	iShares FTSE NAREIT Residential	REZ	0.48%	FTSE NAREIT Residential	⊞	P S	C F
Sector U.S. REITs	iShares FTSE NAREIT Industrial/Office	FIO	0.48%	FTSE NAREIT Industrial/Office	⊞	P S	C F
Sector U.S. REITs	iShares FTSE NAREIT Retail	RTL	0.48%	FTSE NAREIT Retail	⊞	P S	C F
U.S. REITS	iShares Cohen & Steers Realty Majors	ICF	0.35%	Cohen & Steers Realty Majors	⊞	S M	C C
Int'l REITS	WisdomTree International Real Estate Sector Fund	DRW	0.58%	WisdomTree Int'al Real Estate	⊞	S F	F D
	Average Fee—REIT ETFs		**0.43%**				

Appendix A is an abbreviation guide for security selection and weighting methodologies used in each index in Table 12.1. Selection and weighting methodologies are the best fit given information available to the public through the ETF companies by way of each fund's Prospectus.

Summary

Investors have plenty of choices when selecting industry sector ETFs. They come in a variety of index strategies, ranging from market indexes to custom indexes, and the ETFs cover both the U.S. market and the international markets.

Industry sectors ETFs have a variety of uses. They can fill an industry gap in a portfolio, be used to gain greater exposure to an industry sector that is expected to outperform, or be sold short to reduce exposure to an industry. REIT ETFs are particularly useful in portfolio diversification because their underlying operating structure and collateral is significantly different from common stocks and bonds.

Competing index providers divide markets in different ways. The two main industry classification methodologies are the Global Industry Classification Standard (GICS) and Industry Classification Benchmark (ICB). They have more similarities than differences. If you do invest in market industry sector funds, it is better to pick funds that use one classification methodology or the other. Selecting one standard ensures that there is no overlap of stocks in the sector funds you own.

ETFs based on custom industry indexes are available from a variety of providers. Some funds are simply equal weighted versions of S&P 500 industry sectors, others are advanced quantitatively selected indexes that have a goal of beating the passive selected market indexes. Whether the custom index ETFs outperform market index ETFs or not remains to be seen, particularly when the custom index funds have significantly higher management fees.

CHAPTER

13

Special Equity ETFs

Special equity is an interesting category of ETFs. They represent unique, a little quirky, and sometimes expressive investment strategies. These funds make a statement. Some say, "We are environmentally friendly"; others say, "We can cure the world's diseases"; and still others say, "We know a new way to beat the market."

Whatever the message of the ETF, it is sure to be different from broad-based market index ETFs. Every special equity ETF is based on a customized index, and that alone makes a statement—higher fees. The expense ratios of special equity ETFs are about three times higher than the average market index ETF. Although the costs are comparatively high to other types of ETFs, special equity ETFs are still only half the cost of comparable open-end mutual funds that have similar investment strategies.

Six examples of special equity ETFs types are provided in this chapter. There are many more not covered and those are listed in the database link at www.theetfbook.com. The special equity strategies reviewed here are theme funds, sector rotation funds, stock picker funds, leveraged funds, and short funds.

Theme funds follow indexes that focus on a particular idea, such as the environment or corporate governance. Sector rotation funds attempt to move ahead of the masses by rotating stocks around various industry sectors. Stock picker indexes are derived from the Wall Street analyst buy rating lists. Leveraged ETFs put a market index on steroids by providing two times the price movement, while short ETFs move in the opposite direction.

Some special equity ETFs are as close to active management as an ETF can become without actually being labeled an actively managed ETF (see Chapter 5). In fact, the selection methodology of a few special equity index providers can be viewed only as active stock picking. Technically, however, they are index funds because they follow a stock picker's index.

Thematic Investing

Thematic investing follows certain social, economic, corporate, demographic, or other themes that are popular in society. The opportunity comes when more people believe in the same themes and investment is driven in the direction of these companies. The shift of capital could ultimately drive superior performance in a thematic portfolio if the companies in the indexes benefit from the business.

Thematic investing is controversial. Critics see these types of strategies as marketing gimmicks to attract fast money rather than as a viable investment strategy. They say these funds harm investors by encouraging them to chase the latest fad, only to be hurt when economic reality sets in.

We all remember the Internet stock bubble of the late 1990s. Dozens of newly hatched technology and aggressive growth funds pulled in billions of investor dollars. The inevitable bubble burst took down a huge number of individual investors. At the same time, mutual fund companies quietly closed their high-octane tech funds and went on to the next trend.

Other people see thematic investing as an effective strategy because it concentrates securities in an idea that is still misunderstood and underappreciated in the marketplace. As such, those companies involved in the theme will exhibit better than average returns as more investors realize their potential and money is moved into that sector.

In my opinion, there is a little of both going on in thematic investing. There are certainly performance-chasing funds launched in the ETF industry solely for the purpose of gathering hot money, and there are also some genuinely interesting ideas that have long-term viability.

The ETF themes covered next give you an idea of the investment strategy. The themes covered are environmental and clean investing, fighting disease, socially responsible investing, following corporate actions, and tracking company dynamics.

Clean Investing

Companies that clean the environment and those that are in environmentally clean businesses are very popular themes with investors. Several ETF companies offer interesting investment opportunities around that idea. There are many indexes focused on clean water, clean energy, clean air, and companies that are environmentally friendly. All the clean index providers approach the subject differently, and it takes work to figure out which indexes are the cleanest by your standards.

The leader in clean investing has been PowerShares. The PowerShares WilderHill Clean Energy ETF (symbol: PBW) has nearly $1 billion invested in it. A priority of the WilderHill Index is to define and track the clean energy sector, specifically businesses that stand to benefit from a society's transition toward the use of cleaner energy and conservation. Stocks and sector weightings within the WilderHill Clean Energy Index are based on business policies and other qualitative issues. Companies are weighted in the index on the basis of their commitment to clean energy, their technological influence, and efforts to prevent pollution in the first place.

The Claymore/LGA Green ETF (symbol: GRN) seeks to track the Light Green Eco Index. The index is designed to identify companies with the best combination of environmental performance trends in their respective businesses. The index provider seeks a diversified group of liquid, major market stocks with representation from all economic sectors that are demonstrable environmental leaders in regard to waste minimization, clean production, pollution and spill prevention, and consistent compliance with environmental laws.

Van Eck Global recently launched the Market Vectors–Global Alternative Energy ETF (symbol: GEX). The fund tracks the Ardour Global Index. It includes the stocks of 30 publicly traded companies engaged in the entire chain of alternative energy production, including alternative energy fuels and resources (solar, wind, biofuels, water, and geothermal), environmental technologies, energy efficiency, and enabling technologies.

Investing in Fighting Disease

Health is always on the minds of investors, particularly when we are personally affected. HealthSource has created indexes based on various illnesses that are common in the United States and in

Europe. The indexes represent specific areas of health care, life science, and biotechnology.

XShare Funds is the company behind HealthShares ETFs. Each ETF invests in a distinct subsegment of the health care industry, such as the diagnosis and treatment of specific therapeutic areas (for example, cardiology, cancer, infectious disease, and so on) and the development of medical devices (for example, orthopedic repair, cardio devices, and so on). The idea behind HealthShares is to allow investors to align their investments with the technologies that may directly affect their health in the future, and also to assist health insurance providers by creating an equity hedge against payments on those illnesses.

Examples of ETFs include HealthShares Dermatology and Wound Care (symbol: HRW), which focuses on companies that deal with dermatology and the skin. The Metabolic-Endocrine Disorders ETF (symbol: HHM) and the Emerging Cancer ETF (symbol: HHJ) follow companies providing solutions in those markets. HealthShares Neuroscience ETF (symbol: HHN) invests in health care, life sciences, and biotechnology companies that have been identified as neuroscience companies. In total, HealthShares has several dozen ETFs benchmarked to various health-related issues and enterprises.

When the funds were first launched, industry analysts were quick to nickname them "disease funds." Skeptics joked that a few ETF firms were promoting their products so aggressively that you would think ETFs could cure cancer, but now it seems they can! Joking aside, the disease funds have attracted a fair amount of capital.

Some unique HealthShares ETFs may deliver better returns than a market index ETF, but certainly with increased volatility. Each fund has only 22 to 25 holdings of equal weight. The risk of owning only 25 companies in the same industry is clearly higher than that of owning a broad market ETF.

Socially Responsible ETFs

Some investors have a moral dilemma with the products some companies make or the businesses they are in. Rather than selecting companies to invest in, socially responsible indexes attempt to gain broadbased equity exposure while excluding companies that do not pass certain social criteria tests. Examples of screens include eliminating companies in the tobacco, alcoholic beverages, and pornography industries. In addition, socially responsible screens may extend into labor practices, human rights, and even animal rights.

Investors in socially screened ETFs should be aware of what industries are being screened out of an index. You may not agree with what is being called socially irresponsible. For example, most indexes screen out weapons manufacturers and defense companies. As a retired U.S. Marine Corps officer, I have an objection to the providers of those indexes stating that companies in the business of protecting our families, our freedom, and our way of life are socially unacceptable.

Different index providers have different views as to what they believe is socially responsible, and those views are constantly changing. For more information on social indexes, including a list of filters used by each provider, visit www.socialinvest.org. The mutual fund screening tool is particularly helpful.

The iShares KLD Select Social ETF (symbol: KLD) follows the KLD Select Social Index. The index methodology starts with the Russell 1000, excluding tobacco stocks. KLD then evaluates the social and environmental performance of companies in the universe by analyzing community relations, diversity, employee relations, human rights, product quality and safety, the environment, and corporate governance. Companies are scored based on these factors. An optimization process is used to determine index holdings and weights. Companies with high scores in the index have higher weights and companies with low scores have lower weights.

The iShares KLD 400 Social ETF (symbol: DSI) follows the Domini 400 Social index. The index methodology starts with the S&P 500 as its core universe and adds to it 100 non-S&P companies chosen for sector diversification and market capitalization. An additional 50 companies are added that KLD believes exhibit exemplary social and environmental records. Companies involved in alcohol, tobacco, firearms, gambling, and nuclear power are excluded. Military contractors are also excluded. Companies that do not meet KLD's financial screens (market capitalization, earnings, liquidity, stock price, and debt-to-equity ratio) are also ineligible for inclusion.

Corporate Action ETFs

Corporate actions are the decisions made by the board of directors that affect the structure of a company. One company might go public in an initial public offering (IPO) and at the same time two other companies are merging and another is going private in a buyout. The dynamics of corporate actions make for some interesting indexes and ETFs.

The First Trust IPOX-100 Index Fund (FPX) has the objective to replicate as closely as possible, before fees and expenses, the price and yield of the U.S. IPOX-100 Index. The index is a rules-based, value-weighted index measuring the average performance of U.S. IPOs during the first 1,000 trading days. Index constituents are selected on the basis of proprietary quantitative screens. The index is capitalization weighted, with a cap of 10 percent on any issue. Google would have dominated that index without the constraint.

The Claymore/Clear Spin-Off ETF (symbol: SCD) seeks to invest in companies with potentially superior risk and return profiles as determined by Clear. The index is designed to actively represent the stock of a group of companies that have recently been spun off from larger corporations and have the opportunity to better focus on their core market.

PowerShares Buyback Achievers (symbol: PKW) follows the Share Buyback Achievers Index. The index is designed to track the performance of companies that are incorporated in the United States, trade on a U.S. exchange, and must have repurchased at least 5 percent or more of its outstanding shares for the trailing 12 months. The portfolio is rebalanced quarterly and reconstituted annually.

In addition, corporate insiders are constantly buying and selling shares of their company's stock and exercising stock options before stock options expire. Their buying and selling activity is tracked by index providers who use it to create custom indexes that are the basis of ETFs.

The Claymore/Sabrient Insider ETF (symbol: NFO) follows that Sabrient Insider Sentiment Index. The objective of the index is to actively represent a group of stocks that reflect favorable corporate insider buying trends (determined through the public filings of such corporate insiders) or Wall Street analyst earnings estimate increases.

Corporate Dynamics ETFs

IndexIQ Exchange-Traded Funds, Inc. has a different twist on corporate watchdogging. The new ETF company is launching 20 IndexIQ

ETFs that track indexes based on intangible measures like "Most In-novation," "Most Elite Workforces," "Customer Loyalty Leaders," "Most Productive," and "Best Operating Companies." IndexIQ believes that these attributes are too often overlooked in equity analysis, but represent many of the strongest drivers of corporate growth and equity returns.

According to the SEC filing, a "powerful" company is a company that demonstrates favorable results across multiple metrics, such as sales and margin, related to achieving significant economies of scale and establishing barriers to entry that are not eliminated by competition over time. The IndexIQ Most Powerful Companies Index is typically composed of more than 400 companies that have market capitalizations of at least $1.5 billion.

IndexIQ, Inc. and S&P will jointly manage IndexIQ indexes and BNY will do the actual day-to-day management of the funds. IndexIQ Exchange-Traded Funds is a subsidiary of XShares Group, LLC, which is the same company that launched HealthShares ETFs in early 2007.

Actively Managed Indexes

Actively managed indexing may sound like an oxymoron to a traditional market index investor. How can an index be both passive and actively managed? The second group of special equity funds clearly illustrates that custom indexes are anything but passive. Analyst stock picking indexes and sector rotation indexes employ the same methods used by many active managers in open-end mutual funds.

Stock Analyst ETFs

Wall Street employs thousands of securities analysts who attempt to select superior investments through fundamental and technical analysis. So, why shouldn't they have their own indexes and ETFs that track them? They do now.

Claymore has teamed up with Best Investors Research (BIR) to offer a series of ETFs based on Wall Street analyst research. BIR compiles data from five leading independent research firms and creates an overall master list. Each research company ranks its stocks on a 10-point scale on multiple fundamental factors including valuation, leverage, earnings growth, and price momentum.

The BIR research team produces the master list by blending the individual rankings of each independent research company to establish a composite score. Several ETFs are formed from the master list. The Claymore/BIR Leaders 50 (symbol: BST) follows the BIR Leaders 50 index, which represent the stocks with the highest rankings. The Claymore/BIR Leaders Mid Cap Value (symbol: BMV) and the Claymore/BIR Leaders Small Cap Core (symbol: BES) follow BIR subsectors that represent those areas on the master list.

The First Trust Value Line Equity Allocation ETF (symbol: FVI) seeks investment results that correspond generally to the price and yield the Value Line Equity Allocation Index. The index is designed to objectively identify and select those stocks that appear to have the greatest potential for capital appreciation from the universe of stocks. Value Line gives a "Timeliness," "Safety" or "Technical" ranking of 1 or 2, using the Value Line ranking systems.

Stocks in the database are separated by size and style. The stocks in each style are ranked, using multiple factors including price-to-cash flow, price-to-book, return on assets, and price appreciation. The 25 highest ranked stocks in each of the six styles are selected and equally weighted within each classification. The Value Line Equity Allocation Index is rebalanced semiannually each February and August through the reapplication of the stock selection process.

The PowerShares DWA Technical Leaders Portfolio (symbol: PDP) is based on the Dorsey Wright Technical Leaders Index. The index includes approximately 100 U.S.-listed companies that have demonstrated above-average relative price strength. Dorsey Wright takes into account the performance of each of the 3,000 largest U.S.-listed companies as compared to a broad market index, as well as industry sectors and subsectors. The index is reconstituted and rebalanced quarterly, using the same methodology described earlier.

Undiscovered stocks have strong appeal with some very savvy investors, as my years in the brokerage business will attest. The fewer analysts following a company, the more reason to get excited about it.

The Claymore/Sabrient Stealth ETF (symbol: STH) follows the Sabrient Stealth Index. It is a different twist because the index provider is looking for companies that are not heavily followed by analysts. The objective of the index is to actively represent a group of stocks that are flying under the radar screen of Wall Street's analysts, yet have displayed robust growth characteristics that give them the potential to outperform the Russell 2000 index.

Sector Rotation ETFs

Sector rotation strategies are in many ways the opposite of thematic investing. In contrast to thematic investing, where investors hold narrow slices of the market and wait for long-term gains, sector rotation ETFs frequently shift money from one industry sector to another.

Sector rotation index providers use different methods to shift money from one industry to another. Some providers use a top-down economic model to predict future industry gainers while others rely on price momentum and technical analysis. A brief explanation of those active management strategies is provided in Chapter 19.

Claymore Zacks Sector Rotation (symbol: XRO) follows the Zacks Sector Rotation Index. Zacks uses a quantitative formula to overweight industry sectors they believe will deliver potentially superior returns profiles to the S&P 500 index.

Zacks uses a multifactor model. First, they use a top-down macroeconomic method to isolate where the economy is in the business cycle. Then they employ a bottom-up approach to decide sector weighting based on relative value, insider trading, price momentum, earnings growth, earnings estimate revision, and earnings surprise. Exposure for any one sector may range from 0 percent to a maximum of 45 percent of the index. No individual stock may consist of more than 5 percent of the total index. The index is adjusted quarterly.

PowerShares ValueLine Industry Rotation ETF (symbol: PYH) follows the ValueLine Industry Rotation Index. The index comprises 75 stocks chosen on the basis of both their ValueLine Timeliness rank and their industry Timeliness rank. ValueLine selects the highest ranked stock for Timeliness from each of the 50 highest rated industries, as well as the second highest Timeliness ranked stock from each of the 25 highest rated industries. The index is reconstituted and rebalanced quarterly.

Leveraged and Short ETFs

The third category of special equity covers leveraged and short investing. Leveraged ETFs are designed to return twice the return of a market index price and a daily basis (not including dividends), albeit with twice the daily volatility of the index. Short (or inverse)

ETFs are designed to return the inverse (opposite) of the market price return. Leveraged short ETFs return double the opposite of an index price return as measured daily.

An important factor when judging these funds is their daily objective because doubling the volatility on a daily basis results in lower compounded returns over the long term. As such, do not expect a fund that uses 100 percent leverage to return double the price gain over a one-year period. It cannot theoretically happen when there is volatility in the day-to-day numbers.

Daily price volatility affects annual returns. The more volatility a fund has over a period, the lower the long-term compounded return for the period. Since leveraged funds have twice the volatility of a nonleveraged fund, the expected long-term return is lower than double the price return, minus fees. The ProShares prospectus for the Ultra ProShares ETFs dated June 19, 2006, heeds this warning in its leveraged funds:

> Over time, the cumulative percentage increase or decrease in the net asset value of the Fund may diverge significantly from the cumulative percentage increase or decrease in the multiple of the return of the Underlying Index due to the compounding effect of losses and gains on the returns of the Fund. For periods greater than one day, investors should not expect the return of the Fund to be twice the return of the underlying index. In addition, in trendless or flat markets, it is expected that the Fund will underperform the compounded return of twice its benchmark index.

At the end of 2006, there were only a handful of leveraged ETFs and no inverse ETFs. One year later, there are 174 leveraged and inverse ETFs on either the market or in SEC registration from ProShares and Rydex alone. The Rydex funds were in registration as of this writing.

There are high expense ratios associated with leverage and inverse ETFs. ProShares charges 0.95 percent annually in expenses, making those funds some of the costliest in the ETF marketplace. The Rydex ETF series is expected to have lower expenses, although the expenses will likely still be high compared to other ETF categories.

How leveraged ETFs work is relatively simple. First, there is an index as a reference point, such as the S&P 500. The fund owns shares of the index such as ExxonMobil, Microsoft, General Electric, and so on. To double the daily return, leveraged ETFs use a variety of derivatives such as futures contracts and index swaps. Those securities require little cash output. Often the fund manager will borrow against stock in the fund to finance the derivative transactions. The derivatives leverage-up the fund and give it twice as much market exposure than the individual stocks in the portfolio.

The price index return of an index does not include dividends. For all practical purposes, the dividend is given up to pay for the leverage and fees, plus some. That is another reason to expect leveraged funds to underperform twice an index total return in the long term.

Leveraged ETFs are available for popular market index and industry sectors. Examples of market-leveraged funds include the Ultra S&P 500 ETF (symbol: SSO), leveraged to the S&P 500 index, and the Ultra QQQ ETF (symbol: QLD), leveraged to NASDAQ-100 index.

There are nearly a dozen leveraged ProShares ETFs benchmarked to Dow Jones U.S. sector industry indexes. Examples include the Ultra Basic Materials ETF (symbol: UYM) and Ultra Technology ETF (symbol: ROM), both expected to return double the price performance of their respective Dow Jones sector indexes on a daily basis, minus fees.

Short ETFs move in the opposite direction of the index price they track. For example, the Short S&P 500 ETF (symbol: SH) seeks investment results that corresponds to the inverse (opposite) performance of the S&P 500 price index on a daily basis. The Short QQQ ProShares seeks investment results that correspond to the inverse performance of the NASDAQ-100 Price Index.

Leveraged short ETFs are one of the most esoteric and risky funds in the ETF universe. They basically act the same as a short ETF but with twice the punch. If the price of the S&P 500 index is down by 1 percent in one day, then the ProShares UltraShort S&P 500 ETF (symbol: SDS) with 200 percent leverage should go up by 2 percent, and vice versa. Industries can also be double short. ProShares has leveraged short industry ETFs that track all the basic Dow Jones sectors.

Buying a leveraged short ETF allows you to hedge the market risk, otherwise known as beta. If you own an industry ETF but are bearish on the stock market overall, buying a leveraged short ETF on a market index will hedge the market risk inherent in the industry ETF you own, and make a profit for your portfolio from the falling market. Technically speaking, you are net short beta in the portfolio. The trade sounds great in theory, but it can really do damage if you are wrong. Your portfolio will be hit twice if your industry ETF underperforms while the stock market heads higher.

Leveraged and short investments of any type are not for novices. Investors should study the mechanics of these leveraged and short ETFs thoroughly before investing. Make sure you understand how an ETF is expected to react under different market scenarios both in the short term and long term.

Hedging with ETFs

Hedge funds are designed to produce investment profits regardless of whether the stock market is going up or down, thus the name *hedge*. That is not always the case anymore. Hedge funds cover a wide range of investment strategies, some of which are much riskier than the stock market. Money can be made or lost very fast.

The number of hedge funds has proliferated in recent years, reaching a crescendo in 2006 with nearly $1 trillion invested in approximately 10,000 funds. New funds open and old funds sink every year. It is a high stakes, rapid turnover business.

Regardless of how many funds come to the market, they still are closed to all except people with a lot to invest. You need a lot of money to look at hedge funds because the minimums are very high, and it takes money to buy good advice and diversify properly. In addition, most funds have a lock-up period that does not allow any withdrawal of funds for many years.

Hedge funds may be fine for those with a bankroll, but ETFs may soon be the poor man's hedge fund. Right now, ETFs give you the building blocks to construct your own simple hedging strategies. But I believe some day there will be sophisticated hedge fund ETFs that anyone can purchase.

Today, there is one hedge fund of sorts. In May 2007, Barclays Global Investors (BGI) expanded its iPath family of exchange-traded notes (ETNs) with the launch of the iPath CBOE S&P 500 BuyWrite Index ETN (symbol: BWV). The new product tracks the CBOE S&P 500 BuyWrite Index.

The CBOE BuyWrite Index was launched in 2002 and represents the performance of a buy-write investment strategy as applied to the S&P 500. In a buy-write strategy, an investor buys stocks and then writes covered call options on them. The funds make money from the premiums on the calls, which in most cases, is paid out on a quarterly basis. The strategy does best in sideways markets and offers some protection against down markets, however it lags considerably when the markets are rallying.

Launching a sophisticated hedge fund in ETF format may be a ways off. However, today firms are replicating hedge fund returns with ETFs by employing computer models that combine assets in a way that mimic hedge fund returns. Goldman Sachs, Merrill Lynch, and JPMorgan are all working in the space, and IndexIQ is hoping to launch a synthetic hedge fund-of-funds that will use portfolios of ETFs to track the performance of the ten investable Tremont Hedge Fund subindexes. The group plans to offer low-cost mutual funds and separately managed accounts that will track each of the ten indexes.

Hedge funds may not be your interest. But here are a couple of ways you can use ETFs today to hedge events in your life.

Are you into numismatics and have collected rare gold coins as an investment? Historically, the scarcity of the coins boosted their value by a far greater amount than the value of the gold itself. Using ETFs, you can short the value of the gold in the coins and retain the upside potential of the rarity of the coins themselves.

StreetTRACKS Gold Shares (symbol: GLD) and iShares COMEX Gold Trust (symbol: IAU) seeks to reflect the price of gold and gold bullion respectively, minus the expenses of operations. The ETFs are designed for investors who want a cost-effective and convenient way to invest in gold or short the gold market. See Chapter 15 for more details.

Thinking of going to Europe this summer but afraid that the dollar may sink so low that it torpedoes your vacation? Invest in the Euro Currency Trust (symbol: FXE) that allows you to buy Euros today that might cost more by July. There is also the tax-efficient iPath EUR/USD (symbol: ERO). Both investments pay money market interest. See Chapter 15 for more details on these currency investments.

Special Equity ETFs List

Table 13.1 offers a partial list of Special Equity ETFs available on U.S. exchanges. There are many funds to choose from, and more are being introduced each week. The list is a good starting point to finding an ETF that might pique your interest. For a complete list of Special Equity ETFs, including the Index Strategy Box database, visit www.theetfbook.com and www.etfguide.com.

Table 13.1 is divided into three sections. The first section includes thematic ETFs; the second list includes stock picker, sector rotation, and buy-write funds; and the third list includes leveraged and short ETFs. All the funds in this chapter follow a custom index.

Appendix A is an abbreviation guide for security selection and weighting methodologies used in each index in Table 13.1. Selection and weighting methodologies are the best fit given information available to the public through the ETF companies by way of each fund's Prospectus.

Table 13.1   Special Equity ETFs

Thematic ETFs

Theme	ETF Name	Ticker	Expense Ratio	Index	Strategy Box	Sec. Select	Sec. Weight
Disease	HealthShares Autoimmune-Inflammation	HHA	0.75%	HealthShares Autoimmune-Inflammation	▦	S T	X F
Disease	HealthShares Cancer	HHK	0.75%	HealthShares Cancer	▦	S T	X F
Disease	HealthShares Cardio Devices	HHE	0.75%	HealthShares Cardio Devices	▦	S T	X F
Disease	HealthShares Cardiology	HRD	0.75%	HealthShares Cardiology	▦	S T	X F
Disease	HealthShares Diagnostics	HHD	0.75%	HealthShares Diagnostics	▦	S T	X F
Disease	HealthShares Emerging Cancer	HHJ	0.75%	HealthShares Emerging Cancer	▦	S T	X F
Disease	HealthShares GI/Gender Health	HHU	0.75%	HealthShares GI/Gender Health	▦	S T	X F
Disease	HealthShares Infectious Disease	HHG	0.75%	HealthShares Infectious Disease	▦	S T	X F
Disease	HealthShares Metabolic-Endocrine Disorders	HHM	0.75%	HealthShares Metabolic-Endocrine Disorders	▦	S T	X F
Disease	HealthShares Neuroscience	HHN	0.75%	HealthShares Neuroscience	▦	S T	X F

Table 13.1 *(continued)*

Theme	ETF Name	Ticker	Expense Ratio	Index	Strategy Box	Sec. Select	Sec. Weight
Disease	HealthShares Ophthalmology	HHZ	0.75%	HealthShares Ophthalmology		S T	X F
Disease	HealthShares Respiratory/Pulmonary	HHR	0.75%	HealthShares Respiratory/Pulmonary		S T	X F
Social Issues	iShares KLD Select Social Index	KLD	0.50%	KLD Select Social		S S	F S
Social Issues	iShares KLD 400 Social Index	DSI	0.50%	Domini 400 Social		S S	F S
Environmental	Claymore LGA Green	GRN	0.60%	Light Green Advisors Eco Index		Q Q	C F
Environmental	Global Alternative Energy ETF	GEX	0.65%	Ardour Global Index		S T	C F
Environmental	Claymore S&P Global Water	CGW	0.65%	S&P Global Water Index		S T	C C
Environmental	PowerShares Water Resources	PHO	0.60%	Palisades Water Index		S T	C F
Environmental	PowerShares WilderHill Clean Energy	PBW	0.60%	WilderHill Clean Energy Index		S T	C C
Environmental	PowerShares WilderHill Progressive Energy	PUW	0.60%	WilderHill Progressive Energy Index		S T	X M
Environmental	PowerShares Cleantech	PZD	0.60%	Cleantech Index		S T	X E
Corporate Dynamics	IndexIQ Best Corporate Governance All Cap	NA	NA	IndexIQ Best Corporate Governance		Q M	F Q
Corporate Dynamics	IndexIQ Best Operating Companies All Cap	NA	NA	IndexIQ Best Operating Companies		Q M	F Q
Corporate Dynamics	IndexIQ Competitive Momentum Leaders All Cap	NA	NA	IndexIQ Competitive Momentum Leaders		Q M	F Q
Corporate Dynamics	IndexIQ Customer Loyalty Leaders All Cap	NA	NA	IndexIQ Customer Loyalty Leaders		Q M	F Q
Corporate Dynamics	IndexIQ Fastest Growing Companies All Cap	NA	NA	IndexIQ Fastest Growing Companies		Q M	F Q
Corporate Dynamics	IndexIQ Most Elite Workforces All Cap	NA	NA	IndexIQ Most Elite Workforces		Q M	F Q
Corporate Dynamics	IndexIQ Most Innovative Companies All Cap	NA	NA	IndexIQ Most Innovative Companies		Q M	F Q

(continued)

Table 13.1   *(continued)*

Theme	ETF Name	Ticker	Expense Ratio	Index	Strategy Box	Sec. Select	Sec. Weight
Corporate Dynamics	IndexIQ Most Powerful Companies	NA	NA	IndexIQ Most Powerful Companies	⊞	Q M	F Q
Corporate Dynamics	IndexIQ Most Productive Companies All Cap	NA	NA	IndexIQ Most Productive Companies	⊞	Q M	F Q
Corporate Dynamics	IndexIQ Most Sustainable Companies All Cap	NA	NA	IndexIQ Most Sustainable Companies	⊞	Q M	F Q
Corporate Action	PowerShares Buyback Achievers	PKW	0.70%	Share BuyBack Achievers Index	⊞	S C	C C
Corporate Action	Claymore Clear Spin-Off	CSD	0.60%	Clear Spin-off Index	⊞	Q M	C C
Corporate Action	First Trust IPOX100 Index Fund	FPX	0.60%	U.S. IPOX-100 Index	⊞	Q M	C C
Insider Trading	Claymore Sabrient Insider	NFO	0.60%	Sabrient Insider Sentiment Index	⊞	S C	X E
Private Equity	PowerShares Listed Private Equity	PSP	0.70%	Red Rocks Capital Listed Private Equity	⊞	S C	C C
Patent Protected	Claymore Ocean/Tomo Patent	OTP	0.60%	Ocean Tomo 300 Patent Index	⊞	F T	C F
Patent Protected	Claymore/Ocean Tomo Growth Index	OTR	0.60%	Ocean Tomo 300 Patent Growth Index	⊞	F T	C F
Nano Technology	PowerShares LUX Nanotech	PXN	0.60%	Lux Nanotech Index	⊞	F T	C C
	Average Fee		**0.67%**				

Stock Picker, Sector Rotation, and Buy-Write Funds

Strategy	ETF Name	Ticker	Expense Ratio	Index	Strategy Box	Sec. Select	Sec. Weight
Analyst Picks	Claymore/BIR Leaders 50	BST	0.60%	BIR Leaders 50	⊞	Q M	X M
Analyst Picks	Claymore/BIR Leaders Mid Cap Value	BMV	0.60%	BIR Leaders Mid Cap Value	⊞	Q M	X M
Analyst Picks	Claymore/BIR Leaders Small Cap Core	BES	0.60%	BIR Leader Small Cap Core	⊞	Q M	X M

Table 13.1 (continued)

Strategy	ETF Name	Ticker	Expense Ratio	Index	Strategy Box	Sec. Select	Sec. Weight
Analyst Neglect	Claymore Sabrient Stealth	STH	0.60%	Sabrient Stealth Index		Q M	X M
Sector Rotation	Claymore Zacks Sector Rotation	XRO	0.60%	Zacks Sector Rotation Index		P S	F F
Sector Rotation	PowerShares ValueLine Industry Rotation	PYH	0.65%	ValueLine Industry Rotation Index		Q M	X E
Sector Rotation	First Trust ValueLine Equity Allocation	FVI	0.70%	ValueLine Equity Allocation Index		Q M	X E
Buy-Write	iPath CBOE S&P 500 Buy-Write ETN	BWV	0.75%	CBOE S&P 500 Buy-Write		P S	X N
	Average Fee		**0.68%**				

Leveraged, Short, and Short Leveraged ETFs

Strategy	ETF Name	Ticker	Expense Ratio	Index	Strategy Box	Sec. Select	Sec. Weight
Leveraged	Ultra Dow 30	DDM	0.95%	Dow Jones Industrial Average (200%)		P S	X L
Leveraged	Ultra Russell 1000 Growth	UKF	0.95%	Russell 1000 Growth (+ 200%)		P S	X L
Leveraged	Ultra Russell 1000 Value	UVG	0.95%	Russell 1000 Value (+ 200%)		P S	X L
Leveraged	Ultra Russell 2000	UWM	0.95%	Russell 2000 (+ 200%)		P S	X L
Leveraged	Ultra Russell 2000 Growth	UKK	0.95%	Russell 2000 Growth (+ 200%)		P S	X L
Leveraged	Ultra Russell 2000 Value	UVT	0.95%	Russell 2000 Value (+ 200%)		P S	X L
Leveraged	Ultra Russell Mid Cap Growth	UKW	0.95%	Russell Mid Cap Growth (+ 200%)		P S	X L
Leveraged	Ultra Russell Mid Cap Value	UVU	0.95%	Russell Mid Cap Value (+ 200%)		P S	X L
Leveraged	Ultra S&P 500	SSO	0.95%	S&P 500 (+ 200%)		P S	X L
Leveraged	Ultra Small Cap 600	SAA	0.95%	S&P Small Cap 600 (+ 200%)		P S	X L
Leveraged	Ultra Mid Cap 400	MVV	0.95%	S&P Mid Cap (+ 200%)		P S	X L
Leveraged	Ultra QQQ	QLD	0.95%	NASDAQ-100 (+ 200%)		S E	X L
Leveraged	Ultra Basic Materials	UYM	0.95%	Dow Jones Basic Materials (+ 200%)		P S	X L

(continued)

Table 13.1   *(continued)*

Strategy	ETF Name	Ticker	Expense Ratio	Index	Strategy Box	Sec. Select	Sec. Weight
Leveraged	Ultra Consumer Goods	UGE	0.95%	Dow Jones Consumer Goods (+ 200%)		P S	X L
Leveraged	Ultra Consumer Services	UCC	0.95%	Dow Jones Consumer Services (+ 200%)		P S	X L
Leveraged	Ultra Financials	UYG	0.95%	Dow Jones Financials (+ 200%)		P S	X L
Leveraged	Ultra Health Care	RXL	0.95%	Dow Jones Health Care (+ 200%)		P S	X L
Leveraged	Ultra Industrials	UXI	0.95%	Dow Jones Industrials (+ 200%)		P S	X L
Leveraged	Ultra Oil & Gas	DIG	0.95%	Dow Jones Oil & Gas (+ 200%)		P S	X L
Leveraged	Ultra Real Estate	URE	0.95%	Dow Jones Real Estate (+ 200%)		P S	X L
Leveraged	Ultra Semiconductors	USD	0.95%	Dow Jones Semiconductors (+ 200%)		P S	X L
Leveraged	Ultra Technology	ROM	0.95%	Dow Jones Technology (+ 200%)		P S	X L
Leveraged	Ultra Utilities	UPW	0.95%	Dow Jones Utilities (+ 200%)		P S	X L
Short	Short Dow 30	DOG	0.95%	Dow Jones Industrial Average (−100%)		P S	X S
Short	Short Mid Cap 400	MYY	0.95%	S&P Mid Cap 400 (−100%)		P S	X S
Short	Short QQQ	PSQ	0.95%	NASDAQ 100 (−100%)		S E	X S
Short	Short Russell 2000	RWM	0.95%	Russell 2000 (−100%)		P S	X S
Short	Short S&P 500	SH	0.95%	S&P 500 (−100%)		P S	X S
Short	Short Small Cap 600	SBB	0.95%	S&P Small Cap 600 (−100%)		P S	X S
Short Leveraged	UltraShort Russell 1000 Growth	SFK	0.95%	Russell 1000 Growth (−200%)		P S	X S
Short Leveraged	UltraShort Russell 1000 Value	SJF	0.95%	Russell 1000 Value (−200%)		P S	X S
Short Leveraged	UltraShort Russell 2000	TWM	0.95%	Russell 2000 (−200%)		P S	X S
Short Leveraged	UltraShort Russell 2000 Growth	SKK	0.95%	Russell 2000 Growth (−200%)		P S	X S

Table 13.1 *(continued)*

Strategy	ETF Name	Ticker	Expense Ratio	Index	Strategy Box	Sec. Select	Sec. Weight
Short Leveraged	UltraShort Russell 2000 Value	SJH	0.95%	Russell 2000 Value (−200%)	▦	P S	X S
Short Leveraged	UltraShort Russell Mid Cap Growth	SDK	0.95%	Russell Mid Cap Growth (−200%)	▦	P S	X S
Short Leveraged	UltraShort Russell Mid Cap Value	SJL	0.95%	Russell Mid Cap Value (−200%)	▦	P S	X S
Short Leveraged	UltraShort S&P 500	SDS	0.95%	S&P 500 (−200%)	▦	P S	X S
Short Leveraged	UltraShort Small Cap 600	SDD	0.95%	S&P Small Cap 600 (−200%)	▦	P S	X S
Short Leveraged	UltraShort Dow 30 ETF	DXD	0.95%	Dow Jones Industrial Average (−200%)	▦	P S	X S
Short Leveraged	UltraShort Mid Cap 400	MZZ	0.95%	S&P Mid Cap 400 (−200%)	▦	P S	X S
Short Leveraged	UltraShort QQQ	QID	0.95%	NASDAQ-100 (−200%)	▦	S E	X S
Short Leveraged	UltraShort Basic Materials	SMN	0.95%	Dow Jones Short Basic Materials (−200%)	▦	P S	X S
Short Leveraged	UltraShort Consumer Goods	SZK	0.95%	Dow Jones Short Consumer Goods (−200%)	▦	P S	X S
Short Leveraged	UltraShort Consumer Services	SCC	0.95%	Dow Jones Short Consumer Services (−200%)	▦	P S	X S
Short Leveraged	UltraShort Financials	SKF	0.95%	Dow Jones Short Financials (−200%)	▦	P S	X S
Short Leveraged	UltraShort Health Care	RXD	0.95%	Dow Jones Short Health Care (−200%)	▦	P S	X S
Short Leveraged	UltraShort Industrials	SIJ	0.95%	Dow Jones Short Industrials (−200%)	▦	P S	X S
Short Leveraged	UltraShort Oil & Gas	DUG	0.95%	Dow Jones Short Oil & Gas (−200%)	▦	P S	X S
Short Leveraged	UltraShort Real Estate	SRS	0.95%	Dow Jones Short Real Estate (−200%)	▦	P S	X S
Short Leveraged	UltraShort Semiconductors	SSG	0.95%	Dow Jones Short Semiconductors (−200%)	▦	P S	X S
Short Leveraged	UltraShort Technology	REW	0.95%	Dow Jones Short Technology (−200%)	▦	P S	X S
Short Leveraged	UltraShort Utilities	SDP	0.95%	Dow Jones Short Utilities (−200%)	▦	P S	X S
	Average Fee		**0.95%**				

Summary

Special equity ETFs focus on interesting and unusual themes that might have real potential in the future. Generally, theme investing is a long-term strategy because it can take years for the concept to materialize. An ETF theme may be environmental, social, or based on corporate actions. Whatever the theme of an ETF, it will be costly following that theme investing in a market index ETF.

ETFs are sliding into active management through sector rotation and analyst stock picking. Industry sector rotation indexes are designed to move money around various industry sectors in hopes of placing money in profitable ones while avoiding less profitable ones. Analyst stock pick indexes are very similar to actively managed strategies used by actively managed open-end mutual funds.

Leveraged and short ETFs give investors an opportunity to profit more from market movements in either direction. Leveraged ETFs provide nearly twice the daily price return of various market indexes while short ETFs move in the opposite direction. A leveraged short ETF moves at twice the speed of short funds that are not leveraged.

Public hedge funds are just starting to be talked about in the ETF industry. Several fund-of-funds are on the drawing board to emulate hedge fund strategies. Today, hedging with ETFs is done by individual investors trying to enhance returns or protect assets they believe may fall in value.

CHAPTER

14

Fixed Income ETFs

Thus far in Part III, all of the chapters have addressed investing in the equity markets. This chapter addresses a larger part of the financial markets—fixed income.

Fixed income plays a crucial role in most investors' portfolio because the asset class offers stability and income. On average, individual investors place more than 50 percent of their long-term savings in fixed income securities. That means proper fixed income ETF analysis and selection plays an important role in portfolio management.

By dollar weight, the nearly $30 trillion public U.S. fixed income market is far greater in size than the public U.S equity market. But that is not evident from the number of fixed income ETFs available to investors. Less than 5 percent of the U.S. ETF issues track fixed income indexes. Also, of the funds that are available, there is a lot of overlap in indexes.

The lack of fixed income ETFs is due to the greater difficulties managing fixed income portfolios using an ETF structure. The underlying bonds in a fund must have adequate liquidity so that authorized participants (AP) can easily trade these securities (see Chapter 2). It would not be possible for the APs to create complete creation baskets that include all of the individual securities in the indexes without adequate liquidity, including an active derivatives market. The costs to buy and sell securities would be too large, and that would be reflected in ETF spreads.

Fortunately, bond issuers are starting to focus on the ETF market as a new area of distribution. As such, new liquid fixed income indexes and products are slowly being introduced into the marketplace. The success of those new products will entice more ETF providers to develop fixed income funds, which will create a dynamic marketplace.

Bond Market Structure

The U.S. fixed income market is composed of many types of securities. They include, but are not limited to, Treasury issues, government agency issues, mortgages, corporate bonds, municipal bonds, asset-backed securities, and inflation protected securities.

Bonds are generally categorized by type, maturity, and credit rating. The Morningstar Fixed Income Style Box in Figure 14.1 illustrates how maturity and creditworthiness are represented in their mutual fund research. Their methods are typical of most bond categorization techniques.

Bond indexes divide maturities into three ranges. Short-term indexes hold bonds that have an average maturity of three years or less, intermediate-term indexes hold bonds with an average maturity of four to nine years, and long-term indexes hold bonds that have an average maturity of 10 years or longer. If an index has an average maturity of five years, it does not mean all bonds in the fund mature in five years. The bonds could mature from one year through 10 years or any combination thereof. Read the prospectus of the ETF you are interested in so you understand how the index is designed.

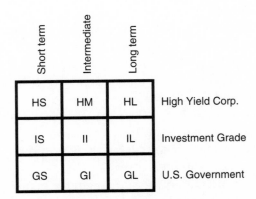

Figure 14.1 Morningstar Fixed Income Style Box

Bond index average duration is an important characteristic. Duration is a measure of interest rate risk. If interest rates move higher, ETFs benchmarked to indexes with longer durations will go down more in value than ETFs benchmarked to indexes that have shorter durations. In the long term, since there is more risk in long-duration bonds, you should expect indexes with long durations to generate a higher total return than indexes with a short duration.

The credit risk of a bond index is more complex than its interest rate risk. Credit risk is a reflection of the financial strength of the issuer. The higher the credit risk, the greater the chance of a default, and the higher the interest rate needs to be to compensate for that risk. The credit risk of U.S. government and government agencies is very low. Corporate bonds that are investment grade are higher, and at the top of the risk level are high yield junk bonds. These funds invest in below-investment grade debt because they have a higher probability of running into trouble.

Figure 14.2 illustrates the risk and return tradeoffs in bond indexes. As the duration of indexes increases and as credit quality decreases, the expected long-term return of a bond index increases to compensate for those extra risks.

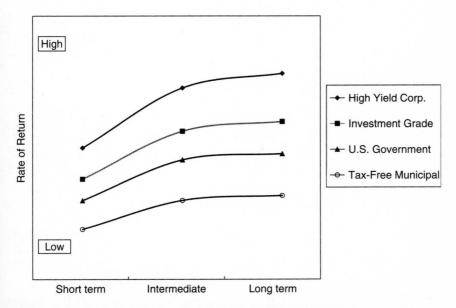

Figure 14.2 Term Risk, Credit Risk, and Expected Return

Fixed Income Indexes

There are several providers of indexes used in fixed income ETFs. A major player in the ETF market is Lehman Brothers. The company constructs hundreds of fixed-income indexes covering all the global bond markets. A growing number of those indexes are used as the basis for ETFs.

The basic structure of the U.S. investment grade market index is as follows:

1. Government/Credit Markets
   A. Government Bills, Notes, and Bonds
      i. Treasury, including inflation-protected securities
      ii. Agency (FNMA and FHLMC bonds, and so on)
   B. Corporate (investment grade, BBB, or better)
      i. Industrial
      ii. Finance
      iii. Utility
      iv. Yankee bonds (foreign bonds trading in U.S. dollars)
2. Mortgage Market
   A. Government National Mortgage Association (GNMA)
   B. Federal Home Loan Mortgage Corporation (FHLMC)
   C. Federal National Mortgage Association (FNMA)
3. Asset-Backed Securities
   A. Credit card receivables
   B. Auto loans
   C. Bank loans
   D. Home equity loans

Lehman requires a bond to have an issue size of at least $100 million before it is used in an index. But that may not be big enough for ETF management. ETF managers typically sample the largest and most liquid bonds from the indexes.

Sampling the Fixed Income Markets

Most bond indexes were not created to be used as the benchmark for an ETF portfolio. They were created as a measure of the fixed income marketplace to be used by economists, analysts, and as a benchmark to measure active bond management strategies against.

It is difficult for ETF companies to track many indexes that were created for other reasons. Many bonds in the traditional indexes are not available on the market, and the turnover of bonds in the indexes is high because of maturing bonds and redemptions from call options. The Lehman Aggregate Bond Index tracks over 6,000 fixed income securities, and a large portion of them do not trade on a regular basis. The index has on average more than 30 percent turnover per year.

Since a full replication of traditional bond market indexes such as the Lehman Aggregate Bond Index is not possible, ETF managers resort to a sampling technique. The fund managers attempt to create portfolios of liquid securities that trade frequently and replicate the risk and return characteristics of the bond index.

Sampling is a complex methodology. It requires fund managers to categorize each bond in an index into different quadrants, using multiple factors. These factors include industries, issue size, credit rating, maturity, and bond coupon, as well as many others. The sorted bonds go into the correct quadrant with similar bonds. The manager then selects a few liquid bonds from each quadrant to represent all bonds in that block.

Once a portfolio of bonds is created, the sampled portfolio is optimized and tested to see whether there was a significant difference in the past risk and return of portfolio and the index the portfolio is trying to track. If the tracking error with the indexes is too high, bonds are replaced in the portfolio. The procedure continues until the tracking error of the portfolio is within an acceptable tolerance. A successful sampling and optimization strategy should require only a few hundred bonds to bring the tracking error within an acceptable level.

Treasury Indexes

The Treasury bond market is the most liquid fixed income market in the world. Trillions of dollars are traded in U.S. Treasury securities each year. There are several indexes that track the U.S. Treasury market. Lehman Brothers provides the most popular Treasury indexes used as benchmarks for U.S. fixed income ETFs.

Vanguard has also filed with the SEC for three Treasury ETFs that do not follow Treasury bond indexes, although the structure is very close. The three ETFs will be a share class of their open-end Short-term Treasury Fund, Intermediate-term Treasury

Fund, and Long-term Treasury Fund. The Vanguard ETFs would sample the Treasury bonds in the open-end funds and be composed of 40 percent to 50 percent of those securities. See Chapter 3 for details about the Vanguard ETF structure.

Lehman Treasury Indexes

The securities in Lehman Treasury Indexes must be publicly issued U.S. Treasury securities denominated in U.S. dollars and must be fixed rate and nonconvertible. In addition, the securities must be rated investment grade, and have $250 million or more of outstanding face value. Excluded from the index are state and local government series bonds and coupon issues that have been stripped from bonds included in the index. The indexes are market capitalization weighted and the securities in the index are updated on the last calendar day of each month.

The Lehman Brothers Treasury indexes are separated by maturities. The 1–3-Year U.S. Treasury Index measures the performance all publicly issued U.S. Treasury securities that have a remaining maturity of greater than or equal to one year and fewer than three. The 7–10-Year U.S. Treasury Index measures the bonds that have a remaining maturity of greater than or equal to 7 years and fewer than 10 years. The 20+-Year U.S. Treasury Index measures the performance of public obligations of the U.S. Treasury that have a remaining maturity of 20 or more years. There are ETFs that are benchmarked to all these indexes.

Ryan ALM Treasury Indexes

Ameristock Funds has five fixed-income ETFs tracking Treasury indexes managed by Ryan ALM, Inc. The indexes differ from Lehman Treasury indexes in that Ryan indexes are bullets. They are isolated to one bullet maturity year rather than a range of years. For example, the Ryan Five-Year Treasury Index includes only five-year Treasury notes, as opposed to another index that might hold a two-year note and an eight-year note that has an overall average of five years to maturity. That being said, the Ameristock/Ryan Five-Year Treasury ETF (symbol: GKC) does have the ability to expand the range. Ameristock samples the Treasury market while still attempting to replicate the risk and return of the Ryan Five-Year Treasury index.

Treasury Inflation Protected Securities (TIPS)

Inflation erodes the purchasing power of an investor's portfolio. Treasury Inflation Protected Securities provide a hedge against that inflation.

TIPS are direct obligations of the U.S. Treasury even though they differ from conventional Treasury bonds in many ways. A conventional bond is issued close to its par value, makes regular fixed interest payments during the life of the bond, and pays the par value of the bond at maturity. TIPS are issued at the prevailing par value at the time, provide interest payments that are adjusted over time to reflect a rise (inflation) or a drop (deflation), and then pay an inflation-adjusted par value when they mature.

The Lehman Brothers U.S. TIPS Index measures the performance of the inflation protected public obligations of the U.S. Treasury. The index includes all publicly issued TIPS in the U.S. and are included in the Barclays Global Investors (BGI) iShares Lehman TIPS ETF (symbol: TIP).

State Street Global Advisors (SSGA) has the SPDR Barclays Capital TIPS ETF (IPE), which tracks the Barclays U.S. Government Inflation-Linked Bond Index. The index is basically the same as the Lehman Brothers U.S. TIPS index in its constituents. It is ironic that SSGA is licensing its competitor's index.

Vanguard has filed for a TIPS ETF that will also follow the TIPS market closely. It is not an index fund and will not be constrained to an index. See Chapter 5 for details.

Mortgages

The Government National Mortgage Association (GNMA) and the Federal National Mortgage Association (FNMA) are two government-regulated organizations that sell pass-through certificates representing part ownership in a pool of mortgage loans. GNMA mortgages are supported by the full faith and credit of the U.S. government. Securities issued by FNMA and other U.S. government agencies are not guaranteed by the U.S. Treasury, but there is an implied guarantee because the government set up those organizations after World War II to stimulate home purchases.

Mortgages have higher yields than direct government bonds because of their prepayment risk. That occurs as homeowners refinance their mortgages during a period of falling interest rates. Investors in mortgages get their money back faster than expected from the prepayment of mortgages, and are forced to reinvest the proceeds at lower interest rates. When interest rates rise, prepayment of mortgages slow, and investors in mortgages become locked into lower-than-current market interest rates.

The iShares Lehman MBS Fixed Rate ETF (symbol: MBB) is the fund at this time that invests specifically in mortgage pass-through certificates. It is benchmarked to the Lehman Mortgage-Backed Securities Fixed Rate index.

Asset-Backed Securities

Asset-backed securities are a type of bond that is issued on the basis of pools of assets or is collateralized by the cash flows from a broad pool of underlying assets. Assets are pooled to make otherwise minor and uneconomical investments worthwhile and reduces the risk by diversifying among several issuers. The securitization of loans and leases makes these securities available to a broad range of investors. These asset pools can be made of receivables including credit card payments, auto loans, mortgages, aircraft leases, royalty payments, and even Hollywood movie revenues.

Currently, there are no ETFs that follow the asset-backed market directly. However, many broad bond market indexes are followed by fixed income ETFs that include asset-backed securities.

Investment Grade Corporate Bonds

The first investment grade corporate bond ETF was launched in July 2002. The iBoxx $ Investment Grade Corporate ETF (Symbol: LQD) is managed by BGI and is reasonably priced at only 0.15 percent per year.

The iBoxx U.S. Dollar Liquid Investment Grade index measures the performance of a fixed number of highly liquid, U.S.-traded investment grade corporate bonds. There are about 100 bonds included in the index. Several of the bonds are Yankee bonds. They are issued by foreign companies and trade in U.S. dollars on U.S. exchanges.

Lehman Brothers has a series of corporate bond indexes. The Lehman Brothers Short-term Credit Index, Intermediate-term

Credit Index, and Credit Index all hold investment grade corporate bonds of varying maturities. There are several ETFs benchmarked to those indexes available from Vanguard and BGI. Lehman names the indexes credit indexes instead of calling them a corporate index because of the asset-backed securities included. Credit card debt and other types of asset-backed securities are not considered direct corporate debt.

High-Yield Corporate Bonds

Less than investment grade corporate bonds are known as high yield or junk bonds. They are the speculative part of the fixed income universe. Most companies that issue junk bonds are not in the best financial condition. Nor are those companies whose rating has been cut to a junk status by S&P, Moody's, and other independent credit rating agencies. Since there is a higher risk that these issuers will not meet their financial obligations, the high yield sector offers high returns in the form of higher interest payments. As a group, junk bonds are expected to achieve a return higher than investment grade bonds but lower than the broad stock market.

In 2007, the iShares iBoxx $ High Yield Corporate ETF (symbol: HYG) was the first high yield ETF to the market. It tracks the iBoxx $ High Yield Corporate Bond Index, an equal weighted index of 50 liquid high yield corporate securities. There is a high price fee for the fund of 0.5 percent per year.

Composite Indexes

Fixed income composite indexes combine different types of bonds into one index. The securities in the Lehman Brothers (LB) Government/Credit Indexes have government bonds, corporate bonds, asset-backed securities, and Yankee bonds (no mortgages). All securities in the LB indexes must be denominated in U.S. dollars and must be fixed-rate and nonconvertible. The indexes are market capitalization weighted and the securities in the indexes are updated on the last calendar day of each month.

There are several investment grade LB Government/Credit Indexes separated by the average maturity of bonds. The 1–5-Year Government/Credit Index includes bonds that have maturities between one and five years. The 5–10-Year Government/

Credit Index includes bonds that have maturities between 5 and 10 years. The Long Government/Credit Index includes bonds that have maturities of greater than 10 years.

Several Vanguard fixed income ETFs invest in the LB Government/Credit indexes, using a sampling technique. The ETFs are composed of a range of securities that, in the aggregate, approximates the full index in the form of key risk factors and other characteristics.

Lehman Aggregate Bond Index

The broadest and most popular index in the LB fixed income series is the Lehman Aggregate Bond Index. The investment grade index tracks over 7,000 U.S. Treasury securities, government agency bonds, mortgages, corporate bonds, and Yankee bonds. The index measures the performance of the U.S. investment grade bond market, which includes investment grade U.S. Treasury bonds, government-related bonds, investment grade corporate bonds, mortgage pass-through securities, commercial mortgage-backed securities and asset-backed securities that are publicly offered for sale in the United States.

The securities in the Lehman Aggregate Bond Index must have $250 million or more of outstanding face value and must have at least one year remaining to maturity. In addition, the securities must be denominated in U.S. dollars and must be fixed-rate and nonconvertible. The index is market capitalization weighted and the securities in the index are updated on the last calendar day of each month.

Bonds in the Lehman Aggregate Bond Index have an average maturity of about seven years, which places the index in the intermediate-term category. Bonds in the index also have a high average rating of AA by S&P. More than 70 percent of the Aggregate Bond Index holdings are in U.S. Treasuries, agency, and government-backed mortgages. Almost 27 percent are investment grade corporate bonds, and about 3 percent are Yankee bonds.

Three ETFs track the Lehman Aggregate Bond Index: the iShares Lehman Aggregate (symbol: AGG), the Vanguard Total Bond Market ETF (symbol: BND), and the SPDR Lehman Aggregate Bond (LAG). All funds use a sampling technique to replicate the index. The difference in performance between one fund and another is the manager's ability to sample the index effectively and the fees charged.

iShares changes 0.20 percent per year for its fund while the SPDR charges 0.1345 percent and Vanguard is only 0.11 percent.

Preferred Stock ETFs

In addition to corporate bonds, financial companies frequently issue preferred stock. Preferred stock falls between fixed income and common equity on a corporate balance sheet. Preferred stocks pay high quarterly income like corporate bonds, but taxes on the income may receive preferential treatment from the IRS. In addition, the dividend on preferred stock may be cut or eliminated without the company defaulting on the issue.

Like common stock, preferred stocks represent partial ownership in a company, although preferred stock shareholders do not enjoy any of the voting rights of common stockholders. Unlike common stock, a preferred stock pays a fixed dividend that does not fluctuate (unless it is cut or eliminated). In that sense, it is like a debt. However, unlike debt securities, dividend payments on a preferred stock typically must be declared by the issuer's board of directors. An issuer's board of directors is generally not under any obligation to pay a dividend (even if such dividends have accrued), and may suspend payment of dividends on preferred stock at any time.

There are benefits to owning preferred stock. First is the high income from dividends. Since preferred investors are lower on the pecking order than bond holders, they should earn more income. And although that dividend may be cut or eliminated, preferred shareholders always receive their dividends first before the common stockholders. A second advantage is the tax benefit of some issues. Qualified dividend income (QDI) preferred stocks pay dividends that receive a tax preference. The dividend is taxed the same as a common stock dividend, which is at a federal tax rate of no more than 15 percent. Be careful with what you buy, because not all preferred stock is QDI eligible.

The PowerShares Financial Preferred Portfolio (symbol: PGF) is benchmarked to the Wachovia Hybrid & Preferred Securities Financial index. There are 30 securities in the index. The ETF samples the index and attempts to use only QDI preferred stocks.

PGF is unique in that PowerShares recognized the benefit of QDI preferred stocks. However, there are two disadvantages. First, the fee is high at 0.6 percent per year. The high fees are hard to swallow, given no capital appreciation should be expected from the securities. Second, QDI preferred stocks are dominated by financial sector issuers, meaning the portfolio lacks industry diversification. I believe the concentration in financials is a minor point, but it should be considered.

The iShares S&P U.S. Preferred Stock (symbol: PFF) is benchmarked to the S&P U.S. Preferred Stock Index. The PFF has greater industry diversification than the PowerShares fund and a lower cost (0.48 percent). However, the big disadvantage is that only about half the securities are QDI-eligible. The index includes trust-preferred securities and various other hybrid issues. As such, ordinary income taxes will be due on that portion for investors who hold the fund in taxable accounts.

More Fixed Income on the Way

State Street launched a series of ETFs to round out their product line around the time this book went to press. The funds are to be benchmarked to Lehman fixed income indexes. Also, Morningstar recently introduced a family of investable bond indexes they want to license as ETFs and other investment products. The Chicago investment research firm's stock indexes are already the benchmarks for several BGI equity ETFs.

The iShares S&P National Municipal Bond ETF (symbol: MUB) tracks the S&P National Municipal Bond Index, a comprehensive index of state and local municipal bonds with investment grade ratings of BBB or better. The expense ratio is 0.25 percent. Standard & Poor's is the Index Provider.

First international and global fixed income ETFs where filed with the SEC in the summer of 2007. The SPDR Lehman International Treasury Bond ETF and the SPDR Barclays Global TIPS ETF are expected to be popular additions to investor's portfolios.

Fixed Income ETF List

Table 14.1 offers a list of Fixed Income ETFs available on U.S. exchanges. There are several funds to choose from, although many overlap. New funds should be introduced in the coming year to broaden the list. To stay on top of new issues, visit the web site listed in the "ETF Resource List" in Appendix B. For lists of all

Table 14.1 Fixed Income ETFs

Category	ETF Name	Ticker	Expense Ratio	Index	Strategy Box	Sec. Select	Sec. Weight
Treasury–Short	iShares Lehman Short U.S. Treasury	SHV	0.15%	LB Short U.S. Treasury	▦	P S	C A
Treasury–Short	iShares Lehman 1–3 YR U.S. Treasury	SHY	0.15%	LB 1–3 YR U.S. Treasury Bond	▦	P S	C A
Treasury–Inter-mediate	iShares Lehman 3–7 YR U.S. Treasury	IEI	0.15%	LB 3–7 YR U.S. Treasury Bond	▦	P S	C A
Treasury–Inter-mediate	iShares Lehman 7–10 YR U.S. Treasury	IEF	0.15%	LB 7–10 YR U.S. Treasury Bond	▦	P S	C A
Treasury–Long	iShares Lehman 10–20 YR U.S. Treasury	TLH	0.15%	LB 10–20 YR U.S. Treasury Bond	▦	P S	C A
Treasury–Long	iShares Lehman 20 + -Year U.S. Treasury	TLT	0.15%	LB 20 + -Year U.S. Treasury	▦	P S	C A
Treasury–Short	Ameristock/ Ryan 1-Year U.S. Treasury	GKA	0.15%	Ryan Adjusted 1-Year U.S. Treasury	▦	P S	C A
Treasury–Short	Ameristock/ Ryan 2-Year U.S. Treasury	GKB	0.15%	Ryan 2-Year U.S. Treasury	▦	P S	C A
Treasury–Inter-mediate	Ameristock/ Ryan 5-Year U.S. Treasury	GKC	0.15%	Ryan 5-Year U.S. Treasury	▦	P S	C A

(continued)

Table 14.2 *(continued)*

Category	ETF Name	Ticker	Expense Ratio	Index	Strategy Box	Sec. Select	Sec. Weight
Treasury–Long	Ameristock/ Ryan 10-Year U.S. Treasury	GKD	0.15%	Ryan 10-Year U.S. Treasury		P S	C A
Treasury–Long	Ameristock/ Ryan 20-Year U.S. Treasury	GKE	0.15%	Ryan 20-Year U.S. Treasury		P S	C A
Treasury–Bills	SPDR Lehman 1–3 Month T-Bill	BIL	0.13%	LB 1–3 Month U.S. Treasury T-Bill		P S	C A
Treasury–Intermediate	SPDR Lehman Intermediate-Term U.S. Treasury	ITE	0.13%	LB Intermediate-Term U.S. Treasury		P S	C A
Treasury–Long	SPDR Lehman Long-Term U.S. Treasury	TLO	0.13%	LB Long U.S. Treasury		P S	C A
Inflation Protected	iShares Lehman TIPS	TIP	0.20%	LB U.S. Treasury TIPS		P A	C A
Inflation Protected	SPDR Barclays Capital TIPS	IPE	0.18%	Barclays U.S. Treasury TIPS		P A	C A
Mortgages	iShares Lehman MBS Fixed Rate	MBB	0.25%	LB U.S. MBS Fixed Rate		P S	C A
Government/ Credit–Intermediate	iShares Lehman Intermediate Government/ Credit	GVI	0.20%	LB Intermediate U.S Government/ Credit		P S	C A

Table 14.3 *(continued)*

Category	ETF Name	Ticker	Expense Ratio	Index	Strategy Box	Sec. Select	Sec. Weight
Government/ Credit– Long	iShares Lehman Government/ Credit	GBF	0.20%	LB U.S. Government/ Credit	⊞	P S	C A
Government/ Credit– Short	Vanguard Short-Term	BSC	0.11%	Lehman 1–5 Year Government/ Credit	⊞	P S	C A
Government/ Credit– Inter- mediate	Vanguard Inter- mediate- Term	BIV	0.11%	Lehman 5–10 Year Government/ Credit	⊞	P S	C A
Gov/ Credit– Long	Vanguard Long-Term	BLV	0.11%	Lehman Long Government/ Credit	⊞	P S	C A
Aggregate Bond	Vanguard Total Bond Market	BND	0.11%	Lehman Brothers U.S. Aggregate	⊞	P S	C A
Aggregate Bond	SPDR Lehman Aggregate Bond	LAG	0.13%	Lehman Brothers U.S. Aggregate	⊞	P S	C A
Aggregate Bond	iShares Lehman Aggregate	AGG	0.20%	Lehman Brothers U.S. Aggregate	⊞	P S	C A
Corporate– Short	iShares 1–3 YR Credit	CSJ	0.20%	LB 1–3 YR US Credit	⊞	P S	C A
Corporate– Inter- mediate	iShares Lehman In- termediate Credit	CIU	0.20%	LB Intermedi- ate US Credit	⊞	P S	C A

(continued)

Table 14.4   (continued)

Category	ETF Name	Ticker	Expense Ratio	Index	Strategy Box	Sec. Select	Sec. Weight
Corporate–Inter-mediate	iShares iBoxx $ Invest-ment Grade Cor-poration	LQD	0.15%	iBoxx U.S. Dlr Liquid Investment Grade	⊞	P S	C A
Corporate–Long	iShares Lehman Credit	CFT	0.20%	LB U.S. Credit	⊞	P S	C A
Corporate–High Yield	iShares iBoxx $ High Yield Corporate	HYG	0.50%	iBoxx $ Liquid High Yield	⊞	P S	X M
Preferred Stocks	iShares S&P U.S. Preferred Stock	PFF	0.48%	S&P U.S. Preferred Stock	⊞	P S	C A
Preferred Stocks	PowerShares Financial Preferred	PGF	0.60%	Wachovia Hybrid & Preferred Financial	⊞	P S	C A
	Average Fee—Fixed Income ETFs		**0.19%**				

fixed income ETFs, including the Index Strategy Box database, visit www.theetfbook.com and www.etfguide.com.

Appendix A is an abbreviation guide for security selection and weighting methodologies used in each index in Table 14.1. Selection and weighting methodologies are the best fit given information available to the public through the ETF companies by way of each fund's Prospectus.

Summary

One way to capture fixed income exposure in your portfolio is to invest in a bond ETF that follows a broad bond market index. Unfortunately, the number of fixed income ETFs is small compared to the burgeoning equity ETF market. In addition, several funds overlap. There are three separate funds following the Lehman Aggregate Bond Index. Fortunately, providers are starting to focus on this important area of investing and are starting to introduce innovative products. Preferred stock and high yield bond ETFs are two areas of innovation in the past year. More innovation is around the corner.

CHAPTER 15

Commodity and Currency ETFs

ETF issuance has been expanded well beyond stock and bond indexing. Funds are now available in several alternative asset classes, including individual commodities, commodity futures, futures indexes, and foreign currencies. These new products are playing an expanding role in portfolio management.

The advantage of adding an alternative asset class such as commodities to your portfolio is that they tend to exhibit a low correlation with traditional stock and bond investments (see Chapter 17). Low correlation between two asset classes means that when one is going up, the other may or may not be following, and could be heading in the opposite direction. That lowers overall portfolio volatility.

In addition, individual commodity sectors tend to have low correlations with one another. Thus, the theory is that diversifying into many commodities through a commodity futures index may be more beneficial than owning single commodity ETFs.

The disadvantages of owning commodity products in a portfolio are several. They include the cost of investing in that asset class, the lack of a real expected long-term return from the asset class, and low tax efficiency of commodities and futures.

Commodities Basics

Commodities are common products such as food, basic materials, and energy-related items that are used every day. Food products include items such as sugar, corn, and oats; basic materials include items such as steel and aluminum; energy is traded in the form of crude oil, natural gas, and electricity. Another category includes precious metals such as gold, which has little manufacturing value, and silver, which has slightly more. All together, these resources make up the global commodities market.

- Energy: crude oil, heating oil, natural gas, electricity
- Industrials: copper, steel, cotton
- Precious Metals: gold, platinum, silver, aluminum
- Livestock: live cattle, lean hogs
- Grains and oilseeds: corn, soybeans, wheat
- Softs: cocoa, coffee, orange juice, sugar

The global commodities market is as wide as it is deep. Commodities tend to be dug up, manufactured, or grown in almost every nation in the world, and that creates hundreds of markets and around-the-world trading. Commodities are being bought and sold someplace in some market 24 hours a day, 7 days a week. If you want to buy an ounce of gold at 10:00 PM on a Sunday night, that can be arranged. If you want to buy 10,000 bales of cotton at 3:00 AM on a Tuesday morning, just pick up the phone or make a few clicks on your computer.

By definition, the word *commodity* means abundance. Although some commodities are more rare than others, there is a lot of the stuff around and more that can be grown, dug up, or manufactured. There are occasional shortages in sectors that create a temporary jump in prices, but those shortages tend to be marginalized over time. If corn prices rise because of greater demand from ethanol manufactures, farmers will grow more corn next season, and keep growing corn until the supply exceeds demand and prices fall again (along with oil prices). If a building boom causes a shortage of steel, prices will rise, producers will mine more ore, mini-mills will recycle more scrap, and new producers will come on line all over the world; and then the building boom will end and steel prices will plummet. Whenever a commodity is priced high enough to make a large enough profit, more of the commodity is created or harvested by current suppliers, and new competitors bring more supply.

It may take several years for the new supply of commodities to meet demand. Start-up costs are high and the discovery of new reserves take time, but supply eventually catches up and the commodity price does eventually come down. A spike in prices tends to not be good for long-term commodity producers because more often than not, a spike in prices eventually leads to oversupply, which leads to a rapid decline in prices and operating losses. Such is the boom-and-bust nature of the business.

Spot and Forward Contract

Before a practical discussion of commodities and currency ETFs can take place, a discussion is required of physical commodities and spot prices, and claims on future commodities and forward prices.

Trading of most physical commodities is not an option for individuals. Unless you own a silo where you can store 10,000 bushels of corn or a large tank to store 1,000 gallons of crude oil, a direct investment in most commodities is not practical. There are exceptions, such as gold and silver, but they are the exception rather than the rule. To make investing in commodities practical, most people invest in contracts that lock in future prices. Those contracts are called futures, forwards, and other acts.

Commodity futures do not represent direct ownership to actual commodities. They are an obligation to buy commodities in the future based on a price that is negotiated today. A contract is a standardized agreement to buy or sell a specific commodity type and quantity at the future delivery date and at a price agreed upon when the contract is purchased. Only a small amount of money is needed to secure the contract and that gives commodity futures investors a large amount of leverage.

Futures prices are different from spot prices, although they are used to estimate future prices. The futures price starts with the current spot price and adjusts for interest rates, known seasonal changes that affect supply and demand, possible storage expenses, and other costs-of-carry expenses.

If spot prices are expected to be much higher at the maturity of the futures contract than they are today, the current futures price will be set at a high level relative to the current spot price. That is known as a market in *contango*. Lower-than-expected spot prices in the future will be reflected in a low current futures price. That is known as a market in *backwardation*. Figure 15.1 is an example of the oil future market in contango and backwardation. It is based on a $60 per barrel expected spot price for oil.

When commodity futures are in backwardation, it has been profitable at times to buy inexpensive futures contracts and to

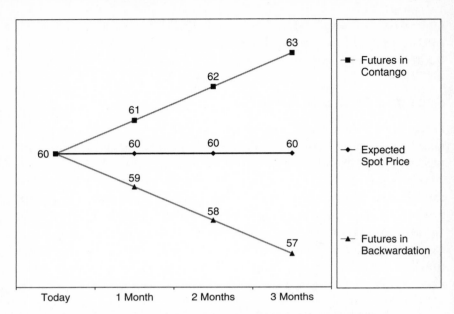

Figure 15.1   Oil Futures Prices in Backwardation and Contango

invest your cash in T-bills. The return has been higher than buying commodities at the spot prices and waiting for higher prices.

The opposite is true when commodity futures are in contango. It is cheaper to buy physical commodities and pay with cash than to buy those commodities by buying futures at a premium. You will incur a cost to carry the physical commodity, but that cost is less expensive than the premium on the futures contract.

Does Buying Futures Earn Free Money?

There is raging debate about the value of investing in commodities futures. Some studies suggest the returns are comparable to stocks even though the return of the spot market has not achieved those results. Other academic studies show that futures returns tend to be closer to the inflation rate. The issue revolves around the period studied, and who is doing the study. Many recent studies showing high returns have concentrated on the last couple of decades. Other studies show much lower returns.

Logically, if commodity futures spend half their time in contango and half their time in backwardation, there should be no advantage to buying the spot or buying the futures. The total return should be the same whether you buy the physical commodity and store it or buy the futures contract and invest your cash in short-term T-bills.

ETFs that invest in futures must roll contracts from one month to the next month to avoid gallons of oil showing up at the fund company's doorstep on the futures expiration date. The roll yield can be positive or negative, depending on the relationship of next month's futures prices to near-term futures prices. In a simplistic sense, if the second month contract is less expensive than the first month (backwardation), buyers of futures earn a profit, and if the second month contract is more expensive than the first month (contango), buyers of futures lose out.

For many years, energy futures buyers made money from an oil market stuck in backwardations. According to data from Barclays Capital, oil was in a state of backwardation about 57 percent of the time between 1983 and 2007. However, the gains earned during those times became losses in 2006 when the market went into contango. That hurt ETF investors. The United States Oil Fund (symbol: USO) was the first crude oil ETF on the U.S. market. USO began trading on April 10, 2006, at $68.25, a price roughly equal to that of a barrel of oil at the time. The fund closed one year later at $52.01, representing a decline of 23.8 percent. During that same period, however, the U.S. benchmark price of crude oil fell only a modest 6.5 percent. Much of the extra loss in USO was a loss due to the negative roll yield from an oil futures market that moved into contango.

There is no way of telling how long the oil market will remain in contango. However long it does last, investors in ETFs that are based on commodities futures will bear the extra expense of a negative roll yield.

Commodity ETFs

Commodities truly are a trading vehicle, not a long-term investment vehicle. Timing is everything. Over the last 30 years, there have been only two major runs in commodities prices. One occurred during the high inflation years of the 1970s, which coincided with the U.S. release of fixed gold prices, and the second occurred during the first decade of the new millennium. Figure 15.2 illustrates the value of gold and oil adjusted for inflation from 1977 to 2006. The two spikes

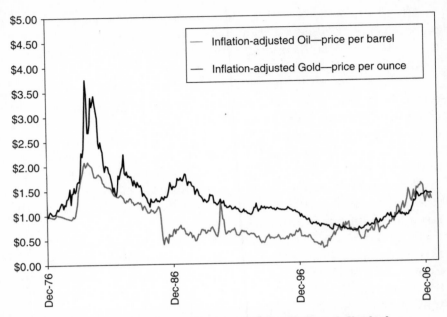

Figure 15.2 $1 in Oil and Gold since 1977, Inflation Adjusted
Source: Commodity Research Bureau

are clearly evident in the figure. The rest of the years' commodity prices were characterized by flat or falling values.

Investors with a good sense of timing may have a chance of making more money in commodities than simply staying in stocks and bonds, but that is not an easy task. Nonetheless, the run-up in commodities prices during the 2000 to 2006 time prompted huge interest from individuals, and index providers and ETF companies were happy to accommodate those investment dollars.

Oil ETFs

The United States Oil Fund (symbol: USO) investment objective is for the NAV of its units to reflect the performance of the spot price of West Texas Intermediate light, sweet crude oil. USOF invests primarily in oil futures contracts, and seeks to have its aggregate NAV approximate at all times the outstanding value of the oil futures contracts. As we have discussed, futures do not track spot prices one for one.

The iPath S&P GSCI Crude Oil Total Return ETN (symbol: OIL) tracks the performance of a nonleveraged investment in West Texas Intermediate crude futures, plus the return that would be earned by an investment of collateral assets in Treasuries.

The PowerShares DB Oil Fund (symbol: DBO) attempts to track the performance of the Deutsche Bank Liquid Commodity Index—Optimum Yield Energy Excess Return Index. Isn't that a mouthful? The index is a rules-based index composed of futures contracts on some of the most heavily traded energy commodities in the world.

The Barclays iPath oil ETN (symbol: OIL) follows the Goldman Sachs Crude Oil Total Return Index of futures contracts. ETNs are debt-linked instruments that trade much like traditional exchange-traded funds. The chief difference is that ETNs do not actually hold a stake in the underlying commodity or commodities futures. ETNs are senior debt notes from Barclays PLC, under which Barclays promises to pay you the exact return of the underlying commodity index, minus an expense ratio of 0.75 percent per year.

The Claymore MACROshares Oil Up Tradeable Trust (symbol: UCR) takes a long positioning on oil futures swap contracts. The shares are designed to track the settlement price of a designated NYMEX division light sweet crude oil futures contract. The Claymore MACROshares Oil Down Tradeable Trust (symbol: DCR) takes the opposite position on the same swap contract.

The two MACROshares are supposed to move opposite each other, and also closely track the price of a barrel of oil. But the funds have not performed as their originators have expected for many technical reasons that go beyond the scope of this chapter. Perhaps the 1.5 percent annual fee has something to do with it.

Gold and Silver ETFs

streetTRACKS Gold Shares (symbol: GLD) offer investors a way to access the gold market without the necessity of taking physical delivery of gold, and to buy and sell that interest through the trading of a security on a regulated stock exchange. The trust holds gold, issues baskets in exchange for deposits of gold, and distributes gold in connection with the redemptions of baskets. Each ETF share represents one tenth of an ounce of gold, backed by bullion held in a vault. The investment objective of the Trust is for the Shares to reflect the performance of the price of gold bullion, less the 0.40% expense.

iShares Comex Gold Trust (symbol: IAU) corresponds to one-tenth of a troy ounce of gold. The ETF's trustee, the Bank of New York, will value the trust's gold on the basis of that day's announced Comex settlement price for the spot month gold futures contract. The shares of the trust will reflect the price of the gold owned by the trust, minus expenses and liabilities. The annual management fee is 0.40 percent.

iShares Silver Trust (symbol: SLV) is backed by physical silver. Each share is equal to about 10 ounces of silver. The custodian of the trust is JPMorgan Chase, although the silver itself is held in the vault of the Bank of England. The annual management fee is 0.50 percent.

There are disadvantages to directly owning gold and silver through an ETF. Since there is no income in the trusts, the expenses are paid by liquidating a portion of the fund's assets. That means selling 0.40 percent of the gold trusts and 0.50 percent of the silver trust. As a result, over time, each share's claim will represent a smaller and smaller amount of gold and silver. If no new shares were to be created, the gold funds, which started at 0.1 ounces per share, would only hold a little more than 0.095 ounces per share after 10 years. By the way, those sales to pay fees are taxable events for U.S. investors.

Speaking of taxes, a second disadvantage of investing directly in gold and silver is a higher tax bill if you sell shares at a profit. Unlike the 15 percent maximum capital gains on equity ETFs held more than one year, gold and silver investments are considered collectibles. As such, gains are taxed at the higher 28 percent maximum capital gains rate. Check with your tax adviser for changes to the tax code.

You can invest in precious metals through funds that use futures contracts. There are three PowerShares funds benchmarked to precious metals futures. The PowerShares DB Gold Fund (symbol: DGL) is based on the Deutsche Bank Liquid Commodity Index—Gold. The PowerShares DB Silver Fund (symbol: DBS) is based on the Deutsche Bank Liquid Commodity Index—Optimum Yield Silver Excess Return Index. The PowerShares DB Precious Metals Fund (symbol: DBP) is based on the Deutsche Bank Liquid Commodity Index—Optimum Yield Precious Metals Excess Return Index. It is a rules-based index composed of futures contracts on gold and silver. The fee for these funds is 0.79 percent.

Commodities Indexes

Commodities mutual funds invest in derivatives of commodity total return indexes. Therefore, investors in those funds should understand how commodity indexes are constructed. There are several competing commodity total return indexes. Like stock indexes, each commodity index provider has its own methodology for calculating returns and its reasons for believing that its system is superior to everyone else's.

Four popular indexes for measuring commodity futures prices are the S&P GSCI (GSCI), Dow Jones-AIG Commodity Index (DJ-AIGCI), and the Deutsche Bank (BD LCI). The most important difference between the indexes is their approach to weighting the different commodity sectors and the periodic rebalancing of those sectors.

The word *index* is used in this chapter even more liberally than with custom equity indexes. All commodity indexes are customized to some degree. There is at least one commodity index provider that changes the weightings of the commodities in its index on an ongoing basis based on that provider's view of the markets. Others engage in an annual rebalancing process to take into account changes in the level of global commodity production or consumption. Still other index providers make regular schedule rebalancing adjustments to the weightings in accordance with index rules set in advance.

The commodity indexes described in this section are futures price indexes. They reflect the change in price of commodity futures, not the change in commodity prices. There is a big difference. There are many factors that drive each market. Spot prices could be flat and futures prices could be going up or down, or vice versa. If you see the price of gas go up at the pumps, it is not guaranteed that your commodities fund is making money.

Total return indexes are designed to replicate the return of fully collateralized commodity futures. The total return is the price return on the commodity futures, plus the difference in price between old futures contract near expiration and new futures prices on the day contracts are rolled to the next month, plus the income from the Treasury bills where the collateral sits. In essence, all ETFs that follow commodities indexes are based on total return indexes, and returns are based on the earlier-mentioned formula.

S&P GSCI Total Return Index

The S&P GSCI was created in 1991 by Goldman Sachs and is widely considered to be the most heavily followed commodity benchmark. In 2007, Goldman Sachs sold the index methodology and rights to Standard and Poor's (S&P). The index is world-production-weighted, which means that the quantity of each commodity in the index is determined by the average value of production in the last five years of available data, and adjusted for liquidity. Weights are reestablished annually and put into effect the first day of January.

The S&P GSCI index tracks the price of 24 commodities, based on overall market value. There are six energy products, five industrial metals, eight agricultural products, three livestock products, and two precious metals. The S&P GSCI methodology produces an index heavily weighted to energy, since the total value of oil produced globally dominates the value of all other commodities. A small rise in the price of crude oil has a significant impact on the S&P GSCI index.

iShares S&P GSCI Commodity-Indexed Trust (symbol: GSG) seeks to correspond generally to the performance of the S&P GSCI-ER Index before the payment of expenses and liabilities. GSG uses commodities futures to accomplish that goal. The iPath S&P GSCI Total Return Index ETN (symbol: DJP) is also linked to the S&P GSCI Total Return Index. Unlike its sister product, DJP provides exposure to the return of the index using unsecured debt issued by Barclays Bank PLC.

Dow Jones–AIG Commodity Index

The DJ-AIGCI strategy was created in 1998 and has a large following among individual and institutional investors. The index is derived from the movements of 20 different commodity futures.

The DJ-AIGCI is not a market index in that its does not measure the gain or loss in value of the commodities futures market. Rather, the custom index is an investment strategy. There are strict rules on sector and security weights. No commodity sector starts the year with more than a 33 percent position (for example, energy) and no single group component may be more than 15 percent of the group or 2 percent of the index (for example, W.T.I. crude oil). The index weights are rebalanced every January. Based on hypothetical data, Dow Jones claims that their investment strategy has outperformed a market index of commodity futures.

The iPath Dow Jones–AIG Commodity Index Total Return ETN (symbol: DJP) is linked to the Dow Jones–AIG Commodity Index Total Return Index. It is designed to return an investment in the futures contracts on physical commodities comprising the index plus the rate of interest that could be earned on cash collateral invested in specified Treasury Bills, before fees.

Deutsche Bank Liquid Commodity Index

Deutsche Bank Liquid Commodity Index (DBLCI) was created in 2003 and is intended to reflect the performance of a handful of the most liquid globally traded commodities. Commodities in the index are set weights comprising crude oil (35 percent), heating oil (20 percent), aluminum (12.5 percent), gold (10 percent), corn (11.25 percent), and wheat (11.25 percent). The percentages of each commodity included in the index are broadly in proportion to historic levels of the world's production and stocks. Deutsche Bank says the limited number of commodities is not important since price movements for commodities in the same sector tend to be highly correlated.

The PowerShares DB Commodity Index Tracking Fund (symbol: DCB) is based on the Optimum Yield version of the Deutsche Bank Liquid Commodity Index. The index has an unusual policy on rebalancing. Positions in energy futures, namely W.T.I. crude oil and heating oil, are rebalanced each month while positions in the other four contracts are rebalanced once a year. The dual rebalancing policy is supposed to increase the roll return, or reduce the negative effect of rolling the futures contracts.

A Progression of New Funds

A natural progression of commodity index fund offerings was to move from broad-based indexes to sectors and subsectors. BGI will manage two sector funds. The iShares GS Commodity Industrial Metals Index Trust tracks a production-weighted index of copper, aluminum, zinc, nickel, and lead futures. iShares GS Commodity Livestock Indexed Trust is designed to provide exposure to the livestock components of the commodities universe.

Taking energy down a notch is the goal of the other two BGI funds. The iShares S&P GS Commodity Light Energy Indexed Trust reduces S&P GSCI energy exposure from 77 percent to just

39 percent. iShares S&P GS Commodity Non-Energy Indexed Trust takes things one step further and excludes energy altogether, allowing investors to track the performance of the ex-energy component of the commodities total return index.

Disadvantages of Commodity ETFs

The disadvantages of owning commodity products in a portfolio are several. They include the cost of investing in that asset class, the lack of a real expected long-term return from the asset class, and low tax-efficiency of commodities and futures. The average cost to invest in commodity ETFs is 0.75 percent per year (see Table 15.2 at the end of the chapter). That makes commodity ETFs the most expensive of all ETF categories.

An Asset Class with No Real Return

Proponents of commodities point to the diversification benefits of adding this asset class to a stock and bond portfolio because it lowers overall portfolio risk. But do commodity ETFs make good *investments*?

Over the long run, an investment in physical commodities and individual commodity futures has returned about the Treasury bill rate before taxes and expenses. The number was recently verified by Claude B. Erb from Trust Company of the West, and Campbell R. Harvey of Duke University and the National Bureau of Economic Research. In their study, *Tactical and Strategic Value of Commodity Futures*, published on January 12, 2006, Erb and Harvey review the history of commodities research and calculate their own data. Their conclusion is that "historically, the average annualized excess return of individual commodity futures has been approximately zero."

My belief is that commodities do not make good long-term investments for people interested in a passive portfolio management (see Chapter 17). Having a lower portfolio risk is a noble goal, but not at the expense of lower expected returns. There is a saying on Wall Street that fits perfectly with my belief on a long-term investment in commodities, "You can't eat risk-adjusted returns."

There is a place for commodities in some investor's portfolios. Commodity funds make great trading tools for people who want to pursue active investment strategies (see Chapter 19). If your timing is good, you can make a lot of money with commodity ETFs and ETNs.

Taxing Issues

There are tax issues that commodity investors need to be aware of. There is no delaying of gains on commodity futures. The IRS requires that all contracts be marked-to-market at year's end, which has the same effect as if they were sold. That includes the futures contracts sitting in ETFs. It does not apply to ETN investments (see Chapter 3.)

Any gains or losses generated throughout the year or from the mark-to-market are taxed as 60 percent long-term—40 percent short-term gains, regardless of the holding period. That works out to a maximum 23 percent capital gains rate, which is higher than stocks, but lower than collectibles, as you read earlier. Interest income is also taxable because it is passed right through.

Tax laws change quickly. Consult your tax adviser before you take any investment action that may affect your IRS Form 1040.

Currencies

Institutional investors have traditionally dominated the currency markets. With ETFs and ETNs, individual investors can now easily invest in a fund that has the sole objective of reflecting the price of the currency held by the fund.

There is a small interest rate paid in the exchange-traded portfolios while money is held in trust, but the main attraction remains the currency exposure. If the currency held by a fund appreciates relative to the U.S. dollar and a shareholder sells shares, the shareholder will earn a profit. If the currency held by a fund depreciates relative to the U.S. dollar and a shareholder sells shares, the shareholder will incur a loss.

Currency ETFs

Rydex Investments launched the first currency ETF, the Euro Currency Trust on the New York Stock Exchange in December 2005. Rydex has since added more ETFs benchmarked to other currencies. Those currencies include many of the United States' largest trading partners. Each ETF holds a different foreign currency with an overseas branch of JPMorgan Chase Bank. The funds track the price of their underlying currency based on the Federal Reserve Noon Buying Rate.

The PowerShares DB US Dollar Bullish Fund (symbol: UUP) and the PowerShares DB US Dollar Bearish Fund (symbol: UDN) are based on the Deutsche Bank Long USD Futures Index and the Deutsche Bank Short USD Futures Index, respectively. The USDX futures contract is designed to replicate the performance of being long or short for the U.S. dollar against the following currencies: the Euro, Japanese yen, British pound, Canadian dollar, Swedish krona, and Swiss franc.

Barclays Bank expanded its lineup of exchange-traded notes (ETNs) in May 2007 with the launch of three currency funds. The notes provide exposure to Euros, British pounds, and Japanese yen, respectively.

- iPath EUR/USD (symbol: ERO)
- iPath GBP/USD (symbol: GBB)
- iPath JPY/USD (symbol: JYN)

The ETNs earn interest income based on the prevailing rates in the foreign country, minus 0.40 percent fee. However, you do not get the cash. Recall from Chapter 3 that ETNs do not pay dividends or any interest income. It is a total return vehicle. The note value increases over time. In contrast, the CurrencyShares pay monthly dividends that are subject to taxation as ordinary income. Table 15.1 is an example of the hypothetical interest paid on the iPath notes compared to the interest paid on CurrencyShares. The table was provided by a great resource for ETF investors, www.indexuniverse.com. The rates that follow were in effect on May 8, 2007.

Table 15.1   Interest on iPath and CurrencyShares Compared

Currency Fund Comparison	Interest Rate
iPath EUR/USD (ERO)	3.6%
CurrencyShares Euro Trust (FXY)	3.5%
iPath GBP/USD (GBB)	5.0%
CurrencyShares British Pound Sterling Trust (FXB)	4.9%
iPath JPY/USD (JYN)	0.3%
CurrencyShares Japanese Yen Trust (FXY)	0.2%

Source: www.indexuniverse.com; May 8, 2007 data

There is an interesting twist to this product. The iPath ETNs have a tax advantage when it comes to long-term gains as well. Barclays bank has received an opinion that is *reasonable* to account for its ETNs as prepaid contracts with respect to their indexes. Based on that opinion, ETN investors would not have to pay any taxes until they sold or redeemed the notes, and then those gains would be subject to long-term capital gains tax rates that are currently 15 percent maximum.

In contrast, the IRS considers any and all currency gains as ordinary income. That means any and all gains on CurrencyShares ETFs are subject to ordinary income taxes, which is at 35 percent today.

So, if you buy a $1,000 in CurrencyShares and sell them for $1,080 one year later plus earning $20 interest, you have to treat that $100 gain as ordinary income. The tax bite would be $35, assuming a 35 percent federal tax rate. That is an after-tax return of 6.5 percent. Contrast that to buying a $1,000 in iPath currency notes and selling them for $1,100 (interest embedded): You have to treat that $100 gain as long-term capital gains, which is taxed at 15 percent. That is an after-tax return of 8.5 percent!

Some people believe that the Barclays tax decision is aggressive. Talk to your own tax adviser and see what he or she says.

Long/Short Currency Investing

PowerShares DB G10 Currency Harvest Fund (symbol: DBV) is an interesting currency/interest rate ETF. The fund is benchmarked to the Deutsche Bank G10 Currency Harvest Index. The index is composed of long futures contracts on the three G10 currencies associated with the highest interest rates and short futures contracts on the three G10 currencies associated with the lowest interest rates. Cash is invested in U.S. government securities. The fund will not establish a long or short futures position in U.S. dollars because it is the fund's home currency. The index reevaluates interest rates quarterly and, based on the evaluation, reweights futures contracts.

Immediately after each reweighting, the index will reflect an investment on a two-to-one leveraged basis in the three long futures contracts and in the three short futures contracts. By entering into long and short positions, the index is expected to provide more consistent and less volatile returns than could be obtained by taking only long currency positions or only short positions.

The Future of Futures ETFs

ETF providers have just begun to issue new products benchmarked to new and interesting alternative asset class indexes. One key to development is an active derivatives market in the product the fund companies are trying to introduce. Where there is an active derivatives market, there can be successfully traded ETFs.

What new developments are in the future? How about mutual funds that track the average market price of homes in your city? The Case-Shiller indexes represent movements in housing price values in 10 major metropolitan areas across the country. The 10 cities include Boston, Chicago, Denver, Las Vegas, Los Angeles, Miami, the New York Commuter Index, San Diego, San Francisco, and Washington D.C.

Futures contracts launched in the second quarter of 2006 track the Case-Shiller indexes. Perhaps homebuyers and sellers will soon be able to hedge their exposure to rising or falling home prices in the city of their choice.

Commodity and Currency Fund List

Table 15.2 offers a list of commodity and currency ETFs and ETNs available on U.S. exchanges. It is divided into two sections. The first section lists currency funds and the second lists commodity funds.

There are a growing number of currency and commodity ETFs and ETNs, and new alternative asset class funds will be introduced in the coming years. To stay on top of the news, visit the web sites listed in the ETF Resource List in Appendix B. For a current list of all commodity and currency ETFs and ETNs, including the Index Strategy Box database, visit www.theetfbook.com and www.etfguide.com.

Appendix A is an abbreviation guide for security selection and weighting methodologies used in each index in Table 15.2. Index descriptions, security selection, and weighting methodologies are the best fit given the information available.

Summary

The growth of ETFs in alternative asset classes has exploded in recent years. Low-cost funds are now available in individual commodities, commodity indexes, and currencies. These new opportunities may

Table 15.2   Commodity and Currency Funds

Currency ETFs and ETNs

Category	Fund Name	Ticker	Expense Ratio	Currency	Strategy Box	Sec. Select	Sec. Weight
Single Country	CurrencyShares Australian Dollar Trust	FXA	0.40%	Australian Dollar		P A	C A
Single Country	CurrencyShares British Pound Sterling Trust	FXB	0.40%	British Pound		P A	C A
Single Country	CurrencyShares Canadian Dollar Trust	FXC	0.40%	Canada Dollar		P A	C A
EURO Zone	CurrencyShares Euro Trust	FXE	0.40%	Euro		P A	C A
Single Country	CurrencyShares Japanese Yen	FXY	0.40%	Japanese Yen		P A	C A
Single Country	CurrencyShares Mexican Peso Trust	FXM	0.40%	Mexican Peso		P A	C A
Single Country	CurrencyShares Swedish Krona Trust	FXS	0.40%	Swedish Krona		P A	C A
Single Country	CurrencyShares Swiss Franc Trust	FXF	0.40%	Swiss Franc		P A	C A
EURO Zone	iPath EUR/USD ETN	ERO	0.40%	Euro		P A	C A
Single Country	iPath GBP/USD ETN	GBB	0.40%	British Pound		P A	C A
Single Country	iPath JPY/USD ETN	JYN	0.40%	Japanese Yen		P A	C A
USD – Long	PowerShares DB U.S. Dollar Index Bullish Fund	UUP	0.50%	DB Long USD Futures Index		P A	C A
USD – Short	PowerShares DB U.S. Dollar Index Bearish Fund	UDN	0.50%	DB Short USD Futures Index		P A	X S
MultiCurrency –Long/Short	PowerShares DB G10 Currency Harvest Fund	DBV	0.75%	DB G10 Currency Future Harvest		P A	X N
	Average Currency Fee		**0.44%**				

(continued)

Table 15.2 *(continued)*

Commodity ETFs and ETNs

Category	Market ETF Name	Ticker	Expense Ratio	Commodity or Index	Strategy Box	Sec. Select	Sec. Weight
Precious Metals	iShares Silver Trust	SLV	0.50%	Silver Spot Price		P A	C A
Precious Metals	iShares Comex Gold Trust	IAU	0.40%	Gold Spot Price		P A	C A
Precious Metals	streetTRACKS Gold Shares	GLD	0.40%	Gold Spot Price		P A	C A
Precious Metals Futures	PowerShares DB Silver Fund	DBS	0.54%	DBLCI-OY Silver Excess Rtn		P A	C A
Precious Metals Futures	PowerShares DB Precious Metals Fund	DBP	0.79%	DBLCI-OY Precious Metals ER		P A	C A
Precious Metals Futures	PowerShares DB Gold Fund	DGL	0.54%	DBLCI-OY Gold Excess Return		P A	C A
Commodity Futures	PowerShares DB Agriculture Fund	DBA	0.91%	DBLCI-OY Agriculture Excess Return		P A	C A
Commodity Futures	PowerShares DB Base Metals Fund	DBB	0.78%	DBLCI-OY Ind'l Metals Excess Return		P A	C A
Commodity Futures	PowerShares DB Energy Fund	DBE	0.78%	DBLCI-OY Energy Excess Return		P A	C A
Commodity Futures	Barclays iPath oil ETN	OIL	0.75%	GS Crude Oil Total Return		P A	C A
Commodity Futures	PowerShares DB Oil Fund	DBO	0.54%	DBLCI-OY Base Metals Excess Return		P A	C A
Commodity Futures	United States Oil Fund	USO	0.50%	West Texas Intermediate Light Spot		P S	C A
Commodity Swaps	Claymore MACROshares Oil Up Tradeable Trust	UCR	1.50%	Bull – NYMEX Light Sweet Ftr		P A	C A
Commodity Swaps	Claymore MACROshares Oil Down Tradeable Trust	DCR	1.50%	Bear – NYMEX Light Sweet Ftr		P A	C A
Total Return Index	iShares S&P GSCI Commodity Indexed Trust	GSG	0.75%	S&P GSCI Total Return		P A	C A
Total Return Index	PowerShares DB Commodity Index Tracking Fund	DBC	0.83%	DB Liquid Commodity–DBLCI		P A	P A

Table 15.2 *(continued)*

Category	Market ETF Name	Ticker	Expense Ratio	Commodity or Index	Strategy Box	Sec. Select	Sec. Weight
Total Return Index	Dow Jones–AIG Commodity Index Total Return ETN	DJP	0.75%	DJ–AIG Commodity Index Total Return	⊞	P A	C A
Total Return Index	The iPath S&P GSCI Total Return Index ETN	GSP	0.75%	S&P GSCI Total Return	⊞	P A	P A
	Average Commodity Fee		**0.75%**				

play an expanded role in portfolio management in the future as the cost is driven down by competition.

There are advantages and disadvantages to adding alternative asset class ETFs to a portfolio. One advantage is that an investment in commodities tends to exhibit a low correlation with traditional stock and bond investments. That lowers the risk of a portfolio overall. However, the disadvantages include the cost of investing, the lack of a real expected return over fees and inflation and low tax efficiency.

More ETFs in alternative asset classes will be introduced as innovation continues in the financial markets. Some of those products will enter new and exciting markets, such as housing prices and possibly the art market. Hopefully, the fees to invest in those products will be low enough so that they benefit buy-and-hold portfolios as well as an active trading portfolio. It is an exciting time for index fund investors who seek a broadly diversified portfolio.

PART

IV

PORTFOLIO MANAGEMENT
USING ETFs

16

Portfolio Management Strategies

All of the chapters in Part IV are provided to help you select and manage your ETF portfolio. Four basic methods of portfolio management are introduced so you can compare and contrast strategies.

The information in this section is intended to be a starting point for research and analysis. More study is recommended before making a final decision on which strategy is best for you. The ETF Research List in the appendix provides an excellent point to begin your search for more information.

The four investment strategies reviewed in this section cover passive investing, life-cycle investing, active management, and special uses. Selected ETF portfolios for each strategy are provided. The ETF selected are examples, not endorsements. There are many fine ETFs not included in this book because there is not enough space, and the marketplace is quickly evolving. Each investor should investigate several competing funds before ultimately deciding on the ones that are appropriate for their unique situation.

Of course, there is always the option of hiring a professional investment adviser to assist in ETF selection and the management of your portfolio. An educated investment professional should be able to explain the differences between ETF types and styles, including the advantages and disadvantages of the indexes they follow.

Passive Investing

Chapter 17 explains the elegantly but effective passive investment strategy of buy-and-hold investing. It is an easy and effective strategy that any individual investor can implement. Millions of individual investors have opted for this low maintenance approach.

Passive investing is a straightforward strategy. It begins by choosing an assortment of broad asset classes that fit your long-term financial goals, and constructing a target asset allocation using those asset classes that are consistent with your goals. The next step is to select low-cost ETFs that represent those chosen asset classes and to buy them in the correct quantity in your portfolio. The target asset allocation is maintained through regular rebalancing of the ETFs to bring the portfolio back in line with your goals. There is no attempt to market-time or predict the next winning sector within the markets.

One reason a buy-and-hold works is because the costs are low. Many passive investors select ETFs that follow market indexes. As such, the expense ratio of ETFs is significantly lower than ETFs that follow custom indexes. Commission costs are also moderated because passive management does not require frequent trading, with the exception of an occasional rebalancing of asset classes.

A derivative of passive investing is known as core and explore, also known as core and satellite. Investors following this strategy own a core portfolio of market index ETFs that charge low fees, and they add in a few ETFs that follow custom indexes or try to time a style or sector. The idea is the latter ETFs will achieve superior returns over market indexes while the portfolio does not deviate from a market return by too large an amount.

Life Cycle Investing

Life changes over time, and so do attitudes about investing. Rather than holding a set asset allocation in certain asset classes for the long term, a life-cycle strategy adjusts a portfolio as investors move through various stages in life. Life cycle investing is a passive approach in that the allocation to asset classes remains constant at each stage for the duration of the stage.

People often invest more aggressively when they are young and become conservative later in life. Young people can afford to be more aggressive. They tend to have little money at stake and a lot of time to make up for mistakes. That attitude changes around mid-Life when the realization of mortality and retirement set in. At retirement age, the driving factor of investing is to provide a necessary stream of income that lasts longer than we do. Finally, in the late stage of retirement, people often find a compromise between their own income needs and growth needs of those who will inherit what is left.

In one of my previous books, *Protecting Your Wealth in Good Times and Bad* [McGraw-Hill 2003], I categorized investors by four general age groups: Early Savers, Mid-Life Accumulators, Early Retirees, and Late Retirees. Those stages are the basis for the portfolio recommendations in Chapter 18.

Active Portfolio Strategies

Active investing is all about achieving returns that are superior to the financial markets. That goal is the crème de la crème for some investors. Unfortunately, it is very difficult to beat the market. Few people can do it consistently enough to achieve the long-term returns needed to justify the time and expense. Nonetheless, if you are ambitious, and failing frequently does not faze you or affect your lifestyle, then perhaps an active strategy is appropriate.

There are millions of ways to try to beat the market using ETFs. They range from large shifts in the stock and bond allocations based on economic forecasts to sector rotation strategies based on price momentum. In your quest for market dominance, you may discover a new market-beating method. If that happens, don't tell anyone. Once the word gets out, your system is destined for mediocrity as other people exploit the idea.

Nominal and Risk Adjusted Returns

Beating the market is not just achieving a higher return. There are two ways an investor can measure investment performance: nominally and risk-adjusted. Beating the market nominally means outperforming on a percentage basis. Superior risk adjusted performance means beating the market after accounting for portfolio risk.

Nominal return is how most individual investors measure their success. If the broad U.S. stock market gained 10 percent in total return during the year and your portfolio gained 12 percent, you beat the market nominally. I would venture to guess that 99 percent of individual investors look at only nominal returns before deciding to buy an investment product.

Risk adjusted returns are a more sophisticated approach to measuring the performance of a portfolio or fund. If the broad

U.S. stock market gained 10 percent in total return during the year and your portfolio gained 12 percent, it may have underperformed the market if the portfolio risk as measured by price volatility was substantially higher than the risk of the stock market. On the other hand, if your portfolio returned only 8 percent while the market achieved 10 percent, the portfolio may have outperformed on a risk-adjusted basis if the risk in the portfolio was substantially lower than market risk. One formula for calculating risk adjusted returns is the Sharpe Ratio. The formula for the Sharpe Ratio is provided in Chapter 19.

Active strategies may or may not achieve the goal of beating the markets. One fact about active strategies, however, is certain: They are more expensive than passive strategies in many ways. First, ETFs that follow custom indexes have higher fees than market indexes. You will pay more if you attempt to beat the market with custom index ETFs. Second, an active strategy tends to have a higher turnover of ETFs in a portfolio. That results in higher commissions. Third, active strategies take time. It takes many hours of research and analysis to correctly sort out the avalanche of information that has a bearing on your active strategy. The fourth cost is emotional. By default, active management means making frequent decisions based on vague information. In the fog of financial war, many decisions will be wrong, and wrong decisions can cost you emotionally as well as monetarily.

Chapter 19 covers the basics of active management using different approaches. The first two are fundamental and the second two are technical. The top-down method starts with a birds-eye view of the global economy and works its way down into countries, asset class styles, and individual industries. The bottom-up approach starts with a fundamental analysis of each industry or country and moves up into tactical asset class selections and dynamic country allocations. Momentum investing looks at the acceleration of earnings trends and price trends to predict future gains. Technical analysis, or charting, looks for established patterns in past price data to predict future prices.

Comparing Active Strategies to Benchmarks

Active portfolio strategies attempt to beat the markets. As such, the return of any active strategy should be compared to appropriate market benchmarks. Those benchmark indexes use passive security selection and capitalization weighting.

A benchmark index may be a single indicator, such as the S&P 500 index, or it may be a combination of several indexes based on the asset allocation of a portfolio. For example, a portfolio that holds a large company U.S. ETF, an international developed market ETF, and a general bond market ETF might be benchmarked to a comparable blended benchmark comprising the S&P 500, the MSCI EAFE index, and the Lehman Brothers Aggregate Bond index.

An active investor may use market timing or tactical asset allocation to beat the blended benchmark. Market timing is wholesale moves completely in and out of stocks, bonds, and cash, while tactical asset allocation is the gradual movement between asset classes in smaller amounts. While the portfolio shifts based on the investor perception, the benchmark does not shift. The allocation of asset classes in the benchmark stays at fixed percentages.

For example, a tactical asset allocation portfolio might shift from 70 percent in stocks and 30 percent in bonds to 30 percent in stocks and 70 percent in bonds. The benchmark, however, is always maintained in the middle at 50 percent in stocks and 50 percent in bonds. The static benchmark allows a comparison of the investor's ability to accurately time the markets to a constant blend.

Figure 16.1 illustrates the amount of variability from a benchmark that investors should expect when using various portfolio management strategies. At the two extremes are buy-and-hold and market timing. A buy-and-hold investor should expect very little tracking error against the benchmark because she is trying to achieve the returns of the markets. Market timing strategies create a large tracking error as investors try to outmaneuver the markets with large asset allocation changes.

Special Strategies and Uses

Chapter 20 touches on ETF use in special situations. You may find a use for an ETF as asset class gap fillers that are not covered by your other investments, or as hedges to illiquid equity positions, or to manage currency risks.

Filling a gap is a common use for sector and country ETFs. For example, Canadian stocks represent 5 percent of the international equity market, but you will not find that country as a holding in

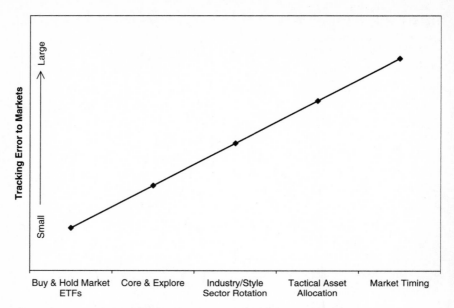

Figure 16.1   ETF Portfolio Strategies and Tracking Errors

Source: Portfolio Solutions, LLC

ETFs that follow the popular MCSI EAFE index (see Chapter 11). A small allocation to the iShares MSCI Canada (symbol: EWC) would fill the gap.

ETFs can be used to hedge illiquid stock positions. For example, you may own company stock that is restricted from sale or you may own stocks that have a cost basis so low that selling it would create a large tax burden. In those cases, shorting an ETF in the industry group that the stock belongs to may give you a partial hedge against a downturn in the stock. If the industry falls and along with it the price of the concentrated stock position, the value of the short position would rise and offset some of the loss.

Currency ETFs have many uses in portfolio management as well as personal planning. Assume you are taking a trip to Germany next summer and are concerned that the value of the dollar will fall against the Euro before you go. You could purchase a few thousand dollars in the CurrencyShares Euro Trust (symbol: FXE) or the iPath EUR/USD (symbol: ERO) and lock in today's exchange rate. If the Euro does strengthen, the money you put aside for the trip is hedged.

Tips for ETF Investors

Chapter 21 provides useful tips for ETF investors. Several trading methods are discussed that can reduce your investment expenses and management time, and increase your investment return and investment satisfaction. Also discussed are the benefits and drawbacks in hiring a professional investment manager to assist in portfolio management.

ETFs are bought and sold on securities exchanges, and where you trade is important. Selecting an appropriate broker can save you time and money. Discount brokers are lower cost but generally provide less service than full service firms. While cost is an important factor in making brokerage decisions, it should not be the only factor. Full service brokerage firms have research staffs that offer clients written proprietary information and trading strategy. Those services may be important to more active ETF investors.

Taxes are an expense that investors can do without. ETFs are inherently tax efficient because of their operating methods. In addition, several portfolio management techniques are suggested that can be used to lower the tax burden further. Those methods include asset location and tax-loss harvesting.

Many people would rather pay someone to do the investment research and portfolio management. Fee-only investment advisers are compensated on the basis of the value of an account rather than the commissions generated during trading. There are many firms to choose from including my own, Portfolio Solutions in Troy, Michigan. The fees for professional management vary from firm to firm. I suggest hiring an adviser who is easy to work with and is reasonably priced.

Summary

Part IV brings together all the elements of good portfolio management, using ETFs. Those elements include various strategies and money saving portfolio management ideas. The investment strategies discussed in this section offer many different approaches, although they can only scratch the surface. There are many ways to use ETFs. The methods are only limited to the imagination of investors.

The four investment strategies reviewed in this section are passive, life cycle, active, and special uses. Selecting ETFs for a passive buy-and-hold strategy is the most popular strategy involving a static asset allocation and occasional rebalancing of investments. Life cycle investing employs a changing asset allocation that follows a person through the four stages of wealth accumulation. Active management is more complex and costly, but can result in greater returns for successful investors.

Choosing the right broker and possibly hiring the right investment manager can make ETF management easier. Trading commissions are an important factor when choosing a broker, but that should not be the only factor in decision making. Other factors include the depth of investment research available and quality of the adviser's advice. If you decide not to manage your own money, for a reasonable annual fee you can hire a qualified investment adviser who will build and maintain a prudent ETF portfolio designed for your needs.

CHAPTER 17

Passive ETF Portfolios

Passive investing is a simple and effective portfolio management technique. It is also difficult to maintain because the strategy requires strict discipline. As such, to be a successful passive investor, you need to have an unwavering belief that the strategy will work in the long term.

Passive investing is all about holding a portfolio of ETFs that mostly follow low-cost market indexes. The portfolio is designed on the basis of an investor's long-term goals, and the investments are held for a very long time. Passive investors do not attempt to time markets by forecasting economic changes or charting prices. Nor do they attempt to rotate among market sectors or styles in search of superior returns. The only trading done in the portfolio is when asset class rebalancing is needed or when cash is added or withdrawn.

The return objective of passive management is to achieve the return of the markets. Successful passive investors realize that natural returns of the global stock and bond markets are worthy returns. They also understand how difficult it is to beat the markets, and that few people actually accomplish that feat during their lifetime.

Unfortunately, passive investing typically starts with good intentions but does not always end that way. Maintaining a set allocation for many years requires conviction and emotional discipline. Many would-be successful passive investors sway from their convictions at some point because they think the strategy may not be working. That usually occurs during poor market conditions. It is at those times that the less faithful abandon the strategy in search of greener pastures. Inevitably, changing investment strategies during rough market periods is the wrong move and results in lower returns and higher risk than maintaining the passive approach through the bad patch.

Passive investing is straightforward. Choose the broad market asset classes you want to have in a portfolio based on your long-term financial goals, and then select low-cost ETFs to represent those asset classes. Over time, the global financial markets will move in different directions and the portfolio will drift from its original allocation. The integrity of the allocation is maintained through a regular rebalancing of ETFs, thus bringing the portfolio back to its original mix.

Investors who understand passive strategies but are not ready for a full market matching approach may divide their portfolio into a portion that uses only ETFs that track market indexes and ETFs that are more aggressive. The core and explore technique (also know as core and satellite) is a strategy whereby investors own a core portfolio of market index ETFs that charge low fees and also buy a few costlier ETFs that follow custom indexes. The hope is to achieve market performance in the core portfolio and achieve superior returns in the custom portion. In the worst case, the total portfolio return will not fall far from a market index return.

Buy and Hold

A buy-and-hold strategy is almost self-explanatory. Based on your investment objectives, you create a diversified portfolio of low-cost ETFs that follow market indexes and hold them for a very long time. Trading is done only annually to rebalance a portfolio back to its target asset allocation, or when cash is added or withdrawn. No attempt is made to predict the return of any market, or to gain excess returns by moving from one investment style or sector to another.

The most important long-term decision you will make in a buy-and-hold strategy is the long-term mix between stock and bond index funds. That decision will explain a majority of portfolio risk and return over the long term. It is thus very important to select a good allocation right from the start when using a buy-and-hold strategy.

Asset Allocation Explained

Asset allocation is a polished way of saying, ''Don't put all your eggs in one basket.'' Global diversification across several types of investments is at the core of the strategy. Which investments you choose is critical to the long-term return expectations of the portfolio. An analysis of returns and asset class correlation is at the center of that decision. This chapter is an introduction to the basic tools and concepts used in asset allocation, and for an advanced understanding, read *All About Asset Allocation*, by Richard A. Ferri [McGraw-Hill, 2005].

Correlation is the tendency of one investment to affect the movement of another. If one investment moves in harmony with another, they have a positive correlation. If the two investments move in opposite directions they have a negative correlation. If the two investments move independent of each other they have no correlation.

The challenge of investors has always been to find ETFs that track indexes that will have a lower correlation to each other in the future. If that can be done, the portfolio will have some investment zigging while others are zagging, and that will lower overall portfolio risk.

There is no benefit to diversifying into two ETFs that invest in the same asset class and have a high positive correlation with each other. For example, if you already own the Vanguard Total U.S. Stock Market ETF (symbol: VTI), it makes no sense to also buy the iShares Russell 3000 (symbol: IWV). The securities that underlie those two ETFs are basically the same, and therefore by default are always highly correlated.

Figure 17.1 illustrates a portfolio that is invested in two ETFs that have similar risk and return characteristics. ETF A and ETF B have a positive correlation with each other. Assuming that rebalancing is done annually, there is no risk reduction in a portfolio that invests 50 percent in EFT A and 50 percent in ETF B. The portfolio behaves the same as either of the two investments.

It would be great to find two ETFs that have a negative correlation of return. Figure 17.2 shows that ETF A and ETF B moving in the opposite direction of each other, and both offer positive returns over the long term. A portfolio of 50 percent in ETF A and 50 percent in ETF B rebalanced annually results in a smooth return compared to either of the two investments individually.

When two ETFs move randomly with each other they have low correlation. Low correlation among unrelated asset classes is much more common than finding two asset classes that have constant negative correlation. Figure 17.3 is an example of two asset classes that have had low correlation. The two ETFs move independent of

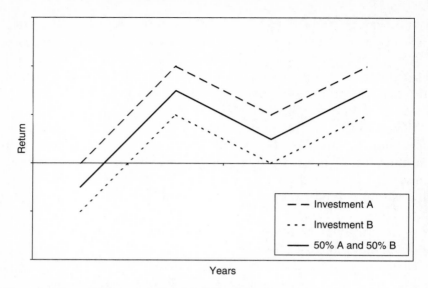

Figure 17.1   Positive Correlation between ETFs

each other most of the time. That is a good set of investments to place in a portfolio providing each is expected to deliver a long-term return over the inflation rate.

Correlation in Reality

In practice, there are not very many ETFs that offer consistently low correlation all of the time and offer positive long-term returns over inflation. They either have a varying correlation and positive real returns or a low correlation with no real expected returns after inflation. The best you will do is to find a few ETFs that have low or negative correlation some of the time, and expected positive long-term returns all of the time.

Figure 17.4 illustrates the rolling 10-year correlation between the returns of U.S. stocks and intermediate-term U.S. Treasuries. When the line is in the top of the chart the correlation is positive and when the line is in the lower half it is negative. As you can see, the correlation varies between positive and negative over time. The chart is typical of many other asset classes. As long as the return outlook of the asset class is positive after inflation, and the correlation between that asset class and another is varying, then it should be included in a portfolio.

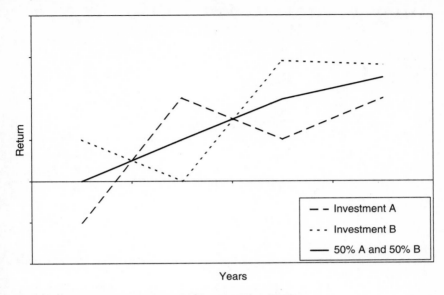

Figure 17.2   Negative Correlation between ETFs

Here are a few realities about correlation and asset class selection:

1. It is very difficult to find major asset classes that have consistently negative or low correlation with one another and are expected to deliver returns higher than the rate of inflation.
2. The correlation between asset classes change, sometimes frequently and suddenly. Investments that once offered good diversification benefits may not have those benefits in the future.
3. During a time of crisis, the correlation between major asset classes increase, for example, global stocks. When the World Trade Center was destroyed by terrorists in September 2001, stock markets around the world fell by more than 5 percent. Global diversification did not help during that horrific period in history.

The topic of asset allocation is not as clear as some advisers preach. There is no mathematic formula that works all the time. Building a portfolio of buy-and-hold investments in the real world requires more common sense than it does quantitative number crunching. The key is to create a good allocation, implement that

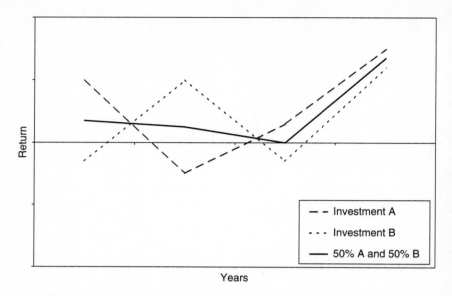

Figure 17.3   Low Correlation between ETFs

allocation, and stay with that allocation. Everything else will eventually fall into place.

Buy-and-Hold Portfolio Examples

A portfolio's allocation to stocks and bonds explains a majority of portfolio performance over the long term. Thus, selecting an appropriate allocation between fixed income and equities is the most important decision you will make. The following asset allocations are the backbone of buy-and-hold strategies using low-cost market ETFs. The five strategic allocations to stocks and bonds represent five different levels of risk and expected return (see the end of the chapter for methodology on the expected return of asset classes).

Following the five strategic allocations are ETF selections representing the equity portion and the fixed income portion of the allocation. The strategic allocations and ETF selections are not meant to be right for everyone, but they are a good place to start building a portfolio that fits your needs.

The return estimates are based on my own historic analysis of asset class risks and returns provided at the end of this chapter. Inflation is imbedded in all asset class returns. The estimates assume

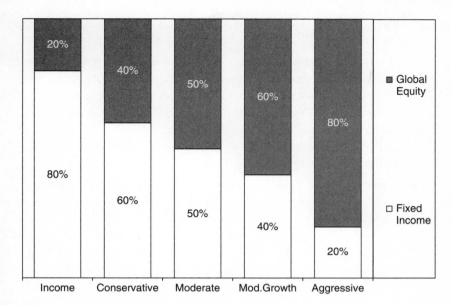

Figure 17.4 Strategic Allocations
Source: Portfolio Solutions, LLC

a 3 percent long-term inflation rate. The return estimates would move higher if the anticipated inflation increased and vice versa.

> *Income Oriented:* Characteristics—lowest volatility and highest cash flow. The expected long-term total return is approximately 5.8 percent, net of expenses and before taxes. The allocation to diversified fixed income ETFs would be approximately 80 percent and the allocation to equity ETFs, including real estate, will be approximately 20 percent.
>
> *Conservative:* Characteristics—low volatility and moderately high cash flow. The expected long-term total return is approximately 6.4 percent, net of expenses and before taxes. The allocation to diversified fixed income ETFs would be approximately 60 percent and the allocation to equity ETFs, including real estate, will be approximately 40 percent.
>
> *Moderate:* Characteristics—controlled volatility and moderate cash flow. The expected long-term total return is approximately 6.7 percent, net of expenses and before taxes. The allocation to diversified fixed income ETFs would be

approximately 50 percent and the allocation to equity ETFs, including real estate, will be approximately 50 percent.

Modest Growth: Characteristics—moderate volatility in difficult markets and low cash flow. The expected long-term total return is approximately 7.0 percent, net of expenses and before taxes. The allocation to diversified fixed income ETFs would be approximately 40 percent and the allocation to equity ETFs, including real estate, will be approximately 60 percent.

Aggressive: Characteristics—periods of high volatility and lowest cash flow. The expected long-term total return is approximately 7.7 percent, net of expenses and before taxes. The allocation to diversified fixed income ETFs would be approximately 20 percent and the allocation to equity ETFs, including real estate, will be approximately 80 percent.

Building a portfolio using the strategic asset allocation and the individual ETFs listed in Table 17.1 is a simple process. Whatever the strategic allocation to equity is, multiply that amount by the equity allocation. Do the same with fixed income. For example, in Table 17.1 the allocation to REITS is 10 percent. If the strategic stock and bond allocation you choose is 50 percent in equity, then the allocation to REITs is only 5 percent ($10\% \times 50\% = 5\%$).

Core and Explore

Some critics of an all-passive ETF management say that the problem with the strategy is that it achieves *only* the market averages. There is no opportunity for superior returns. The critics are correct. No passive portfolios will ever beat the markets. On the other hand, there is no opportunity to underachieve the market either, net of fees. Nonetheless, if an investor wants to take more risk and explore other options, a core and explore strategy is a good compromise between passive and active management.

Core and explore (or core and satellite) blend together the low-cost simplicity of market index ETFs with the chance to beat the market using active strategies. There are two ways to explore. First, use an allocation to custom index ETFs in areas of the global financial markets you believe are inefficient. Second, try to time

Table 17.1 Sample of Market Index ETFs in a Portfolio

Equity Portion of 100%		ETF Name	Symbol	Fee
45%	U.S. Total Stock Market	Vanguard Total Stock Market ETF	VTI	0.07%
15%	U.S. Small Value	iShare S&P 600 Small Cap Value	IJS	0.25%
10%	Real Estate	Vanguard REIT ETF	VQN	0.12%
12%	European Markets	Vanguard European Index ETF	VGK	0.18%
12%	Pacific Rim Markets	Vanguard Pacific Index ETF	VPL	0.18%
6%	Emerging Market	Vanguard Emerging Markets ETF	VWO	0.30%

Fixed Income of 100%		ETF Name	Symbol	Fee
60%	Total Bond Market	Vanguard Total Bond Market ETF	BND	0.11%
20%	Corporate Bond	IBoxx $ InvesTop Invest Grade Corp.	LQD	0.15%
20%	Inflation Protected Securities	iShares Lehman TIPS Bond Fund	TIP	0.20%

Source: Portfolio Solutions, LLC

industry sectors, styles, or countries using a variety of ETFs that track those areas.

The explore side of a portfolio will be more expensive than the core side. ETFs that follow custom indexes have expense ratios up to five times higher than market index ETFs. Or, if a market timing or sector rotation strategy is used on the explore side, the turnover will be higher, as will the commission cost. Either way, explore strategies have to make up their higher expenses before delivering a benefit to your portfolio.

Realistic Returns from Passive Portfolios

It is possible to estimate long-term portfolio returns when using a passive approach to ETF management. The estimated returns can be forecast using long-term relationships between the risks and returns of asset classes, and by analyzing how markets are related to expected long-term economic growth.

There are many methods for predicting market returns, and none will be exact. At best the predictions will be close to reality. Despite the inexact science of forecasting, we must do it anyway so that we can put together an asset allocation based on the forecast. If your forecast is conservative, you have a better chance of achieving your financial goal. I believe it is better to keep expectations low and possibly be pleasantly surprised than have unrealistic expectations and fall short of your financial goals.

One method of forecasting returns projects past performance and risks into the future with adjustments for today's interest rates, corporate earnings levels, and tax rates. A second method of market prediction starts with economic forecasts and assesses the probability of market returns using those forecasts. A third method is to combine past market data with a conservative estimate of long-term economic growth.

No one knows for certain what the returns will be in the financial markets. Combining the technical aspects of past market returns with the fundamental inputs from economic estimates may be the best way to form an opinion. The market forecasts put forth in Table 17.2 (see page 291) later in this chapter are based on that combination.

Inflation Is in Every Estimate

No sensible person would put money into any investment knowing that the expected return was below the rate of inflation. The inflation rate is always part of the expected return of all investments. That rate is added to the expected premium for taking risks in various markets.

The inflation rate has averaged about 3 percent annually since the middle of the 1980s. That is slightly higher than the historic inflation rate of about 2 percent annually that dates back several centuries. It is not an easy task to predict inflation. A 3 percent rate of inflation is assumed in this analysis and the market return estimates provided in Table 17.2.

Equity Return Expectations

The primary driver behind stock prices is earnings. The more money companies make, the more money shareholders make and stocks go up in value.

One way to forecast earnings growth is to start with the expected growth in overall economic activity. Gross domestic product (GDP) is the single best measure of economic activity. Real GDP is the sum total of all goods and services produced in the United States during the year adjusted for inflation. It is composed of four components: consumer spending, government spending, business spending, and exports minus imports. There is a direct and consistent relationship between GDP growth and corporate earnings growth. Figure 17.5 illustrates that relationship by showing that earnings growth follows GDP growth.

Cash Dividends. The second part of calculating equity returns is to consider the cash payment of stock dividends. Dividends are currently not as large a part of the total return equation as they used to be but remain important to the performance of stocks in the long term. U.S. stocks are currently paying less than 2 percent per year in dividend yields, as measured by the S&P 500 Index.

Speculation (PE Expansion and Contraction). The third driver of total return is speculation. If most investors believe that corporate earnings will increase faster than the average, the price of stock will increase in anticipation of the greater earnings growth. This is exactly the reason Internet stocks kept going higher and higher in

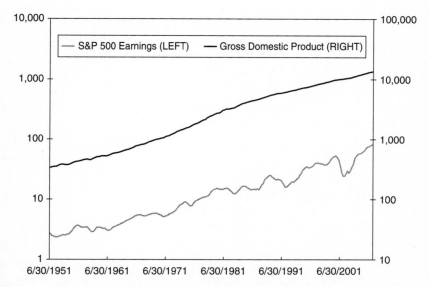

Figure 17.5   GDP and S&P 500 Corporate Earnings Growth
Source: Federal Reserve, S&P

the late 1990s and real estate stocks expanded during this decade. The prices of those stocks were simply adjusting to the earnings forecasts of analysts and investors. In the case of Internet stocks, when real earnings came in substantially below forecasts, the value of that industry collapsed.

Speculation creates about 10 times more volatility in the market than actual earnings changes and about 100 times more volatility than dividend changes. If you have a crystal ball and can predict the mind of the masses, then you can make a lot of money on changing market valuation. Personally, I have never had any luck doing that.

In the short run, speculation creates the volatility in stock prices, but in the long run, the speculative noise tends to cancel out any economic growth drivers of stock prices. Speculation is not predictable, so there is no sense trying to input that variable into a long-term forecast. It is impossible to predict what investors will think about the value of the markets next week, next month, or next year, let alone 30 years from now. For the following forecasts, we assume the price-to-earnings ratios of the stock market are held constant at current levels, thereby eliminating speculative noise.

Bond Return Expectations

The expected return on bonds is much easier to read than the expected return for stocks. An expected Treasury bond return equals interest payments, plus the reinvestment of interest, plus or minus unexpected changes in the expected inflation before the bond matures. There is a fourth and fifth pricing factor when a corporate bond is being evaluated. They are the credit quality of the corporate bond and the call option of the issuer.

There is a direct and inverse relationship between the inflation rate and the price of all bonds. When inflation is rising, bond prices are falling, and when inflation is falling, bond prices are rising. Figure 17.6 highlights the relationship between long-term inflation and intermediate-term Treasury bond returns.

Figure 17.6 illustrates one of the most volatile periods in U.S. bond market history, when inflation soared to double digits percent in the early 1980s and interest rates followed. Over the long term, the returns from intermediate-term Treasury bonds have achieved a 2 percent return over the inflation rate despite the lag in returns due to changes in inflation.

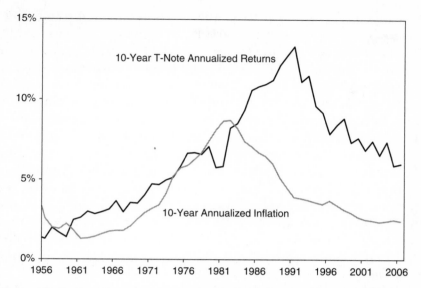

Figure 17.6   Ten-Year Annualized Inflation and Treasury Bond Returns
Source: Federal Reserve

The 2-percent-over-inflation return is known as the bond risk premium. That is the number used for the forecast in Table 17.2. ETFs have investment costs. Assuming the cost is 0.5 percent per year, intermediate-term Treasury bond ETFs are therefore expected to achieve about 1.5 percent more in the long run, net of expenses.

Corporate bonds have a higher risk than Treasury bonds because of the possibility of default. As such, the expected return is higher. The default risk premium has historically been about between 0.5 and 0.8 percent higher than the return from comparable maturity Treasuries. Thus, the expected risk premium for corporate bond ETFs is 2.0 percent over the inflation rate, net of fees.

The Forecast

The forecasts in Table 17.2 were calculated using the primary drivers of market returns: inflation, earnings growth, historic risk premiums, interest, and dividends. It would require a book much thicker than this to detail the mechanics behind the forecasting methods used in Table 17.2. Although the table is likely to have errors, it is a place to start.

No portfolio in this chapter holds commodity or currency ETFs because this author believes that pure commodity and currency investments reduce the long-term expected return of a portfolio. The results of academic studies on commodity returns are so inconsistent that it is difficult to conclude what the *past* performance was, let alone the expected future return. In this book, commodities and currencies are viewed as trading vehicles rather than as long-term investments. Commodity investments are included as part of Chapter 19 on active portfolio management strategies.

Passive investing primarily uses a static stock and bond allocation. Table 17.2 helps you estimate the return from an asset allocation of market index ETFs. If you create a core and explore portfolio, the more exploring you do, the higher the cost goes with no guarantee of higher returns. There is a possibility that you will choose the right explore strategy and enhance your return above the added portfolio risk.

Table 17.2   30-Year Estimates of Market Index ETF Returns

Expected Long-term ETF Returns*	Real Return	With 3% Inflation
Government-Backed Fixed Income ETFs		
Intermediate-term U.S. Treasury Notes	1.5	4.5
Long-term U.S. Treasury Bonds	2.0	5.0
GNMA Mortgages	2.0	5.0
Intermediate Tax-free (AA Rated)	1.0	4.0
Corporate Bonds ETFs		
Intermediate High Grade Corporate	2.0	5.0
Preferred Stocks	3.0	6.0
High Yield Corporate	4.0	7.0
U.S. Equity ETFs		
U.S. Large Stocks	5.0	8.0
U.S. Micro Cap Stocks	7.0	10.0
U.S. Small Value Stocks	7.0	10.0
REITs (Real Estate Investment Trusts)	5.0	8.0

Table 17.2   *(continued)*

Expected Long-term ETF Returns*	Real Return	With 3% Inflation
International Equity ETFs		
International Developed Country Stocks	5.0	8.0
International Small Country Stocks	6.0	9.0
International Emerging Country Stocks	7.0	10.0
Commodities ETFs	0.0	3.0
Gross Domestic Product Growth	3.0	6.0

*These are estimates of returns. No guarantees are implied or to be inferred.
Source: Portfolio Solutions, LLC

Summary

Passive investing is all about holding a portfolio of mostly market index ETFs for a very long time, and only trading when rebalancing a portfolio or when cash is added or withdrawn. The return objective of a passive portfolio is to achieve the return of the markets rather than trying to beat the markets.

Passive investing is straightforward. Choose the broad market asset classes you want to have in a portfolio based on your long-term financial goals, and then select low-cost ETFs to represent those asset classes. Do not attempt to time markets by forecasting economic changes or charting prices. Over time markets will move and the portfolio will drift from its original allocation. The integrity of the allocation is maintained through regular rebalancing of the ETFs, thus bringing the portfolio back to its original mix.

Many people are not ready for a purely passive investment strategy. That is where core and explore strategies can help. Investors who want to take a little more risk in an attempt to beat the markets can divide their portfolio into market index ETFs and more aggressive strategies. The goal is to achieve market performance on the core side and beat the market in the explore portion. Seeking higher returns by using core and explore is a worthy objective, although difficult to achieve and more costly.

CHAPTER 18

Life Cycle Investing

Life is short and constantly changing. The most appropriate ETF portfolio for your needs today may not be the one you will need twenty years from now. The life cycle method of investing adjusts your ETF allocation in various asset classes as you move through life's stages.

The life cycle method is intuitive, because it follows traditional portfolio management wisdom concerning changing risks and re-turns preferences as we age. The ETF portfolio examples that follow market indexes provided in this chapter are a good starting point for portfolio construction and are designed to be adjusted as needed. The examples are not meant to be one-size-fits-all model portfolios because they do not take into consideration the many nuances of each person's life and unique financial situation.

Chapter 17 introduced the theory of asset allocation and passive investing. Academic studies have shown that asset allocation accounts for a vast majority of your portfolio's risks and returns over the long term. As such, your asset allocation is the single most important decision you will make in portfolio management.

Life cycle investing is a technique that adjusts the asset allocation of a portfolio over various stages in life. Often people are more aggressive investors when they are young because they have little invested and have an abundance of working years ahead of them to make up any losses. Investors grow more conservative as they enter middle age and realize the limits of their mortality. People are the most conservative when nearing retirement. Preparing for retirement often includes selling a business or taking a large rollover from a pension fund. Older retirees have other issues, such as preparing to pass on the family wealth.

Life Cycle Models

The definition of aggressive and conservative investing varies from person to person. One 40-year-old may think that allocating 65 percent to stocks is aggressive while the next 40-year-old thinks allocating 80 percent to stocks is conservative. This chapter takes the middle of the road approach. Each life stage and asset allocation recommendation is neither overly conservative nor overly aggressive for that period. Rather, it is a moderate allocation. Your allocation may be very different. Only you can decide whether an allocation is too conservative or aggressive for your tastes.

People of different ages have different financial needs and perceptions on investing. In a previous book, *Protecting Your Wealth in Good Times and Bad* [McGraw-Hill 2003], I categorized investors into four general groups based on age. Those groups are Early Savers, Mid-Life Accumulators, Preretirees and Active Retirees, and Mature Retirees. The material in this chapter uses similar ages with slight modifications.

Many of the market index ETFs in the portfolios can be substituted with custom index ETFs, if you are interested in a core-and-explore strategy. The difference will be a higher cost of investing and increased tracking error against market indexes.

The Four Life Phases of Investing

There are four life phases of investing reviewed in this chapter. They are Early Savers, Mid-Life Accumulators, New Retirees, and Mature Retirees. New Retirees also includes a five-year period leading up to retirement.

> **Early Savers** are investors who are in the beginning stages of their careers and families. They start their savings plan with few assets and a lot of ambition. The group generally spans ages 20 to 39. Early savers can and should be as aggressive in their asset allocation as they are comfortable with. The risk for this group is overextending their portfolios beyond the emotional tolerance for risk.

Mid-Life Accumulators are investors who are established in their careers and family life. They are accumulators of many things from cars to homes to appliances to children. From ages 40 to 59, accumulators know where they stand on career and family, and have a good idea about what to expect in the future. Generally, mid-life accumulators begin to reduce their exposures to riskier assets, particularly as they approach their mid to late fifties.

New Retirees covers people near retirement, those transitioning into retirement, and active retirees who are enjoying the fruits of their labors. It is the first stage where accumulation of wealth slows or stops and the distribution of wealth begins. As such, it is the first stage where a cash component is needed in the asset allocation. This stage generally covers people between ages 60 and 75.

Mature Retirees or fully retired investors, are not as active as they used to be. They have different needs, ranging from long-term care to estate planning issues. At this stage, financial matters are often jointly decided with children and other family members. Gifts to heirs and charities are common.

Investors in all stages have some similar financial goals and similar concerns. Similar goals include a desire for financial security and the desire to pay less income tax. Similar concerns include the fear of running out of money and the fear of not having adequate health care coverage when needed. These common goals and concerns are considered in every asset allocation regardless of stage.

Investors have more differences than similarities. Those differences include personal investment experiences, career challenges, education levels, health issues, family situations, risk tolerance differences, personality strengths and weaknesses, and, sometimes, legal issues.

Figure 18.1 represents typical life cycle investing models, using an allocation of stocks, bonds, and cash. Only liquid retirement assets are shown, not emergency cash or home ownership. Those models are middle of the road. They are not right for everyone. The right asset allocation for you should be whatever mix gives you the highest probability of achieving your financial goals while at the same time is within your tolerance for financial risk.

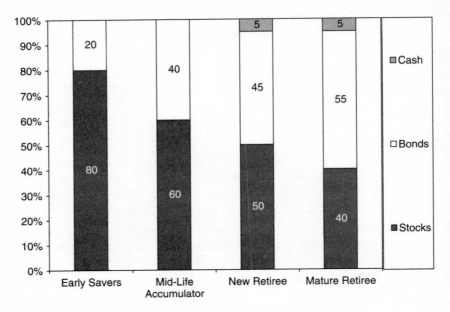

Figure 18.1 **Life Cycle Asset Allocation Guide**

ETF Portfolios for Each Stage

Two portfolios are provided for each stage in the life cycle. The first uses only low-cost market index ETFs and the second uses only customized index ETFs. The market index ETF portfolios are low-cost market-based index funds in each category or style. Customized index ETF portfolios represent alternative investment options, albeit at higher costs than market index ETF portfolios.

The custom index ETFs selected in the second portfolio at each phase represent examples of the types of investments that could replace market index ETFs. Investors who wish to incorporate a core and explore strategy can combine the first portfolio with the second. More aggressive investors may choose to have an all-custom index ETF portfolio.

The custom index ETF choices become more conservative through the life cycle examples. Aggressive growth ETFs were selected as equity funds for the early saver's portfolio, while conservative dividend-paying ETF funds are emphasized in the new retiree portfolio. The fixed income choices also grow progressively more conservative, although many fixed income funds still follow market indexes because there are only a few fixed income ETFs that follow custom indexes.

The customized index ETFs in the portfolios represent examples of funds that can be used. The mention of those funds should not be mistaken as an endorsement of those products. While I believe that many of those ETFs are fine products, including some very unique theme funds, there is no way to know if those funds will achieve their stated goal of outperforming market indexes, particularly since there are higher costs involved.

The market index portfolios in this chapter are a good place to start the process of designing a mix of funds that is right for you. First, tweak the asset allocation to your needs. Second, add or take away funds to suit your personal needs and desires.

Considerations for investment selection should at the least reflect your income level, savings rate, tax rate, fixed employee retirement plan options, estate planning concerns, special family situations, and your tolerance for investment risk. For more information on those topics, including detailed portfolio design and asset allocation recommendation, read *All About Asset Allocation* [McGraw-Hill 2005].

No portfolios in this chapter hold commodity or currency ETFs for the same reason they were not included in Chapter 17 on passive investing. This author believes that pure commodity and currency investments reduce the long-term expected return of a portfolio. Commodity investments are included as part of the trading vehicle in active portfolio management strategies in Chapter 19.

Phase 1—Early Savers

The key component for starting to accumulate wealth is savings consistency. For early savers, the most important component of investing is a consistent savings plan. The management of those savings is also important, but having a regular savings plan comes beforehand. Ideally, a young person will start a savings plan at the same time he lands his first full-time job.

Young investors can and should be aggressive in their investment allocation because they have many years before they will use the money in retirement. A more aggressive portfolio is expected to compound at a higher rate of return, thus providing more money at retirement.

Young investors also have a time advantage that allows them to make up for past investment mistakes. They also have a valuable commodity that retirees no longer have. That is their human capital. Young people can and should invest in their education and training, thus increasing the rate of return on their most valuable possession, which is the value of their labor.

On the other hand, young investors have the unfortunate position of being the most inexperienced investors in the marketplace, and that often costs them dearly. A new investor does not know their personal tolerance for financial risk. Many young investors think they can handle the volatility of 100 percent in aggressive stocks. But rarely can a person stand a portfolio that volatile of 100 percent in aggressive stocks 100 percent of the time. That can lead to the wrong investment decisions at downturns in the markets.

Early savers should probably limit their equity allocation to 80 percent of their long-term investments. An 80 percent allocation to equity and 20 percent to fixed income has about the same long-term return as 100 percent equity, but with less volatility. An 80 percent position in equity also allows investors to buy more stock during a rebalancing when the stock market falls.

Phase 2—Mid-Life Accumulators

People mature physically, emotionally, professionally, and financially as they progress through life. Mid-life investors develop a different attitude about their money than they had as early savers. As such, different asset allocations are needed to help them tailor their portfolio to the changing environment.

In mid-life, most people see that there are ceilings to their careers, their lifestyles, and their private matters. A person typically reaches the halfway mark in their working life during their early forties. They have worked full-time for about 20 years or more and will likely work full-time for another 20 years. Hopefully, their compensation is increasing and retirement savings are starting to accumulate.

In addition, they have been in a few jobs in perhaps a few industries. They have made investment mistakes, have seen economic recessions, and have watched interest rates and the stock market flip-flop up and down.

Mid-life is a point in life when a person sees her financial future with more clarity than ever before. She forms her first coherent

Table 18.1   ETF Ideas for Early Savers

Early Savers Market Index ETF Portfolio Example

Asset Class	Percent	Market Index ETFs	Fee	Symbol
U.S. Stocks & REITs	**45**			
Total U.S. Market	25	Vanguard Total Market ETF	0.07	VTI
Small Value	15	iShares S&P 600 Small Value	0.25	IJS
Micro Cap	5	First Trust DJ Select Micro Cap	0.50	FDM
Real Estate	**10**	Vanguard REIT ETF	0.12	VNQ
International Stocks	25			
Pacific Rim	10	Vanguard Pacific ETF	0.18	VPL
Europe	10	Vanguard European ETF	0.18	VGK
Emerging Markets	5	Vanguard Emerging Mkt ETF	0.30	VWO
Fixed Income	**20**			
Total U.S. Bond	10	Vanguard Total Bond ETF	0.11	BND
Inflation Protected	5	iShares Lehman TIPS	0.20	TIP
High Yield Corporate	5	iShares iBoxx High Yield Corporate	0.50	HYG

Early Savers Customized Index ETF Portfolio Example

Asset Class	Percent	Customized Index ETFs	Fee	Symbol
U.S. Stocks & REITs	**45**			
Quant Fund	30	PowerShares Dynamic Aggressive Growth	0.60	PGZ
Theme Fund	10	Claymore Ocean/Tomo Patent	0.60	OTP
Small Cap	5	PowerShares Zacks Micro Cap	0.60	PZI
Real Estate	**10**	SPDR DJ Wilshire International Real Estate	0.59	RWX
International Stocks	**25**			
Global Theme	10	SPDR FTSE/Macquarie Global Infrastructure	0.60	GII
Int'l Small	10	SDPR S&P International Small Cap	0.60	GWX
Emerging Markets	5	Claymore BNY BRIC ETF	0.60	EEB
Fixed Income	**20**			
High Yield Corporate	10	iShares iBoxx High Yield Corporate	0.50	HYG
Preferred Stocks	10	iShares S&P U.S. Preferred Stock Index	0.48	PFF

Source: Portfolio Solutions, LLC

vision of what retirement will look like, and begins to calculate how much money she will need to retain a lifestyle in retirement to be comfortable.

An informal financial review leads mid-life accumulators to a change in their savings and investment plan so that it better matches their long-term vision. Along with those changes are refinements to their portfolio. Speculative investing generally diminishes, and the core elements of a portfolio become more pronounced. Table 18.2 provides examples or what a mid-life accumulator's portfolio might hold.

Phase 3—New Retirees

There are two phases of being a new retiree: preretirement planning and postretirement enjoyment. A person typically enters the preretirement planning stage two to five years before leaving full-time employment. Preretirement is as much an attitude adjustment as it is a financial process.

Many questions need to be answered in preretirement, and some are perplexing. Will you have enough to retire? Will the money run out before your time on Earth runs out? How much should you or can you withdraw each year? Can you still donate to the charities you support? Can you help pay for the grandchildren's educations? Since the answers to those questions are estimates at best, people become the most conservative they will ever be as they close in on retirement.

Many preretirees shift their portfolios to conservative investments that they believe best suits their future. Sometimes the switch is too conservative. Some people allocate a large portion of their savings in low-yielding cash and short-term fixed income investments. Then, when they are comfortably in retirement, they reverse part of their holdings back into equities. That type of unintentional market timing is not advised. Preretirees need to look beyond the first year or two of retirement and allocate their portfolios accordingly.

One question asked by most people in preretirement is how much they can safely withdraw from their portfolios without touching the principal. There have been several academic studies on this question, and they all point to about a 4 percent withdrawal rate. However, that rate assumes you intend to spend the same amount of inflation-adjusted dollars each year as you age. It also assumes you

Table 18.2 ETF Ideas for Mid-Life Accumulators

Mid-Life Accumulator Market Index ETF Portfolio Example

Asset Class	Percent	Market Index ETFs	Fee	Symbol
U.S. Stocks & REITs	**30**			
Total U.S. Market	15	Vanguard Total Market ETF	0.07	VTI
Small Value	10	iShares S&P 600 Small Value	0.25	IJS
Micro Cap	5	First Trust DJ Select Micro Cap	0.50	FDM
Real Estate	**10**	Vanguard REIT ETF	0.12	VNQ
International Stocks	**20**			
Pacific Rim	8	Vanguard Pacific ETF	0.18	VPL
Europe	8	Vanguard European ETF	0.18	VGK
Emerging Markets	4	Vanguard Emerging Mkt ETF	0.30	VWO
Fixed Income	**40**			
Total U.S. Bond	26	Vanguard Total Bond ETF	0.11	BND
Inflation Protected	7	iShares Lehman TIPS	0.20	TIP
High Yield Corporate	7	iShares iBoxx High Yield Corporate	0.50	HYG

Mid-Life Accumulator Customized Index ETF Portfolio Example

Asset Class	Percent	Customized Index ETFs	Fee	Symbol
U.S. Stocks & REITs	**30**			
Large Value	15	PowerShares FTSE RAFI U.S. 1000	0.60	PRF
Theme Growth	10	Claymore/Great Companies Large Cap Growth	0.60	XGC
Small Cap	5	Claymore Sabrient Stealth	0.60	STH
Real Estate	**10**	SPDR DJ Wilshire International Real Estate	0.59	RWX
International Stocks	**20**			
Global Value	10	PowerShares International Dividend Achievers	0.50	PID
Small Value	5	WisdomTree International Small Cap Dividend	0.58	DLS
Global Theme	5	Global Alternative Energy ETF	0.60	GEX
Fixed Income	**40**			
Corporate	20	iShares Lehman Credit	0.20	CFT
Mortgages	20	iShares Lehman MBS Fixed Rate	0.25	MBB

Source: Portfolio Solutions, LLC

intend to leave your entire inflation-adjusted retirement nest egg to your heirs. Neither one of those assumptions is probably accurate. Most people spend more in the first few years of retirement and less in the later years. In addition, spending principal during retirement is fine if it is not your intent to pass your retirement savings to your heirs.

Cash for income during retirement can be produced in a portfolio in many ways. Interest and dividend income are two sources. There is also the annual rebalancing in a portfolio. You can easily calculate the amount of income the investments will give you, and then take any shortfall during a rebalancing.

The transition from full-time work to retirement signals a new investment phase in a portfolio. The portfolio will convert from accumulation to distribution. That means investors will soon stop putting money in and soon start taking some out. Accordingly, new retirees will probably want to reduce their allocation to riskier assets and build up some cash. Table 18.3 highlights two ETF portfolios based on an appropriate asset allocation for people entering retirement and in early retirement.

Phase 4—Mature Retirees

The good news is that Americans are living longer; the bad news is we all have to go sometime. The Fountain of Youth has still not been discovered. That means we eventually need to get our financial affairs in order to prepare those who will look after us when we can't care for ourselves, and possibly prepare heirs to inherit whatever wealth we leave them.

Choosing a person or persons to take over your finances is something to do far in advance, while you're still capable of making those decisions. Once a helper has been chosen, they should be fully informed of your financial situation, including any insurance policies and far-flung business arrangements that you may have entered into. An understanding of your estate plan is also critical, and especially important is the location of your wills, trusts, and other important documents.

The investment asset allocation of a mature retiree's portfolio can vary considerably, depending on how much money there is and who is going to get it. Classical thinking on the subject points to a conservatively managed portfolio to carry a retiree through the remainder of her life.

Table 18.3 ETF Ideas for New Retirees

New Retiree Market Index ETF Portfolio Example

Asset Class	Percent	Market Index ETFs	Fee	Symbol
U.S. Stocks & REITs	**30**			
Total U.S. Market	23	Vanguard Total Market ETF	0.07	VTI
Small Value	7	iShares S&P 600 Small Value	0.25	IJS
Real Estate	**5**	Vanguard REIT ETF	0.12	VNQ
International Stocks	15			
Pacific Rim	6	Vanguard Pacific ETF	0.18	VPL
Europe	6	Vanguard European ETF	0.18	VGK
Emerging Markets	3	Vanguard Emerging Markets ETF	0.30	VWO
Fixed Income	**45**			
Total U.S. Bond	30	Vanguard Total Bond ETF	0.11	BND
Inflation Protected	10	iShares Lehman TIPS	0.20	TIP
High Yield Corporate	5	iShares iBoxx High Yield Corporate	0.50	HYG
Cash	**5**			

New Retiree Customized Index ETF Portfolio Example

Asset Class	Percent	Market Index ETFs	Fee	Symbol
U.S. Stocks & REITs	**30**			
Large Value	18	First Trust Large Cap Value Opprt. AlphaDEX	0.70	FTA
Small Value	7	Rydex S&P 600 Small Cap Pure Value	0.35	RZV
Technical	5	PowerShares DWA Technical Leaders Portfolio	0.60	PDP
Real Estate	**5**	iShares Cohen & Steers Realty Majors	0.35	ICF
International Stocks	**15**			
Int'l Value	5	WisdomTree DIEFA Fund	0.48	DWM
Global Growth	5	Claymore/Robeco Developed World Equity	0.65	EEW
Small Value	5	WisdomTree International Small Cap Dividend	0.58	DLS
Fixed Income	**45**			
Treasuries	20	Ameristock/Ryan 5-Year Treasury	0.15	GKC
Corporate Bond	20	iShares Lehman Intermediate Credit	0.20	CIU
Inflation Protected	5	Vanguard TIPS ETF	0.11	(TBD)
Cash	**5**			

Source: Portfolio Solutions, LLC.

Deeper thought on wealth management in later years brings in all aspects of estate planning. Asset allocation in the investment portfolio is part of that process. If a retiree is not going to need all of his liquid assets, the portfolio allocation should probably reflect

Table 18.4   EFT Ideas for Mature Retirees

Mature Retiree Market Index ETF Portfolio Example

Asset Class	Percent	Market Index ETFs	Fee	Symbol
U.S. Stocks & REITs	**30**			
Total U.S. Market	20	Vanguard Total Market ETF	0.07	VTI
Small Value	5	iShares S&P 600 Small Value	0.25	IJS
REITs	5	Vanguard REIT ETF	0.12	VNQ
International Stocks	**10**			
Pacific Rim	5	Vanguard Pacific ETF	0.18	VPL
Europe	5	Vanguard European ETF	0.18	VGK
Fixed Income	**55**			
Total U.S. Bond	45	Vanguard Total Bond ETF	0.11	BND
Inflation Protected	10	iShares Lehman TIPS	0.20	TIP
Cash	**5**			

Split-Allocation Market Index ETF Portfolio Example

Asset Class	Percent	Market Index ETFs	Fee	Symbol
U.S. Stocks & REITs	**35**			
Total U.S. Market	23	Vanguard Total Market ETF	0.07	VTI
Small Value	7	iShares S&P 600 Small Value	0.25	IJS
REITs	5	Vanguard REIT ETF	0.12	VNQ
International Stocks	**15**			
Pacific Rim	6	Vanguard Pacific ETF	0.18	VPL
Europe	6	Vanguard European ETF	0.18	VGK
Emerging Markets	3	Vanguard Emerging Mkt ETF	0.30	VWO
Fixed Income	**48**			
Total U.S. Bond	38	Vanguard Total Bond ETF	0.11	BND
Inflation Protected	10	iShares Lehman TIPS	0.20	TIP
High Yield Corporate	5	iShares iBoxx High Yield Corporate	0.50	HYG
Cash	**2**			

Source: Portfolio Solutions, LLC

in part the investment objectives of the heirs who will inherit the portfolio. As such, the asset allocation and investment selections should include a combination of both the needs of the retiree and the needs of the beneficiaries.

Here is an example of a combined asset allocation. Assume a 75-year-old retiree has named her two adult children as the beneficiaries of her retirement portfolio. The children's ages are 41 and 43. An appropriate asset allocation for the retiree may be 40 percent in stocks and 60 percent in bonds and cash. An appropriate allocation for the beneficiaries may be 60 percent in stocks and 40 percent bonds. Assume the retiree needs little income from the portfolio because she has other sources of income. Instead of using the retiree's allocation of 40 stocks and 60 percent in bonds, a split allocation of 50 percent in stocks and 50 percent in bonds may be more appropriate. That allocation represents a balance between the minimum income needs of the retiree and the long-term growth needs of the beneficiaries.

Table 18.4 provides two examples of ETF portfolios for a mature retiree. The first portfolio assumes that only the retiree's needs are considered in the allocation. The second portfolio assumes the portfolio is a split allocation between the retiree and younger heirs. Cash is included in both portfolios to take care of the account owner's immediate needs.

Summary

Life cycle investing is a well-founded method of portfolio design and management. The strategy works particularly well for people who have the goal of accumulating modest wealth and holding on to that wealth in retirement. Using life cycle investing as the backbone of a lifelong investment plan provides structure and continuity to a portfolio.

Young investors can be aggressive with their savings because they have many years ahead to make up the mistakes. Also, young investors do not have a lot at stake because they have not accumulated a large amount of wealth. The most important asset they have is their time.

Investors' risk preferences change as they grow older. At middle age, people begin to look forward and for the first time think about retirement at the end of their careers. Investors are the most conservative when they are nearing retirement and during the first year as a retiree. Many mature retirees require income from their portfolio. Others who have more than enough to sustain themselves often use a split allocation for the sake of their heirs.

CHAPTER 19

Active Portfolio Management with ETFs

Active portfolio management using ETFs is a strategy of selecting funds for a portfolio with the intent to outperform a market benchmark. Active portfolio strategies are in stark contrast to the passive strategies discussed in previous chapters where ETFs are selected that have the objective to achieve returns close to the benchmark.

Active portfolio management remains the dominant method of investment selection in the financial markets today. That is ironic since the scorecard between the active strategies and passive strategies clearly favors passive methods. It is very difficult to outperform market indexes. Even so, a large number of investors have the undying belief that one day they will eventually find an active method that consistently generates superior results.

There are literally millions of ways that investors can select ETFs in an active management portfolio. It is impossible to discuss all those methods in these few pages. However, I have attempted to group several of them into a few basic categories.

The four active management strategies discussed in this chapter are: top down, bottom up, momentum, and technical. Top-down analysis starts with an examination of the global economic outlook when deciding on which ETFs to purchase. Bottom-up methods focus on detecting the quality of earnings in an industry to decide which have the most value. Momentum investors buy ETFs that have had high returns and accelerating fundamentals. Technical analysis involves the study of ETF price trends and patterns to make investment decisions.

All four active strategies tend to overlap in some way. For example, if an industry is ripe for growth based on a top-down analysis, the earning fundamentals are typically improving, which means momentum is present in earnings and price movement, and their stock chart shows a favorable pattern. Active investors may use a combination of methods when selecting ETFs to watch and ultimately purchase. You could find attractive investments using top-down or bottom-up analysis, and then time your trades by using momentum indicators and technical patterns.

All active strategies work some of the time, but no strategy works all of the time. Whichever active strategy you decide to use, be consistent, be cost conscious, be patient, and be realistic about your prospects for beating the market.

Nominal and Risk Adjusted Returns

There are two ways an investor can beat the market: nominally and risk adjusted. The return of an ETF, or a portfolio of ETFs, can be misunderstood if the return is not compared to the performance of an appropriate passive market benchmark using both nominal and risk adjusted factors.

Nominal returns are quoted in the financial press. Beating the market nominally means outperforming on a percentage basis only. For example, if an ETF gained 12 percent and a comparable market index gained 10 percent, the ETF outperformed the market nominally by 2 percent. Most people would make a positive judgment about the ETF based on that information.

A comparison of nominal returns is only half the story; risk is the other half. Investment risk is an important factor to compare when judging the performance of an active strategy against a market benchmark. Risk adjusted returns compare the performance of an ETF to the market on two levels. If an ETF gained 12 percent with substantial volatility and a comparable market index gained 10 percent with low volatility, the ETF may have underperformed the index on a risk adjusted basis. On the other hand, if an ETF returned only 8 percent while the market achieved 10 percent, the ETF may have outperformed the market on a risk adjusted basis if the volatility of the fund was substantially less than the volatility of the market.

Table 19.1 Nominal and Risk Adjusted Returns

	Annual Return	Standard Deviation	Sharpe Ratio	Nominal Return	Risk Adjusted Return
Portfolio A	8	10	0.40	Lowest	Highest
Portfolio B	12	30	0.27	Highest	Lowest
Benchmark	10	17	0.33		
T-Bills	4				

There are many ways to measure the risk adjusted return of a portfolio. Table 19.1 illustrates the difference using the Sharpe Ratio. It is a measure of risk adjusted returns developed by William F. Sharpe, the 1990 recipient of a Nobel Prize in Economic Sciences. Briefly, the Sharpe Ratio compares the risk and return of an investment to the risk and return of an appropriate index. Outperforming investments achieved more return per unit of risk than their benchmark.

The definition of the Sharpe Ratio is:

$$S(x) = (rx - RF)/StdDev(x)$$

Where:
x is an investment
rx is the average annual rate of return of the investment
Rf is the rate of return of Treasury bills
StdDev(x) is the volatility of rx as measured by standard deviation

Active portfolio management has one goal—beat the benchmark. The accomplishment of the mission should be measured both nominally and risk adjusted after the deduction of all fees and expenses. Ideally, the active strategy you choose will achieve both nominal and risk adjusted return benefits. Having only a better risk adjusted return is fine, but if the nominal return is not high enough you may not achieve your financial objectives.

Top-Down Strategies

Top-down investors begin with a space shuttle view of the global economy. The idea is to find the macroeconomic trends in the global marketplace and try to determine which countries and which industries will benefit most from those trends. An ETF investor would then select funds that represent those industries and countries. If the analysis is correct, the portfolio will outperform its benchmark.

Price changes in securities markets are in part related to changes taking place in an economy. That makes economic press releases by public agencies and private research firms important information for top-down investors. Those releases include wide ranging data, such as factory production, employment trends, monetary policy figures, tax revenue data, balance of trade figures, commodity supplies, and wholesale prices.

As a macroeconomic picture forms, investment themes begin to develop. Assume, for example, the global supply of oil is building and prices are falling rapidly. A reduction in the price of oil will cause the operating profits of energy companies to fall. Consequently, you may decide to underweight energy companies in a portfolio by selling energy-related ETFs or buying an ETF that shorts energy stocks. The beneficiaries of lower oil prices are transportation, shipping, and utility companies. Overweighting airlines, automobile manufacturers, and utility stocks may provide excess returns if your analysis is correct.

Country allocation is another way to play the global supply of oil. A drop in oil prices would hurt the exports of some commodity-driven economies and help the countries that import oil. Central America, Canada, and Russia have natural resource-driven economies that would be hurt by a drop in natural resource prices while western Europe, Japan, and the United States are large importers of oil and other natural resources. An investor could sell or short Canadian, Central American, and Russian ETFs and buy broad market Japanese and European ETFs as well as overweight U.S. exposure.

Commodities prices are only one minor part of top-down analysis. There are many themes on a macro basis that can be exploited if the analysis is correct. Some of those themes are the aging of the population in various countries, how technology is changing business and trade, global warming and other environmental issues, and political changes and their effects on business, trade, and taxes. A space shuttle view of the global economy can help you position your portfolio to take advantage of global changes and potentially produce returns that are higher than a passive benchmark without taking more risk.

Economic Cycle Analysis

Boom to bust economic cycles occur at varying times, lengths, and amplitudes in every country in the world. Even large developed countries move from prosperity to recession and back to prosperity again. Emerging economies tend to have more volatile cycles because their economies are not as diversified as a developed market. In some countries, economic declines have persisted for several years and even decades.

The business cycle is measured using Gross Domestic Product (GDP), which is the level of business output in a country. The GDP of a nation is never stable. It is either growing faster or slower, or contracting.

The GDP cycle is illustrated using a wave type pattern. The wave is divided into four stages: expansion, prosperity, contraction, and recession. After business contraction that leads to a recessionary phase, growth begins again, leading to the expansionary phase. Figure 19.1 is an illustration of the economic wave. The buy and sell points for asset classes are discussed later in the chapter.

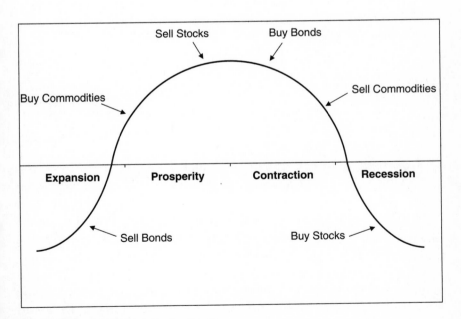

Figure 19.1 The Economic Cycle

Source: Portfolio Solutions, LLC

The phases of the business cycle are characterized by changing employment, industrial productivity, and interest rates. Asset price changes sometimes precede business cycle stages, and sometimes they move in unison with them. Consequently, the economic cycle provides a method for tracking and predicting economic activity and making appropriate asset class investments.

The following is a summary of how the classic economic cycle develops:

Prosperity: The economy is strong; people are employed and making money. The demand for goods and services increases. At some point, the demand outstrips supply, and that causes a rise in general consumer prices (inflation). As prices increase, people ask for higher wages and more benefits. As the cycle progresses, higher employee costs translate into accelerated price increases on products sold and services offered.

Contraction: When price pressure accelerates, the Federal Reserve raises interest rates to cool economic growth. Increased borrowing rates slow spending by consumers and businesses. Consequently, the decrease in demand causes a slowdown in business growth, and prices begin to stabilize.

Recession: If interest rates remain high for too long, demand decreases too much and companies cut back production. Workers are laid off. Layoffs decrease demand further as employed workers start to fear for their own jobs and postpone spending. That leads to more layoffs and eventually a real decline in national output.

Expansion: The Federal Reserve makes credit easier by lowering interest rates. Demand begins to increase again when prices become low enough and borrowing costs decline. The increase in demand requires a greater supply of goods and services. Companies hire, people become optimistic, spending increases, and the cycle begins again.

When the business cycle doesn't run smoothly there can be disastrous consequences. The Great Depression between 1929 and 1932 was a result of too much growth too fast in the 1920s. High inflation and low unemployment, coupled with a series of ill-timed taxes imposed by Congress on our trading partners put the country in a prolonged recession better known as a depression. The country came out of the depression in the early 1930s after a massive government borrowing and spending program.

Governments try to manage their economies in two ways: fiscal policy run by the government (tax and spend) and monetary policy run by the Federal Reserve Bank (interest rate adjustments). If it appears that inflation is rising too quickly, the Federal Reserve (the central bank of the United States charged with handling monetary policy) may decide to raise interest rates to curtail consumer and business spending. In addition, the president, along with Congress, may also decide to raise income taxes to take money out of the economy and create a disincentive for businesses to expand and hire more workers. On the other hand, if the economy is performing poorly, the Federal Reserve may lower interest rates and the government may lower taxes to spur spending and increase business investment.

Interest rates play a very important role in shaping economic activity. Changes in borrowing costs are also eventually reflected in stock prices. Companies must pay more to borrow money for equipment and to fund daily business operations. Individuals pay more for mortgages as well as other loans to purchase products such as automobiles. The higher cost of borrowing reduces money available for spending in other areas of the economy. That slows overall economic growth and cools the stock market. In addition, as interest rates rise, investor preferences shift from the uncertainty of stock returns to the higher interest rates from bonds. That puts further pressure on stock prices.

Markets and the Economic Cycle

Understanding the economic cycle is a key element in making macro decisions about asset allocation. Being in the right market at the right time will make money for you when stocks are rising, and save money when stocks are falling. There are better times than others to invest in stocks, bonds, and commodities. If you have the foresight to predict where an economy is in the business cycle, and when the cycle will shift, you could position a portfolio accordingly and possibly outperform a passive buy-and-hold strategy.

Figure 19.1 illustrates the points in the cycle where those major asset allocation shifts would occur. Tactical asset allocation attempts to move money to asset classes expected to outperform and form asset classes that are expected to underperform.

A word of caution about tactical asset allocation using the business cycle: there is no hard evidence that asset classes always follow the cycle as illustrated in Figure 19.1. And don't assume the economy at one stage or another is based on the performance of asset classes. There is an old saying on Wall Street, "The stock market has forecast ten out of the last four recessions."

Sector Rotation by the Business Cycle

Some investors need to maintain a consistent asset allocation to stocks and bonds. They are not able (or allowed by charter) to rotate around asset classes as depicted in Figure 19.1. The goal of sector rotation is to vary exposure to various styles and types within stock and bond asset classes based on different periods in the business cycle in an attempt to outperform a passive strategy using market indexes.

As the economy expands and contracts, value stocks and growth stocks act differently as much as large stocks and small stocks do. Bond maturities and types also have cycles that are intertwined with the business cycle. Long-term bonds react well right after the economy has peaked. Short-term bonds conserve wealth when the economy has been expanding for several quarters. By shifting between corporate bonds and Treasuries at the right time, an investor can also benefit from narrowing credit spreads. Figure 19.2 illustrates a simple rotation strategy that can be created, using ETFs benchmarked to equity style indexes and fixed income indexes.

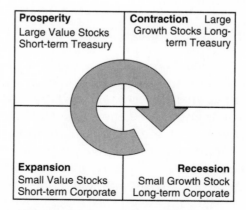

Figure 19.2   The Business Cycle Applied to Styles and Bonds
Source: Portfolio Solutions, LLC

Table 19.2 Timing Industry Sector ETFs

Expansion	Prosperity	Contraction	Recession
Industrials	Commodities	Financials	Health Care
Consumer Durables	Energy	Services	Financials
Energy	Basic Materials	Transportation	Technology
Real Estate	Real Estate	Utilities	Transportation
Technology	Services	Health Care	Utilities

Source: Portfolio Solutions, LLC

Table 19.2 illustrates the approximate points in the business cycle when selected industry sectors have historically provided the highest returns relative to other sectors. An industry rotation strategy is accomplished by overweighting specific industry ETFs during their most productive periods and avoiding them during less productive periods. The strategy is very popular and is widely used in the investment industry. Consequently, what everyone expects to happen usually does not. Let the buyer beware.

Bottom-Up Analysis

Proven experts such as Warren Buffett generally favor a bottom-up approach to investment selection. Bottom-up ETF investors conduct extensive research on industries and countries to build value-based opinions. Economic factors do matter, but fundamentals matter more. In fact, a downturn in the stock market may provide bottom-up investors with the safety margin they need to buy an attractive industry ETF.

Fundamental analysis is a dynamic exercise that includes studying earnings growth drivers, product competitiveness, return on equity equations, and dividend yields. An important aspect of fundamental analysis is the growth potential of the industry or a country over the next few years. Ideally, investors want to own ETFs in industries or countries with underappreciated growth prospects.

Here are some points of analysis for bottom-up industry ETF investors:

Sales, Earnings, and Book Value: Current price-to-sales, price-to-earnings, and price-to-book ratios are compared to the average long-term ratios for the industries. Industries to accumulate are trading below historic averages and industries to avoid are trading substantially above their historic averages.

Balance Sheet: Clean or improving corporate balance sheets are a factor in bottom-up industry investing because they show management effectiveness and prudent allocation of capital. Industries with decreasing debt relative to equity are favorable. Companies with increasing debt loads relative to equity should be avoided.

Cash Flow: Strong free cash flow in an industry shows that companies in that industry are able to fund their operations without adding more debt, and leaves room for potential dividend increases in the future.

One method of bottom-up industry analysis involves rankings using a comparison of relative fundamental criteria. Table 19.3 represents an example of bottom-up sector rotation strategy using a scoring system. Each industry receives a score in each category. A score of five means an industry is trading at its normal long-term valuation. A score below five means the industry is trading above its normal valuation and a score above five means the industry is trading below its normal valuation. Industries with the highest total scores are considered attractive, based on bottom-up fundamental analysis.

Investment styles (large/small/growth/value) can also be measured using relative valuation. When a style is trading above its normal valuation, it is thought to be expensive and when it is trading below its normal valuation, it is thought to be inexpensive.

Figure 19.3 illustrates the ratio comparing the price-to-book ratio (P/B) of small cap stocks versus large cap stocks. The valuation of large company stocks became very expensive relative to small company stocks during most of the 1990s. By early 2000, the valuation of large cap was the highest it had ever been relative to small cap. Prices cannot climb to the moon, however. Large cap stocks underperformed small stocks for five years following the peak, and a comparison of P/Bs actually fell below historic norms.

It is very difficult to time the exact tops and bottoms of industries and styles using fundamental analysis. Even though the data are telling you a style or industry is attractive, it may be years before

Table 19.3 ETF Industry Rotation using a Bottom-Up Strategy

	Basic Materials	Cyclical	Energy	Financials	Industrials	Real Estate	Services	Technology	Transportation	Utilities
Price to Sales	4	5	3	7	6	2	7	9	7	6
Price to Earnings	3	5	3	6	7	3	8	7	8	4
Price to Book	4	6	4	7	6	4	7	5	5	4
Free Cash Flow	5	6	7	8	5	4	8	7	4	5
Dividend Yield	6	6	5	6	3	4	6	5	5	5
Debt to Equity	5	7	5	4	4	1	9	5	3	6
Return on Equity	5	4	7	5	5	3	8	7	4	5
Total Average Score*	4.6	5.6	4.9	6.1	5.1	3.0	7.6	6.4	5.1	5.0

*Buy highest score, sell lowest score.
Source: Portfolio Solutions, LLC

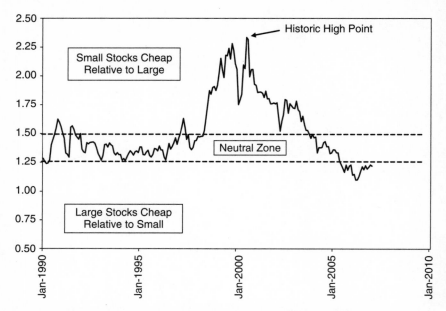

Figure 19.3   The Ratio of Russell 1000 P/B to Russell 2000 P/B
Source: Portfolio Solutions, LLC

a reversal takes place. Be prepared to underperform the markets with your portfolio while other people continue to make money in overvalued sectors. Eventually, you will probably be correct in your evaluation. But to make money doing this type of active investing, you have to have conviction and unnerving patience.

Momentum Investing

Momentum investing is a strategy best explained by Isaac Newton's first law of motion, "A body in rest tends to stay at rest, and a body in motion tends to stay in motion, unless the body is compelled to change." To momentum investors, the trend is your friend. When an industry is experiencing above-average sales and earnings growth, those trends tend to persist.

Momentum investing is a price-timing strategy. The momentum investor waits for an established upward trend in prices backed by favorable earnings news. Favorable earnings momentum is when industry growth is accelerating and beating Wall Street analyst estimates.

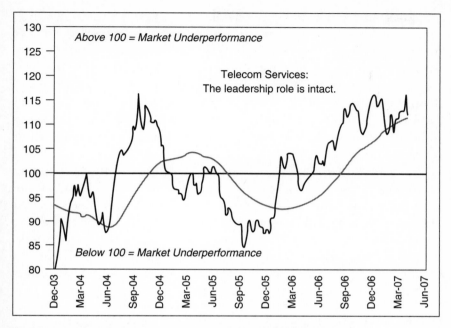

Figure 19.4   S&P Telecom Services Relative Strength
Source: Standard and Poor's

One method of measuring relative price momentum is to assign a score to each industry based on price gains. Using a market baseline with a score of 100, a higher score means higher price momentum in that industry and a lower score means a below-average price momentum.

Figure 19.4 illustrates a 12-month relative strength score of 115 for telecom services. The score means the telecom services industry sector has outperformed the market over a 12-month period ending in June 2007. A 200-day moving average is also included in the figure as a technical indicator (see next section). Telecom Services is a subsector of the Technology Select Sector SPDR (symbol: XLK).

Price momentum tends to be strongest in the short term (fewer than 12 months). As such, momentum strategies require constant monitoring of ETF prices and frequent turnover of sectors. It is not unusual for an industry ETF portfolio to turn over 100 percent or more per year when price momentum is the primary trigger for trading.

Earnings momentum is also a common investment strategy when used in conjunction with price momentum. Earnings are the key driver behind stock prices, and earnings momentum typically confirms price momentum. Wall Street analysts forecast future industry earnings and growth rates. Sectors are then ranked by growth rates from the fastest growing earnings to the slowest growing. When an industry is growing earnings faster then analysts expect, it is a good indication that stock prices in that industry will also continue their upward trend.

There is a danger in momentum investing. As more investors jump on a rising trend, it can drive prices artificially high. When the earnings momentum of an industry decelerates and meets analyst estimates, or worse, all momentum investors head for the exit at the same time. Unfortunately, not everyone can get out fast enough. Overwhelming sell volume can pound stock prices and cause a downward spiral that affects all stocks in that industry. That results in large losses over a short period of time.

Technical Analysis

Technical analysis is the study of stock price patterns for the purpose of forecasting future price trends. Price charts are the primary tool in technical analysis. A chart graphically represents the price movement over a specific period of time. Trading volume can also be included to verify the strength of a trend.

The simplest use of technical analysis it to monitor the up-trend of an ETF. An up-trend line is a straight line passing through the troughs of an up-move as shown in Figure 19.5 for the Energy Select SPDR (symbol: XLE). The importance of a trend line increases with every test when a correction in price takes place. The longer a trend line lasts, the more significant it becomes. Breaking the trend line is a violation and a sell signal for a technical investor.

Many technical investors prefer to use moving averages to confirm a trend or the breaking of a trend. For example, a 200-day moving average is a popular technical indicator. An ETF is held in a portfolio as long as the closing price stays above its 200-day moving average. It is sold if it falls below the 200-day moving average. Figure 19.5 shows the 200-day moving average for Energy Select SPDR (symbol: XLE).

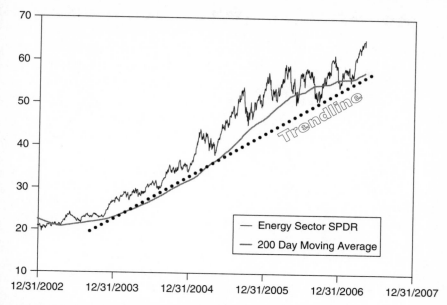

Figure 19.5   Energy Select SPDR Price Chart and Trend
Source: American Stock Exchange (AMEX)

Chart Formations

History repeats itself, or at least that is what investors using technical analysis hope. Predictions of future prices are made when certain patterns develop in stock charts. Profits can be earned if those patterns hold true and are detected early enough. Some of the formations indicate a trend reversal (reversal formation) and others a continuation of the trend (continuation formation).

There are many different formations with sometimes strange-sounding names. Head-and-shoulders, cup and saucer, rounding bottoms, triangles and ascending triangles, flags, and gaps are just a few odd-sounding names, though the granddaddy of all formations is the Elliott Wave.

Ralph Nelson Elliott (1871–1948) was an accountant by profession. He was also an avid market watcher and chartist. Elliott was convinced that stock market activity was a part of a much larger law governing all of human activity. He claimed that the stock market

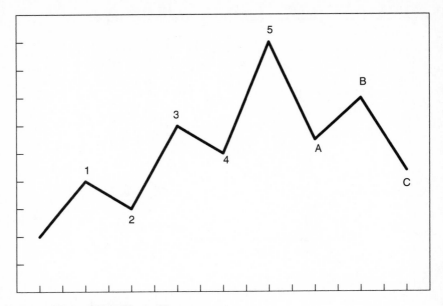

Figure 19.6   Elliot Wave Theory

follows a repetitive rhythm of an advance followed by a decline (see Figure 19.6). Every impulse wave can be subdivided into a five-wave structure (1-2-3-4-5), while the corrective wave can be subdivided into a three-wave structure (A-B-C).

The theory gets much, much deeper. There are fractal waves, which are waves within waves, and rules for wave count, and so on. To this day there are diehard Elliott Wave Theory followers who swear by the pattern.

Head and shoulders is a common technical pattern that, when formed, signals the security is likely to move against the previous trend. The head-and-shoulders top is a signal that a security's price is set to fall, once the pattern is complete, and is usually formed at the peak of an upward trend. The second version, the head-and-shoulders bottom (also known as inverse head and shoulders), signals that a security's price is set to rise and usually forms during a downward trend. Figure 19.7 is an example of an inverse head and shoulders pattern form in the Financial Select Sector SPDR (symbol: XLF) between May 2006 and September 2006. The price breakout occurred in mid-September.

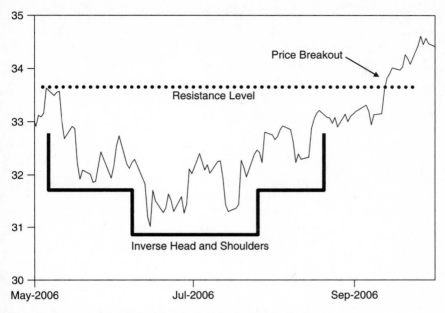

Figure 19.7   XLF Inverse Head and Shoulders Pattern

Technical Analysis Critics

To say technical analysis is controversial would be an understatement. It is rare to find one major academic mind that believes technical patterns in stock prices reveal futures price trends. Burton G. Malkiel, Professor and Chair of Economics at Princeton, systematically tears down technical analysis in his classic book *A Random Walk Down Wall Street*. Malkiel shows how past price movements do not give any useful indication about what will happen in the future, even over short periods of time. Benjamin Graham, a famous value investor and Warren Buffett's mentor, had this to say about technical analysis in his classic book, *The Intelligent Investor*:

> In our own stock-market experience and observation, extending over fifty years, we have not known a single person who has consistently or lastingly made money by thus "following the market." We do not hesitate to declare that this approach is as fallacious as it is popular.

Will technical analysis work for you? It is difficult not to look at a chart before committing capital. We all would like to believe that the chart will give us some indication of the future. Realistically, who knows? I have never had any success.

Prudence is Recommended

Do any active strategies work? Yes, all strategies work sometime, and No, nothing works all the time. There will be periods when you can point to a favored active strategy and say it worked. But there are just as many periods when that strategy did not work.

The strategies discussed in this chapter are for informational purposes only. They are not endorsed or recommended. I personally do not use active strategies in my own portfolio, and my company does not use active strategies in the portfolios we manage for clients.

If you do believe there is an active strategy out there that will work in your benefit over the long term, don't put all your eggs in one basket. Core and explore is a more prudent approach when using active management techniques (see Chapter 17). A core and explore approach ensures at least a portion of your portfolio will achieve market returns minus minimal fees while you attempt to outperform with the other portion.

Summary

Active investment strategies are all about beating the returns of the financial markets. That goal can be accomplished nominally or on a risk-adjusted basis. Ideally, an active portfolio will beat the market both nominally and risk adjusted. That way you do not underachieve your financial goals by sacrificing lower nominal returns for better risk adjusted returns.

There are an infinite number of ways to manage an ETF portfolio using active management. The four basic strategies outlined in this chapter are just the tip of the iceberg. Fundamental analysis is either top down or bottom up. Momentum analysis is the study of price and earnings acceleration. Technical analysis is the study of price patterns.

If you decide to use an active approach to managing your portfolio, you must do significant research, be dedicated, and above all, have patience. A core and explore approach may be the most prudent method because it ensures diversification. But even then, there is no guarantee. The only thing certain about active management is that the cost is higher than with passive strategies. If you decide to go the active route, be prepared to be wrong frequently, humbled regularly, and rewarded occasionally.

Special Portfolio Strategies

The evolution of ETFs offer an increasing number of investment opportunities. ETFs are versatile. They can be optioned, shorted, hedged, and bundled into other securities. Those features have led to an array of strategies that were not easily achieved or feasible with traditional open-end mutual funds. There are four special uses discussed in this chapter. Those uses are:

- Hedging strategies to reduce risk in a portfolio that is over exposure to an industry. The technique is useful for people who work in an industry and are paid with restricted securities or company stock options.
- Speculation using pairs trading by purchasing one ETF you think will increase in value and selling the same amount of another you think will decrease in value, or not increase as much. The result is a small gain earned from the performance difference.
- Currency trading using ETFs and ETNs is a growing area of interest. Strategies can hedge the currency risk for global travelers as well as businesses that are buying and selling abroad. Currency speculators may also find ETFs and ETNs easier to trade and more economical than buying currencies directly.
- Tax swapping is a simple and effective way to increase the after-tax performance of a taxable portfolio. If an ETF in your portfolio is at a loss, there is likely a similar fund that you can swap. The sell and buy creates a tax loss. Harvested losses can

be used to offset future capital gains, or be used to reduce ordinary income subject to taxation.

Those are just a few alternative ETF strategies. There is a large and growing volume of techniques that can potentially enhance portfolio returns or hedge other financial risk. As the number of ETFs expands, their versatility will lead to many more ideas and strategies.

Unique Characteristics of ETFs

ETFs have unique characteristics that most open-end mutual funds do not have. These characteristics allow the creation of new and interesting trading strategies. ETFs can be leveraged or shorted, and many are paired with options. The following is a brief explanation of those characteristics.

Leverage: ETFs can be leveraged using margin. Margin is borrowing money from a brokerage firm to buy securities. Minimum account levels are required and enforced by the NASD, the NYSE, and by individual brokerage firms. Investing on margin can be profitable for investors if their profits from securities purchased overcome the interest charges and commission costs.

Options: While not an ETF per se, ETF options can give investors control over a large number of ETF shares with little money down. Albeit, options use substantial leverage and thus can mean substantially higher risks. There are two types of options: call options and put options. A call option gives you the right to buy shares of ETFs at a specific price for a specific period of time, and put options give you the right to sell shares of ETFs for a specific price over a specific period of time. The price of an option consists of its intrinsic value and a speculative premium. The speculative premium diminishes as the option approaches its expiration date.

Shorting: ETFs can be shorted like individual stocks. Shorting involves selling borrowed shares an investor does not own in expectation the price of an ETF will decline in value. If the ETF does decrease in value, it can be bought back by the short seller at a lower price. That results in a profit. You can buy ETFs that do the shorting for you. That avoids completing extra brokerage paperwork and the possibility your short stock will be called in by the owner.

Using ETFs to Reduce Industry Risk

Industry sector funds are used as hedging tools for many investors. They are particularly useful for investors with a single concentrated position in one industry. Perhaps you are an employee at a company that pays you in part with stock options or restricted stock. Or perhaps you own a large equity position in a stock but are reluctant to sell for tax reasons. If this sounds like your situation, hedging with an industry ETF or ETN may reduce your risk.

One way to hedge a large position in a single company is to build a portfolio of industry ETFs around the position. Assume that you have 10 percent of your liquid net worth in one technology stock. You bought the stock years ago at a greatly reduced price and selling it would result in a large tax liability. Instead of selling the stock, build a portfolio of nontech industry ETFs around the position. The result is a portfolio that closely tracks the stock market while maintaining the single position.

Figure 20.1 illustrates an example of what a build-around portfolio might look like. Assume again a large holding in one technology stock that represented 10 percent of a portfolio. There are 10 basic industries in the U.S. stock market (see Chapter 12). Based on a build-around strategy, an industry ETF is purchased for each industry based on its market weight with the exception of technology (using 2007 weights). Since the single technology company represents 10 percent of a portfolio, it becomes one of the technology industry holdings. Assume technology is 16 percent of the total U.S. equity market. That means 6 percent of the portfolio would be allocated to a technology ETF.

Once a build-around portfolio is established, industry weightings can be adjusted as needed. One reason that would occur is if there is an opportunity to harvest losses in one industry sector and offset those losses with gains from the sale of the concentrated stock holding. An explanation of tax-loss harvesting is provided at the end of this chapter.

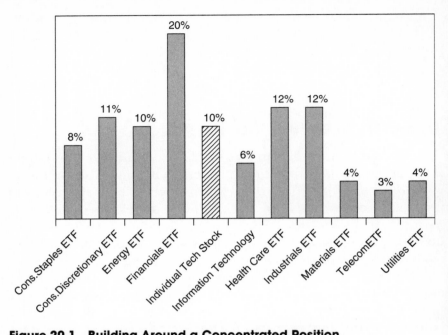

Figure 20.1   Building Around a Concentrated Position
Source: Portfolio Solutions, LLC

Many people face overexposure to financial risk in the industry they work in. Stock options and restricted stock is often part of a complete compensation package and that adds specific risk to personal wealth. In addition, a person's human capital, as measured by salaries, bonuses, and job security, is also exposed to the same industry risk. One way to hedge industry risk is to short an ETF that is specific to the industry. Shorting an industry ETF would help mitigate the risk without violating restrictive trading rules placed on company options and restricted stock.

Figure 20.2 provides an example of ETF shorting against an industry position. Assume that you have liquid net worth of $500,000. Approximately $100,000 of the amount is held in the restricted stock of one technology company. The rules prohibit you from selling the stock, but you can sell a technology ETF that holds the stock. Figure 20.2 illustrates the selling of $100,000 in a technology industry ETF and the purchase of $500,000 in a diversified total U.S. stock market ETF. The strategy is not a perfect hedge, but it does offer some protection against a decline in the technology industry.

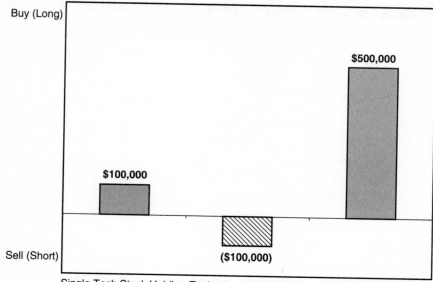

Buy (Long)

$500,000

$100,000

Sell (Short)

($100,000)

Single Tech Stock Holding   Technology ETF (Short)   Total U.S. Market ETF

Figure 20.2   Reducing Risk by Shorting an Industry ETF
Source: Portfolio Solutions, LLC

There are other ways to reduce industry risk exposure using ETFs. Instead of shorting an ETF, investors can *buy* an ETF that does the industry shorting for you. ProShares and Rydex have several inverse industry ETFs that short industry sectors.

Another defensive approach is to use options on ETFs. Buying protective put options on ETFs in the industry would partially insure a portfolio against price declines in an industry.

Finally, ETFs are being introduced that leave out industries. For example, First Trust NASDAQ-100 Ex-Tech Sector (symbol: QQXT) invests in all the NASDAQ-100 stocks except technology. An investor could use one fund with a built-in technology gap to hedge their single stock holding.

There are some caveats to these strategies. If you sell short an ETF, you will have to pay the dividend paid by the fund. If you buy a put to hedge industry risk, you have to deal with buying new puts over and over as options expire. That means paying a speculative premium and commission each time. Those costs will slowly whittle away at profits.

Pairs Trading and Market Neutral Strategies

Pairs trading and market neutral strategies have been made easier with the large variety of ETFs on the market. Both strategies short one or more ETFs and buy one or more others. The idea is to make money from a divergence in total return.

Pairs trading is the selling short of one category of ETF while buying another category by an equal amount. You win when the ETF you bought outperforms the one you sell. Figure 20.3 represents two examples of pairs trading. The first example is an industry sector rotation play and the second example is a bond yield play.

In the first pairs trading example, you believe the economy is beginning to turn down. Health care stocks typically perform better than energy stocks when a contraction in the economy begins. To take advantage of the divergence, you short an energy stock ETF and buy a health care stock ETF. If you are correct on the timing, your profit is the difference in total return of the two ETFs.

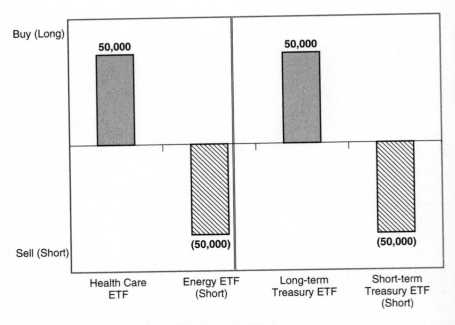

Figure 20.3   Examples of ETF Pairs Trading
Source: Portfolio Solutions, LLC

In the second example, you believe that the Federal Reserve Bank will continue to raise short-term interest rates even though you forecast a downturn in the economy. If your analysis is correct, long-term bond yields will fall (long-term bond prices rise) as short-term bond yields rise (short-term bond prices fall). If you are correct, ETFs invested in long-term bonds will outperform ETFs invested in short-term bonds and your profit will be the difference.

A market neutral strategy is similar to a pairs trade except that a broad market ETF is sold short rather than an industry ETF. The trade is done when you believe an industry will outperform the broad market. If your hunch is correct, you earn the difference between the superior return of the ETF following an industry and the return of the ETF following the broad market index. The trade will create a portfolio that is market neutral, meaning all of the stock market risk is taken out of the trade.

A second way to create a market neutral trade is to short an ETF that invests in an industry that you believe will underperform the market, and buy an ETF that follows a broad market index. If you

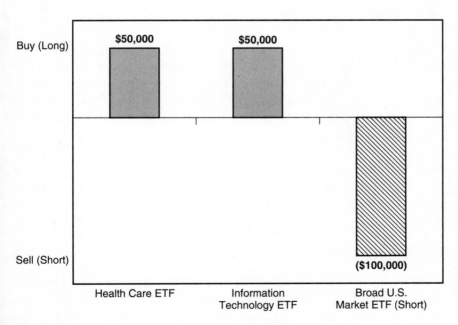

Figure 20.4   Example of a Market Neutral ETF Trade
Source: Portfolio Solutions, LLC

are correct on the industry-versus-market performance differential, you will earn a profit when the total return of the market index ETF outperforms the industry.

Figure 20.4 is an example of a market neutral trade. You believe health care and technology stocks are undervalued compared to the rest of the stock market. Accordingly, you buy health care and technology ETFs and sell a comparable amount of a broad U.S. market ETF. If you are correct on your industries, you gain the difference in return between the market and the industry, minus investment expenses.

Currency Hedging and Speculation

Currency trading using ETFs is a growing area. Hedging currencies using ETFs and ETNs can reduce the financial risk for global travelers and small companies doing business abroad. Currency speculation has also been made much easier for individual investors because of the trading flexibility of ETFs and ETNs. The securities pay a money market rate of interest based on the currency they are in while hedging against a decline in the U.S. dollar.

Are you planning a trip abroad and want to hedge the U.S. dollars you have saved for the event? Or perhaps you are saving for a villa in Italy? For a small annual fee, you can lock in the value of the currency you will be using for the event and receive interest on your money based on the interest rates prevailing in that region. Before leaving for the trip or closing on your villa, simply sell the ETF or ETN and withdraw U.S. dollars.

Are you a speculator at heart? Do you have a hunch that the Euro will decline against the yen? If so, short a Euro fund and buy a yen fund. If you are correct, the difference in total return from those funds goes in your pocket, minus commission costs.

Tax Loss Harvesting

Tax loss harvesting is a common tax-reduction method that can be used with ETF management in a taxable account. The idea is to sell money-losing ETFs and use the losses to offset taxable gains from profitable trades. If done successfully, tax loss harvesting will increase an investor's after-tax returns.

One roadblock to this strategy is the wash sale rule. The IRS will not allow you to take a tax loss if you sell a fund and buy it back within 30 days. *It* is defined as not only the exact security you just sold, but anything "substantially identical" as well.

Fortunately, the plethora of ETFs has given investors many options that may be similar, but not substantially identical to the investments you are selling. Wash sale rules don't permit investors to harvest a tax loss if they repurchase the same ETF immediately, but the wash sale rule can be avoided by redeploying the loss proceeds into a similar ETF. This allows investors to harvest the loss and still maintain market exposure.

Suppose in December of 2003, you purchased $10,000 worth of the iShares Russell 3000 ETF (symbol: IWV) in a taxable account. IWV attempts to match the performance of the Russell 3000 Index, which is a market weighted index that covers approximately 3,000 of the largest U.S. stocks.

Because of a decline in stock prices over the next 12 months your IWV position had a market value of only $8,000. Consequently, you sell IWV and buy $8,000 worth of the Vanguard Total U.S. Market ETF (symbol: VTI). That ETF is benchmarked to the MSCI U.S. Broad Market Index, which represents about 3,500 of the largest U.S. stocks. The trade captures a $2,000 tax loss and retains your position in the stock market.

IWV and VTI have performed similarly to each other over the years, yet both are managed by two unrelated fund companies and they track two distinctly different indexes. Thus, the funds are not substantially identical. That means you can harvest the $2,000 tax loss from IWV and immediately reinvest the proceeds in VTI without worrying about being subject to the IRS wash sale tax.

Figure 20.5 illustrates the relative performance of IWV to VTI from December 2001 to December 2003. As you can see, swapping funds around the end of 2002 resulted in nearly identical performance. However, you also have a $2,000 tax loss that can be used to offset gains in other investments, or be used to offset up to $3,000 in ordinary income taxes.

Tax swaps have real benefits for high-income investors. They increase after-tax portfolio performance. Assume you are in a 35 percent federal tax bracket. If the $2,000 tax loss on IWV was used to offset $2,000 in ordinary income, you have saved $700 in federal income taxes. That is a 7 percent return on a $10,000 investment.

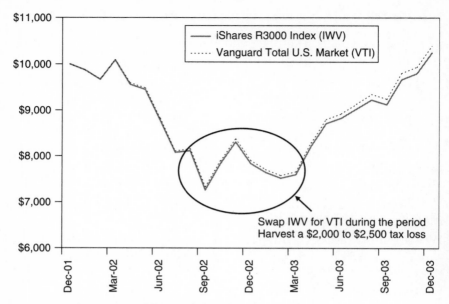

Figure 20.5   ETF Tax Swapping Example
Source: Portfolio Solutions, LLC

Granted, there is a capital gains tax to pay when you sell VTI and make an extra $2,000, but capital gains are taxed at 15 percent, not 35 percent. You would pay back only $300 of the $700 saved in taxes. The net result is a permanent savings of $400. That is a 4 percent free return on a $10,000 investment, courtesy of the federal government.

Check with your tax adviser before using a tax swap strategy. Tax laws change quickly and your tax adviser will be up to date on the restrictions.

Future ETF Strategies

Are you going to buy a home in a few years, but are afraid that home prices in your area may appreciate beyond your means? Or, are you selling a home next year and want to hedge against falling prices? Soon you may be able to purchase (or short) housing ETFs that can be used to hedge an impending purchase (or sale) of a home in your geographical area. As of this writing, housing ETFs are available at this time. But they are eventually going to be part of a robust ETF industry that is just getting started.

Summary

The evolving ETF marketplace has lead to many new and interesting portfolio management strategies. The trading flexibility of ETFs and options on ETFs make sophisticated strategies available to the public that were once the bailiwick of large institutional investors.

There are many strategies mentioned in this chapter and they touch only the surface. Hedging strategies can reduce risk for people who are overexposed to an industry; speculators using pairs trading can buy one industry ETF and short another; currency risks can be hedged for global travelers and businesses that are buying and selling abroad; and tax swapping is a simple and effective way to increase the after-tax performance of a taxable portfolio.

With every new strategy there comes investment risk. Know the limits of your knowledge and trading skill before employing these sophisticated ideas. Also, it is prudent to check with your tax adviser before using ETF tax harvesting.

21

Operational Tips for ETF Investors

Managing your ETF portfolio can be a smooth evolution or a frustrating experience. A lot depends on where you choose to trade and how you trade. Investing in the ETF marketplace without a plan will likely result in higher costs because you will not get good trade execution when buying and selling funds. Your cost of investing can be minimized with just a few trading trips.

An alternative to managing your own account is to hire someone else to do it for you. That can be accomplished through the brokerage firm where you trade or through a fee-only registered investment adviser (RIA). A fee-only RIA is compensated as a percentage of assets under management rather than by trading commissions. In either case, hiring a professional adviser to design, trade, and manage a portfolio is often a better solution for investors who are not interested in managing their account or who are not able to manage their account any longer.

Selecting a Custodian

ETFs trade on stock exchanges. As such, ETFs can be purchased only through a NASD registered brokerage firm. You can use a full service brokerage firm such as Merrill Lynch or Smith Barney, or choose a discount brokerage firm such as Charles Schwab or TD Ameritrade. There are advantages and disadvantages to each type.

A full service brokerage firm has the advantage of a dedicated representative. You will always talk to the same person when you call. The registered rep should be aware of your investment objectives and recommend securities that are suitable. Another advantage of full service brokerage is access to research. If you believe that the stock analysts on Wall Street provide superior research and investment recommendations, then access to a firm's research through a full service broker is important.

There are distinct disadvantages to working with a full service brokerage firm. First, commission costs are high. The commission rate charged by full service firms can be ten times the cost or more of the same trade done through a discount brokerage firm. If you are an active trader, high commission costs will quickly eat into your profits.

A second disadvantage of using a full service broker is the conflict of interest inherent in the industry. Full service brokerage firms serve many masters. They are paid fees and commissions by individual clients that have accounts at the firm, and the firms are paid distribution and marketing dollars by product providers that sell investments through the brokerage network. When a brokerage firm recommends an investment, which client are they truly representing? Do they have your best interest at heart or the firm that is paying them a large fee to market the product being recommended?

If you enjoy doing your own ETF research and do not need a personal relationship with a registered rep at a full service brokerage firm, then a discount brokerage firm can save you a lot of money on trading commissions. Low cost firms include Charles Schwab, TD Ameritrade, Fidelity, Scottrade, FOLIOfn, and a variety of others. Many of these firms offer independent ETF research that is similar to the analysis offered by full service brokerage firms.

The disadvantage of discount brokers is the lack of interaction between you and the company representatives. You will speak with a different person every time you call a discount firm to discuss your account.

Some discount firms now have a higher level of service for clients with larger accounts. Those services allow you to speak to the same person each time your call. But, let the buyer beware. Many times, personal reps are compensated for what they sell either directly or by meeting sales goals. As such, the same conflict of interest that exists at full service firms can also exist at discount brokerage firms. When in doubt, ask. The rep is required by law to disclose conflicts.

Trading ETF Shares

Unlike open-end mutual funds, ETFs are not always bought and sold at prices equal to their intraday value. The intraday value is an estimate of the actual net asset value (NAV) of the fund. The actual NAV of an ETF is published only once per day, after the markets are closed.

ETFs trade at prices set by market forces. The differences between ETF market prices and its intraday values are usually small, although larger spreads can and do arise. An ETF is said to trade at a premium to its intraday value if the ETF market price is greater than the intraday value, and it's said to trade at a discount if the opposite is true.

Stock exchanges, ETF companies, and authorized participants (APs) closely track the spread between ETF prices and intraday values. Each day after the market closes, the closing difference between an ETF and its actual NAV is made available to the public on various web sites. ETFs may trade after the market closes, but those after-hours prices are not part of the premium and discount data. Morningstar.com lists historic ETF premiums and discounts on an ETF Snapshot page and on the Total Returns page.

The premium and discount figures are useful for showing how well or poorly an ETF's closing market price of an ETF tracks its net asset value (NAV) at the end of the day. A timing discrepancy in pricing, however, can lead to an exaggeration or understatement of the data. For example, a stock in an index may have closed early because of a merger announcement. In that case, the buyout price of the closing shares would be reflected in the ETF price but not the NAV. In a second example, there may have been a delayed trade on certain stocks or on the ETF that did not hit the tape until after 4:00 PM. That absence of those trades may cause the spread between an ETF price and NAV to be different from what it actually is.

The spread between an ETF price and its intraday value is often wider right after the opening of the stock market, as market participants wait for all stocks to open. The excess spread can persist for about 30 minutes, at which point all stocks are open and pricing is more accurate. As such, I do not recommend trading ETFs until after 10:00 AM Eastern time. Under normal market conditions, by 10:00 AM Eastern time, the intraday value and ETF price are in line with each other.

The ticker tape can get delayed during volatile market days, and that can widen the spread between ETFs and their intraday values. The excess spread occurs because high volume prevents the reporting of some trades. Thus, the intraday value may be inaccurate.

The spread between the bid and ask of an ETF will widen when the bid and ask spreads in the underlying securities widen. That also occurs on high volatility days. During those times, the spread between an ETF and intraday values can become erratic and traders seek alternative indicators of price. When spreads are widening because of volatility, many traders look to the futures and options markets for help in determining the correct ETF price rather than the delayed intraday price.

If you are not in a hurry, here are three recommendations for trading ETFs. First, trade ETFs after 10:00 AM Eastern time and before 3:30 PM Eastern time. That places a 30-minute no-trade band around the opening and closing bell when spreads are highest. Second, trade on nonvolatile days when there is a stable intraday value. Third, check the futures and options markets if you are trading during a volatile period because the intraday value of an ETF is likely to be inaccurate.

Asset Location Tips

Taxes are an expense to every investor and should be controlled. Several tax-saving strategies using ETFs have already been discussed in this book. They include the inherent tax efficiency within the ETF structure (Chapter 4) and a tax loss harvesting strategy that can be used in the management of a taxable account (Chapter 20).

One final method of tax savings discussed in this chapter is asset location. Chapters 17 and 18 discussed asset allocation at length, whereby ETFs are chosen from different asset classes. Asset location is how those ETFs are spread across different types of investment accounts. Some investment accounts are more tax efficient than others. Asset allocation and asset location can work together to achieve a higher-than-expected after-tax return.

Taxable accounts receive a Form 1099 each year stating the amount of taxable income it generated. Nontaxable accounts do not get 1099s because there are no taxes due on the income. It follows then, that tax efficient ETFs are best held in a taxable account while tax inefficient ETFs are better held in a tax-deferred account.

Taxable Accounts

A taxable account generates an annual Form 1099 that lists all of the dividends, interest, and security transactions that the IRS is expecting you to report on your annual tax returns. Taxable accounts include, but are not limited to, personal accounts, joint accounts, trust accounts, business accounts, and custodian accounts. There are instances when the primary beneficiary of an account may not pay the taxes, such as an irrevocable trust, but the account itself is still taxable and can benefit from tax planning.

The overall asset allocation between stocks and bonds in a portfolio is the most important determinant of portfolio performance. In a taxable account, however, the second most important determinant of performance is tax efficiency. If you can defer taxable gains and reduce taxable dividend and interest income, then the after-tax performance of the account is increased. By creating a tax efficient portfolio, you will pay less in taxes, which automatically increases your wealth.

There are several strategies that reduce taxes in a taxable account. First, select only ETFs that are tax efficient. The SEC mandates that all ETFs report after-tax performance as well as pretax performance. In addition, Morningstar gives ETFs a tax-efficiency rating, which is also useful. Morningstar mutual fund reports are free from most public libraries or can be obtained from the company for an annual fee. There is also an inexpensive online subscription to Morningstar's mutual fund database.

Most equity ETFs are tax efficient. Turnover of securities is low and arbitrage within the fund allows the manager to disperse low-cost-basis stock (Chapter 4). The redemption and creation feature gives the ETF managers an opportunity to pass capital gains on to institutional investors who redeem creation units, thus eliminating capital gains distributions in most ETFs at the end of the year.

Taxable accounts are an ideal place to locate your equity ETFs. The tax efficiency created through the ETF management process, plus the ability to harvest tax losses in a volatile market, makes them a perfect fit. ETNs also make interesting choices for taxable accounts because of their unique structure (Chapter 4). Be cautious of REIT ETFs, though, because they are taxed differently from common equity ETFs. Because REITs distribute a large amount of their gains as ordinary income, taxable accounts are not the ideal location for those securities.

Bonds in a Taxable Account.   The question of placing taxable bond ETFs in a taxable account is always a tricky one because there is no one-size-fits-all solution. Taxable bonds include corporate bonds, government bonds, mortgages, and composite funds that hold a combination of those types.

One school of thought is to put tax efficient equity ETFs in taxable accounts and tax inefficient fixed income ETFs and REIT ETFs in nontaxable accounts. While that is a wise strategy for some people, it may not be practical for others.

Here are three reasons why an investor could have taxable bond ETFs in their taxable accounts:

1. An investor may not have much money in tax-deferred accounts, thus by default, bond ETFs go in the taxable account.
2. An investor with low taxable income and in a low tax bracket may find the after-tax return of bonds in a taxable account is still acceptable; for example, a tax rate on the interest that is less than 30 percent.
3. An investor may not have the psychological makeup to divide his investments by account type, and that would lead to unintended consequences. It is a mistake to view the performance of the equity ETFs in a taxable account in isolation instead of viewing the big picture, because it leads to emotionally based account decisions when the markets are volatile.

The best approach to the question of bonds in a taxable account is to calculate what your tax on the interest would be. To find that answer, simply ask your qualified tax adviser. A second method is to dig out your most recent tax return. Find the line on the second page of your Form 1040 labeled Taxable Income. If you earned $1,000 more in taxable income, how much more would you have to pay in taxes? That information is available in the booklet you may have received with your tax forms, and it is also available on the IRS web site at www.irs.gov.

If you have to pay less than $300 in income taxes on the $1,000 in interest income, your tax rate is below 30 percent. It is then generally okay to have bond ETFs in a taxable account.

If you have to pay $300 or more, your tax rate is 30 percent or more, and it would be costly to have bond ETFs in your taxable account. It might be advantageous to avoid the tax by placing bond ETFs in a nontaxable account.

My recommendation is to talk with a qualified tax adviser. Taxes can be complex and no tax reduction investment strategy should be attempted without the help of a knowledgeable tax specialist.

Nontaxable Accounts

In many ways, developing and managing a nontaxable ETF portfolio is easier than a taxable portfolio because taxes do not get in the way of decision making. You have more freedom to choose between different types of ETFs in a nontaxable portfolio. Nontaxable accounts include Individual Retirement Accounts (IRAs), a Roth IRA, pension accounts, and other entities that either defer taxes or avoid them altogether.

The allocation of REIT ETFs in a nontaxable account is a good idea. REIT ETFs are tax inefficient because of the taxable income they must distribute each year (Chapter 12). If you place 10 percent of the total value of a portfolio in a REIT ETF, try to do it in a nontaxable account.

Managing bond ETFs in a nontaxable account eliminates the burden of paying annual income taxes on the interest. Taxable bond ETFs are diverse. You can select from corporate bond funds, government bond funds, mortgage funds, and composite funds that hold a combination of those types. There are also high yield corporate bond funds that are particularly suitable for nontaxable accounts.

Most commodity and currency ETFs are also tax inefficient. Investors must pay ordinary income taxes on a portion of the gains from futures in commodity funds. Consequently, the overall tax rate is higher than the long-term capital gains rate.

Gold and silver funds are a different tax animal also. The IRS views funds that hold gold, gold bullion, and silver as collectibles. The maximum tax rate on long-term realized gains of collectibles is 28 percent rather than the 15 percent from securities trading.

ETNs are an exception to the commodity tax rules. An ETN is taxed at long-term capital gains rates when you sell rather than taxed on annual distributions from commodity futures contracts. They are the only type of commodity investment that offer tax efficiency and can be placed in taxable accounts. Caveat: To date the IRS has not challenged the tax treatment of ETN. But that could change. Check with your tax adviser for updates.

Investors who choose to use commodities and currencies should carefully consider the tax implications before deciding where to place those investments. In most cases, they should probably be placed in a nontaxable account.

The Hidden Risk of Asset Location

Should you own only stock ETFs in a taxable account and bond ETFs, REITS, and commodities in a nontaxable account, or keep the same balance in both types of accounts? It depends on the investor, not the investments.

Technically, it makes good practice to use an asset location strategy. But from a psychological perspective, it may not. There is a risk to placing all equity ETFs in a taxable account and all bond and REIT ETFs in a nontaxable account. Some clients will start to have "account fixation." They will compare the performance of the two accounts rather than looking at them as one complete portfolio.

Comparing the performance of the taxable account to the nontaxable can have unintended consequences. It is very difficult for people who compare accounts to watch their all-equity ETF taxable account drop during a bear market. Those investors may become emotional and lose sight of the big picture. When that occurs, investors make irrational decisions to sell the equity ETFs in the taxable account.

Emotionally selling equity ETFs in a poor market typically results in lower overall returns and higher overall portfolio risk. If you are prone to compare portfolios, then it is recommended that you forgo asset location and use the same asset allocation across all accounts. If you are disciplined and focused on your entire portfolio rather than its parts, then asset location is a good way to reduce taxes.

Rebalancing ETFs

Global markets go up and global markets go down, and they do not always go in the same direction at the same time or by the same amount. The ETFs in a portfolio that represent different asset classes in your portfolio will shift from their original allocation, starting the day after you purchase them. ETFs need to be rebalanced back to their targets regularly so the drift does not become too large.

Rebalancing also puts the risk of the portfolio back in line with your investment objectives.

It is a good idea to rebalance at least annually, especially if the markets have been particularly volatile. The easiest way to do rebalancing is to pick a time during the year when it will always be done. For example, you can use the first week in January or your birthday. Another method is to check the allocation of the portfolio occasionally to see whether your ETFs are off target by a certain percentage. Five percent is reasonable, for example, when market forces cause a 50 percent stock and 50 percent bond portfolio to be a 53 percent stock and 47 percent bond portfolio.

There are no tax consequences to rebalancing a nontaxable account; they are a consideration, however, when rebalancing a taxable account. Selling some ETF shares that are at a gain, purchasing more ETF shares that are lagging creates capital gains in a taxable portfolio.

There are alternative ways to rebalance a taxable account to minimize taxable events. Consider the following methods:

1. Do not automatically reinvest ETF dividend income. Let the income flow into your cash account rather than automatically buying more shares of the ETF. Once cash has accumulated in your account, manually invest it in ETFs where it is needed.
2. When adding new money to a taxable account, use that opportunity to rebalance the portfolio.
3. If you have a prior tax-loss carryforward or can offset a capital gain through tax-loss harvesting, use those losses to offset the gain from the sale of ETF shares that are at a profit.
4. Sell only those ETF tax lots that have been in your account for more than one year. It is better to pay a lower long-term capital gains tax rate than to pay the higher short-term capital gains rate. If no shares have been held for more than one year, you can wait until they have been held for more than one year before selling.
5. Rebalancing a taxable portfolio does not have to take place on the same date each year. If you have no positions that are at a long-term gain, it is better to wait a week or a month for short-term capital gains to become a long-term gain and lower your tax bill.

Hiring an Investment Manager

This ETF book has covered a lot of ground. If you read this far, I commend you. Now you need to decide who is going to implement all of these great ideas.

Some people opt to hire a professional investment adviser to design, implement, and manage their ETF portfolio. If you are too busy, too uninterested, too confused, or not able to keep up with your portfolio, then hiring an adviser makes sense.

There are two types of investment advisers: registered reps and fee-only. The first works at a brokerage firm and the second is generally independent.

Registered reps (brokers) are employed by brokerage firms. They are paid a commission each time you buy and sell securities. Some brokerage firms also provide a fee-option called a wrap account in lieu of commissions. That is fine as long as the fee is not greater than the commission, which can be the case when managing an ETF portfolio under a brokerage wrap account. You can give your broker trading discretion on an ETF portfolio and they can manage it for you. The disadvantage is that if a broker is paid on commission, there may be a tendency to trade when trading is not needed.

Independent investment advisers are paid on a fee-only basis. For a standard annual fee, they will design, implement, and maintain an ETF portfolio based on your needs. The fee charged is usually based on the value of the assets under management. The fee-only payment method takes out the conflict of interest created by commission sales. That being said, fee-only advisers are not without their own conflicts. Some advisers charge excessive fees or $1\frac{1}{2}$ percent to manage ETF portfolios. No adviser is that good where they can add enough value to make up for an excessive fee.

Services of Advisers

Here is a partial list of services that advisers provide:

1. **Help tailor an investment plan:** Many people need help formulating an investment plan and developing the correct asset allocation for their needs. They may already have a general idea of where they want to go financially but do not have the tools or expertise to put a complete plan together. An

adviser will help clients understand how their needs can be met through ETF investing, and then design, implement, and manage the complete investment plan.

2. **Offers consistency of strategy:** People switch investment strategies about every three years on average (as measured by the Investment Company Institute mutual fund turnover statistics). In the 1990s, growth stocks were hot. A few years later, investors switched to value stocks, then international stocks, and then commodity-driven stocks. Good advisers do not chase markets or returns. The consistency of management style will help achieve higher lifetime results.

3. **Creates a human circuit breaker:** Sometimes investors wake up in the middle of the night because they fear a market collapsed. When that happens, advisers are there to act as a psychologist. This usually means calming investors' fears and talking them out of making emotionally based investment decisions.

4. **Places someone on duty 24/7/365:** There will come a time in your life when you just do not have the time or desire to deal with day-to-day investment decisions. A trusted adviser will do your investment chores for you and ensure that your portfolio is properly maintained.

The right adviser will get the job done in an efficient and cost-saving manner. To gain a better understanding, I suggest contacting the Vanguard Group and asking for a free copy of How to Select a Financial Adviser. The booklet is available online at www.vanguard.com, or it can be obtained by mail by calling 1-800-662-7447.

Another place to ask for references for a knowledgeable investment adviser is through the www.diehards.org web site. The Diehards site is linked to a Morningstar discussion board called Vanguard Diehards and to a public discussion board called Bogleheads. The second board is named in honor of Jack Bogle, founder of the Vanguard Group and a pioneer in the field of index fund management.

Diehards.org is used by like-minded investors who are interested in keeping their costs low. Not all participants are interested in ETFs, but many are knowledgeable about the subject and can pass along the names of other people who are more knowledgeable. I personally participate on the site and am available to answer questions about indexes, ETFs, and low-cost portfolio management.

As the founder and CEO of one of the nation's leading low-cost adviser firms, I believe good advisers serve clients best by creating a workable plan, implementing that plan, and keeping clients focused on that path. It is not an adviser's job to risk a client's money by using exotic strategies. It is an adviser's job to understand the client's financial objectives and create a mix of investments that has the highest probability of meeting those objectives at a reasonable cost and controlled risk.

Summary

There are several steps you can take to make management of your ETF portfolio easier. Choosing the right brokerage firm is essential. Commission costs are important, but the most important attribute of a good brokerage firm is that the people representing you have your best interests at heart.

How and when you trade ETFs can have an impact on your investment performance. I recommend buying and selling during the middle of a trading day and when the markets are relatively calm. Those are the times when an ETF's price is trading closest to its intraday value.

Tax control is an important element in ETF portfolio management. Different types of accounts have different tax issues. The best asset location for your equity ETFs may be in taxable accounts, and the best location for bond ETFs may be in nontaxable accounts. Consult your tax adviser to find out whether asset allocation is to your advantage.

An alternative to managing your own account is to hire someone else to do it for you. That can be accomplished through the brokerage firm where you trade or through a fee-only investment adviser. There are several advantages to hiring an adviser, including piece of mind and the assurance that an investment strategy will be followed. The right adviser will guide you toward your financial goals effectively and efficiently while keeping costs under control.

Index Strategy Box
Abbreviation Guide

The left column lists abbreviations for security selection categories and the primary weighting methodology and the right column lists abbreviations for security weighting categories and the primary weighting methodology. See the Glossary for definitions of categories and methodologies.

Security Selection Abbreviations	Security Weighting Abbreviations
P A – Passive / Full Replication	C A – Capitalization / Full Cap
P B – Passive / Buy and Hold	C C – Capitalization / Constrained
P S – Passive / Sampling	C F – Capitalization / Free Float
P I – Passive / Single Security	C L – Capitalization / Liquidity
	C P – Capitalization / Production
S C – Screened / Corporate Actions	
S E – Screened / Exchange Listing	F D – Fundamental / Dividends
S F – Screened / Fundamentals	F E – Fundamental / Earnings
S M – Screened / Multiple Factor	F F – Fundamental / Multifactor
S P – Screened / Price Trends	F M – Fundamental / Momentum
S S – Screened / Social Issues	F P – Fundamental / Security Prices
S T – Screened / Thematic (x-social)	F Q – Fundamental / Qualitative
	F S – Fundamental / Social Issues
Q C – Quantitative / Technical	
Q E – Quantitative / Economic Cycle	X E – Fixed Weight / Equal
Q F – Quantitative / Fundamentals	X F – Fixed Weight / Equal – then float
Q M – Quantitative / Multi-factor	X L – Fixed Weight / Leveraged
Q P – Quantitative / Proprietary*	X N – Fixed Weight / Long-Short
Q Q – Quantitative / Qualitative	X M – Fixed Weight / Modified Equal
Q X – Quantitative / Momentum	X S – Fixed Weight / Short (inverse)

*Not enough information on index available

Index Strategy Boxes

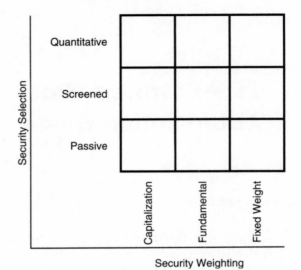

Figure A.1 Index Strategy Boxes™

APPENDIX B

ETF Resource List

Books on ETF Investing

Active Index Investing by Steven A. Schoenfeld (2004)

All About Asset Allocation by Richard Ferri (2005)

All About Index Funds, 2nd Edition by Richard Ferri (2007)

All About Exchange Traded Funds by Archie Richards Jr. (2002)

The Bogleheads' Guide to Investing by Taylor Larimore, Mel Lindauer, Michael LeBoeuf, and John C. Bogle (2006)

ETF Investing Around the World by Carlton T Delfeld (2007)

ETF Trading Strategies Revealed by David Vomund and Linda Raschke (2006)

Exchange Traded Funds as an Investment Option by A. Seddik Meziani (2005)

Exchange Traded Funds: An Insider's Guide to Buying the Market by Jim Wiandt (2001)

Exchange-Traded Funds for Dummies by Russell Wild (2006)

Getting Started in Exchange Traded Funds by Todd Lofton (2007)

Investing with Exchange-Traded Funds Made Easy by Marvin Appel (2006)

Morningstar ETF 150: 2007 by Morningstar Inc. and Dan Culloton (2007)

The New Global Investor by Carlton T. Delfeld (2004)

New Investment Frontier: A Guide to Exchange Traded Funds for Canadians by Howard J. Atkinson and Donna Green (2006)

Power Investing With Basket Securities by Peter Madlem & Larry D. Edwards (2001)

The Smart Investor's Guide for Investing by Nachman Bench PH. D. (2003)

Understanding Exchange-Traded Funds by Archie Richards Jr. (2007)

Someone Will Make Money on Your Funds by Gary L. Gastineau (2005)

ETF Web Sites of Interest

News and Research

theetfbook.com: updates to this book and a source of links to important ETF sites.

etfguide.com: a comprehensive exchange-traded fund database that includes *Index Strategy Box* data, market research, breaking news, and commentary.

indexuniverse.com: a clearinghouse for news, information, and data. The company also publishes the *ETFR* (Exchange-Traded Funds Report) and the *Journal of Indexing*.

marketwatch.com: breaking news on the ETF industry with commentary.

morningstar.com: detailed database, research, commentary, and discussion boards.

etf.stock-encyclopedia.com: database of ETFs with links to providers.

etfzone.com: comprehensive ETF database, commentary, and discussion board.

indexinvestor.com: in-depth analysis of index fund investing, including ETFs.

seekingalpha.com: ETF articles, news, and advice for both active and passive investors.

Major ETF Product Providers

bldrsfunds.com: BLDRS is a series of ETFs based on The Bank of New York ADR Index.

claymore.com/etfs: Claymore Securities offers a lineup of ETFs that track key market segments.

dbcfund.db.com: Deutsche Bank is the sponsor of the DB Commodity Index Tracking Fund (Amex: DBC).

ftportfolios.com: First Trust Portfolios ETFs track market segments and quantitative indexes.

holdrs.com: HOLDRs are a group of unmanaged sector portfolios developed by Merrill Lynch.

healthsharesinc.com: Therapeutic theme ETFs in pharmaceuticals, health services, life sciences, and biotech.

ishares.com: iShares are a family of ETFs managed by Barclays Global Investors.

ishares.ca: iShares Canadian ETF information managed by Barclays Global Investors.

nasdaq.com/oneq: Fidelity Management & Research Company manages the ONEQ exchange-traded fund.

powershares.com: The PowerShares are a family of quantitative ETFs that offer a diverse product lineup.

proshares.com: ProShares offer leveraged and inverse ETFs and are a unit of ProFunds Group.

rydexfunds.com: Rydex Investments offers a lineup of ETFs that track key market segments. Also see currencyshares.com for information on currency ETF pricing.

ssgafunds.com: State Street Global Advisors manages a diverse lineup of ETFs.

vanguard.com: Vanguard ETFs are a share class of Vanguard index mutual funds.

vaneck.com: Van Eck Global is a sponsor of a few ETFs, including the Gold Miners.

wisdomtree.com: WisdomTree offers ETFs that fundamentally select and weight global equities.

Major Market Index Providers

djindexes.com: Dow Jones is the developer and owner of benchmark indexes used for ETFs.

ftse.com: FTSE Group is the developer and owner of benchmark indexes used for ETFs.

indexes.morningstar.com: The indexes reveal meaningful differences in stock style, capitalization, and sectors.

lehman.com: Lehman Brothers is the world's leading provider of fixed income benchmarks.

msci.com: Morgan Stanley Capital International (MSCI) is the developer and owner of benchmark indexes for ETFs.

russell.com: Russell is the developer and owner of benchmark indexes used for ETFs.

standardandpoors.com: Standard & Poor's is the developer and owner of benchmark indexes used for ETFs.

wilshire.com: Wilshire Associates provides the benchmark Wilshire 5000 indexes and many others.

Major U.S. Stock Exchanges

amex.com: The American Stock Exchange was the first exchange to list ETFs in the United States. The web site provides in-depth information and trading data on ETFs that trade on the AMEX and information on Intellidex indexes used by PowerShares.

nasdaq.com: The NASDAQ exchange offers a family of ETFs that consist of the NASDAQ-100 Index, NASDAQ Biotechnology Index fund, and the BLDRs family.

nyse.com: The New York Stock Exchange is the oldest stock exchange in the United States and it lists a number of important ETFs.

Glossary

12b-1 fee: An annual fee charged by some mutual funds to pay for marketing and distribution activities. The fee is taken directly from fund assets, which reduces a shareholder's total return.

accumulated dividends: Dividends paid per ETF share, net of expenses, through and including the previous day's close. Stocks pay dividends throughout the quarter while ETFs pay dividends only once per quarter.

active management: An investment strategy that seeks to outperform the average returns of the financial markets. Active managers rely on research, market forecasts, and their own judgment and experience in selecting securities to buy and sell.

alpha: A measure of performance in percentage above or below what would have been predicted by risk as suggested by its beta. Positive alpha means a fund performed greater than its risk would suggest, while negative alpha means the fund underperformed. An ETF of alpha 1.5 outperformed its index by 1.5 percent as predicted by its beta.

annual turnover: Percentage of value of stocks in a portfolio that are sold and replaced with new stocks each year.

annualize: To make a period of less than a year apply to a full year, usually for purposes of comparison. For instance, a portfolio turnover rate of 36 percent over a 6-month period could be converted to an annualized rate of 72 percent.

AP: see *authorized participant.*

asked price: The price at which a security is offered for sale. For a no-load mutual fund, the asked price is the same as the fund's net asset value per share. Also called offering price.

authorized participant: An institutional investor that is authorized to buy and sell ETF creation units directly with a fund company.

automatic reinvestment: An arrangement by which the dividends or other earnings from an investment are used to buy additional shares in the investment vehicle.

average effective maturity: A weighted average of the maturity dates for all securities in a money market or bond fund. (The maturity date is the date that a money market instrument or bond buyer will be repaid by the security's issuer.) The longer the average maturity, the more a fund's share price will move up or down in response to changes in interest rates.

back-end load: A sales fee charged by some mutual funds when an investor sells fund shares. Also called a contingent deferred sales charge.

benchmark index: An index that correlates with a fund, used to measure a fund manager's performance.

beta: A measure of the magnitude of a portfolio's past share-price fluctuations in relation to the ups and downs of the overall market (or appropriate market index). The market (or index) is assigned a beta of 1.00, so a portfolio with a beta of 1.20 would have seen its share price rise or fall by 12 percent when the overall market rose or fell by 10 percent.

bid-ask spread: The difference between what a buyer is willing to bid (pay) for a security and the seller's ask (offer) price.

book value: A company's assets minus any liabilities and intangible assets.

broad market index: A basket of securities that covers all securities on an entire market, or samples the spectrum of securities to achieve a return close to the market. Examples would be the Russell 3000 Index and the Lehman Brothers Aggregate Bond Index.

broker/broker-dealer: An individual or firm that buys or sells mutual funds or other securities for the public.

buy and hold: An investment strategy of investing in securities and holding them for the long term. Also defines HOLDRs, an ETF structure that buys securities one time in a portfolio and does not replace or rebalance those securities.

capital gain or loss: The difference between the sale price of an asset, such as a mutual fund, stock, or bond, and the original cost of the asset.

capital gains distributions: Payments to ETF shareholders of gains realized during the year on securities that the fund has sold at a profit, minus any realized losses.

capped: see *constrained indexes.*

cash investments: Short-term debt instruments, such as commercial paper, banker's acceptances, and Treasury bills, that mature in less than one year. Also known as money market instruments or cash reserves.

closed-end fund: A mutual fund that has a fixed number of shares, usually listed on a major stock exchange.

commodities: Unprocessed goods such as grains, metals, and minerals traded in large amounts on a commodities exchange.

commodity futures: see *futures.*

constrained indexes: Portfolios that are constrained or capped to restrict the amount any security can be represented in an index or an ETF.

consumer price index (CPI): A measure of the price change in consumer goods and services. The CPI is used to track the pace of inflation.

corporate actions: Decisions made by the board of directors of a corporation that affect the shareholders of that corporation.

cost basis: The original cost of an investment plus its associated purchase expenses and capital improvements . For tax purposes, the cost basis is subtracted from the sales price to determine any capital gain or loss.

country risk: The possibility that political events (a war, national elections), financial problems (rising inflation, government default), or natural disasters (an earthquake, a poor harvest) will weaken a country's economy and cause investments in that country to decline.

coupon/coupon rate: The interest rate that a bond issuer promises to pay the bondholder until the bond matures.

creation unit: A set of shares or securities that makes up one unit of the fund held by the trust that underlies an exchange traded fund (ETF). One creation unit is the denomination of underlying assets that can be redeemed for a certain number of ETF shares.

credit rating: A published ranking, based on a careful financial analysis, of a creditor's ability to pay interest or principal owed on a debt.

credit risk: The possibility that a bond issuer will fail to repay interest and principal in a timely manner. Also called default risk.

currency risk: The possibility that returns could be reduced for Americans investing in foreign securities because of a rise in the value of the U.S. dollar against foreign currencies. Also called exchange rate risk.

custodian: Either (1) a bank, agent, trust company, or other organization responsible for safeguarding financial assets, or (2) the individual who oversees the mutual fund assets of a minor's custodial account.

declaration date: The date the board of directors of a company or mutual fund announces the amount and date of its next dividend payment.

default: A failure to pay principal or interest when due.

depreciation: A decrease in the value of an investment.

derivative: A financial contract whose value is based on, or "derived" from, a traditional security (for example, a stock or bond), an asset (for example, a commodity), or a market index (for example, the S&P 500 Index).

discount broker: A brokerage that executes orders to buy and sell securities at commission rates lower than a full-service brokerage.

distributions: Payments of dividends and/or capital gains by an ETF.

dividend yield: The annual rate of return on a share of stock, determined by dividing the annual dividend by its current share price. In a stock mutual fund, this figure represents the average dividend yield of the stocks held by the fund.

dollar-cost averaging: Investing equal amounts of money at regular intervals on an ongoing basis. This technique ensures that an investor buys fewer shares when prices are high and more shares when prices are low.

earnings per share: A company's earnings divided by the number of common shares outstanding.

economic cycle: Refers to the fluctuations of economic activity about its long-term growth trend. The cycle involves shifts over time between recovery and prosperity and contraction or recession. The fluctuations are often measured using the real gross domestic product (GDP).

efficient market: The theory, disputed by some experts, that stock prices reflect all market information that is known by all investors. Also states that investors cannot beat the market because it is impossible to determine future stock prices.

enhanced index fund: An index fund that is designed to generally track an index but also to outperform it through the use of leverage, futures, trading strategies, capital gains management, and other methods.

equal weighted: A portfolio-weighting scheme whereby each security in a basket has the same percentage allocation. Also see *modified equal weighted*.

equal, then float: A portfolio-weighting scheme whereby each security in a basket is initially allocated the same percentage and then the securities are left to float with market capitalization changes to those securities. Used in HOLDRs.

estimated cash amount: The amount of estimated cash embedded in each creation unit. The estimated cash amount per creation unit is designed to give authorized participants an idea of approximately how much cash per creation unit will be needed to create or redeem ETF shares on a given day.

exchange: The physical location or a computer-based system used to trade public securities between buyers and sellers.

exchange-traded fund(ETF): An exchange-traded fund is an index fund that trades on the stock market. A common ETF is Standard & Poor's Depositary Receipts (SPY), which tracks the S&P 500.

ex-dividend date: The date when a distribution of dividends and/or capital gains is deducted from a mutual fund's assets or set aside for payment to shareholders. On the ex-dividend date, the fund's share price drops by the amount of the distribution (plus or minus any market activity). Also known as the reinvestment date.

expense ratio: The percentage of a portfolio's average net assets used to pay its annual expenses. The expense ratio, which includes management fees, administrative fees, and any 12b-1 fees, directly reduces returns to investors.

factors: Can represent a broad assortment of fundamentals, qualitative, and quantitative measures of a security's value. Financial ratios are common factors.

Federal Reserve: The central bank that regulates the supply of money and credit throughout the United States. The Fed's seven-member board of governors, appointed by the president, has significant influence on U.S. monetary and economic policy.

fee-only adviser: An arrangement in which a financial adviser charges an hourly rate, annual retainer or an agreed-upon percentage of assets under management for financial services.

free float: Shares of a public company that are freely available to the investing public. A free float index does not include the value of shares held by large owners or stock with sales restrictions (restricted stock that cannot be sold until they become unrestricted stock).

full capitalization (or full cap): A market capitalization method that uses all stock outstanding regardless of who holds it and where it is held.

full replication: An ETF strategy that fully replicates the securities and weighting of an underlying index. Typical of unit investment trusts (UITs).

front-end load: A sales commission charged at the time of purchase by some mutual funds and other investment vehicles.

fund family: A group of mutual funds sponsored by the same organization, often offering exchange privileges between funds and combined account statements for multiple funds.

fundamentals: Financial information about a company derived from its balance sheet, income statement, statement of cash flow, and other publicly released information.

fundamental analysis: A method of examining a company's financial statements and operations as a means of forecasting stock price movements.

futures: A contract to buy or sell specific amounts of a specific commodity (for example, grain or foreign currency) for an agreed-upon price at a certain time in the future.

global fund: A mutual fund that invests in stocks of companies in the United States and foreign countries.

grantor trust: An ETF that at creation follows an index but remains static and does not attempt to track it. HOLDRs are main adherents to this form of ETF.

gross domestic product (GDP):   The value of all goods and services provided by U.S. labor in a given year. One of the primary measures of the U.S. economy, the GDP is issued quarterly by the Department of Commerce. Formerly known as the gross national product (GNP).

hedge: A strategy in which one investment is used to offset the risk of another security.

high yield fund: A mutual fund that invests primarily in bonds with a credit rating of BB or lower. Because of the speculative nature of high yield bonds, high yield funds are subject to greater share price volatility and greater credit risk than other bond funds.

HOLDRs: HOLding Company Depositary Receipts are securities that represent an investor's ownership in the common stock or American Depositary Receipts (ADR) of specified companies in a particular industry, sector, or group.

indexing: An investment strategy to match the average performance of a market or group of stocks. Usually this is accomplished by buying a small amount of each stock in a market.

index providers: Companies that construct and maintain stock and bond indexes. The main providers are S&P, Dow Jones, Lehman Brothers, MSCI, Russell, and Wilshire.

indicative optimized portfolio value: see *intraday value.*

inflation risk: The possibility that increases in the cost of living will reduce or eliminate the returns on a particular investment.

interest rate risk: The possibility that a security or mutual fund will decline in value because of an increase in interest rates.

international fund: A mutual fund that invests in securities traded in markets outside the United States. Foreign markets present additional risks, including currency fluctuation and political instability. In the past, these risks have made prices of foreign stocks more volatile than those of U.S. stocks.

intraday value: An ongoing estimate of the underlying value of securities and cash that make up ETF shares that is quoted every 15 seconds by the exchange listing the ETF. In various places, it is also called the Intraday Indicative Value, Underlying Trading Value, Indicative Optimized Portfolio Value.

inverse fund: A fund designed to go in the opposite direction of the stock or bond market. Also see *short funds*.

investment adviser: A person or organization that makes the day-to-day decisions regarding a portfolio's investments.

investment grade: A bond whose credit quality is considered to be among the highest by independent bond-rating agencies.

junk bond: A bond with a credit rating of BB or lower. Also known as high yield bonds because of the rewards offered to those who are willing to take on the additional risks of a lower quality bond.

large cap: A company whose stock market value is generally in excess of $10 billion, although the range varies according to the index provider.

leveraged index fund: An index fund that is designed to move more than the market, but in proportion to the market. A leveraged S&P 500 fund that has a 2-to-1 ratio will go up or down twice as much as the S&P 500 index.

liquidity: The degree of a security's marketability; that is, how quickly the security can be sold at a fair price and converted to cash.

load fund: A mutual fund that levies a sales charge either when shares are bought (a front-end load) or sold (a back-end load).

long-term capital gain: A profit on the sale of a security or mutual fund share that has been held for more than one year.

long-short: The buying of long securities that are expected to increase in value and the selling of short securities that are expected to decrease in value.

management fee: Also called an advisory fee, the amount a mutual fund pays to its investment adviser for the work of overseeing the fund's holdings.

market capitalization: Or market cap, is a measurement of corporate or economic size equal to the stock price times the number of shares outstanding of a public company. Determined by multiplying the total number of company stock shares outstanding by the price per share.

market neutral: An investment strategy that buys equity investments believed to achieve superior returns and shorts an equal amount of a broad market index fund, negating the impact of market returns on the portfolio.

maturity date: The date when the issuer of a bond agrees to repay the principal, or face value, to the buyer.

median market cap: The midpoint of market capitalization (market price multiplied by the number of shares outstanding) of the stocks in a portfolio. Half the stocks in the portfolio will have higher market capitalizations, and half will have lower.

mid cap: A company whose stock market value is generally between $2 billion and $10 billion, although the range varies according to the index provider.

modified equal weighted: A portfolio-weighting scheme whereby securities in a portfolio are assigned fixed percentages, based on a fundamental factor for each security or their ranking in a quantitative model.

momentum: Refers to the statistical strength of price and earnings trends. It can also be applied to the direction and strength of analyst convictions, using earnings estimates and the revision of those estimates.

Morningstar Style Box: Morningstar, Inc. has broken down the world of domestic mutual funds into small, medium, and large cap funds and by objective growth, value, or blend. A funds style is illustrated using a tic tac toe–type categorization figure.

municipal bond fund: A mutual fund that invests in tax-exempt bonds issued by state, city, and local governments. The interest obtained from these bonds is passed through to shareholders and is generally free of federal, state, and local income taxes.

National Association of Securities Dealers (NASD):   An organization of brokers and dealers designed to protect the investing public against fraudulent acts.

net asset value (NAV):   The market value of a mutual fund's total assets, minus liabilities, divided by the number of shares outstanding. The value of a single share is called its share value or share price.

no-load fund: A mutual fund that charges no sales commission or load.

nominal return: The return on an investment before adjustment for inflation.

open-end fund: An investment entity that has the ability to issue or redeem the number of shares outstanding on a daily basis. Prices are quoted once per day, at the end of the day, at the net asset value of the fund (NAV).

operating expenses: The amount paid for asset maintenance or the cost of doing business. Earnings are distributed after operating expenses are deducted.

optimization: A mathematical process of selecting and weighting a portfolio of securities in an attempt to achieve the highest probability of achieving a certain desired risk-and-return outcome.

option: A contract in which a seller gives a buyer the right, but not the obligation, to buy or sell securities at a specified price on or before a given date.

payable date: The date when dividends or capital gains are paid to shareholders. For mutual funds, the payable date is usually within two to four days of the record date. The payable date also refers to the date on which a declared stock dividend or bond interest payment is scheduled to be paid.

portfolio composition file (PCF): A daily list of the exact names and quantity of the underlying securities and cash that need to be turned in by an authorized participant to receive one creation unit.

portfolio transaction costs: The expenses associated with buying and selling securities, including commissions, purchase and redemption fees, exchange fees, and other miscellaneous costs. In a mutual fund prospectus, these expenses would be listed separately from the fund's expense ratio. Does not include the bid/ask spread.

premium: An amount that exceeds the face value or redemption value of a security or of a comparable security or group of investments. It may indicate that a security is favored highly by investors. Also refers to a fee for obtaining insurance coverage.

price-to-book ratio (P/B): The price per share of a stock divided by its book value (that is, net worth) per share. For a portfolio, the ratio is the weighted average price-to-book ratio of the stocks it holds.

price-to-earnings ratio (P/E): The share price of a stock divided by its per-share earnings over the past year. For a portfolio, the weighted average P/E ratio of the stocks in the portfolio. P/E is a good indicator of market expectations about a company's prospects; the higher the P/E, the greater the expectations for a future growth in earnings.

product description: A written document containing important information about ETF fees, objectives, and mechanics of share purchase in the secondary market. Not intended to be a substitute for a prospectus.

production weighted: Based on the average quantity of production of each commodity in the index over a specific period, normally five years.

proprietary: An opaque investment strategy used by index providers and investment managers. The strategy is intentionally not fully disclosed to investors. The lack of transparency means investors can never be entirely sure why investments are being added or replaced in an index or a fund.

prospectus: A legal document that gives prospective investors information about a mutual fund, including discussions of its investment objectives and policies, risks, costs, and past performance. A prospectus must be provided to a potential investor before he or she can establish an account and must also be filed with the SEC.

proxy: Written authorization by a shareholder giving someone else (for example, fund or company management) authority to represent his or her vote at a shareholder meeting.

qualitative: A process of rating securities based on nonfinancial information such as the treatment of employees, the quality of products, the remaining patent life on those products, and the level of environmental stewardship.

quantitative analysis: In securities, an assessment of specific measurable factors (for example, the cost of capital or the value of assets) and projections of sales, costs, earnings, and profits. Combined with more subjective or qualitative considerations (for example, management effectiveness), quantitative analysis can enhance investment decisions and portfolios.

real estate investment trust (REIT): A company that manages a group of real estate investments and distributes to its shareholders at least 95 percent of its net earnings annually. REITs often specialize in a particular kind of property. They can, for example, invest in real estate such as office buildings, shopping centers, or hotels; purchase real estate (an equity REIT); and provide loans to building developers (a mortgage REIT).

real return: The actual return received on an investment after factoring in inflation. For example, if the nominal investment return for a particular period was 8 percent and inflation was 3 percent, the real return would be 5 percent.

record date: The date used to determine who is eligible to receive a company or fund's next distribution of dividends or capital gains.

redemption: Authorized participant turns in an ETF creation unit and receives an in-kind distribution of shares.

redemption fee: 1) A fee charged by some open-end mutual funds when an investor sells shares within a short period of time. 2) A fee charge to authorized participants for creation unit redemption.

registered investment adviser (RIA):   An investment professional who is registered with, but not endorsed by, the Securities and Exchange Commission (SEC) or the state the RIA does business in. They recommend investment products and manage accounts.

registered investment company (RIC):   Common type of ETF that tracks indexes closely, allows sampling (not every stock in an index is necessarily purchased) and derivatives in its operations. Examples include iShares and Sector SPDRs.

reinvestment: The use of investment income to buy additional securities. Some ETF structures allow managers to reinvest dividends paid by holdings in the fund while other structures do not allow reinvestment.

replication: see *full replication.*

return of capital: A distribution that is not paid out of earnings and profits. It is a return of the investor's principal.

risk tolerance: An investor's ability or willingness to endure declines in the prices of investments while waiting for them to increase in value.

sampling: A strategy of selecting securities from a market or index that represents the characteristics of that market or index without owning all of the securities that trade on the market or index.

sector diversification: The percentage of a portfolio's stocks from companies in each of the major industry groups.

sector fund: A mutual fund that concentrates on a relatively narrow market sector. These funds can experience higher share price volatility than some diversified funds because sector funds are subject to issues specific to a given sector.

Securities and Exchange Commission (SEC):   The agency of the federal government that regulates mutual funds, registered investment advisers, the stock and bond markets, and broker-dealers. The SEC was established by the Securities Exchange Act of 1934.

shares outstanding: The number of ETF shares issued as of the closing on the previous trading day. It is the number used to calculate the NAV.

Since ETFs are constantly being created and redeemed during a trade day, shares outstanding change from day to day.

Sharpe ratio: A measure of risk adjusted return. To calculate a Sharpe ratio, an asset's excess returns (its return in excess of the return generated by risk-free assets such as Treasury bills) are divided by the asset's standard deviation. Should be compared to an appropriate benchmark.

short funds: A mutual fund or ETF that seeks to provide investment results that will inversely correlate to the daily price performance of an index.

short sale: Sale of a security or option contract not owned by the seller, usually to take advantage of an expected drop in the price of the security or option. In a typical short-sale transaction, a borrowed security or option is sold, and the borrower agrees to purchase replacement shares or options at the market price on or by a specified future date. Generally considered a risky investment strategy.

short-term capital gain: A profit on the sale of a security or mutual fund share that has been held for one year or less. A short-term capital gain is taxed as ordinary income.

small cap: A company whose stock market value is generally less than $2 billion, although the range varies according to the index provider.

spread: The difference between the bid (sell) price and the ask (buy) price of a security.

standard deviation: A measure of the degree to which a fund's return varies from its previous returns or from the average of all similar funds. The larger the standard deviation, the greater the likelihood (and risk) that a security's performance will fluctuate from the average return.

Statement of Additional Information (SAI): The SAI goes into detail about many matters found in a mutual fund prospectus, particularly the tax consequences of fund distributions.

swap agreement: An arrangement between two parties to exchange one security for another, to change the mix of a portfolio or the maturities of the bonds it includes, or to alter another aspect of a portfolio or financial arrangement, such as interest rate payments or currencies.

tax deferral: Delaying the payment of income taxes on investment income. For example, owners of traditional IRAs do not pay income taxes on the interest, dividends, or capital gains accumulating in their retirement accounts until they begin making withdrawals.

tax free: An investment or account where the interest or gains are free from federal income taxes, even after withdrawals.

tax swapping: Creating a tax loss by the simultaneous sale of one index fund and the purchase of a similar fund.

tax-exempt bond: A bond, usually issued by municipal, county, or state governments, whose interest payments are not subject to federal, and in some cases, state and local income tax.

thematic: A strategy of portfolio management that tends to be based on an emotionally charged topic. Examples include clean air and water, corporate actions, and social responsibility.

total cash required: The cash required per creation unit for creations and redemptions executed the previous day to ensure that those trades occur at NAV. Cash required ensures that existing ETF shares do not experience any dilution in value as a result of creation and redemption activity.

total return: A percentage change, over a specified period, in a mutual fund's net asset value, with the ending net asset value adjusted to account for the reinvestment of all distributions of dividends and capital gains.

trading spread: see *spread*.

transaction fee/commission: A charge assessed by an intermediary, such as a broker-dealer or a bank, for assisting in the sale or purchase of a security.

Treasury security: A negotiable debt obligation issued by the U.S. government for a specific amount and maturity. Treasury bills (1 year or less), Treasury notes (1 to 10 years), and Treasury bonds (over 10 years).

turnover rate: An indication of trading activity during the past year. Portfolios with high turnover rates incur higher transaction costs and are more likely to distribute capital gains.

unit investment trust (UIT): Common type of ETF that requires exact duplication of an index and prohibits derivatives in operation, like Management Investment Trusts. Examples include SPY and QQQQ.

underlying trading value: see *intraday value*.

unrealized capital gain or loss: An increase (or decrease) in the value of a security that is not "real" because the security has not been sold. Once a security is sold by the portfolio manager, the capital gains or losses are realized by the fund, and any payment to the shareholder is taxable during the tax year in which the security was sold.

volatility: The degree of fluctuation in the value of a security, mutual fund, or index. Often expressed as a mathematical measure such as standard deviation or beta. The greater a fund's volatility, the wider the fluctuations between its high and low prices.

wash sale rule: The IRS regulation that prohibits a taxpayer from claiming a loss on the sale of an investment if that investment, or a substantially identical investment, is purchased within 30 days before or after the sale.

yield curve: A line plotted on a graph that depicts the yields of bonds of varying maturities, from short-term to long-term. The line, or curve, shows the relationship between short- and long-term interest rates.

yield-to-maturity: The rate of return an investor would receive if the securities held by a portfolio were held to their maturity dates.

About the Author

Richard Ferri is the founder and CEO of Portfolio Solutions, LLC, a fee-only investment firm in Troy, Michigan. The company manages investment portfolios for clients using index funds and ETFs as part of its low-cost asset allocation strategy. Portfolio Solutions manages over $1 billion in separate accounts for high-net-worth individuals, families, nonprofit organizations, and corporate pension plans.

Ferri earned a Bachelor of Science degree in Business Administration from the University of Rhode Island and a Master of Science degree in Finance from Walsh College. He also holds the designation of Chartered Financial Analyst (CFA). Before joining the investment community in 1988, Ferri served as an officer and fighter pilot in the U.S. Marine Corps and is now retired from the Marine Corps Reserve.

Index

Note: ETF(s) in index refers to exchange-traded funds.